P9-CFP-162

PRODUCTS LIABILITY

IN A NUTSHELL

Eighth Edition

By

DAVID G. OWEN
Carolina Distinguished Professor of Law
University of South Carolina

Mat # 40506948

Nutshell Series, In a Nutshell, the Nutshell Logo and West Group are trademarks registered in the U.S. Patent and Trademark Office.

COPYRIGHT © 1974, 1981, 1988, 1993 WEST PUBLISHING CO.
© West, a Thomson business, 1998, 2003, 2005
© 2008 Thomson/West
      610 Opperman Drive
      P.O. Box 64526
      St. Paul, MN 55164–0526
      1–800–328–9352

Printed in the United States of America

ISBN 978–0–314–17086–6

 TEXT IS PRINTED ON 10% POST
CONSUMER RECYCLED PAPER

For Ethan, Wendy, and Megan

*

PREFACE

PRODUCTS LIABILITY IN A NUTSHELL explores the ever-changing terrain of this field of law, including its essential history, developments, policies, and tensions. Succinctly yet comprehensively, this work examines the classic cases, illustrative and provocative case developments, and the most important state and federal legislation on such matters as grounds of liability; definitions and proof of product defect; rules for expert testimony, including recent Supreme Court decisions and changes in the Federal Rules of Evidence; how courts and legislatures have dealt with the perplexing issue of "state of the art"; how the evolving jurisprudence on federal preemption affects this field of law; recent developments in various special types of litigation, such as prescription drugs, toxic contaminants, and post-sale duties to warn or recall; and changes wrought by the RESTATEMENT (THIRD) OF TORTS: PRODUCTS LIABILITY.

This book is the successor to DAVID G. OWEN & JERRY J. PHILLIPS, PRODUCTS LIABILITY IN A NUTSHELL (7th ed. 2005), which itself followed two editions of a Nutshell by Dix Noel and Jerry Phillips and, more recently, four editions by Jerry Phillips alone. Because of vast changes in products liability law since Professors Noel and Phillips published the first Nutshell in 1974, the seventh edition reconstructed this field of law from the ground up to reflect how the discipline was reconceived in recent years. The Nutshell draws heavily upon and abridges my more extensive work, OWEN, PRODUCTS LIABILITY LAW (2d ed., Thomson-West 2008) (available at westlaw.com and amazon.com), to which the reader is referred for fuller discussion and citation of authority on matters discussed here.

Thanks for editorial work on this edition of the Nutshell are due to my eagle-eyed research assistant, William Mills. For editorial and many other enhancements, I am especially grateful for the tireless efforts of Karen Miller, my trusty research associate, who meticulously adapted hornbook revisions to this edition of the Nutshell. I remain grateful to Doug Powell for supporting this project before he even saw the manuscript for the hornbook-treatise from which this Nutshell was to spring. And Roxanne Birkel deserves high credit for applying her usual magic, with characteristic grace and skill, in guiding the manuscript of this little book through the perils of production.

DAVID G. OWEN

Cashiers, North Carolina
August 2008

SUMMARY OF CONTENTS

Page

PREFACE --V
TABLE OF CONTENTS --IX
TABLE OF CASES --XVII

1. **Introduction** --------------------------------------1

PART I: THEORIES OF LIABILITY

2. **Negligence**--45
3. **Tortious Misrepresentation**--------------------72
4. **Warranty** ---86
5. **Strict Liability in Tort**------------------------126

PART II: PRODUCT DEFECTIVENESS

6. **Nature and Proof of Defectiveness** ------173
7. **Manufacturing Defects** -----------------------206
8. **Design Defects**------------------------------------221
9. **Warning Defects** --------------------------------261
10. **Limitations on Defectiveness**---------------298

PART III: CAUSATION

11. **Cause in Fact**---------------------------------------337
12. **Proximate Cause** ----------------------------------361

PART IV: DEFENSES

13. User Misconduct Defenses -------------------383
14. Special Defenses ---------------------------------415

PART V: SPECIAL ISSUES

15. Special Types of Defendants ----------------431
**16. Special Types of Transactions and
        Products**--457
17. Automotive Litigation ----------------------------485
18. Punitive Damages ---------------------------------505

INDEX --539

VIII

TABLE OF CONTENTS

Page

PREFACE --V
SUMMARY OF CONTENTS--VII
TABLE OF CASES --XVII

Chapter 1. INTRODUCTION

§ 1.1 Products Liability Law ------------------------------1
§ 1.2 Early Law ---5
§ 1.3 Modern American Law ----------------------------11
§ 1.4 Foreign Law---42

PART I: THEORIES OF LIABILITY

Chapter 2. NEGLIGENCE

§ 2.1 Negligence—Generally ---------------------------45
§ 2.2 The Standard of Care ----------------------------48
§ 2.3 Proof of Negligence—Industry Standards ----56
§ 2.4 Proof of Negligence—Violation of Statute----58
§ 2.5 Proof of Negligence—Res Ipsa Loquitur ------64
§ 2.6 The Resurgence of Negligence ------------------69

Chapter 3. TORTIOUS MISREPRESENTATION

§ 3.1 Misrepresentation—Generally ------------------72
§ 3.2 Fraud ---74
§ 3.3 Negligent Misrepresentation --------------------81
§ 3.4 Strict Liability for Misrepresentation----------83

Chapter 4. WARRANTY

Page

§ 4.1 Warranty—Generally -----------------------------86
§ 4.2 Express Warranty------------------------------------88
§ 4.3 Implied Warranty of Merchantability----------93
§ 4.4 Implied Warranty of Fitness for Particular
       Purpose ---96
§ 4.5 Privity of Contract and Third–Party
       Beneficiaries--100
§ 4.6 Notice of Breach -----------------------------------105
§ 4.7 Disclaimers --106
§ 4.8 Limitations of Remedy---------------------------117
§ 4.9 Anti-Disclaimer and Other Warranty
       Reform Legislation -----------------------------121

Chapter 5. STRICT LIABILITY IN TORT

§ 5.1 Strict Liability in Tort—Generally----------------126
§ 5.2 The Path to Strict Liability in Tort ----------127
§ 5.3 Restatement (Second) of Torts § 402A ------134
§ 5.4 Policies and Rationales --------------------------143
§ 5.5 Liability Tests -------------------------------------149
§ 5.6 The Consumer Expectations Test ------------150
§ 5.7 The Risk–Utility Test ---------------------------155
§ 5.8 Alternative Tests ---------------------------------160
§ 5.9 Comparison with Other Liability Theories --164

PART II: PRODUCT DEFECTIVENESS

Chapter 6. NATURE AND PROOF OF DEFECTIVENESS

§ 6.1 Defectiveness—Generally -----------------------173

§ 6.2 The Three Types of Defect ----------------------175
§ 6.3 Proof of Defect—Expert Testimony ----------180
§ 6.4 Proof of Defect—Recurring Issues ------------192
§ 6.5 Restatement (Third) of Torts: Products
       Liability ---198

Chapter 7. MANUFACTURING DEFECTS

§ 7.1 Manufacturing Defects—Generally ----------206
§ 7.2 Theories and Tests of Liability ----------------209
§ 7.3 Departure from Design Specifications ------211
§ 7.4 Product Malfunction -----------------------------212
§ 7.5 Food and Drink------------------------------------217

Chapter 8. DESIGN DEFECTS

§ 8.1 Design Defects—Generally ----------------------221
§ 8.2 Theories and Tests of Liability ----------------224
§ 8.3 The Consumer Expectations Test ------------224
§ 8.4 The Risk–Utility Test ----------------------------228
§ 8.5 Proof of a Reasonable Alternative Design --233
§ 8.6 Combining Consumer Expectations and
       Risk–Utility ---------------------------------------239
§ 8.7 Constructive Knowledge—The Wade–Keeton
       Test --246
§ 8.8 The Third Restatement ------------------------248
§ 8.9 Optional Safety Devices -------------------------251
§ 8.10 Prescription Drugs and Medical Devices --255

Chapter 9. WARNING DEFECTS

§ 9.1 Warning Defects—Generally--------------------261

§ 9.2 Theories and Tests of Liability ----------------265
§ 9.3 Adequacy--268
§ 9.4 Persons to Be Warned --------------------------277
§ 9.5 Sophisticated Users and Bulk Suppliers ----281
§ 9.6 Prescription Drugs and Medical Devices ----285

Chapter 10. LIMITATIONS ON DEFECTIVENESS

§ 10.1 Limitations on Defectiveness—Generally --298
§ 10.2 Obvious Dangers --------------------------------299
§ 10.3 Inherent Product Hazards ------------------305
§ 10.4 State of the Art ----------------------------------309
§ 10.5 Prenatal Harm -----------------------------------327
§ 10.6 Deterioration -------------------------------------329
§ 10.7 Disposal and Salvage --------------------------330
§ 10.8 Post–Sale Duties to Warn, Repair, or Recall 332

PART III: CAUSATION

Chapter 11. CAUSE IN FACT

§ 11.1 Cause in Fact—Generally ----------------------337
§ 11.2 Tests and Proof of Causation------------------338
§ 11.3 Multiple Defendants --------------------------346
§ 11.4 Warnings Cases—Special Causation Issues--356

CHAPTER 12. PROXIMATE CAUSE

§ 12.1 Proximate Cause—Generally ----------------361
§ 12.2 Foreseeability and Other "Tests"------------363
§ 12.3 Intervening and Superseding Causes ------370

PART IV: DEFENSES

Chapter 13. USER MISCONDUCT DEFENSES

Page

§ 13.1 User Misconduct Defenses—Generally ----383
§ 13.2 Contributory Negligence-----------------------386
§ 13.3 Comparative Fault--------------------------------389
§ 13.4 Assumption of Risk ------------------------------396
§ 13.5 Misuse--402
§ 13.6 Defenses to Warranty Claims ----------------409
§ 13.7 Defenses to Misrepresentation Claims ----412

Chapter 14. SPECIAL DEFENSES

§ 14.1 Special Defenses—Generally ------------------415
§ 14.2 Compliance with Contract Specifications;
        Government Contractors--------------------416
§ 14.3 Compliance with Statutes and Regulations--419
§ 14.4 Federal Preemption ------------------------------422
§ 14.5 Statutes of Limitations and Repose --------428

PART V: SPECIAL ISSUES

Chapter 15. SPECIAL TYPES OF DEFENDANTS

§ 15.1 Special Types of Defendants—Generally --431
§ 15.2 Retailers and Other Non-Manufacturing
        Sellers---432
§ 15.3 Raw Material and Component Part
        Suppliers---437
§ 15.4 Parent and Apparent Manufacturers;
        Franchisers -------------------------------------439

§ 15.5 Successor Corporations ------------------------443
§ 15.6 Employers as Manufacturers------------------446
§ 15.7 Miscellaneous Marketing Participants ----450

Chapter 16. SPECIAL TYPES OF TRANSACTIONS AND PRODUCTS

§ 16.1 Special Types of Transactions and
              Products—Generally -------------------------457
§ 16.2 Lease, Bailment, and License Transactions --458
§ 16.3 Service Transactions ---------------------------464
§ 16.4 Repaired, Rebuilt, and Reconditioned
              Products --------------------------------------469
§ 16.5 Used Products ----------------------------------471
§ 16.6 Electricity --473
§ 16.7 Real Estate--474
§ 16.8 Publications --------------------------------------476
§ 16.9 Blood---480
§ 16.10 Miscellaneous Transactions and
              Products --------------------------------------481

Chapter 17. AUTOMOTIVE LITIGATION

§ 17.1 Automotive Litigation—Generally ------------485
§ 17.2 Defects That Cause Accidents ----------------486
§ 17.3 Crashworthiness --------------------------------488
§ 17.4 Indivisible Harm and Damages
              Apportionment --------------------------------494
§ 17.5 Plaintiff Fault------------------------------------497

Chapter 18. PUNITIVE DAMAGES

§ 18.1 Punitive Damages—Generally ----------------505

TABLE OF CONTENTS

§ 18.2 Functions of Punitive Damages --------------509
§ 18.3 Forms of Manufacturer Misconduct --------513
§ 18.4 Basis of Liability ---------------------------------518
§ 18.5 Problems and Recurring Criticisms --------521
§ 18.6 Judicial and Legislative Reform --------------521
§ 18.7 Constitutional Limitations --------------------528

INDEX ---539

*

TABLE OF CASES

References are to Pages

A

ACandS, Inc. v. Abate, 121 Md.App. 590, 710 A.2d 944 (Md.App. 1998), *468*

Accordini v. Security Cent., Inc., 283 S.C. 16, 320 S.E.2d 713 (S.C.App.1984), *362*

Adams v. Northern Illinois Gas Co., 211 Ill.2d 32, 284 Ill.Dec. 302, 809 N.E.2d 1248 (Ill.2004), *48*

Altria Group, Inc. v. Good, ___ U.S. ___, 128 S.Ct. 1119, 169 L.Ed.2d 846 (2008), *426*

Anderson v. Owens–Corning Fiberglas Corp., 281 Cal.Rptr. 528, 810 P.2d 549 (Cal.1991), *323*

Anderson vs. General Motors Corporation, 1999 WL 1466627 (Cal.Superior 1999), *493*

Auld v. Sears, Roebuck & Co., 261 A.D. 918, 25 N.Y.S.2d 491 (N.Y.A.D. 2 Dept.1941), *329*

Ault v. International Harvester Co., 117 Cal.Rptr. 812, 528 P.2d 1148 (Cal.1974), *197*

Austin v. Will–Burt Co., 361 F.3d 862 (5th Cir.2004), *268*

Axen v. American Home Products Corp. ex rel. Wyeth–Ayerst Laboratories, 158 Or.App. 292, 974 P.2d 224 (Or.App.1999), *514*

Azzarello v. Black Bros. Co., Inc., 480 Pa. 547, 391 A.2d 1020 (Pa.1978), *160*

B

Baker v. City of Seattle, 79 Wash.2d 198, 484 P.2d 405 (Wash. 1971), *459*

TABLE OF CASES

Barban v. Rheem Textile Systems, Inc., 2005 WL 387660 (E.D.N.Y.2005), *136*

Barker v. Lull Engineering Co., 143 Cal.Rptr. 225, 573 P.2d 443 (Cal.1978), *161, 241*

Barnett v. La Societe Anonyme Turbomeca France, 963 S.W.2d 639 (Mo.App. W.D.1997), *509*

Barry v. Quality Steel Products, Inc., 263 Conn. 424, 820 A.2d 258 (Conn.2003), *382*

Bartkewich v. Billinger, 432 Pa. 351, 247 A.2d 603 (Pa.1968), *300*

Bass v. Air Products & Chemicals, Inc., 2006 WL 1419375 (N.J.Super.A.D.2006), *360*

Bastian v. Wausau Homes Inc., 620 F.Supp. 947 (N.D.Ill.1985), *475*

Bates v. Dow Agrosciences LLC, 544 U.S. 431, 125 S.Ct. 1788, 161 L.Ed.2d 687 (2005), *427*

Baxter v. Ford Motor Co., 168 Wash. 456, 12 P.2d 409 (Wash. 1932), *83*

Beattie v. Beattie, 786 A.2d 549 (Del.Super.2001), *462*

Beauchamp v. Dow Chemical Co., 427 Mich. 1, 398 N.W.2d 882 (Mich.1986), *449*

Bednarski v. Hideout Homes & Realty Inc., a Div. of United States Homes & Properties, Inc., 711 F.Supp. 823 (M.D.Pa. 1989), *475*

Bell v. Industrial Vangas, Inc., 179 Cal.Rptr. 30, 637 P.2d 266 (Cal.1981), *448*

Bell v. T.R. Miller Mill Co., Inc., 768 So.2d 953 (Ala.2000), *212*

Bell ex rel. Estate of Bell v. Precision Airmotive Corp., 42 P.3d 1071 (Alaska 2002), *471*

Bellotte v. Zayre Corp., 531 F.2d 1100 (1st Cir.1976), *379*

Bellotte v. Zayre Corp., 116 N.H. 52, 352 A.2d 723 (N.H.1976), *154*

Bericochea–Cartagena v. Suzuki Motor Co., Ltd., 7 F.Supp.2d 109 (D.Puerto Rico 1998), *180*

Berish v. Bornstein, 437 Mass. 252, 770 N.E.2d 961 (Mass.2002), *62*

Beshada v. Johns–Manville Products Corp., 90 N.J. 191, 447 A.2d 539 (N.J.1982), *28, 318*

Bexiga v. Havir Mfg. Corp., 60 N.J. 402, 290 A.2d 281 (N.J.1972), *252*

Biss v. Tenneco, Inc., 64 A.D.2d 204, 409 N.Y.S.2d 874 (N.Y.A.D. 4 Dept.1978), *254*

Blaha v. Stuard, 640 N.W.2d 85 (S.D.2002), *482*

Blevins v. New Holland North America, Inc., 97 F.Supp.2d 747 (W.D.Va.2000), *121*

BMW of North America, Inc. v. Gore, 517 U.S. 559, 116 S.Ct. 1589, 134 L.Ed.2d 809 (1996), *529*

Bocci v. Key Pharmaceuticals, Inc., 189 Or.App. 349, 76 P.3d 669 (Or.App.2003), *524*

Bockrath v. Aldrich Chemical Co., Inc., 86 Cal.Rptr.2d 846, 980 P.2d 398 (Cal.1999), *341*

Borel v. Fibreboard Paper Products Corp., 493 F.2d 1076 (5th Cir.1973), *264*

Boryszewski ex rel. Boryszewski v. Burke, 380 N.J.Super. 361, 882 A.2d 410 (N.J.Super.A.D.2005), *497*

Bourgeois v. Garrard Chevrolet, Inc., 811 So.2d 962 (La.App. 4 Cir.2002), *488*

Bowen v. Cochran, 252 Ga.App. 457, 556 S.E.2d 530 (Ga.App. 2001), *398*

Boyle v. United Technologies Corp., 487 U.S. 500, 108 S.Ct. 2510, 101 L.Ed.2d 442 (1988), *418*

Brandt v. Boston Scientific Corp., 204 Ill.2d 640, 275 Ill.Dec. 65, 792 N.E.2d 296 (Ill.2003), *465*

Braun v. Soldier of Fortune Magazine, Inc., 968 F.2d 1110 (11th Cir.1992), *477*

Breast Implant Product Liability Litigation, In re, 331 S.C. 540, 503 S.E.2d 445 (S.C.1998), *467*

Bren–Tex Tractor Co., Inc. v. Massey–Ferguson, Inc., 97 S.W.3d 155 (Tex.App.-Hous. (14 Dist.) 2002), *433*

Bridgestone/Firestone North America Tire, L.L.C. v. A.P.S. Rent–A–Car & Leasing, Inc., 207 Ariz. 502, 88 P.3d 572 (Ariz.App. Div. 2 2004), *442*

Briscoe v. Amazing Products, Inc., 23 S.W.3d 228 (Ky.App.2000), *379*

Brooks v. Beech Aircraft Corp., 120 N.M. 372, 902 P.2d 54 (N.M.1995), *324*

Brown v. Superior Court, 245 Cal.Rptr. 412, 751 P.2d 470 (Cal.1988), *286, 323*

Browning–Ferris Industries of Vermont, Inc. v. Kelco Disposal, Inc., 492 U.S. 257, 109 S.Ct. 2909, 106 L.Ed.2d 219 (1989), *526*

Bruce v. Martin–Marietta Corp., 544 F.2d 442 (10th Cir.1976), *310, 313*

Bruzga v. PMR Architects, P.C., 141 N.H. 756, 693 A.2d 401 (N.H.1997), *465*

Bryant v. Hoffmann–La Roche, Inc., 262 Ga.App. 401, 585 S.E.2d 723 (Ga.App.2003), *257, 258*

Bryant v. Tri–County Elec. Membership Corp., 844 F.Supp. 347 (W.D.Ky.1994), *473*

Buckman Co. v. Plaintiffs' Legal Committee, 531 U.S. 341, 121 S.Ct. 1012, 148 L.Ed.2d 854 (2001), *427*

Buell–Wilson v. Ford Motor Co., 73 Cal.Rptr.3d 277 (Cal.App. 4 Dist.2008), *524*

Buford v. Toys R' Us, Inc., 217 Ga.App. 565, 458 S.E.2d 373 (Ga.App.1995), *105*

Bullara v. Checker's Drive–In Restaurant, Inc., 736 So.2d 936 (La.App. 3 Cir.1999), *218*

Burton v. R.J. Reynolds Tobacco Co., 397 F.3d 906 (10th Cir. 2005), *49, 77*

C

Calles v. Scripto–Tokai Corp., 224 Ill.2d 247, 309 Ill.Dec. 383, 864 N.E.2d 249 (Ill.2007), *152, 153, 166*

Campbell v. State Farm Mut. Auto. Ins. Co., 98 P.3d 409 (Utah 2004), *533*

Campo v. Scofield, 301 N.Y. 468, 95 N.E.2d 802 (N.Y.1950), *299*

Carbone by Carbone v. Alagna by Alagna, 239 A.D.2d 454, 658 N.Y.S.2d 48 (N.Y.A.D. 2 Dept.1997), *434*

Carillo v. Ford Motor Co., 325 Ill.App.3d 955, 259 Ill.Dec. 619, 759 N.E.2d 99 (Ill.App. 1 Dist.2001), *491*

Carroll Towing Co., United States v., 159 F.2d 169 (2nd Cir. 1947), *15, 51, 157, 230*

Castaldi v. Land Rover North America, Inc., 69 Fed. R. Serv.3d (E.D.N.Y.2007), *487*

CEF Enterprises, Inc. v. Betts, 838 So.2d 999 (Miss.App.2003), *218*

Christiana v. Southern Baptist Hosp., 867 So.2d 809 (La.App. 4 Cir.2004), *481*

Cintrone v. Hertz Truck Leasing and Rental Service, 45 N.J. 434, 212 A.2d 769 (N.J.1965), *459*

Cipollone v. Liggett Group, Inc., 505 U.S. 504, 112 S.Ct. 2608, 120 L.Ed.2d 407 (1992), *424*

City of (see name of city)

Comstock v. General Motors Corp., 358 Mich. 163, 99 N.W.2d 627 (Mich.1959), *333*

Condos v. Musculoskeletal Transplant Foundation, 208 F.Supp.2d 1226 (D.Utah 2002), *467*

Conner v. Quality Coach, Inc., 561 Pa. 397, 750 A.2d 823 (Pa.2000), *419*

Connick v. Suzuki Motor Co., Ltd., 275 Ill.App.3d 705, 212 Ill.Dec. 17, 656 N.E.2d 170 (Ill.App. 1 Dist.1995), *91*

Conway v. A.I. DuPont Hosp. for Children, 2007 WL 560502 (E.D.Pa.2007), *467*

Cooper Industries, Inc. v. Leatherman Tool Group, Inc., 532 U.S. 424, 121 S.Ct. 1678, 149 L.Ed.2d 674 (2001), *530*

Cooper Tire and Rubber Co. v. Tuckier, 826 So.2d 679 (Miss. 2002), *487*

Cotton v. Buckeye Gas Products Co., 840 F.2d 935, 268 U.S.App. D.C. 228 (D.C.Cir.1988), *276*

Crane v. Bagge & Son, Inc., 2005 WL 1576544 (Cal.App. 2 Dist.2005), *97*

Crankshaw v. Piedmont Driving Club, Inc., 115 Ga.App. 820, 156 S.E.2d 208 (Ga.App.1967), *366*

Cremeans v. Willmar Henderson Mfg. Co., a Div. of Waycrosse, Inc., 57 Ohio St.3d 145, 566 N.E.2d 1203 (Ohio 1991), *399*

Crosswhite v. Jumpking, Inc., 411 F.Supp.2d 1228 (D.Or.2006), *153*

Cunningham v. MacNeal Memorial Hospital, 47 Ill.2d 443, 266 N.E.2d 897 (Ill.1970), *480*

D

Daly v. General Motors Corp., 144 Cal.Rptr. 380, 575 P.2d 1162 (Cal.1978), *395, 503*

Daubert v. Merrell Dow Pharmaceuticals, Inc., 509 U.S. 579, 113 S.Ct. 2786, 125 L.Ed.2d 469 (1993), *26, 183*

Davidson v. Time Warner, Inc., 1997 WL 405907 (S.D.Tex.1997), *479*

Davila v. Goya Foods, Inc., 2007 WL 415147 (S.D.N.Y.2007), *219*

Daye v. General Motors Corp., 720 So.2d 654 (La.1998), *499*

Deed v. Walgreen Co., 50 Conn.Supp. 339, 927 A.2d 1001 (Conn.Super.2007), *295*

Deemer v. A.H. Robins Co., Case No. C-26420 (Kan. Dist. Ct. Sedgwick Cty. 1975), *515*

Denny v. Ford Motor Co., 639 N.Y.S.2d 250, 662 N.E.2d 730 (N.Y.1995), *170*

Dillard v. Pittway Corp., 719 So.2d 188 (Ala.1998), *399*

Douglas v. E. & J. Gallo Winery, 69 Cal.App.3d 103, 137 Cal. Rptr. 797 (Cal.App. 5 Dist.1977), *448*

Dow Corning Corp., In re, 2007 WL 186303 (9th Cir.2007), *465*

Duchess v. Langston Corp., 564 Pa. 529, 769 A.2d 1131 (Pa. 2001), *198*

Ducko v. Chrysler Motors Corp., 433 Pa.Super. 47, 639 A.2d 1204 (Pa.Super.1994), *215*

E

East River S.S. Corp. v. Transamerica Delaval, Inc., 476 U.S. 858, 106 S.Ct. 2295, 90 L.Ed.2d 865 (1986), *139*

Edward W. Knoster, Estate of v. Ford Motor Co., 200 Fed.Appx. 106 (3rd Cir.2006), *488*

Elliott v. Kraft Foods North America, Inc., 118 S.W.3d 50 (Tex. App.-Hous. (14 Dist.) 2003), *218*

Escola v. Coca Cola Bottling Co. of Fresno, 24 Cal.2d 453, 150 P.2d 436 (Cal.1944), *128*

Estate of (see name of party)

Evans v. General Motors Corp., 359 F.2d 822 (7th Cir.1966), *490*

Exxon Shipping Co. v. Baker, ___ U.S. ___, 128 S.Ct. 2605 (2008), *525*

F

Falada v. Trinity Industries, Inc., 642 N.W.2d 247 (Iowa 2002), *314*

Feldman v. Lederle Laboratories, 97 N.J. 429, 479 A.2d 374 (N.J.1984), *28, 286, 318, 321*

Flagstar Enterprises, Inc. v. Davis, 709 So.2d 1132 (Ala.1997), *218*

Fletcher v. Atex, Inc., 68 F.3d 1451 (2nd Cir.1995), *440*

Fluor Corp. v. Jeppesen & Co., 170 Cal.App.3d 468, 216 Cal.Rptr. 68 (Cal.App. 2 Dist.1985), *478*

Folsom v. Kawasaki Motors Corp. U.S.A., 509 F.Supp.2d 1364 (M.D.Ga.2007), *314*

Forbes v. General Motors Corp., 935 So.2d 869 (Miss.2006), *88*

Ford Motor Co. v. General Acc. Ins. Co., 365 Md. 321, 779 A.2d 362 (Md.2001), *99*

TABLE OF CASES

Ford Motor Co. v. Moulton, 511 S.W.2d 690 (Tenn.1974), *111*
Ford Motor Co. v. Rushford, 868 N.E.2d 806 (Ind.2007), *48*
438 Main Street v. Easy Heat, Inc., 99 P.3d 801 (Utah 2004), *342*
Fox v. Ford Motor Co., 575 F.2d 774 (10th Cir.1978), *496*
Frank v. DaimlerChrysler Corp., 292 A.D.2d 118, 741 N.Y.S.2d 9 (N.Y.A.D. 1 Dept.2002), *140*
Freightliner Corp. v. Myrick, 514 U.S. 280, 115 S.Ct. 1483, 131 L.Ed.2d 385 (1995), *426*
Frey v. Harley Davidson Motor Co., Inc., 734 A.2d 1 (Pa.Super.1999), *472*
Frye v. United States, 293 F. 1013 (D.C.Cir.1923), *182*
Fuentes v. Shin Caterpillar Mitsubishi, Ltd., 2003 WL 22205665 (Cal.App. 6 Dist.2003), *273*

G

Gaines–Tabb v. ICI Explosives, USA, Inc., 160 F.3d 613 (10th Cir.1998), *61, 381*
Garcia v. Halsett, 3 Cal.App.3d 319, 82 Cal.Rptr. 420 (Cal.App. 1 Dist.1970), *462*
Garcia v. Joseph Vince Co., 84 Cal.App.3d 868, 148 Cal.Rptr. 843 (Cal.App. 2 Dist.1978), *348*
Gardiner v. Gray, 1815 WL 1401 (Assizes 1815), *93*
Gaston v. Bobby Johnson Equipment Co., Inc., 771 So.2d 848 (La.App. 2 Cir.2000), *471*
Geier v. American Honda Motor Co., Inc., 529 U.S. 861, 120 S.Ct. 1913, 146 L.Ed.2d 914 (2000), *425*
General Elec. Co. v. Joiner, 522 U.S. 136, 118 S.Ct. 512, 139 L.Ed.2d 508 (1997), *186*
General Motors Corp. v. Edwards, 482 So.2d 1176 (Ala.1985), *235*
General Motors Corp. v. Hopkins, 548 S.W.2d 344 (Tex.1977), *403*
General Motors Corp. v. Saenz on Behalf of Saenz, 873 S.W.2d 353 (Tex.1993), *277*
General Motors Corp. v. Sanchez, 997 S.W.2d 584 (Tex.1999), *396, 488*
Genereux v. American Beryllia Corp., 518 F.Supp.2d 306 (D.Mass.2007), *283*
Gibson v. Wal–Mart Stores, Inc., 189 F.Supp.2d 443 (W.D.Va. 2002), *63*

Gillham v. Admiral Corp., 523 F.2d 102 (6th Cir.1975), *506*

G.J. Palmer v. Espey Huston & Associates, Inc., 84 S.W.3d 345 (Tex.App.-Corpus Christi 2002), *465*

Glittenberg v. Doughboy Recreational Industries, 441 Mich. 379, 491 N.W.2d 208 (Mich.1992), *178, 305*

Golonka v. General Motors Corp., 204 Ariz. 575, 65 P.3d 956 (Ariz.App. Div. 1 2003), *313, 360*

Golt by Golt v. Sports Complex, Inc., 644 A.2d 989 (Del.Super.1994), *462*

Goodman v. Stalfort, Inc., 411 F.Supp. 889 (D.N.J.1976), *406*

Gray v. Badger Min. Corp., 676 N.W.2d 268 (Minn.2004), *269, 282, 283*

Green v. Denney, 87 Or.App. 298, 742 P.2d 639 (Or.App.1987), *366*

Green v. Smith & Nephew AHP, Inc., 245 Wis.2d 772, 629 N.W.2d 727 (Wis.2001), *313, 325*

Greenfield v. Suzuki Motor Co. Ltd., 776 F.Supp. 698 (E.D.N.Y. 1991), *367*

Greenman v. Yuba Power Products, Inc., 59 Cal.2d 57, 27 Cal. Rptr. 697, 377 P.2d 897 (Cal.1963), *11, 18, 131*

Greenwood v. Busch Entertainment Corp., 101 F.Supp.2d 292 (E.D.Pa.2000), *462*

Griggs v. BIC Corp., 981 F.2d 1429 (3rd Cir.1992), *55, 237*

Grimshaw v. Ford Motor Co., 119 Cal.App.3d 757, 174 Cal.Rptr. 348 (Cal.App. 4 Dist.1981), *493*

Grover v. Eli Lilly & Co., 63 Ohio St.3d 756, 591 N.E.2d 696 (Ohio 1992), *329*

H

Haase v. Badger Mining Corp., 266 Wis.2d 970, 669 N.W.2d 737 (Wis.App.2003), *282*

Hall v. E. I. Du Pont De Nemours & Co., Inc., 345 F.Supp. 353 (E.D.N.Y.1972), *353*

Hammes v. Yamaha Motor Corp. U.S.A., Inc., 2006 WL 1195907 (D.Minn.2006), *335*

Hanberry v. Hearst Corp., 276 Cal.App.2d 680, 81 Cal.Rptr. 519 (Cal.App. 4 Dist.1969), *82, 450*

Hanus v. Texas Utilities Co., 71 S.W.3d 874 (Tex.App.-Fort Worth 2002), *473*

Hardy v. General Motors Corp., 126 Ohio App.3d 455, 710 N.E.2d 764 (Ohio App. 6 Dist.1998), *499*

Harrison v. B.F. Goodrich Co., 881 So.2d 288 (Miss.App.2004), *443*

Hebel v. Sherman Equipment, 92 Ill.2d 368, 65 Ill.Dec. 888, 442 N.E.2d 199 (Ill.1982), *441*

Helicoid Gage Division of Am. Chain & Cable Co. v. Howell, 511 S.W.2d 573 (Tex.Civ.App-Hous (14 Dist.) 1974), *155*

Henningsen v. Bloomfield Motors, Inc., 32 N.J. 358, 161 A.2d 69 (N.J.1960), *9, 11, 101, 121, 130, 486*

Hickman v. William Wrigley, Jr. Co., Inc., 768 So.2d 812 (La.App. 2 Cir.2000), *219*

High v. Westinghouse Elec. Corp., 610 So.2d 1259 (Fla.1992), *332*

Hill v. Wyeth, Inc., 2007 WL 674251 (E.D.Mo.2007), *257*

Hiner v. Deere and Co., Inc., 340 F.3d 1190 (10th Cir.2003), *334*

Hinojasa v. Automatic Elevator Co., 92 Ill.App.3d 351, 48 Ill.Dec. 150, 416 N.E.2d 45 (Ill.App. 1 Dist.1980), *468*

Hopkins v. Dow Corning Corp., 33 F.3d 1116 (9th Cir.1994), *516*

Hubbard–Hall Chemical Co. v. Silverman, 340 F.2d 402 (1st Cir.1965), *274*

Huddell v. Levin, 537 F.2d 726 (3rd Cir.1976), *495*

I

In re (see name of party)

Irion v. Sun Lighting, Inc., 2004 WL 746823 (Tenn.Ct.App.2004), *232*

J

James v. Meow Media, Inc., 300 F.3d 683 (6th Cir.2002), *479*

James v. Meow Media, Inc., 90 F.Supp.2d 798 (W.D.Ky.2000), *379*

Jappell v. American Ass'n of Blood Banks, 162 F.Supp.2d 476 (E.D.Va.2001), *453*

Jarke v. Jackson Products, 258 Ill.App.3d 718, 197 Ill.Dec. 230, 631 N.E.2d 233 (Ill.App. 1 Dist.1994), *225*

Jarvis v. Ford Motor Co., 283 F.3d 33 (2nd Cir.2002), *488*

Jenkins v. General Motors Corp., 446 F.2d 377 (5th Cir.1971), *210*

Jett v. Ford Motor Co., 192 Or.App. 113, 84 P.3d 219 (Or.App. 2004), *385, 396*

Johnson v. American National Red Cross, 276 Ga. 270, 578 S.E.2d 106 (Ga.2003), *481*

Johnson v. American Standard, Inc., 74 Cal.Rptr.3d 108, 179 P.3d 905 (Cal.2008), *303*

Johnson v. Raybestos–Manhattan, Inc., 69 Haw. 287, 740 P.2d 548 (Hawai'i 1987), *313, 324*

Johnson v. Stanley Bostitch, Inc., 2000 WL 709480 (E.D.Pa. 2000), *462*

Johnson Controls Battery Group, Inc. v. Runnels, 2003 WL 21191063 (Tex.App.-Tyler 2003), *53*

Jonas v. Isuzu Motors Ltd., 210 F.Supp.2d 1373 (M.D.Ga.2002), *488*

Jones v. Amazing Products, Inc., 231 F.Supp.2d 1228 (N.D.Ga. 2002), *56, 306*

Jones v. Ford Motor Co., 263 Va. 237, 559 S.E.2d 592 (Va.2002), *410*

Jones v. Rath Packing Co., 430 U.S. 519, 97 S.Ct. 1305, 51 L.Ed.2d 604 (1977), *423*

Jones v. United Metal Recyclers, 825 F.Supp. 1288 (W.D.Mich. 1993), *332*

Jonescue v. Jewel Home Shopping Service, 16 Ill.App.3d 339, 306 N.E.2d 312 (Ill.App. 2 Dist.1973), *266*

Jordan v. Sunnyslope Appliance Propane & Plumbing Supplies Co., 135 Ariz. 309, 660 P.2d 1236 (Ariz.App. Div. 1 1983), *472*

Jorgensen v. Meade Johnson Laboratories, Inc., 483 F.2d 237 (10th Cir.1973), *328*

K

Kaneko v. Hilo Coast Processing, 65 Haw. 447, 654 P.2d 343 (Hawai'i 1982), *475*

Kaplan v. C Lazy U Ranch, 615 F.Supp. 234 (D.Colo.1985), *482*

Karim v. Tanabe Machinery, Ltd., 322 F.Supp.2d 578 (E.D.Pa. 2004), *400*

Karl, State v., 220 W.Va. 463, 647 S.E.2d 899 (W.Va.2007), *292*

Keeler v. Richards Mfg. Co., Inc., 817 F.2d 1197 (5th Cir.1987), *207*

Kelleher v. Marvin Lumber & Cedar Co., 152 N.H. 813, 891 A.2d 477 (N.H.2005), *139*

Killeen v. Harmon Grain Products, Inc., 11 Mass.App.Ct. 20, 413 N.E.2d 767 (Mass.App.Ct.1980), *262*

King v. National Spa and Pool Institute, Inc., 570 So.2d 612 (Ala.1990), *454*

Kirk v. Michael Reese Hosp. and Medical Center, 117 Ill.2d 507, 111 Ill.Dec. 944, 513 N.E.2d 387 (Ill.1987), *375*

Klein v. Sears Roebuck and Co., 773 F.2d 1421 (4th Cir.1985), *98*

Kolarik v. Cory Intern. Corp., 721 N.W.2d 159 (Iowa 2006), *220*

Korean Air Lines Disaster of Sept. 1, 1983, In re, 1985 WL 9447 (D.D.C.1985), *381*

Korean Air Lines Disaster of Sept. 1, 1983, In re, 664 F.Supp. 1463 (D.D.C.1985), *381*

Kotz v. Hawaii Elec. Light Co., Inc., 83 P.3d 743 (Hawai'i 2004), *472*

Kumho Tire Co., Ltd. v. Carmichael, 526 U.S. 137, 119 S.Ct. 1167, 143 L.Ed.2d 238 (1999), *187*

L

LaBelle ex rel. LaBelle v. Philip Morris, Inc., 243 F.Supp.2d 508 (D.S.C.2001), *314*

Laidlow v. Hariton Machinery Co., Inc., 170 N.J. 602, 790 A.2d 884 (N.J.2002), *449*

Larkin v. Pfizer, Inc., 153 S.W.3d 758 (Ky.2004), *289*

Larsen v. General Motors Corp., 391 F.2d 495 (8th Cir.1968), *490*

Leake v. Meredith, 221 Va. 14, 267 S.E.2d 93 (Va.1980), *459*

Leary ex rel. Debold v. Syracuse Model Neighborhood Corp., 799 N.Y.S.2d 867 (N.Y.Sup.2005), *266*

Levey v. Yamaha Motor Corp., 361 N.J.Super. 312, 825 A.2d 554 (N.J.Super.A.D.2003), *275*

Levine v. Sears Roebuck and Co., 200 F.Supp.2d 180 (E.D.N.Y. 2002), *471*

Lewis v. Lead Industries Ass'n, Inc., 342 Ill.App.3d 95, 276 Ill.Dec. 110, 793 N.E.2d 869 (Ill.App. 1 Dist.2003), *356*

Lewis v. Sea Ray Boats, Inc., 119 Nev. 100, 65 P.3d 245 (Nev. 2003), *266*

Liebeck v. McDonald's Restaurants, P.T.S., Inc., 1995 WL 360309 (N.M. Dist.1994), *507*

Lillebo v. Zimmer, Inc., 2005 WL 388598 (D.Minn.2005), *54*

Lloyd v. General Motors Corp., 397 Md. 108, 916 A.2d 257 (Md.2007), *140*

Lohrmann v. Pittsburgh Corning Corp., 782 F.2d 1156 (4th Cir.1986), *345*

Lovick v. Wil–Rich, 588 N.W.2d 688 (Iowa 1999), *518*

M

MacDonald v. Ortho Pharmaceutical Corp., 394 Mass. 131, 475 N.E.2d 65 (Mass.1985), *290*

MacPherson v. Buick Motor Co., 217 N.Y. 382, 111 N.E. 1050 (N.Y.1916), *10, 127, 208, 210, 486*

Madison v. American Home Products Corp., 358 S.C. 449, 595 S.E.2d 493 (S.C.2004), *295*

Maize v. Atlantic Refining Co., 352 Pa. 51, 41 A.2d 850 (Pa. 1945), *275*

Maneely v. General Motors Corp., 108 F.3d 1176 (9th Cir.1997), *81*

Martens v. MCL Const. Corp., 347 Ill.App.3d 303, 282 Ill.Dec. 856, 807 N.E.2d 480 (Ill.App. 1 Dist.2004), *474*

Martinez v. Duke Energy Corp., 130 Fed.Appx. 629 (4th Cir. 2005), *474*

Massey v. Cassens & Sons, Inc., 2007 WL 2710490 (S.D.Ill.2007), *461*

Maybank v. S. S. Kresge Co., 46 N.C.App. 687, 266 S.E.2d 409 (N.C.App.1980), *180*

Mazda Motor Corp. v. Lindahl, 706 A.2d 526 (Del.Supr.1998), *500*

Mazetti v. Armour & Co., 75 Wash. 622, 135 P. 633 (Wash.1913), *8, 101*

McCarthy v. Olin Corp., 119 F.3d 148 (2nd Cir.1997), *233*

McConkey v. McGhan Medical Corp., 144 F.Supp.2d 958 (E.D.Tenn.2000), *440*

McGuire v. Davidson Mfg. Corp., 398 F.3d 1005 (8th Cir.2005), *49*

McGuire v. Davidson Mfg. Corp., 258 F.Supp.2d 945 (N.D.Iowa 2003), *67*

Medtronic, Inc. v. Lohr, 518 U.S. 470, 116 S.Ct. 2240, 135 L.Ed.2d 700 (1996), *427*

Meneely v. S.R. Smith, Inc., 101 Wash.App. 845, 5 P.3d 49 (Wash.App. Div. 3 2000), *453*

Menendez v. Paddock Pool Const. Co., 172 Ariz. 258, 836 P.2d 968 (Ariz.App. Div. 1 1991), *476*

Menz v. New Holland North America, Inc., 507 F.3d 1107 (8th Cir.2007), *342*

Mercer v. Uniroyal, Inc., 49 Ohio App.2d 279, 361 N.E.2d 492 (Ohio App. 6 Dist.1976), *447*

Mesman v. Crane Pro Services, 512 F.3d 352 (7th Cir.2008), *53*

Micallef v. Miehle Co., Division of Miehle–Goss Dexter, Inc., 384 N.Y.S.2d 115, 348 N.E.2d 571 (N.Y.1976), *301*

Mickle v. Blackmon, 252 S.C. 202, 166 S.E.2d 173 (S.C.1969), *330*

Milford v. Commercial Carriers, Inc., 210 F.Supp.2d 987 (N.D.Ill. 2002), *465*

Miller v. McDonald's Corp., 150 Or.App. 274, 945 P.2d 1107 (Or.App.1997), *442*

Mitchell v. Volkswagenwerk, A.G., 669 F.2d 1199 (8th Cir.1982), *496*

Moning v. Alfono, 400 Mich. 425, 254 N.W.2d 759 (Mich.1977), *434*

Monsanto Co. v. Reed, 950 S.W.2d 811 (Ky.1997), *331*

Moore ex rel. Moore v. Memorial Hosp. of Gulfport, 825 So.2d 658 (Miss.2002), *296*

Moore ex rel. Moore v. Mississippi Valley Gas Co., 863 So.2d 43 (Miss.2003), *339*

Mounds View, City of v. Walijarvi, 263 N.W.2d 420 (Minn.1978), *465*

Myers v. Philip Morris Companies, Inc., 123 Cal.Rptr.2d 40, 50 P.3d 751 (Cal.2002), *307*

N

Nelson v. Superior Court, 50 Cal.Rptr.3d 684 (Cal.App. 3 Dist. 2006), *484*

New Texas Auto Auction Services, L.P. v. Gomez De Hernandez, 249 S.W.3d 400 (Tex.2008), *455*

Nichols v. Agway, Inc., 280 A.D.2d 889, 720 N.Y.S.2d 691 (N.Y.A.D. 4 Dept.2001), *476*

Nicholson v. American Safety Utility Corp., 346 N.C. 767, 488 S.E.2d 240 (N.C.1997), *410*

Nissan Motor Co. Ltd. v. Nave, 129 Md.App. 90, 740 A.2d 102 (Md.App.1999), *491*

Nunnally v. R.J. Reynolds Tobacco Co., 869 So.2d 373 (Miss. 2004), *232*

TABLE OF CASES

O

Ogletree v. Navistar Intern. Transp. Corp., 269 Ga. 443, 500 S.E.2d 570 (Ga.1998), *302*

Olshansky v. Rehrig Intern., 872 A.2d 282 (R.I.2005), *67*

Ostendorf v. Clark Equipment Co., 122 S.W.3d 530 (Ky.2003), *334, 335*

P

Pabon v. Hackensack Auto Sales, Inc., 63 N.J.Super. 476, 164 A.2d 773 (N.J.Super.A.D.1960), *81*

Pacific Mut. Life Ins. Co. v. Haslip, 499 U.S. 1, 111 S.Ct. 1032, 113 L.Ed.2d 1 (1991), *528*

Pack v. Damon Corp., 434 F.3d 810 (6th Cir.2006), *120*

Palmer v. Massey–Ferguson, Inc., 3 Wash.App. 508, 476 P.2d 713 (Wash.App. Div. 2 1970), *301*

Parish v. Jumpking, Inc., 719 N.W.2d 540 (Iowa 2006), *306*

Parris v. M. A. Bruder & Sons, Inc., 261 F.Supp. 406 (E.D.Pa. 1966), *388*

Patterson v. Central Mills, Inc., 2003 WL 2007941 (6th Cir.2003), *411*

Pavlides v. Galveston Yacht Basin, Inc., 727 F.2d 330 (5th Cir.1984), *269*

Pemberton, Estate of v. John's Sports Center, Inc., 35 Kan. App.2d 809, 135 P.3d 174 (Kan.App.2006), *60*

Pennsylvania Dept. of General Services v. U.S. Mineral Products Co., 587 Pa. 236, 898 A.2d 590 (Pa.2006), *167*

Perez v. Wyeth Laboratories Inc., 161 N.J. 1, 734 A.2d 1245 (N.J.1999), *291*

Peterson v. Lou Bachrodt Chevrolet Co., 61 Ill.2d 17, 329 N.E.2d 785 (Ill.1975), *472*

Philip Morris USA v. Williams, ___ U.S. ___, 127 S.Ct. 1057, 166 L.Ed.2d 940 (2007), *534*

Philip Morris USA Inc. v. Williams, ___ U.S. ___, 128 S.Ct. 2904 (2008), *535*

Philip Morris USA Inc. v. Williams, 540 U.S. 801, 124 S.Ct. 56, 157 L.Ed.2d 12 (2003), *534*

Phillips v. Cricket Lighters, 584 Pa. 179, 883 A.2d 439 (Pa.2005), *95*

Phillips v. Kimwood Mach. Co., 269 Or. 485, 525 P.2d 1033 (Or.1974), *247*

Pillars v. R. J. Reynolds Tobacco Co., 117 Miss. 490, 78 So. 365 (Miss.1918), *217*

Polemis, In re, 1921 WL 15985 (CA 1921), *365*

Port Authority of New York and New Jersey v. Arcadian Corp., 189 F.3d 305 (3rd Cir.1999), *380*

Potter v. Chicago Pneumatic Tool Co., 241 Conn. 199, 694 A.2d 1319 (Conn.1997), *162, 240, 315*

Potter v. Ford Motor Co., 213 S.W.3d 264 (Tenn.Ct.App.2006), *235*

Price v. Blaine Kern Artista, Inc., 111 Nev. 515, 893 P.2d 367 (Nev.1995), *379*

Purvis v. American Motors Corp., 538 So.2d 1015 (La.App. 1 Cir.1988), *180*

R

Ramirez v. Plough, Inc., 25 Cal.Rptr.2d 97, 863 P.2d 167 (Cal. 1993), *273, 421*

Raney v. Honeywell, Inc., 540 F.2d 932 (8th Cir.1976), *229*

Ray v. Alad Corp., 136 Cal.Rptr. 574, 560 P.2d 3 (Cal.1977), *445*

Reed v. Chrysler Corp., 494 N.W.2d 224 (Iowa 1992), *500*

Reeder v. Bally's Total Fitness Corp., 963 F.Supp. 530 (E.D.Va. 1997), *462*

Rhoads v. Service Mach. Co., 329 F.Supp. 367 (E.D.Ark.1971), *49*

Ricci v. AB Volvo, 2004 WL 1686936 (9th Cir.2004), *404*

Rice v. Paladin Enterprises, Inc., 128 F.3d 233 (4th Cir.1997), *478*

Richelman v. Kewanee Machinery & Conveyor Co., 59 Ill.App.3d 578, 16 Ill.Dec. 778, 375 N.E.2d 885 (Ill.App. 5 Dist.1978), *367*

Riegel v. Medtronic, Inc., ___ U.S. ___, 128 S.Ct. 999, 169 L.Ed.2d 892 (2008), *427*

Rivera v. Philip Morris, Inc., 395 F.3d 1142 (9th Cir.2005), *137*

RLI Ins. Co. v. Union Pacific R. Co., 463 F.Supp.2d 646 (S.D.Tex. 2006), *62*

Robinson Helicopter Co. v. Dana Corp., 129 Cal.Rptr.2d 682 (Cal.App. 2 Dist.2003), *519*

Rogers v. Ingersoll–Rand Co., 144 F.3d 841, 330 U.S.App.D.C. 198 (D.C.Cir.1998), *178*

Roney v. Gencorp, 431 F.Supp.2d 622 (S.D.W.Va.2006), *75*

Rose v. Brown & Williamson Tobacco Corp., 855 N.Y.S.2d 119 (N.Y.A.D. 1 Dept.2008), *306*

Rosendin v. Avco Lycoming Div., Civ. No. 202,715 (Cal. Super. Ct. Santa Clara Cty. 1972), *514*

Ruzzo v. LaRose Enterprises, 748 A.2d 261 (R.I.2000), *120, 460*

S

Samuel Friedland Family Enterprises v. Amoroso, 630 So.2d 1067 (Fla.1994), *460*

Sanders v. Acclaim Entertainment, Inc., 188 F.Supp.2d 1264 (D.Colo.2002), *378, 479*

Sanders v. Hartville Mill. Co., 14 S.W.3d 188 (Mo.App. S.D.2000), *212*

Sanns v. Butterfield Ford, 94 P.3d 301 (Utah App.2004), *433*

Sappington v. Skyjack, Inc., 512 F.3d 440 (8th Cir.2008), *190, 460*

Schaerrer v. Stewart's Plaza Pharmacy, Inc., 79 P.3d 922 (Utah 2003), *296*

Scher v. Bayer Corp., 258 F.Supp.2d 190 (E.D.N.Y.2003), *480*

Schipper v. Levitt & Sons, Inc., 44 N.J. 70, 207 A.2d 314 (N.J.1965), *475*

Schwarz, Estate of v. Philip Morris Inc., 206 Or.App. 20, 135 P.3d 409 (Or.App.2006), *74*

Sears, Roebuck & Co. v. Kunze, 996 S.W.2d 416 (Tex.App.-Beaumont 1999), *517*

September 11 Litigation, In re, 280 F.Supp.2d 279 (S.D.N.Y. 2003), *380*

September 11 Litigation, In re, 265 F.Supp.2d 208 (S.D.N.Y. 2003), *95, 233, 380*

Shipler v. General Motors Corp., 271 Neb. 194, 710 N.W.2d 807 (Neb.2006), *166*

Silicone Gel Breast Implants Products Liability Litigation, In re, 887 F.Supp. 1447 (N.D.Ala.1995), *440*

Simeone v. Bombardier–Rotax GmbH, 360 F.Supp.2d 665 (E.D.Pa.2005), *440*

Simonetta v. Viad Corp., 137 Wash.App. 15, 151 P.3d 1019 (Wash.App. Div. 1 2007), *266*

Sindell v. Abbott Laboratories, 163 Cal.Rptr. 132, 607 P.2d 924 (Cal.1980), *349*

Small v. Pioneer Machinery, Inc., 329 S.C. 448, 494 S.E.2d 835 (S.C.App.1997), *373*

Smith v. Alza Corp., 400 N.J.Super. 529, 948 A.2d 686 (N.J.Super.A.D.2008), *70*

Smith v. Brown & Williamson Tobacco Corp., 2007 WL 2175034 (Mo.App. W.D.2007), *235*

Smith v. Florida Power and Light Co., 857 So.2d 224 (Fla.App. 2 Dist.2003), *474*

Smith v. Ford Motor Co., 215 F.3d 713 (7th Cir.2000), *487*

Smoot v. Mazda Motors of America, Inc., 469 F.3d 675 (7th Cir.2006), *68*

Solo v. Trus Joist MacMillan, 2004 WL 524898 (D.Minn.2004), *96*

Soufflas v. Zimmer, Inc., 474 F.Supp.2d 737 (E.D.Pa.2007), *53*

Soule v. General Motors Corp., 34 Cal.Rptr.2d 607, 882 P.2d 298 (Cal.1994), *162, 243, 491*

Sprietsma v. Mercury Marine, a Div. of Brunswick Corp., 537 U.S. 51, 123 S.Ct. 518, 154 L.Ed.2d 466 (2002), *427*

Springmeyer v. Ford Motor Co., 71 Cal.Rptr.2d 190 (Cal.App. 1 Dist.1998), *438*

Stahlecker v. Ford Motor Co., 266 Neb. 601, 667 N.W.2d 244 (Neb.2003), *378*

Stanley Industries, Inc. v. W.M. Barr & Co., Inc., 784 F.Supp. 1570 (S.D.Fla.1992), *273*

State ex rel. v. _____ (see opposing party and relator)

State Farm Mut. Auto. Ins. Co. v. Campbell, 538 U.S. 408, 123 S.Ct. 1513, 155 L.Ed.2d 585 (2003), *531*

Sternhagen v. Dow Co., 282 Mont. 168, 935 P.2d 1139 (Mont. 1997), *325*

Stillie v. AM Intern., Inc., 850 F.Supp. 960 (D.Kan.1994), *470*

St. Joseph Hospital v. Corbetta Const. Co., Inc., 21 Ill.App.3d 925, 316 N.E.2d 51 (Ill.App. 1 Dist.1974), *78*

Strothkamp v. Chesebrough–Pond's, Inc., 1993 WL 79239 (Mo. App. E.D.1993), *274*

Sufix, U.S.A., Inc. v. Cook, 128 S.W.3d 838 (Ky.App.2004), *516*

Summers v. Tice, 33 Cal.2d 80, 199 P.2d 1 (Cal.1948), *350*

Sutowski v. Eli Lilly & Co., 82 Ohio St.3d 347, 696 N.E.2d 187 (Ohio 1998), *351*

T

The T.J. Hooper, 60 F.2d 737 (2nd Cir.1932), *58*

Thornton v. Gray Automotive Parts Co., 62 S.W.3d 575 (Mo.App. W.D.2001), *392*

Tillman v. Vance Equipment Co., 286 Or. 747, 596 P.2d 1299 (Or.1979), *472*

Tobacco Cases II, In re, 113 Cal.Rptr.2d 120 (Cal.App. 4 Dist. 2001), *82*

Toole v. Richardson–Merrell Inc., 251 Cal.App.2d 689, 60 Cal. Rptr. 398 (Cal.App. 1 Dist.1967), *506*

Torres–Rios v. LPS Laboratories, Inc., 152 F.3d 11 (1st Cir. 1998), *273*

Townsend v. Sears, Roebuck and Co., 227 Ill.2d 147, 316 Ill.Dec. 505, 879 N.E.2d 893 (Ill.2007), *313, 325*

Treadwell Ford, Inc. v. Campbell, 485 So.2d 312 (Ala.1986), *60*

Trull v. Volkswagen of America, Inc., 145 N.H. 259, 761 A.2d 477 (N.H.2000), *497*

Turner v. Bituminous Cas. Co., 397 Mich. 406, 244 N.W.2d 873 (Mich.1976), *444*

Turner v. International Harvester Co., 133 N.J.Super. 277, 336 A.2d 62 (N.J.Super.L.1975), *472*

Tuttle v. Lorillard Tobacco Co., 377 F.3d 917 (8th Cir.2004), *454*

U

United States v. _____ (see opposing party)

Universal Underwriters Ins. Group v. Public Service Elec. & Gas Co., 103 F.Supp.2d 744 (D.N.J.2000), *473*

V

Van Bracklin v. Fonda, 12 Johns. 468 (N.Y.Sup.1815), *218*

Vandermark v. Ford Motor Co., 61 Cal.2d 256, 37 Cal.Rptr. 896, 391 P.2d 168 (Cal.1964), *436*

Vassallo v. Baxter Healthcare Corp., 428 Mass. 1, 696 N.E.2d 909 (Mass.1998), *323*

Velleca v. Uniroyal Tire Co., Inc., 36 Mass.App.Ct. 247, 630 N.E.2d 297 (Mass.App.Ct.1994), *410*

Venezia v. Miller Brewing Co., 626 F.2d 188 (1st Cir.1980), *411*

Verge v. Ford Motor Co., 581 F.2d 384 (3rd Cir.1978), *254*

Verret v. American Biltrite, Inc., 2006 WL 2507318 (Tex.App.- Fort Worth 2006), *341*

Vic Potamkin Chevrolet, Inc. v. Horne, 505 So.2d 560 (Fla.App. 3 Dist.1987), *434*

Vincer v. Esther Williams All–Aluminum Swimming Pool Co., 69 Wis.2d 326, 230 N.W.2d 794 (Wis.1975), *152*

W

Waering v. BASF Corp., 146 F.Supp.2d 675 (M.D.Pa.2001), *68*

Walcott v. Total Petroleum, Inc., 964 P.2d 609 (Colo.App.1998), *60*

Wald v. Costco Wholesale Corp., 2005 WL 425864 (S.D.N.Y. 2005), *54*

Walters v. Seventeen Magazine, 195 Cal.App.3d 1119, 241 Cal. Rptr. 101 (Cal.App. 4 Dist.1987), *477*

Warner–Lambert Co., LLC v. Kent, ___ U.S. ___, 128 S.Ct. 1168, 170 L.Ed.2d 51 (2008), *427*

Waters v. NMC–Wollard, Inc., 2007 WL 2668008 (E.D.Pa.2007), *339*

Watson v. Ford Motor Co., 2007 WL 4216975 (Ohio App. 6 Dist.2007), *519*

Watters v. TSR, Inc., 904 F.2d 378 (6th Cir.1990), *479*

Way v. Boy Scouts of America, 856 S.W.2d 230 (Tex.App.-Dallas 1993), *477*

Weisgram v. Marley Co., 528 U.S. 440, 120 S.Ct. 1011, 145 L.Ed.2d 958 (2000), *187*

Whitaker v. Lian Feng Mach. Co., 156 Ill.App.3d 316, 108 Ill.Dec. 895, 509 N.E.2d 591 (Ill.App. 1 Dist.1987), *104*

Whitaker v. T.J. Snow Co., Inc., 953 F.Supp. 1034 (N.D.Ind. 1997), *470*

White v. ABCO Engineering Corp., 221 F.3d 293 (2nd Cir.2000), *438*

Whitmer v. Schneble, 29 Ill.App.3d 659, 331 N.E.2d 115 (Ill.App. 2 Dist.1975), *482*

Williams v. Philip Morris Inc., 344 Or. 45, 176 P.3d 1255 (Or. 2008), *535*

Williams v. Philip Morris Inc., 340 Or. 35, 127 P.3d 1165 (Or. 2006), *534*

Williams v. Philip Morris Inc., 193 Or.App. 527, 92 P.3d 126 (Or.App.2004), *534*

Williams v. Philip Morris Inc., 182 Or.App. 44, 48 P.3d 824 (Or.App.2002), *534*

TABLE OF CASES

Williams v. RCA Corp., 59 Ill.App.3d 229, 17 Ill.Dec. 144, 376 N.E.2d 37 (Ill.App. 1 Dist.1978), *377*

Winnett v. Winnett, 57 Ill.2d 7, 310 N.E.2d 1 (Ill.1974), *367*

Winter v. G.P. Putnam's Sons, 938 F.2d 1033 (9th Cir.1991), *477*

Winterbottom v. Wright, 1842 WL 5519 (Ex Ct 1842), *7*

Wissel v. Ohio High School Athletic Assn., 78 Ohio App.3d 529, 605 N.E.2d 458 (Ohio App. 1 Dist.1992), *455*

Wright v. Brooke Group Ltd., 652 N.W.2d 159 (Iowa 2002), *69, 169*

Wyeth v. Levine, ___ U.S. ___, 128 S.Ct. 1118, 169 L.Ed.2d 845 (2008), *426*

Wyrulec Co. v. Schutt, 866 P.2d 756 (Wyo.1993), *473*

PRODUCTS LIABILITY

IN A NUTSHELL

Eighth Edition

*

CHAPTER 1

INTRODUCTION

Table of Sections

§ 1.1   Products Liability Law.
§ 1.2   Early Law.
§ 1.3   Modern American Law.
§ 1.4   Foreign Law.

———

§ 1.1   PRODUCTS LIABILITY LAW

Products liability law lies at the center of the modern world. To a large extent, persons accomplish their individual and collective objectives, and relate to one another, through the products of technology—automobiles, punch presses, drain cleaners, tractors, prescription drugs, frozen dinners, tennis rackets, perfumes, computers, and airplanes (civilian and military). Matters concerning the creation and exchange of such products of science and technology are addressed by the law of property, patents, contracts, and commerce. Products liability law instead addresses the consequences of modern science and technology gone awry—when products, or the interactions between people and their products, fail. Governing private litigation of product

1

accidents, the rules of products liability law define the legal responsibility of sellers and other commercial transferors of products for damages resulting from product defects and misrepresentations about a product's safety or performance capabilities.

A typical products liability case involves a claim for damages against the product's manufacturer by a person injured while using the product. The plaintiff seeks to prove that the injury was caused by some deficiency in the way the product was made or marketed—that the product was in some manner "defective" or falsely described. In addition, the plaintiff will attempt to demonstrate that he or she used the product properly or at least foreseeably. Typically, damage claims include medical expenses, disability and disfigurement, pain and suffering, lost earnings and earning capacity, perhaps emotional harm, and possibly some kind of property damage, sometimes to the product itself. The defendant usually attempts to show that the product was *not* defective—that it was in fact reasonably made and properly marketed. Further, the defendant often seeks to establish that the plaintiff's injuries resulted principally because the plaintiff or some other person improperly used the product, or perhaps that something other than the product caused the harm.

Mixed Sources of Products Liability Law

Products liability law is full of mixtures. It is a mixture of tort law—negligence, strict liability in tort, and deceit—and of the contract law of sales—

mostly warranty. It is a mixture of common law, now mostly on its tort side, and statutory law, generally on its contract side—notably sales law under the Uniform Commercial Code (UCC). In addition, many state legislatures (and Congress, to a much lesser extent) have enacted products liability "reform" acts which address products liability matters, often functionally apart from tort and contract. Because of these hybrid characteristics of products liability law, plaintiffs often have a variety of available claims. *Negligence, breach of implied warranty*, and *strict liability in tort* are all based on the notion that something was wrong with the product, that it was unduly dangerous or "defective." Remedies for *breach of express warranty* and *fraud* (and possibly other forms of tortious misrepresentation) may be available when a product is more dangerous than it was stated to be, even if it was not defective or unfit under negligence, implied warranty, or strict liability in tort.

Many of the most difficult issues in modern products liability law spring from the doctrinal mixture of tort and contract. Just to name a few of the many issues of this type, the clash of tort and contract doctrines has generated perplexing questions about the standard of liability, the test for design defectiveness, defenses, statutes of limitations, and recoverable damages.

Products Liability Resources

There are many works on products liability law, and the most useful scholarship often resides in law journals. The most useful general reference works in this field of law are listed below.

American Law

Owen, Products Liability Law (2d ed. 2008). This Nutshell is an abridgment of this 1–volume work, published by Thomson/West, an invaluable hornbook/treatise with prolific case and law journal authorities and deeper discussions of the topics discussed herein.

Frumer and Friedman, Products Liability (Sklaren rev. ed., 2008). This is the classic treatise on products liability law, now containing 11 volumes, published by Matthew Bender.

Madden & Owen on Products Liability Law (3d ed. 2000). Published by Thomson/West, available on Westlaw at MOPL, this is a short multi-volume treatise treatment of the field.

Restatement (Third) of Torts: Products Liability (1998). The Restatement contains valuable Reporters' Notes on major topics.

Products Liability Reporter (CCH). This reporter carries full reports of most important cases and statutes.

BNA Product Safety and Liability Reporter. This reporter, now available online, summarizes some of the most important judicial decisions, reports on various product safety agency regulatory matters, and contains the full text of safety statutes and regulations.

Foreign Law

Stapleton, Product Liability (1994). This scholarly study of products liability law, published by Butterworths, remains the best critical, theoretical inquiry into this field of law.

Miller and Goldberg, Product Liability (2d ed. 2004). This comprehensive 1–volume treatise is published by Oxford University Press.

Howells ed., The Law of Product Liability (2d ed. 2007). This is a collection of studies on various aspects of the law, litigation, and regulation.

Whittaker, Liability for Products: English Law, French Law, and European Harmonization (2005). This book focuses on English and French law and how the law of these two nations has adjusted to the European Directives on product liability and product safety.

§ 1.2   EARLY LAW

The roots of modern products liability law reach deep into history, beyond the law of ancient Rome at least to the law of Mesopotamia. The early origins of products liability law are mostly located in the tort–contract hybrid warranties of quality, both express and implied, although there are early signs of seller liability in negligence as well. However, as a broad and coherent set of legal principles for the recovery of product-caused harm, products liability law is of recent origin. With the exception of a few cases involving fraud and the sale of defective medicines and food, the appearance of products liability cases in the law reports coincides with the rise of the Industrial Revolution in the late 1800s. By 1900, such cases began to appear with some frequency. Yet, as late as the 1950s, "products liability" was not even a term of art, much less a field of law.

Roman Law

In early Roman law, products liability was virtually unknown, and the principle (if not the phrase) of *caveat emptor* ("let the buyer beware") ruled supreme. The seller, that is, was not liable for any defects in a product unless he expressly warranted or fraudulently misrepresented that they did not exist. In time, however, some basic principles of seller responsibility for defects in certain types of sales began to emerge, and Justinian's *Digest* in 533 A.D. referred to a basic implied warranty of quality accompanying the sales of goods, imposing strict liability for the sale of defective products.

Early English Law

From the laws of Justinian to early medieval English law, the legal system degenerated from a moderately sophisticated system of sales law to one that was crude at best. By 1600, the principle of *caveat emptor*—that the risk of hidden defects lay with the buyer—had become well established in English law. By the early 1800s, however, English courts finally replaced the *caveat emptor* rule with its opposite doctrine, the implied warranty of quality—that the seller impliedly warrants that its products contain no hidden defects making them unfit for their ordinary purposes. Parliament eventually codified the common-law implied warranty of merchantability in the Sale of Goods Act of 1893.

The other major development in English products liability law in the nineteenth century was the application of the privity-of-contract defense to negligence claims, which served to shield remote sellers from legal responsibility in negligence for harm caused by defects in their products. In *Winterbottom v. Wright*, 152 E.R. 402 (Exch. 1842), the defendant, Wright, a manufacturer and repairer of stagecoaches, supplied a stagecoach to the Postmaster General under a contract to keep it in good repair. The coach broke down and overturned, injuring the driver, Winterbottom, who sued for damages. Ruling that the victim of a product accident could not maintain a negligence action against a seller without privity of contract, the Exchequer Chamber reasoned that allowing such claims would open "an infinity of actions.... Unless we confine the operation of such contracts as this to the parties who entered into them, the most absurd and outrageous consequences, to which I can see no limit, would ensue." Id. at 404–05.

Early American law

Warranty

Caveat emptor. The English doctrine of *caveat emptor* was widely embraced in the American colonies and continued throughout much of the 1800s and, in many states, into the 1900s. Toward the end of the 1800s, various American states began to overrule *caveat emptor* and to apply instead a principle of seller responsibility for hidden defects, sometimes called *caveat venditor*. The courts reasoned that a sale raises an implied warranty against latent defects if the buyer pays fair value for a product fairly expected to be free of defects. By the turn of the twentieth century, enough American states had adopted a common-law implied warranty of quality that the doctrine was reduced to statutory form in the Uniform Sales Act of 1906, patterned after the English Sales of Goods Act.

Privity of contract. As courts began imposing implied warranties of quality on manufacturers in the latter part of the nineteenth century, manufacturers increasingly were handing over the retail function to third-party dealers. This meant that the typical consumer began to deal contractually only with the retailer. Thus, in the late 1800s, manufacturers sued in warranty by consumers of defective products had available the ready-made defense of no privity of contract. But the harshness of this rule in cases of consumer injury was readily apparent, and courts began to riddle it with exceptions, first in the case of defective foodstuffs, in the early 1900s. See *Mazetti v. Armour & Co.*, 135 P. 633 (Wash. 1913).

The breakdown of the remote seller's privity defense in implied warranty cases spread in the 1950s from human food to products for intimate bodily

use (soap, hair dye, etc.). Then, in the late 1950s
and early 1960s, several courts overturned the privity requirement in warranty cases involving durable
goods. In *Henningsen v. Bloomfield Motors, Inc.*,
161 A.2d 69 (N.J. 1960), the privity bar was repudiated in a landmark implied warranty case involving
injuries from a defective automobile. In the words
of Dean William Prosser, *Henningsen* marked the
"fall of the citadel of privity."

Negligence and the Privity Obstacle

As in warranty, the American law of negligence
borrowed from England the formidable privity-of-
contract requirement for consumer recovery for injuries from defective products. This was the principle of *Winterbottom v. Wright*, previously discussed,
which prohibited *negligence* actions against "remote" manufacturers with whom plaintiffs had no
"privity of contract." In an effort to protect America's developing industry from widespread liability,
courts in the late nineteenth and early twentieth
centuries staunchly applied the privity-of-contract
doctrine to bar negligence claims in defective product cases. By 1900, dissatisfaction with the privity-
bar rule had generated certain exceptions, as for
products that were "imminently" or "inherently"
dangerous to human safety. Yet, courts normally
confined these exceptions to products like poisons,
drugs, guns, explosives, and foodstuffs.

In 1911, Donald MacPherson, a stone cutter and
gravestone dealer from a small village near Sarato-
ga Springs, New York, purchased a new Buick Run-

about from the local automobile dealer. Soon there-after, while Mr. MacPherson was driving a sick neighbor to the hospital, the wooden spokes on his Buick's left rear wheel broke, causing the wheel to collapse and the car to go out of control and crash into a ditch, pinning Mr. MacPherson under the axle. In his negligence action against Buick Motor Company, the trial judge refused to bar the claim based on the absence of privity of contract, the jury returned a verdict of $5,000 for MacPherson, and the intermediate appellate court affirmed.

In *MacPherson v. Buick Motor Co.*, 111 N.E. 1050, 1053 (N.Y. 1916), a case that in many re-spects began the modern era of products liability law, the New York Court of Appeals affirmed the decision for the plaintiff. Writing for the majority, Judge Benjamin Cardozo held that the imminent danger rule was not limited to poisons, explosives, and other products which by their nature are imple-ments of destruction. "If the nature of a thing is such that it is reasonably certain to place life and limb in peril when negligently made, it is then a thing of danger." If the manufacturer of such a foreseeably dangerous product knows that it "will be used by persons other than the purchaser, and used without new tests, then, irrespective of con-tract, the manufacturer of this thing of danger is under a duty to make it carefully." Explaining the liberation of tort law from the law of contracts, Judge Cardozo proclaimed:

> We have put aside the notion that the duty to safeguard life and limb, when the consequences of

negligence may be foreseen, grows out of contract and nothing else. We have put the source of the obligation where it ought to be. We have put its source in the law.

Over the next several decades, one jurisdiction after another adopted the new *MacPherson* rule, the last being Maine in 1982.

§ 1.3　MODERN AMERICAN LAW

Once *MacPherson* gave birth to negligence claims against manufacturers, products liability claims slowly began to spread across the nation. By the 1950s, courts were beginning to apply warranty claims to manufacturers of defective food, cosmetics, and similar products. Truly modern products liability law in America arose in the early 1960s, beginning with *Henningsen v. Bloomfield Motors*, 161 A.2d 69 (N.J. 1960), which allowed a non-purchaser injured in an accident caused by a defective car to sue the manufacturer in warranty despite two linchpin warranty law defenses—*privity of contract* and *disclaimer*.

Three years later, the Supreme Court of California decided *Greenman v. Yuba Power Products, Inc.*, 377 P.2d 897 (Cal. 1963), which declared that manufacturers of defective products are strictly liable in tort to persons injured by such products, irrespective of any contract limitations that might inhere in the law of warranty. In 1964, the American Law Institute (ALI) memorialized the rule of strict products liability in tort in § 402A of the *Restatement*

(Second) of Torts, officially promulgated in 1965. Over the next ten to fifteen years, the doctrine of strict products liability in tort, together with a variety of secondary principles, spread like wildfire around the nation. This was the birth of modern products liability law in America.

Yet the products liability law that prevails in the United States in the early twenty-first century is a much different creature than the simple story just related might suggest. First, the law has become much more complex, having evolved and transmogrified in myriad diffuse directions, by many thousands of cases and a proliferation of state "reform" statutes altering various aspects of this area of the law. Also, the significance of products liability law has mushroomed from the 1960s and early 1970s at which time this curious new field of law was little more than an academic curiosity. Further, beginning in the 1980s, the direction of products liability law changed from an expansion of the rights of victims of product accidents to a limitation of those rights.

Today, products liability occupies a central role in American law: products liability litigation and prevention figure prominently in corporate and legal decisionmaking as plaintiffs' lawyers across the nation file thousands of products liability suits each year. In an effort to prevent and manage such high stakes litigation, many major corporations and law firms have established separate teams or departments for products liability matters. In short, products liability now ranks as one of the most important fields of law.

Studies on Products Liability Litigation

While earlier studies suggested an explosion in products liability litigation, studies covering the late 1980s and most of the 1990s showed moderation and, in some instances, declines in case filings (at least in non-asbestos cases), verdicts, and plaintiff success rates. But products liability costs and insurance tend to move in waves, sometimes up and sometimes down. One such study revealed fewer numbers of products liability cases, but a substantial increase in the size of awards—from about $500,000 in 1993 to over $1.8 million in 1999. The study's research indicates that, in the early 2000s, the plaintiff's bar was increasingly limiting its clients to those having more serious injuries and a greater likelihood of success, and that it was refining its litigation techniques and skills, including effective use of expert witnesses.

Reform

From the time manufacturers and insurers first began to feel the impact of modern products liability law in practice during the 1970s, they began to push for its "reform," arguing that the products liability system had developed certain excesses that unfairly increased liability at the expense of everyone except plaintiffs and their lawyers. Since the late 1970s, products liability reform efforts have taken center stage in many state legislatures, the United States Congress, the courts themselves, federal regulatory agencies (like the FDA), and the ALI. In 1996, President Clinton vetoed an act of Congress that would have significantly altered certain aspects of this area of the law, and Congress continues to periodically address selected issues of products liability and safety. In 1998, the ALI provided products liability with its own *Restatement*— the *Restatement (Third) of Torts: Products Liability*. And, in varying ways, state legislatures and courts continue each year to reform this field of law.

To date, most legislative reform has been in the states, several of which have enacted broad products liability statutes that codify the basic principles of products liability law. Topics subject to statutory reform have included theories of liability and of defectiveness in manufacture, design, and warning; defenses, including the effect of a user's fault, assumption of risk, obvious dangers, product alteration and misuse, state of the art, compliance with custom, compliance with statutes and regulations, and statutes of limitation and repose; retailer liability; pleading requirements for compensatory damages; standards for and limitations on punitive damages; and special rules governing specific topics, such as the effect of using seatbelts and child restraint devices, and rules governing various types of products, such as tobacco, alcohol, guns, asbestos, prescription drugs and medical devices, and breast implants.

Products Liability: A Nutshell of a *Nutshell*

Theories of Recovery

Negligence. Negligence in producing or selling a product is the classic products liability claim, and it remains a fundamentally important theory of recovery. Notwithstanding the rise of "strict" theories of manufacturer liability in recent decades, negligence retains a vital role in modern products liability law. Courts in many modern cases, some state legislatures, and the *Restatement (Third) of Torts: Products Liability* have all returned to negligence principles, and sometimes negligence doctrine, as the basis of liability in various products liability contexts.

Negligence commonly is determined by balancing the burden ("costs") of safety precautions against the safety benefit the precautions seek to provide. The type and amount of care reasonably required is generally a function of the type, likelihood, and amount of harm (together viewed as the risk) that precautions (of a particular cost) may be expected to prevent. If the risk posed by the sale and use of a product in a certain condition is great, due care requires that great precautions be taken to avert the risk; if the risk is small, reasonable care requires only small precautionary measures in response.

The "Hand formula," from Judge Learned Hand's opinion in *United States v. Carroll Towing Co.*, 159 F.2d 169 (2d Cir. 1947), assesses the reasonableness of an act or omission by evaluating a calculus of three factors: the burden of taking precautions to avoid a risk of harm, on the one side, balanced against the likelihood that the actor's conduct will produce the harm multiplied by the seriousness of the harm, on the other. By this method, negligence is suggested if $B < P \times L$, where B is the burden (cost) of avoiding accidental loss that foreseeably may result if B is not undertaken, P is the increase in probability of loss if B is not undertaken, and L is the probable magnitude (expected cost) of such loss, or $\mathbf{B} < \mathbf{P} \times \mathbf{L} \Rightarrow \mathbf{N}$: if the cost of taking a particular safety precaution (B) is less than the precaution's expected safety benefits $(P \times L)$, then the manufacturer's failure to adopt the precaution implies its negligence ($\Rightarrow$ N). Thus, in making and marketing its products, a manufacturer is expected to exercise an amount of care in avoiding foreseeable risk proportionate to that risk.

Tortious misrepresentation. A tortious misrepresentation claim may arise if a manufacturer or other seller makes a false and material communication about a product's characteristics to a person who is harmed by reasonably relying on the truth of the communication. If the seller knows that the assertion is false, and intends that others will rely upon its truth, the seller may be liable for fraudulent misrepresentation (''deceit''). If a seller is merely negligent in failing to discover that its statements are false, it may be liable for negligent misrepresentation. Under *Restatement (Second) of Torts* § 402B, a handful of jurisdictions impose strict liability in tort for injuries to person or property from a seller's public misrepresentations about a product's safety—notwithstanding the seller's reasonable belief that the representations are true.

Breach of warranty. Modern products liability warranty law is set forth in the Uniform Commercial Code (UCC), Article 2 (sales law), which prescribes how warranties arise and are defined, to whom they extend, and remedies for their breach. UCC § 2–313 governs express warranties; UCC § 2–314 provides for the implied warranty of merchantability; and UCC § 2–315 addresses implied warranties of fitness for particular purpose.

UCC § 2–313 is similar to strict liability claims for misrepresentation under *Restatement (Second) of Torts* § 402B except that express warranty claims require that a buyer, rather than proving "reliance," prove that the representation was "part of the basis of the bargain." Products liability claims for breach of the implied warranty of merchantability under UCC § 2–314 usually are based on a product's failure to be "fit" for the "ordinary purposes" of products of that type. In most states, "unmerchantable" is the equivalent of "defective" for purposes of strict liability in tort under § 402A of the *Restatement (Second) of Torts*. The implied warranty of fitness for "particular" purpose may arise typically in a retail sale when the seller has reason to know that the buyer is relying on the seller's skill or judgment to select a product that will serve the buyer's special needs.

Three prominent *defenses* to warranty claims in products liability cases are: (1) the absence of *privity of contract*; (2) failing to *promptly notify* the seller of the breach; and (3) contractual *disclaimers*. But the *Magnuson–Moss Federal Warranty Act* substantially restricts a seller's ability to avoid warranty responsibility by disclaimers in cases of *consumer* goods.

Strict liability in tort. Strict liability in tort is widely viewed as the dominant theory of recovery in modern products liability law. Judge Traynor first explicitly applied the doctrine in *Greenman v. Yuba Power Products, Inc.*, 377 P.2d 897 (Cal. 1963), and the ALI adopted this new liability principle in § 402A of the *Restatement (Second) of Torts* in 1964 and promulgated it by publication in 1965. Sweeping across America during the late 1960s and 1970s, courts (and a few legislatures) enthusiastically embraced § 402A and its strict liability in tort for physical harm caused by defective products.

Liability under § 402A was called "strict" because it was grounded not on a manufacturer's fault in producing a defective product but on the frustration of consumer expectations of product safety when a latent product defect causes harm. Yet, as more and more courts during the 1970s and 1980s broadly extended the new principle beyond manufacturing flaws to design and warning cases, the truly strict consumer expectations test increasingly gave way—in design and warning cases—to the principles of risk-utility balancing and foreseeability that underlie the law of negligence. While courts continued to assert that they were applying "strict" liability, and while such liability was indeed strict when applied to manufacturers in cases involving manufacturing defects (and to retailers in most contexts), it became increasingly clear that the liability principles applied in design and warning cases (most of products liability litigation) are truly based on fault.

In 1992, the ALI began work on a new *Restatement of Torts* on the specific topic of products liability law. This new *Restatement* was approved in 1997 and published in 1998 as the *Restatement (Third) of Torts: Products Liability*. While the *Third Restatement* continues to apply strict liability to manufacturing defects, it abandons strict liability for design and warning defects, which it defines functionally in principles of negligence.

Yet modern products liability law in most states still rests squarely on the "strict liability" language of § 402A. While a number of courts have adopted certain key provisions of the *Products Liability Restatement*, and while many courts acknowledge that the principles applied to design and warning cases are similar to negligence, most courts continue to parrot traditional § 402A jurisprudence that broadly calls modern products liability law "strict." In this way, courts have created a disjunction between what they say and what they do. Be that as it may, the principle of inertia suggests that courts for many years will continue to apply principles of negligence to design and warning defect issues while purporting to apply the accumulated "strict" liability doctrine spawned by § 402A.

Product Defectiveness

Regardless of the underlying cause of action, and putting aside cases involving a defendant's misrepresentations of product safety, the plaintiff in nearly every products liability case must prove that the defendant's product contained an unnecessary hazard that caused the harm. All products are dangerous to some extent, at least when put to certain uses. But many product dangers—such as a knife's sharp blade—are impractical, if not impossible, to avoid. For such inherent product risks, *users* rather than makers or suppliers properly must avoid and insure against the possibility of injury. But sometimes products carry foreseeably excessive risks that users and consumers should not have to bear, either because users and consumers do not expect such risks or because manufacturers can cost-effectively and practicably avoid them. In such cases, manufacturers properly bear responsibility for excessive harm their products cause to users and third parties. Products that carry excessive risk are called "defective."

While most states still ground liability on one or more of the traditional causes of action (negligence, breach of implied warranty, strict liability in tort), some courts are beginning to subordinate the formal, *doctrinal* aspects of these traditional liability theories to a *functional* consideration of whether a product was "defective." Most American jurisdictions now divide product defect cases into three categories:

(1) *Manufacturing defects*—production flaws a manufacturer does not intend;

(2) *Design defects*—undue risks that a safety device or other design alternative reasonably would prevent; and

(3) *Warning defects*—undue risks that information on product hazards and how to avoid them reasonably would prevent.

Manufacturing Defects

Manufacturers and other suppliers normally are liable for injuries caused by manufacturing defects in products that they sell. When strict liability principles are applied to defects of this type, liability is *truly* strict, based on proof of some error in production that caused the product to contain an unintended flaw. Most litigation over defectively manufactured goods concerns questions of causation rather than the defectiveness *vel non* of the accident product. When a malfunctioning product is damaged in a resulting accident or lost thereafter, the "malfunction doctrine" may help a plaintiff who is unable to establish the specific defect. Quite like *res ipsa loquitur*, the malfunction doctrine comes into play when circumstances suggest that the accident probably was caused by a product defect, and the plaintiff's evidence eliminates other normal causes of such accidents such as an errant mechanic or driver error.

Defective food cases present the most unappetizing types of manufacturing defect cases, where mice turn up in soft drinks, glass in cans of spinach, clam shells in clam chowder, and maggots in dried pea soup. Today, food is considered defective in its "manufacture" if it contains a hazard the consumer did not reasonably expect, and a food supplier is strictly liable for resulting injuries.

Design Defects

Manufacturers are subject to liability for unreasonable design hazards that injure users and other persons. Because users may put any type of product to dangerous use, no matter how safely it is designed, it is crucial to adopt a definition of design defect that divides products designed with reasonable safety from those that are not. While courts in the 1960s and 1970s widely applied the *Second Restatement*'s definition of design defect—whether a product was more dangerous than an ordinary consumer would contemplate (the "consumer expectations" test)—courts in recent years increasingly have shifted away from this test because it fails to provide a meaningful standard for complex designs and, also, because it shields manufacturers from responsibility for obvious dangers of design. Today, though the consumer expectations test is often stated to be the rule, courts widely use some form of cost-benefit analysis, often referred to as a "risk-utility" or "risk-benefit" test of liability, to make design defect determinations.

When courts apply cost-benefit principles to design defect determinations, they typically claim to
be using a standard of "strict" liability. Yet the
risk-utility test courts employ in such cases is nothing more or less than the risk-utility test applied in
negligence, based on Judge Learned Hand's formula
from the *Carroll Towing* case, discussed above.
That negligence formula, it will be recalled, is B <
P x L ⇒ N. In modern products liability law,
courts have substituted "defect" for "negligence"
(D for N), which adapts the test to the "strict"
products liability task of determining design defectiveness. So reformulated, the defectiveness "equation" becomes:

$$\mathbf{B < P \; x \; L \;\; \Rightarrow \;\; D}$$

which may be restated in cost-benefit terms as:
Costs < (Safety) Benefits ⇒ Defect. That is, a
product's design may be classified as defective if the
costs of improving its safety (including dollar costs
and any lost utility and increased dangers of other
types) are less than the expected safety benefits.
This risk-utility test for design defectiveness, which
ties the measure of precaution to the measure of
risk, grounds design safety determinations in fairness and utility.

Warning Defects

A product is defective if the manufacturer does
not provide adequate information about its hidden
dangers (warnings) and, if not evident, how to
avoid them (instructions). Warnings and instructions must be adequate not only in their content

(substantive adequacy), but in the means by which they are communicated to users and consumers (procedural adequacy). If a hazard is substantial, prudence may require that the warning be placed directly on the product rather than in product literature that may become separated from the product. Sometimes foreign language warnings or symbols would help communicate warning information, but courts generally do not require these special ways to warn. If a product may be expected to cause serious allergic reactions in a substantial number of people, a manufacturer must disclose the product's allergenic tendencies. While manufacturers generally must try to warn consumers directly, manufacturers of prescription drugs normally must warn physicians only, because doctors stand as "learned intermediaries" between drugs and patients with responsibility for connecting appropriate drugs (and medical devices) to appropriate patients, and for passing along whatever information may be appropriate for particular patients to know.

The Products Liability Restatement

In 1998, the American Law Institute adopted the *Restatement (Third) of Torts: Products Liability* to replace the *Second Restatement*'s skeletal treatment of products liability law in § 402A and certain other sections. Under the *Products Liability Restatement*, liability generally arises from selling a product that is defective in one of the three ways mentioned earlier, or from making a misrepresentation of product safety. A product contains a *manufacturing*

defect under the *Third Restatement* if it "departs
from its intended design even though all possible
care was exercised in the preparation and marketing of the product." A product contains a *design
defect* if the product's hazard could have been reduced with "a reasonable alternative design,"
meaning that the danger could have been designed
away cost-effectively without unduly diminishing
the product's usefulness. A product contains a
warning or *instruction defect* if it was not, but
reasonably could have been, equipped with adequate warning of foreseeable product hazards or
instruction on how to avoid them. Other provisions
govern special products, transactions, defendants,
and duties, such as food, used products, prescription
drugs and medical devices, successor corporations,
and post-sale duties to warn or recall.

Although plaintiffs' lawyers widely viewed the
Third Restatement as a conservative reformation of
products liability law, and while it did abandon the
Second Restatement's idea in § 402A of applying
one general principle of "strict" liability for defective products of all types, the *Third Restatement*
largely mirrors the paths that many American
courts had begun to tread in the 1980s and 1990s as
the expansionary doctrines adopted during the
1960s and 1970s began to retreat. Today, while
recovery for product accidents is still formally based
on the underlying theories of recovery—negligence,
breach of the implied warranty of merchantability,
and strict liability in tort—liability principally rests

on proof that a product was defective in manufacture, design, or warning.

Proving Defects

Conceptualizing product defects and proving them are two very different things. The key to proof of product defect necessarily rests on the effective use of experts to explain how a product's dangers are excessive, how the defect reasonably could have been removed, and how its presence caused the plaintiff's harm. Particularly since the Supreme Court sought to rid the law of "junk science" in *Daubert v. Merrell Dow Pharmaceuticals, Inc.*, 509 U.S. 579 (1993), which placed on courts a "gatekeeping" responsibility to evaluate the reliability and relevance of scientific expert testimony offered by the parties before allowing it in evidence, courts and lawyers have been striving to figure out how science and engineering properly may be used to help determine whether a product is defective and, if so, whether the defect caused the plaintiff's harm.

Various evidentiary doctrines affect proof of product defect and causation in modern products liability litigation. For example, if the cause of a product accident is a mystery, but its circumstances suggest the probability that the product was defective, then *res ipsa loquitur* or the malfunction doctrine may establish the product's defectiveness, as discussed above. In other cases, proof that a product violated or complied with a safety standard adopted by industry or the government may help establish whether the product was or was not defective. Sometimes a product's defectiveness may be proved in part by similar failures of the same kind of product, while at other times a long safe history will go to show a product's nondefectiveness. Finally, to avoid discouraging safety improvements, most courts apply the "repair doctrine" to exclude evidence that a manufacturer adopted remedial measures to improve a product's safety after an accident occurred.

Limitations on Defectiveness

Sometimes there are good reasons for shielding a manufacturer from responsibility for accidental harm to users and consumers of its products.

Obvious and inherent hazards. The obviousness of a product hazard does not relieve a manufacturer from taking reasonable steps to *design* a danger out of a product, as by incorporating an inexpensive safety device that does not reduce the product's usefulness. Yet, in most states, there is no duty to *warn* of obvious or widely known product hazards—that sharp knives cut, that cigarettes are addictive, that alcohol causes intoxication, that guns can kill, and that fast food can cause obesity— because little good is served by telling people what they already know. Not only are the hazards of such products obvious, but they also are inherent, meaning they cannot be designed away. Thus, while their manufacturers bear responsibility for unintended production flaws and for failing to warn of hidden dangers, such products are not defective for their obvious, inherent risks.

Unforeseeable risks and "state of the art." During the 1960s and 1970s, there was a widespread belief that "strict" products liability in tort meant that manufacturers were subject to liability even if the risk of harm was unforeseeable or otherwise could not reasonably be prevented. This was the holding in *Beshada v. Johns–Manville Prod. Corp.*, 447 A.2d 539 (N.J. 1982), in which the New Jersey Supreme Court held that a product was defective for not bearing a warning against an unforeseeable risk. The commentators vociferously disagreed with the logic and fairness of such an approach, and the court promptly reversed itself in *Feldman v. Lederle Labs.*, 479 A.2d 374 (N.J. 1984), where it ruled that manufacturers must only warn of risks they reasonably can foresee (dangers within the "state of the art") at the time they sell a product. Together, these two cases marked the pivotal point in modern American products liability law, when courts began to shift their perspective away from trying to fashion truly strict standards of manufacturer liability to imposing standards of responsibility to which manufacturers reasonably might conform.

Today, no matter how dangerous a product may be, it is not "defective" (in all but a few states) if the manufacturer cannot reasonably foresee or avoid the risk when the product is sold. A product's design and warning, in other words, need only be as safe as reasonably possible under the prevailing "state of the art." These two propositions—that manufacturers must guard against risks only if they are *foreseeable*, and that manufacturers must guard against those risks only by precautions that are *reasonable*—are the two central pillars of modern American products liability law.

Other limitations. Courts impose special duty limitations on liability in a number of other situations, including *prenatal harm*, which some courts hold is not the manufacturer's responsibility after the second generation of injuries; *product deterioration*, which courts normally hold is not the manufacturer's responsibility; *post-sale* duties to *warn*, which courts increasingly hold are governed by negligence principles, and to *recall and repair*, which most courts simply reject.

Defenses

Misconduct Defenses

Defenses to negligence and strict liability in tort claims. Manufacturers properly are responsible only for injuries proximately caused by defects in their products, not for injuries caused by a user's improper or deliberately risky product use. The role of *contributory negligence* is diminished in certain strict tort contexts, but it remains an important defense to certain products liability claims—even in *comparative fault* states, most of which bar recovery for the portion of a plaintiff's injuries attributable to his or her own fault and for *all* damages when the plaintiff's fault exceeds the defendant's. Although the *assumption of risk* doctrine is dwindling to some extent, this defense still bars recovery entirely in many states and serves as a damages-reducing factor in other states. Unforeseeable *misuse* normally bars recovery altogether.

Defenses to warranty and tortious misrepresentation claims. The law is quite confused as to the application of tort law misconduct defenses to warranty claims, and generalizations on this issue are not much help. Article 2 of the UCC makes some scattered comments on a buyer's careless use, stating that, if a buyer purchases or uses a product knowing it to contain a dangerous defect, resulting injuries may be the *proximate* result of the plaintiff's use rather than of any unmerchantable condition in the product. But many courts apply the standard tort law misconduct defenses of contributory (and comparative) negligence, assumption of risk, and product misuse to claims for breach of implied warranty, just as they do to claims for negligence and strict liability in tort. In fraud and other tortious misrepresentation actions, the basic misconduct issue is whether the plaintiff's *reliance* was "justifiable" or "reasonable," that is, whether the plaintiff had a "right to rely" (based on reasonableness principles) on the particular representation.

Causation

Cause in Fact

In general. Cause in fact is the actual connection between a product defect and the plaintiff's harm. A plaintiff must always link his or her injury or disease to a defect in a product that the manufacturer made and sold. Thus, the first causal requirement in every case is to show that the challenged product was manufactured by the defendant, since different manufacturers make similar products, and sometimes the product is destroyed in the accident or thrown away.

Proving that a product defect caused the plaintiff's injury usually involves the same *"but-for"* hypothetical inquiry involved in other tort law contexts: a product defect may be a cause in fact of the plaintiff's harm if the defect was a *sine qua non* of the harm—a necessary antecedent without which the harm would not have occurred. Most states use a *"substantial-factor test"* for situations where multiple chemicals or other products combine to cause an injury that would have occurred even if one of them were removed.

Toxic substance issues. In litigation concerning toxic substances (such as asbestos, drugs, and other chemicals), plaintiffs normally must prove: (1) *exposure* to the toxic substance; (2) *general causation*—that the substance is capable of causing the particular disease in humans; and (3) *specific causation*—that the substance actually caused the disease in the plaintiff.

A plaintiff injured by a fungible product, such as a generic drug taken long ago, may be unable to identify the manufacturer. Among the variety of causation theories adopted by several courts to address this problem is the "market share" approach, whereby each manufacturer of the fungible product contributes a proportion of the plaintiff's damages equal to its market share. Most courts reject this theory, and the few that accept it normally restrict it to a particular drug (DES). Other theories of collective responsibility on industries for harms that cannot be traced to particular manufacturers—alternative liability, enterprise liability, concert of action, and civil conspiracy—generally have failed.

Defective warning claims. Inadequate warning claims present special causation problems because of the difficulty of ascertaining whether the plaintiff would have seen an adequate warning if one had been provided and, if so, whether he or she would have acted to avert the injury. Many courts have sought to avoid this problem by employing a rebuttable "heeding presumption" that the purchaser or user would have read and heeded an adequate warning, had one been provided.

Proximate Cause

Proximate cause is a reasonably close connection between the plaintiff's injury and a product defect, which limits recovery, even in strict liability, to foreseeable plaintiffs and foreseeable risks of harm. Ordinary principles of superseding causation also apply to products liability cases, whereby a manufacturer's responsibility for the harm is broken by an intervening force if it was not reasonably foreseeable.

Special Defenses

Regulatory compliance, federal preemption, compliance with contract specifications, and government contractors. Most courts hold that compliance with a safety statute or regulation is some evidence, but not conclusive, of a product's nondefectiveness and the manufacturer's non-negligence. "Federal preemption" may bar a products liability claim if the safety issue, such as the "adequacy" of warnings on cigarettes, has already been resolved by Congress or a federal agency. The "contract specifications defense" protects a manufacturer from design defect liability for merely fabricating a product according to design specifications provided by the buying enterprise, unless the defect was obvious to the fabricator. A special application of this principle is the "government contractor defense," which normally bars recovery for defective design and warning claims against contractors who build products according to designs provided or approved by the government.

Statutes of limitations and repose. Statutes of limitations for tort claims generally, and some for products liability claims in particular, require that actions be filed within some specified period—typically 2 or 3 years—from when the plaintiff reasonably should have discovered the injury and, perhaps, its cause. Under the UCC, warranty claims must be brought within 4 years from when a product first is sold. Some states have statutes of "repose," designed to put products liability claims ultimately to rest, whether discovered or not, within some fairly long period of time—often 10 years after the date of sale. Some states have realty improvement statutes of repose, ranging from 3 to 20 years in length, applying to products attached to realty.

Special Defendants, Transactions, Products, and Litigation

Special Defendants

Products liability defendants who are not manufacturers ordinarily have less control over product safety than the enterprise that designed and manufactured the product, raising the question of whether it is logical or fair to hold a non-manufacturing supplier strictly responsible for injuries from defects in the products it sells.

Retailers. Retailers normally are subject to strict liability in tort, but statutes in some states protect retailers from strict liability if the manufacturer is solvent and within the jurisdiction of the court.

Raw material and component part suppliers. Suppliers of such products are liable for injuries caused by defects in materials or components they provide, but not for the design of the finished product unless they substantially participate in that design.

Parent corporations. Parent corporations normally are not responsible for harm caused by defective products manufactured by their subsidiaries, but a court may allow a parent's "corporate veil" to be "pierced" on grounds of agency and apparent agency, apparent manufacturer, concerted tortious action, and, most importantly, alter ego.

Trademark owners and franchisers. Trademark owners and franchisers are responsible for defective products produced and sold by trademark licensees or franchisees only if the trademark owner or franchiser had substantial control over the product's safety.

Successor corporations. When one company (the successor) purchases the assets of another (the predecessor), the successor normally is *not* responsible for the predecessor's debts, including products liability claims after the sale of assets has occurred, subject to four widely accepted exceptions: (1) when the purchaser expressly or impliedly assumes such liability; (2) when the transaction amounts to a consolidation or merger of the two companies; (3) when the purchaser is a mere continuation of the seller; and (4) when the transaction is a fraudulent attempt to avoid such liability. Some states add one or two new exceptions: (5) when the successor continues the predecessor's product line; and (6) when there is a continuity of enterprise after the transaction.

Employers. If an employer manufactures defective machinery for use in its own enterprise, injuring an employee, the "exclusive remedy" principle of workers' compensation precludes the employee from suing the employer as a manufacturer of a defective product.

Special Transactions and Products

The products liability paradigm rests on the sale of a new chattel, raising the question of whether strict products liability principles should extend to other contexts where other policies and principles may predominate.

Leased, bailed, and licensed products. Courts have applied strict liability in tort (and warranty) to commercial leases of automobiles and other products, reasoning that such transactions involve largely the same policy issues as commercial sales. Yet determining whether strict liability principles should be applied to commercial bailments or licenses for use of a product for a short time—such as ice skates at rinks and grocery carts at supermarkets—has proved problematic. Only if the licensed or bailed product is necessary or "integral" to the sale of some other product (as a wine glass for the sale of wine in a restaurant or bar), whereby it becomes a "tie-in" product, do most courts hold that the transaction may be subject to strict liability in tort.

Sales–service transactions. A doctor who uses a hypodermic needle to inject serum into a patient's arm will probably include as part of the medical fee a charge for the hypodermic needle and the serum. If the needle is defective and breaks while in the patient's arm, or if the serum is defective, the patient might assert a products liability claim against the doctor for "selling" a defective product that caused an injury. In sales-service hybrid cases of this type, most courts determine whether the sale or service aspect predominates, and then apply strict liability principles only if the "essence" of the transaction involved a sale rather than a service.

Repaired, refurbished, reconditioned, rebuilt, and remanufactured products. In deciding whether to apply strict liability principles to these product-improvement situations, courts generally apply some form of the essence-of-the-transaction or predominant-factor test just mentioned. These cases often turn on whether the product that comes out from service is essentially the one that went in, in which case only negligence principles apply, or whether an essentially different product is introduced into the stream of commerce, in which case strict liability principles may apply.

Used products. Most courts hold that only negligence, not strict liability, applies to used products, but many courts do allow strict liability claims.

Electricity. When power surges cause injury or damage, most courts hold that electricity is a "product" that may subject the supplying utility company to strict liability in tort for selling it in a defective condition, assuming it passed through a customer's meter and thus was sold into the stream of commerce. Yet many other courts refuse to apply strict liability to such cases, reasoning that electricity is a unique form of "product," and that its provision is a service rather than a sale.

Real estate. A few early decisions applied strict liability in tort to builder-vendors of mass-produced residential homes and manufacturers of prefabricated homes and structures, and many courts have applied such principles to component fixtures installed in houses and other structures. But most courts refuse to apply strict products liability in tort to claims involving defects in land, houses, and other structures attached to the land, reasoning that products liability law properly applies only to *products*, which are chattels or personal property, not real property.

Publications. Except for aeronautical charts containing false information, courts refuse to apply strict liability to the provision of information—in books, magazines, films, records, computer games, and websites—reasoning that the message (*vs.* its packaging) is not a "product," and they are also often troubled by the difficult First Amendment issues such claims would raise.

Blood. Infected blood and blood products can cause AIDS or hepatitis, but almost all states have enacted "blood shield statutes" that protect blood banks and other suppliers from strict liability in tort or warranty, leaving victims to their proof of negligence in how the blood was gathered or tested for disease.

Animals. A few courts have allowed strict liability claims for diseases transmitted to humans by pets sold in a diseased condition. But most courts hold that living things are not "products" within the scope of the strict tort doctrine because an animal's nature, such as the tendency of a horse to buck or a dog to bite, is not fixed when it leaves the seller's control.

Special Litigation

Motor vehicles. Automotive products liability litigation is governed by the principle of "crashworthiness"—that vehicles must be designed with reasonable safety for the crash environment—making manufacturers subject to liability for "enhanced injuries" to occupants caused by uncrashworthy aspects of a vehicle's design. If an occupant's crash injuries are indivisible (such as paraplegia or death), apportioning the harm between the uncrashworthy aspect of the vehicle and the crash itself is often difficult if not impossible. A growing majority of courts hold manufacturers of uncrashworthy vehicles responsible for all damages from indivisible injuries.

Courts are sharply split on whether a driver's fault in causing an accident may be considered, as a matter of proximate cause or comparative fault, in apportioning damages for enhanced injuries in cases where the driver challenges the crashworthiness of the vehicle. In addition, some courts allow a "seatbelt defense" to establish that the plaintiff is responsible for injuries a seatbelt would have prevented, but the availability of this defense depends on each state's seatbelt statute.

Damages

Compensatory Damages

Injury, death, property damage, and economic loss. Principles of compensatory damages in products liability cases largely track the rules of compensatory damages applied in ordinary tort cases. In particular, the same types of damages normally are recoverable in strict liability in tort as in negligence, including damages for personal injury, wrongful death, and, in most states, property damage. Claims for pure economic loss normally are recoverable only in warranty, not in either negligence or strict liability in tort. Some courts allow claims for an increased risk of disease, but most do not.

Emotional distress and lost consortium. Damages for emotional distress and lost consortium are often allowed in claims for strict products liability in tort, both by direct victims and bystanders, under rules similar to those applied under the law of negligence. Some courts have allowed recovery for fear of diseases such as cancer ("cancerphobia") from contact with a harmful substance, sometimes on narrow rules, while other courts deny such claims.

Medical monitoring. Courts are split on whether to allow recovery for medical monitoring of victims exposed to some toxic substance, or defective medical device, where future harm is possible but difficult to detect.

Punitive Damages

Nature. Punitive damages are available in claims for negligence, fraud, or strict liability in tort (but not warranty), on proof that a manufacturer was guilty of flagrantly disregarding consumer safety, to punish and deter such gross misconduct. Examples include fraudulently marketing unsafe products, or selling a product known to contain a serious hidden hazard without disclosing it to consumers in order to promote the product's sale.

Problems and reform. Punitive damages are criticized for various reasons, including the vague standards for their recovery and for determining their amount. In an effort to control awards of punitive damages, most states have adopted one or more statutory reforms, the most common being to increase the standard of proof from "preponderance of the evidence" to "clear and convincing" proof.

Due process limitations. Beginning in 1991, the Supreme Court has rendered a series of decisions imposing due process constraints on punitive damages, requiring, among other things, that trial courts properly instruct juries on the functions of punitive damages; that trial and appellate courts carefully review the basis of such awards; that such awards not be assessed for conduct outside the state that may be legal elsewhere; and that the ratio of punitive to compensatory awards be reasonable, not unduly large. These Supreme Court decisions are prodding lower courts to reduce high punitive damage awards in some products liability cases.

§ 1.4   FOREIGN LAW

In recent years, modern principles of products liability law have been developing around the world. Viewing products liability from a truly global perspective has just begun, yet it is a perspective that soon may predominate in a world where products are manufactured, distributed, fail, and injure human beings without regard to boundaries of nation states.

Europe's Products Liability Directive

Spurred by the Thalidomide tragedy and the adoption of § 402A in America, the European Economic Community in 1985 adopted a *Directive on Liability for Defective Products*. Each member state in the Economic Community, now including all 27 members of the European Union, must enact national legislation "approximating" this as other EC Directives.

The *Directive* declares that "liability without fault on the part of the producer is the sole means of adequately [protecting] the consumer against damage caused by a defective product." Article 1 of the *Directive* provides, "The producer shall be liable for damage caused by a defect in his product," and Article 6(1) states that a product is "defective" "when it does not provide the safety which a person is entitled to expect, taking all circumstances into account," including the product's presentation, foreseeable uses, and the date of sale.

Article 7 of the *Directive* sets forth certain defenses to products liability claims, including the "development risk" defense, adopted in nearly all European nations. Not unlike the state-of-the-art defense in America, this defense shields a producer from liability if "the state of scientific and technical knowledge at the time when he put the product into circulation was not such as to enable the existence of the defect to be discovered."

Other Nations

In recent years, products liability law has gone global. Japan and many other nations outside Europe have enacted (or introduced) "clones" of the *European Directive,* which is rapidly becoming the worldwide model for products liability legislation outside the United States. And many other nations in recent years have otherwise modernized their products liability laws.

*

PART I
THEORIES OF LIABILITY

CHAPTER 2
NEGLIGENCE

Table of Sections

§ 2.1 Negligence—Generally.
§ 2.2 The Standard of Care.
§ 2.3 Proof of Negligence—Industry Standards.
§ 2.4 Proof of Negligence—Violation of Statute.
§ 2.5 Proof of Negligence—Res Ipsa Loquitur.
§ 2.6 The Resurgence of Negligence.

---

§ 2.1 NEGLIGENCE—GENERALLY

Negligence is the classic claim in American products liability law, and it remains a fundamentally important theory of recovery. Even as its doctrinal significance slipped into the shadows as various "strict" theories of manufacturer liability pushed to center stage in recent decades, negligence retained a prominent place in the developing law of modern products liability. Negligence is still the principal theory of tort recovery in several states (Del., Mass., Mich., N.C., and Va.) that chose not to adopt strict products liability in tort. In states that do recognize strict liability in tort claims, empirical studies show that juries—perhaps because negligence is "hotter" than strict liability—are more likely to find for plaintiffs, and in higher amounts, on negligence rather than on strict liability.

Since the 1980s, there has been a growing movement to return to negligence in design, warning, and other types of cases, leading some state legislatures, courts, and the *Restatement (Third) of Torts: Products Liability* to reassert the central role of negligence principles, and in some cases negligence doctrine, in a variety of products liability contexts.

To prove any products liability claim sounding in negligence, a plaintiff must establish: (1) that the seller owed a duty to the plaintiff; (2) that the seller breached that duty; (3) that the breach of duty was a cause in fact of the plaintiff's injury; (4) that the cause in fact was a proximate cause of the injury; and (5) that damages for the harm suffered are recoverable in negligence. The first two elements are considered here and the last three are treated in later chapters. For a more thorough examination of negligence, see Owen, Products Liability Law ch. 2 (2d ed. 2008).

Duty

Manufacturers have a duty to exercise reasonable care to refrain from selling products that contain unreasonable risks of harm. This duty thus is limited to requiring only *reasonable* care—not perfect care; to protecting only persons *foreseeably* placed at risk—not all persons; and to avoiding only risks that are *foreseeable*—not all risks. In short, the negligence duty is one of reasonableness—not perfection.

In addition to defining the scope of a manufacturer's obligations to persons foreseeably put at risk by product dangers, duty serves another, sharper role of limitation. As a threshold issue of law in every negligence case, the duty element provides courts with an effective screening device for dividing cases into two broad categories—those properly embraced by the negligence system and those properly excluded. Drawing from a broad range of considerations of fairness, justice, and social policy, the duty issue provides courts an opportunity to consider the appropriateness of applying negligence law to various types of claims at the category level. For example, courts have employed no-duty rationales in denying claims against fast food retailers for selling fattening foods to customers who get fat; against pharmacists for failing to warn clients of side effects in prescription drugs; against manufacturers for failing to equip all their products with safety features sold as optional, failing to warn of obvious dangers, and failing to recall dangerous products; and against manufacturers and retailers for selling alcohol to persons who get ill or cause an accident, selling products that may be dangerous when disposed of or dismantled, selling drugs that cause birth defects in the grandchild of the drug's recipient, and for selling handguns in such quantities and locations as to facilitate handgun crime.

Breach

A breach of duty is established by proving that a manufacturer or other product seller failed to conform to the standard of reasonable care that defines the duty. Because the duty required by negligence law is defined in terms of "reasonable" (not perfect) care, the mere fact that a manufactured good is *defective* ordinarily will not establish breach. Instead, to establish breach, a plaintiff normally must prove both defect *and* negligence:

(1) That the product was *defective* (in its design, manufacture, or marketing), *and*

(2) That the manufacturer was *negligent* in some manner in making or selling the product in that defective condition.

This follows from the commonsense idea that, except in certain limited contexts (notably misrepresentation and negligent entrustment), a manufacturer or other seller cannot be negligent for making or selling a product that is good.

§ 2.2 THE STANDARD OF CARE

A manufacturer in negligence is held to a standard of "ordinary care and prudence," see *Adams v. Northern Illinois Gas Co.*, 809 N.E.2d 1248 (Ill. 2004), or "reasonable care," see *Ford Motor Co. v. Rushford*, 868 N.E.2d 806 (Ind. 2007). Sometimes courts tailor the standard to the "care [of] a reasonable manufacturer," see *McGuire v. Davidson Mfg. Corp.*, 398 F.3d 1005 (8th Cir. 2005) (Iowa law), or, further, "a press [or whatever product] manufacturer of ordinary prudence," see *Rhoads v. Service Mach. Co.*, 329 F.Supp. 367 (E.D. Ark. 1971).

Manufacturers Held to Standard of "Expert in the Field"

One of the most fundamental propositions of negligence doctrine in the products liability context is that a manufacturer, having designed, produced, and marketed its products, is held to the level of an *expert* in its field. As such, its conduct is fairly measured against that of a reasonable manufacturer that is an expert in manufacturing that particular type of product. See *Burton v. R.J. Reynolds Tobacco Co.*, 397 F.3d 906 (10th Cir. 2005) (Kan. law) (cigarettes). Accordingly, a manufacturer is charged with the duty of design, manufacture, and marketing commensurate with an expert's awareness of the particular product's foreseeable environments of use and special dangers within that environment.

Responsibility Limited By Reasonable Foreseeability

One of the most basic tenets of all negligence law is that an actor's responsibility is limited to risks and victims foreseeably threatened by the conduct. In other words, if a type of risk or victim lies outside the realm of reasonable foreseeability, the manufacturer or other actor cannot be faulted for failing to take steps to avert the risk or protect the victim. One doctrine used by courts in negligence cases confronting claims of unforeseeability is the doctrine of "constructive knowledge," which holds that a risk (or victim) is deemed foreseeable if a manufacturer in the same position acting reasonably would have foreseen the risk (or victim). In such cases, a court simply implies ("constructs") the knowledge based on the reasonable foreseeability of the risk.

Determining Due Care

Cost–Benefit Analysis

The negligence standard of care—reasonable care in the circumstances—ordinarily may be determined by balancing the burden ("costs") of safety precautions the defendant failed to adopt against the safety benefit the precautions would have achieved. That is, the type and amount of care that reason requires is generally a function of the type, likelihood, and degree of harm (together viewed as the magnitude of the risk) that precautions (of a particular cost) may be expected to prevent. If the risk posed by the sale and use of a product in a certain condition is great, due care normally requires that great precautions be taken to avert the risk; if the risk is small, reasonable care ordinarily requires only small precautionary measures in response.

For example, if the risk at issue concerns the possible failure of an automobile's steering, brakes, or tires at highway speeds, or the possibility that a punch press ram may unexpectedly depress on an operator's hand, "reasonable" care will demand the utmost precautions by the manufacturer to avert the risk. Yet, if the foreseeable risk is relatively minimal, reasonably appearing to involve at most the risk of minor harm to person or property—a scratch, a fabric tear, or a harmless product malfunction—then a manufacturer has little reason to devote more than a modest amount of attention, expense, or other resources to reducing such a trivial risk of harm. This principle of balance, inherent in tort law generally and negligence law in particular, is sometimes referred to as the "calculus of risk."

The "Hand Formula"

The most celebrated formulation of the calculus-of-risk approach for evaluating conduct under the negligence standard of care was offered by Judge Learned Hand in *United States v. Carroll Towing Co.*, 159 F.2d 169 (2d Cir. 1947). In *Carroll Towing*, Judge Hand reasoned that the degree of care appropriate to an occasion often reflects a calculus of three factors: the *burden* of taking precautions to avoid a risk of harm, on the one side, balanced against the *likelihood* that the actor's conduct will produce the harm multiplied by the *seriousness* of that harm, on the other. Negligence is implied if an actor fails to adopt a burden of precaution of less magnitude than the harm the precaution is likely to prevent. Judge Hand expressed this concept algebraically in that negligence is suggested if:

$$B < P \times L$$

where B is the burden (cost) of avoiding accidental loss that foreseeably may result if B is not undertaken, P is the increased probability of loss if B is not undertaken, and L is the probable magnitude of such loss. This is the so-called "Hand formula."

If the Hand formula is supplemented with a symbol for the implication ($\Rightarrow$) of negligence (N), the full formula reads:

$$B < P \times L \Rightarrow N$$

Thus conceived and applied to the products liability context, the Hand formula may be explained as follows: if the cost of taking a particular safety precaution (B) is less than the expected safety benefits (P x L) of the untaken precaution, the manufacturer's failure to adopt the precaution implies its negligence ($\Rightarrow$ N).

The Hand formula expresses algebraically the commonsense idea that people may fairly be required to contemplate the possible consequences of important actions before so acting. That is, nearly all reasoned decisions involve a weighing of the costs and benefits expected to flow from a contemplated course of action, and the decisions of product manufacturers are no different. Thus, prior to making important design, manufacturing, and marketing decisions, a responsible manufacturer should fairly weigh the risks of injury to consumers and bystanders when considering its own interests in maximizing profits. See *Mesman v. Crane Pro Servs.*, 512 F.3d 352 (7th Cir. 2008) (Ind. law) (Posner, J.).

In sum, due care requires a manufacturer to exercise an amount of care proportionate to an expected risk of harm.

Contexts Requiring Due Care

Manufacturing

Manufacturers sometimes make negligent mistakes during some stage of the production process, and such mistakes occasionally cause harm to consumers and other persons foreseeably placed at risk. See *Soufflas v. Zimmer, Inc.*, 474 F.Supp.2d 737 (E.D. Pa. 2007) (polyethylene knee replacement broke); *Johnson Controls Battery Group, Inc. v. Runnels*, 2003 WL 21191063 (Tex. App. 2003) (battery exploded). Beginning with the careful selection and testing of raw materials and component parts, the manufacturing process involves all aspects of the maker's construction, assembly, and preparation of the product for distribution. The manufacturer is bound to exercise reasonable care at each step to reduce the risk of dangerous defects in its products.

Even when a manufacturer exercises the utmost care in production, it is inevitable that some small percentage of products—from time to time and for one reason or another—will contain manufacturing flaws of one type or another that are dangerous to users or third parties. For this reason, manufacturers must exercise reasonable care to catch such defects by designing and implementing quality control ("quality assurance") systems appropriate to the nature and degree of risk, including sampling and testing of products off the assembly line, as appropriate.

Design

In formulating the product concept, a manufacturer makes decisions that will affect the safety of the entire product line: decisions concerning the types and strengths of raw materials and component parts, the manner in which they are combined into the finished product, whether safety devices are included, the overall product concept, and the type and extent of prototype testing to ensure that the product works safely when put to use.

Determining whether the design of any particular product was "adequately" safe—or was, instead, "unreasonably" hazardous—is often a difficult task, particularly since the process usually involves second-guessing (with the benefit of hindsight) the defendant's professional design engineers. Yet, "mistakes" of this type sometimes are made, and resulting injuries are sometimes traceable to a manufacturer's failure to exercise reasonable care in designing its products. See *Wald v. Costco Wholesale Corp.*, 2005 WL 425864 (S.D.N.Y. 2005) (manufacturer of bicycle helmet subject to liability for negligent design); *Lillebo v. Zimmer, Inc.*, 2005 WL

388598 (D. Minn. 2005) (design of hip implant stem).

The usefulness of the Hand cost-benefit formula is most evident in design cases. Here, design engineers regularly evaluate various trade-offs between product usefulness, cost, and safety. As a general proposition, designing more safety into a product decreases its usefulness and/or affordability. That is, safety generally comes at a cost in terms of utility, price, or both—safety devices may interfere with a product's functioning and usually add to its monetary costs. Thus, the duty of due care ordinarily requires that a manufacturer's engineers be guided by the Hand formula's principles of proportionality: the greater the foreseeable risk of harm, the greater the precautions should be to avoid the harm. In this manner, the Hand formula, based on principles of reasonableness, optimality, and balance is especially useful in determining whether a particular design decision was reasonable or unreasonable—whether the manufacturer, in adopting the design, was negligent or not. See *Griggs v. BIC Corp.*, 981 F.2d 1429 (3d Cir. 1992) (Pa. law) (where nearly 1000 people were killed annually in fires started by children playing with butane lighters, jury could find manufacturer negligent in failing to equip lighter with childproof feature at cost of about 70¢).

Proof of negligence in a design case often centers around the availability of a feasible alternative design that would have prevented the accident and

would have been safer overall. Generally, if there is
no reasonable way to the design a particular danger
out of a product, the manufacturer cannot be held
negligent for the product's design.

Warnings and Instructions

As consumers confront a burgeoning variety of
mechanical, chemical, and electrical products of
ever-increasing complexity, they become increasingly dependent on the expert manufacturer to supply
them with information on product dangers and how
to avoid them. A prudent manufacturer must provide whatever information reasonably appears necessary to permit the consumer to use the product
with reasonable safety. A manufacturer consequently may be negligent if it fails to provide consumers
with adequate *warnings* of dangers in its product or
instructions on methods for its safe use. See *Jones
v. Amazing Prods., Inc.*, 231 F.Supp.2d 1228 (N.D.
Ga. 2002) (risk that "Liquid Fire" drain cleaner,
97% sulfuric acid, might melt another container
into which it is transferred).

§ 2.3 PROOF OF NEGLIGENCE— INDUSTRY STANDARDS

Proof that a manufacturer acted unreasonably in
developing, producing, or marketing a defective
product normally involves evidence about the components of the negligence calculus—the nature,
magnitude, and likelihood of a foreseeable risk of
harm, on the one hand, and the various costs and
practicality of mitigating the risk, on the other.

This section and the next two address three major forms of proof of negligence that may be especially germane to a negligence claim: industry custom, applicable safety statutes and regulations, and *res ipsa loquitur*.

Custom—how a community addresses particular situations according to prevailing social norms—is one of the most rudimentary and powerful sources of law. Because the standard of reasonable behavior in negligence law is grounded in community norms, whether an actor who has caused harm to another acted or failed to act as similar actors customarily behave in the same situation goes to the heart of negligence determinations. Hence, the traditional negligence formulation is the failure to exercise "ordinary" care. In products liability cases, evidence of applicable customs may tend to show the foreseeability of the risk as well as the cost, feasibility, utility, and acceptability among consumers of the particular safety measures the plaintiff asserts the defendant negligently failed to adopt.

Accordingly, an actor may well be negligent if he or she *fails* to conform to the customary level of care. Yet, sometimes, a community over time may allow the ordinary level of care for protecting others to fall below the level of care that a reasonable prudent person would provide, in which case an actor would be negligent for *conforming* to the customary level of care. Judge Learned Hand famously articulated the principle that, while industry practice or custom is important evidence of the reasonableness of its members' conduct, it is not conclusive of due care, since the industry as a whole may have "unduly lagged" in adopting precautionary measures dictated by reasonable prudence. See *The T.J. Hooper*, 60 F.2d 737, 740 (2d Cir. 1932). This is now the universal rule in negligence law: a defendant's conformance to or violation of applicable customary standards of care is some evidence, though rarely conclusive, of whether the defendant exercised due care in the circumstances.

§ 2.4 PROOF OF NEGLIGENCE— VIOLATION OF STATUTE

In products liability negligence actions, the trier of fact normally sets the applicable standard of care by applying the general common-law standard of reasonable care and prudence to the facts and circumstances of the particular case. Yet legislatures sometimes specify by statute, and regulatory agencies sometimes specify by regulation, particular safety measures required in certain situations and particular dangerous conditions prohibited in others. Such statutes (or regulations) may provide explicitly for civil damages arising from their breach. More typically, however, safety statutes provide criminal or quasi-criminal penalties for their violation.

If a manufacturer, retailer, or other products liability defendant violates a safety statute in a manner that harms a plaintiff, the doctrine of *negligence per se* may permit the plaintiff to establish the defendant's duty of care and breach thereof by proving the statutory violation. In such situations, a court borrows the specific standard of conduct set forth in the statute, deferring to the legislative determination of proper behavior in substitution for a judicial definition of due care.

Negligence Per Se—**The Two–Pronged Test**

All safety rules, whether statutory, regulatory, or common law, are adopted to protect certain types of persons against certain types of risk of harm, and the reach of all such rules is limited to this extent. Accordingly, most courts will adopt a standard of behavior set by a statute or regulation for use in a negligence action only if:

(1) The plaintiff was injured by a *type of risk* (often referred to as "harm") the statute (or regulation) was intended to *prevent*; and

(2) The plaintiff was in a *class of persons* the statute (or regulation) intended to *protect*.

This is the classic two-pronged test (often unhelpfully stated in reverse order) for deciding whether a safety standard in a criminal safety statute may properly be used as the standard of care in a negligence action under the doctrine of *negligence per se*.

As for the first prong, the *type-of-risk-prevented* requirement, death resulting from an automobile's deficient steering is a type of risk sought to be prevented by the recall provisions of the federal Motor Vehicle Safety Act; whereas a statute requiring that gasoline be dispensed only into safe containers is intended to prevent the risk of leaks, not the risk that gasoline bought in a cup might be thrown on a person to facilitate catching her on fire. See *Walcott v. Total Petroleum, Inc.*, 964 P.2d 609 (Colo. Ct. App. 1998).

As for the second prong, the *class-of-plaintiff-protected* requirement, a state statute requiring manufacturers of toxic products to supply purchasers with a material safety data sheet (MSDS) is designed to protect users of the product, often a purchaser's employees; but an act requiring insurers to return titles and licenses of total-loss vehicles to the Department of Revenue seeks to protect owners of vehicles from thefts, not pedestrians injured by runaway vehicles defectively rebuilt. See *Treadwell Ford, Inc. v. Campbell*, 485 So.2d 312 (Ala. 1986).

Other *Negligence Per Se* Requirements

An essential element of every *negligence per se* action is that the defendant actually *violated* the pertinent statute or regulation, as proof that the safety standard contained therein was breached. See *Estate of Pemberton v. John's Sports Ctr., Inc.*, 135 P.3d 174 (Kan. Ct. App. 2006).

Further, even if a plaintiff establishes that a statute was breached and meets the two-pronged test, so that it may be used to set the relevant standard of care, a plaintiff still must prove each of the other elements of a negligence claim, including cause in fact and proximate cause. For example,

Gaines–Tabb v. ICI Explosives, USA, Inc., 160 F.3d 613, 623 (10th Cir. 1998) (Okla. law), held that the defendant's manufacture and sale of ammonium nitrate used by terrorists to make a bomb to blow up the federal building in Oklahoma City was not a proximate cause of the injuries due to "the intervention of a supervening cause—the unforeseeable, nearly unprecedented, criminal bombing of the Murrah Building. Absent proximate cause there can be no negligence, per se or otherwise."

Whether on grounds of proximate causation or scope of risk, a defendant's violation of a licensing statute generally does not amount to *negligence per se*. Thus, a restaurant's failure to obtain an operating license from the health department, a drug manufacturer's failure to obtain proper FDA approval of a new drug or medical device, or an aircraft manufacturer's failure to obtain proper certification from the FAA for a new airplane, may each subject the manufacturer to administrative penalty, but none of these violations converts the defendant into an outlaw subject to absolute liability.

Excuses

Many courts accept the list of statutory violation excuses set forth in *Restatement (Second) of Torts* § 288A which relieves a defendant of liability in negligence for violating a statute or administrative regulation if the violation is due to the defendant's incapacity, unawareness of a need for compliance, inability to comply, an emergency not due to the defendant's own misconduct, or if compliance would have presented a greater risk of harm than violation.

Procedural Effect

Jurisdictions vary on the procedural effect they accord to a statutory or regulatory violation. Some courts, possibly a majority, hold that such a violation *conclusively* establishes the defendant's negligence—that an unexcused violation of a statute or regulation is negligence in itself, or negligence "per se." See *RLI Ins. Co. v. Union Pac. R.R.*, 463 F.Supp.2d 646 (S.D. Tex. 2006) (unexcused violation is negligence per se).

Many other jurisdictions treat a violation merely as *evidence* of negligence, perhaps the best approach, which the trier of fact may accept or reject as it sees fit. See *Berish v. Bornstein*, 770 N.E.2d 961 (Mass. 2002). In a small number of jurisdictions (Cal., Colo., Kan., Mich., and Vt.), by common law or statute, a violation of a safety statute or regulation creates a rebuttable *presumption* of negligence. And some jurisdictions that give conclusive status to violations of a legislature's statutes give a lesser, mere-evidence effect to violations of a city's ordinances or regulations of administrative agencies, both considered subordinate rule-making bodies.

Federal Law and Federal Courts

Negligence per se claims, being creatures of state tort law, must be distinguished from the federal doctrine prescribing when a private cause of action may be *implied* in a federal statute. More narrow than *negligence per se*, the federal implication doctrine allows private claims only when Congress clearly so intended. See *Gibson v. Wal–Mart Stores, Inc.*, 189 F.Supp.2d 443 (W.D. Va. 2002) (disallowing private claims under Federal Hazardous Substances Act and Poison Prevention Packaging Act). While the federal implication doctrine may be its cousin, *negligence per se* is an independent, substantive doctrine of state tort law applicable in both state courts and federal diversity actions for violations of both state and federal statutes and regulations, regardless of whether the implication doctrine would also allow a private claim.

Compatibility with Ordinary Negligence Claims

While *negligence per se* and ordinary negligence claims are separate and independent, the two claims are quite compatible. Indeed, plaintiffs typically and properly include counts for both ordinary negligence and *negligence per se* in the same complaint, and a plaintiff may prevail by establishing the defendant's breach of its duty of care on either form of negligence claim.

Compliance with Statutory Standards— Evidence of Due Care

A product seller's *compliance* with a statutory or regulatory safety standard in a negligence action is proper evidence of a product's *non*defectiveness and the manufacturer's *due care*, but such compliance is rarely conclusive on these issues. A few state products liability reform statutes (e.g., Colo., Ind.) provide that compliance with a statute or regulation gives rise to a rebuttable presumption that the manufacturer was not negligent. Compliance with safety statutes and regulations is addressed later as a matter of special defense. See § 14.3, below.

§ 2.5 PROOF OF NEGLIGENCE— RES IPSA LOQUITUR

To establish a defendant's negligence, a plaintiff usually must prove, with specificity, the manner in which the defendant was negligent in making or selling a product that injured the plaintiff. Proof merely that a product malfunctioned and caused an accident usually does not suffice. The absence of direct evidence of how or why a product was defective may be due to circumstances beyond the plaintiff's control, as where a product is destroyed in an accident or because there simply is no way for the plaintiff to uncover what went wrong on the assembly line long ago.

Sometimes, as when a plaintiff encounters a bug or a mouse in her Coke or a toe in his chewing tobacco, the circumstantial evidence surrounding the misadventure quite strongly suggests that the product's defective condition resulted from some negligent act or omission by the manufacturer or other supplier. In situations like these, negligence law contains a doctrine of circumstantial evidence that allows a plaintiff to establish a prima facie case without direct evidence of how specifically the product failed or how specifically the defendant may have been negligent—*res ipsa loquitur* ("*res ipsa*").

Limitations

Certain limitations on the *res ipsa* doctrine should be noted. First, this doctrine applies only when the circumstances of an accident are mysterious and unknown. There is no need for a doctrine of circumstantial evidence designed to allow plausible guesses as to how an accident occurred when direct evidence clearly establishes that fact. So, though many courts allow a plaintiff to rely on *res ipsa* even when the plaintiff pleads and offers specific evidence on negligence and causation—particularized proof on how and why a product accident occurred—the need for *res ipsa* vanishes, like a bat in the light, once the plaintiff's evidence specifically and fully explains how the product failed and particularizes reasonable steps the defendant could have taken to prevent the failure. Frequently, however, a plaintiff's proof of how an accident occurred will not be specific and complete, in which case the plaintiff should be entitled to rely upon *res ipsa* in addition to more specific proof.

Second, while *res ipsa* allows an inference of *negligence* and sometimes *causation*, a plaintiff relying on *res ipsa* still has the burden of proving, in almost all states, *all* the elements of a negligence case—the defendant's duty, *breach*, *cause in fact*, proximate cause, and damage.

Third, one should also remember that *res ipsa loquitur* is a rule of *negligence*, not strict products liability, such that the inferences (or presumptions) must point to a probability that the defendant was *negligent* in allowing a product to *become* defective, not merely that the product was defective—such as when a mouse shows up in a bottle of Coke. What must be inferred is the defendant's *negligence* in allowing the defect into the product and in selling it in that condition. And proof, no matter how strong, of the product's defectiveness alone simply will not suffice. For the latter, there is a closely similar, more recent doctrine (the "malfunction doctrine") discussed in § 7.4, below, tailored to proof of defect for purposes of establishing strict products liability.

Elements

Although *res ipsa* is not a cause of action but merely a method of proof, it nevertheless has two or three definite elements. Most traditional formulations of *res ipsa* in America derive from the first edition of *Wigmore on Evidence* (1905), which divided the doctrine into three elements:

(1) The event must be of a kind that ordinarily does not occur in the absence of someone's negligence;

(2) It must be caused by an agency or instrumentality within the exclusive control of the defendant; and

(3) It must not have been due to any voluntary action or contribution on the part of the plaintiff.

In order, these elements raise inferences (1) that *someone* was *negligent*; (2) that the someone was the *defendant*; and (3) that the someone was *not* the *plaintiff*. In combination, these elements mean that a plaintiff may rely on *res ipsa* where the circumstances suggest that an accident probably resulted from the defendant's negligence and not from the actions of the plaintiff or another.

Prompted by the widespread adoption of *comparative fault*, many courts have eliminated the third element, an element that suggests an absence of the plaintiff's contributory fault. Thus, though many courts continue to define the doctrine in terms of the traditional three elements, see *Olshansky v. Rehrig Int'l*, 872 A.2d 282 (R.I. 2005), sounder formulations of *res ipsa* today limit the essential elements to the first two. See *McGuire v. Davidson Mfg. Corp.*, 258 F.Supp.2d 945, 953 (N.D. Iowa 2003) (comparative fault act "abrogates the requirement that the plaintiff show his actions did not contribute to the injury").

Multiple Defendants

The exclusive control element is problematic for plaintiffs in cases with multiple defendants. If more than one defendant handles a product in a way that could cause the injury, no one defendant will have had exclusive control over the product and a *res ipsa* case ordinarily will fail. In such a successive control situation, a plaintiff usually will have to show that the probable negligence was attributable to a particular defendant and not the others—by evidence that implicates the particular defendant, exonerates the other parties, or some combination of the two. See *Waering v. BASF Corp.*, 146 F.Supp.2d 675 (M.D. Pa. 2001) (evidence of negligent packaging by manufacturer of hazardous chemical, with no evidence of negligent shipping by distributors, sufficed to implicate manufacturer and exonerate distributors).

Procedural Effect

The importance of *res ipsa loquitur* lies in its procedural effect. As with other types of circumstantial evidence, a large majority of courts hold that *res ipsa* provides nothing more than an *inference* that the defendant was negligent, an inference the jury is free to accept or reject. See *Smoot v. Mazda Motors of Am., Inc.*, 469 F.3d 675 (7th Cir. 2006) (Wis. law). Yet an inference of this type may be exceedingly important to a plaintiff deprived by circumstances of direct proof of negligence and causation, saving him or her from summary judgment or a directed verdict for the defendant. In a few states, *res ipsa* provides a plaintiff with a "presumption" of negligence, or makes out a prima facie case, which shifts the burden of going forward with the evidence (or the "burden of proof") to the defendant who thereupon must produce some evidence that it was not negligent or lose the case.

§ 2.6   THE RESURGENCE OF NEGLIGENCE

Beginning in the 1980s, negligence theory began a resurgence in American products liability law, albeit sporadic, in both courts and legislatures. This development, visible in some American states more than others, still appears to be resisted in Europe and elsewhere in the world.

Resurgence in the Courts

In adopting strict liability in tort during the 1960s and 1970s, many courts stated or suggested that the new strict products liability doctrine eliminated the need for a separate theory of liability in negligence. But as courts applied the new "strict" products liability doctrine in an expanding array of contexts, they increasingly recognized that liability for design and warning defects is best defined in terms of negligence principles, centered on a balance of foreseeable risk, cost, utility, reasonableness, and such factors as optimality.

Many courts have acknowledged this close similarity, or "functional equivalence," of negligence and "strict" liability in both the design and warning contexts, and a small number boldly apply negligence principles explicitly, rather than those of "strict" liability, in design defect cases. See *Wright v. Brooke Group Ltd.*, 652 N.W.2d 159 (Iowa 2002) (design case). But most courts so far have refused to take the final step and acknowledge that negligence doctrine should displace strict liability as the single, proper liability standard for rendering risk-utility determinations in design and warning defect cases. Though acknowledging that liability in design and warning cases is really little more than negligence, most courts continue to assert that it really *is* something more. See *Smith v. Alza Corp.*, 948 A.2d 686 (N.J. Super. Ct. App. Div. 2008).

Resurgence in the Restatement

These developments in the courts are mirrored by the *Restatement (Third) of Torts: Products Liability* which, though defining liability in terms of "defect," acknowledges that liability for both defective design and defective warning is based on principles of negligence.

In § 2(b), the *Third Restatement* limits *design defects* to "foreseeable risks of harm" that a manufacturer could have avoided with a "reasonable alternative design." Comment *d* recognizes that the liability standard is essentially negligence because it "adopts a reasonableness ('risk-utility balancing') test as the standard for judging the defectiveness of product designs. More specifically, the test is whether a reasonable alternative design would, at reasonable cost, have reduced the foreseeable risks of harm posed by the product and, if so, whether the omission of the alternative design rendered the product not reasonably safe." The necessary "comparison between an alternative design and the product design that caused the injury [is] undertaken from the viewpoint of a reasonable person. That standard is also used in administering the traditional reasonableness standard in negligence."

Section 2(c) similarly limits *warning defects* to "foreseeable risks of harm" that a manufacturer could have avoided with "reasonable instructions or warnings." Comment *i* observes that this liability standard "adopts a reasonableness test for judging the adequacy of product instructions and warnings [and so] parallels Subsection (b)."

Resurgence in Reform Statutes

Negligence principles also figure prominently in the products liability reform legislation enacted in a number of states. A prominent feature of many such statutes is the definition of liability in negligence terms. Several of the statutes (e.g., La.) define design defectiveness in classic risk-utility language, discussed above. In addition, some of the statutes (e.g., Miss., N.J., Ohio) define the liability standard for warning defects, and sometimes design defects as well (e.g., Ind., Wash.), in conventional negligence terms. And North Carolina's statute expressly rejects the strict products liability in tort doctrine.

Thus, in an increasing number of states, negligence principles are returning to the law of products liability as the dominant (and sometimes exclusive) tort law standard of liability in design and warning cases. Endorsed by the *Restatement (Third) of Torts: Products Liability*, this trend may be expected to continue in both courts and legislatures in the years ahead.

CHAPTER 3

TORTIOUS MISREPRESENTATION

Table of Sections

§ 3.1   Misrepresentation—Generally.
§ 3.2   Fraud.
§ 3.3   Negligent Misrepresentation.
§ 3.4   Strict Liability for Misrepresentation.

––––––

§ 3.1   MISREPRESENTATION— GENERALLY

Misrepresentation is the communication of false or misleading information to another. A tortious misrepresentation claim may arise in a products liability context if a manufacturer or other seller communicates a false and material statement of fact about a product to a person who is harmed by reasonably relying on the truth of that communication.

For example, a manufacturer may assert—in an advertisement, operating manual, label, plaque, or oral statement to a buyer—that its crane is "rated to 20,000 lbs." If the crane cannot in fact lift that amount of weight without breaking, and an 18,000 pound load falls on a worker beneath the boom when it collapses, the worker may have a tortious misrepresentation claim against the manufacturer for its false assertion about the crane's weight-bearing capabilities. Or a drug manufacturer may promote a medication as "free of significant side effects" when it does in fact cause such side effects (say, sterility) in many people. Misrepresentation claims thus require no "defect" in the product but are based on the communication of false words that cause harm.

Three separate claims for tortious misrepresentation may arise under the common law, distinct theories of liability that differ principally according to the defendant's state of mind in making the representation: (1) intentional misrepresentation ("fraud" or "deceit"); (2) negligent misrepresentation; and, in a minority of jurisdictions under *Restatement (Second) of Torts* § 402B, (3) strict liability in tort for making public misrepresentations about a product's safety.

Because misrepresentation claims hinge on particular words written or spoken by the defendant, they require the precise identification and close scrutiny of the particular, offending language. Thus, a lawyer considering a misrepresentation claim must first and foremost isolate the exact words challenged, framing the particular context in which they were communicated, in order to assess whether they properly give rise to a misrepresentation claim. For a more thorough examination of tortious misrepresentation, see Owen, Products Liability Law ch. 3 (2d ed. 2008).

§ 3.2 FRAUD

The action of intentional misrepresentation or "deceit," referred to as "fraud," figures prominently (if not frequently) in modern American products liability litigation, often in claims against cigarette manufacturers. Although the precise specification of elements varies from state to state, most courts agree that they in substance include the following:

(1) A *representation*;

(2) Its *falsity*;

(3) Its *materiality*;

(4) The speaker's *knowledge of its falsity* or ignorance of its truth;

(5) The speaker's *intent that it should be acted on* by the hearer;

(6) The hearer's *ignorance of its falsity*;

(7) The hearer's *reliance* on its truth;

(8) The hearer's *right to rely* thereon; and

(9) The hearer's consequent and *proximate injury*.

See *Estate of Schwarz v. Philip Morris Inc.*, 135 P.3d 409 (Or. Ct. App. 2006); Owen, Products Liability Law § 3.2 (2d ed. 2008).

In formulating these requirements for the tort of deceit, some courts condense them into as few as

three, four, or five elements. For example, elements
(7) and (8) in the above formulation may be combined into a single element designated "justifiable
reliance." In contrast, other courts splinter the
various requirements into as many as eleven elements, as by pulling apart element (1) into separate
components of "representation," "existing," and
"fact." Regardless of how they are divided, courts
widely agree that the substance of these components are necessary to establish a claim for fraudulent misrepresentation.

In many states, and under Fed. R. Civ. P. 9(b), a
plaintiff must plead with specificity facts constitut-
ing a fraud (the "who, what, when, and where"
facts), see *Roney v. Gencorp*, 431 F.Supp.2d 622
(S.D. W.Va. 2006), and many jurisdictions apply a
"clear and convincing evidence" standard of proof
to such claims. The plaintiff's burden of proof applies to each element of fraudulent misrepresentation, and such a claim will fail unless the plaintiff
establishes each one of these separate elements. For
these reasons, recovery on fraudulent misrepresentation claims can be particularly difficult, and plaintiffs often shy away from this tort if relief appears
available on some other theory of recovery with
fewer elements and less stringent requirements of
proof, such as breach of express warranty.

Representation

By its very nature, a misrepresentation consists
of the defendant's explicit communication of infor-

mation to the plaintiff or another, usually by words but occasionally by picture (as an illustration of the product performing tasks it cannot safely perform) or conduct (as by painting over a dangerous defect). More difficult conceptually is the question of whether a defendant may be liable in fraud for mere *silence*, that is, for failing to communicate information about some hidden defect or danger lurking in a product. The traditional general rule is that the mere *nondisclosure* of information is not a "representation" and so does not support an action of deceit, a sound rule that prevents any failure to warn from also amounting *ipso facto* to a misrepresentation.

Since a simple no-duty-to-disclose rule is sometimes harsh in application, courts from an early date began to create exceptions to it for special situations, such as allowing claims for "fraudulent concealment." For example, a speaker has a duty to disclose information necessary to cure a "half-truth"—a misconception caused by a defendant's representation that is literally true but that implies facts which themselves are untrue. Another exception to the general no-duty rule sometimes applicable to products liability cases is the duty to correct information believed by the speaker to be true at the time it was communicated but which subsequently is discovered to be false. In addition, the existence of a fiduciary or confidential relationship may impose an affirmative duty on the person entrusted with a special position of power over the other's interests to provide the other with information necessary to protect the other's interests. But the normal relationship between manufacturers and consumers can hardly be characterized as fiduciary or confidential. See *Burton v. R.J. Reynolds Tobacco Co.*, 397 F.3d 906 (10th Cir. 2005) (Kan. law).

Fact

To support a fraud claim, a representation must be of an existing *fact*. The fact represented must exist at the time of the representation, and a fraudulent misrepresentation claim will not lie with respect to predictions of future conditions or events, unless such predictions imply the existence of facts that presently exist. A promise of future performance made with no present intention of keeping it constitutes a misstatement of an existing fact.

The misrepresentation must concern a *fact* as opposed to an *opinion*. That is, the matter misrepresented must be specific and capable of objective determination. By definition, a "puff" is not a representation of fact. Buyers ordinarily view a seller's subjective beliefs concerning the value or quality of a product, including general commendatory characterizations—such as "good," "excellent," "high quality," or "terrific"—as casual sales talk, "puffery" not intended or taken to be factual assertions. Normally, the more specific the assertion, the more likely that it fairly may be regarded as a factual assertion, and the more general it is, the more likely that it should be characterized as an opinion. Thus, to say that a crane is "capable of safely lifting 40,000 pounds" is a statement of fact, but to say that it is "a mighty strong crane" is a statement of opinion.

Falsity

The plaintiff must prove that a fact represented was false, based on the fair meaning of the representation. To determine whether a representation is substantially true or substantially false, the words should be construed in context. As previously mentioned, half-truths are considered false. So, if a manufacturer has its paneling tested for flammability by Underwriters Laboratories, and the paneling miserably fails the test because it is far too flammable to receive any flame-spread rating whatsoever, the manufacturer's statements to a prospective buyer that the paneling is "not flame-spread rated" is false and fraudulent because it suggests that the paneling has not yet been flame-tested, not that it was tested and failed the test. See *St. Joseph Hosp. v. Corbetta Constr. Co.*, 316 N.E.2d 51 (Ill. App. Ct. 1974).

Materiality

To support a claim for fraud, the misrepresentation must be *material*, as distinguished from trivial or irrelevant. One is not likely to rely, nor does one have a right to rely, on information truly insignificant to the transaction. A fact is "material" if a reasonable person would consider it important *or* if the speaker expects the recipient to so consider it. See Rest. (2d) § 538.

"*Scienter*"—Knowledge of Falsity and Intent to Deceive

The central elements of deceit, distinguishing it from negligent and innocent misrepresentation, are a defendant's *knowledge* that its representation is false and its *intent* to deceive the plaintiff thereby. Because of the difficulties in proving this guilty state of mind, plaintiffs in fraud cases often have difficulty establishing this important "*scienter*" component to an intentional misrepresentation claim.

In recent decades, many courts have liberalized the *scienter* requirement if the speaker makes a statement as of his own knowledge without knowing whether it be true or false, in which case the speaker is falsely asserting that he or she knows the matter to be true. While some courts squeeze this type of state of mind into the "intent" mold, others classify it merely as "recklessness." Characterized either way, such a state of mind normally is considered adequate *scienter* to support a claim for fraud.

Justifiable Reliance

The plaintiff, or someone acting on the plaintiff's behalf (such as a parent, employer, or doctor), must in fact learn about and then act somehow in *reliance* on the misrepresentation—as by purchasing the product, using it in a particular manner, or failing to take certain precautions. If a plaintiff fails to establish such reliance, a causal link between the defendant's misrepresentation and the plaintiff's injury normally is not established, and the case will usually fail. So, a smoker's fraud claim will fail if he fails to allege and prove that he saw and relied upon a cigarette manufacturer's representation that the cigarettes were safe.

In contrast to the entirely *subjective* nature of the element of reliance, involving as it does the issue of whether the plaintiff or other representee in fact believed the representation and took action, at least in part, as a result thereof, the *justifiability* of the reliance rests on an *objective* standard of reasonableness in all the circumstances. Thus, for a fraud to be actionable, a plaintiff must not only rely on the misrepresentation, but the reliance must be justifiable or reasonable. Since justifiability is an element of a claim for *intentional* misrepresentation, courts understandably are reluctant to allow a plaintiff's careless trust on a defendant's calculated fraud to bar a claim for this intentional tort. In the end, however, a plaintiff must have had a "right to rely" on the defendant's misrepresentation, and a case for fraud will fail if the plaintiff cannot prove the justifiability of his or her reliance.

Resulting Damage

A plaintiff must prove and may recover damages from relying on a defendant's fraudulent misrepresentation. A claim for deceit is completed by proof of this final element—actual damages proximately resulting from the misrepresentation.

§ 3.3 NEGLIGENT MISREPRESENTATION

The prima facie claim for negligent misrepresentation, a quite uncommon cause of action in products liability cases, closely resembles the claim for intentional misrepresentation, except that the elements of duty and negligence replace the element of fraudulent intent. See *Maneely v. General Motors Corp.*, 108 F.3d 1176 (9th Cir. 1997) (in California, such claims require proof that (1) defendant had duty to exercise due care in providing information, (2) defendant was negligent in its provision, (3) plaintiff reasonably relied on it, and (4) plaintiff was injured as a result).

While manufacturers may be responsible for negligent misrepresentation for false representations on a product's label or in advertising, many of the cases involve retailers, such as sellers of used cars. An early, typical negligent misrepresentation case is *Pabon v. Hackensack Auto Sales, Inc.*, 164 A.2d 773 (N.J. Super. Ct. App. Div. 1960). The plaintiff was injured when the steering on his new automobile locked, causing the car to crash. He had noticed a "clicking" and "chopping" sensation in the steering and had brought it to the attention of the defendant's service manager on three occasions prior to the accident. Each time, without checking the problem, the service manager said something like: "It's a new car. Don't worry about it. It'll wear out." The court held that a jury could find the defendant car dealer liable for negligent misrepresentation on these facts because the service manager made positive assertions without a reasonable basis to know them to be true.

On occasion, certifiers of product quality, such as Underwriters Laboratories (UL), are held subject to liability for negligent misrepresentation. The most prominent case of this type is *Hanberry v. Hearst Corp.*, 81 Cal.Rptr. 519 (Ct. App. 1969), a claim against the publisher of Good Housekeeping magazine by the purchaser of slippery shoes for negligently awarding the shoes the "Good Housekeeping's Consumers' Guaranty Seal" without adequate testing.

Particularly with claims for damages other than personal injury or property damage (such as emotional distress and pure economic loss), courts often state that a negligent misrepresentation claimant must show the additional element that the defendant owed a *duty* to the claimant to impart accurate information. If the relationship between the defendant and plaintiff is too remote (such as a union that paid medical expenses of members whose lung diseases were caused by smoking cigarettes whose safety was misrepresented by the defendant), the manufacturer may have no duty at all. See *In re Tobacco Cases II*, 113 Cal.Rptr.2d 120 (Ct. App. 2001). In addition, some states (Minn., N.C.) limit damages for negligent misrepresentation to pecuniary loss, such that personal injury claims may not be based on negligent misrepresentation, while other states (Cal.) bar emotional distress claims in negligent misrepresentation.

§ 3.4 STRICT LIABILITY FOR MISREPRESENTATION

A manufacturer or other seller who innocently makes a false statement about a product's quality or safety that results in harm may be subject to liability in contract for breach of an express warranty, as discussed in the next chapter. Some states provide an additional claim for such strict or no-fault liability for misrepresentation under a parallel cause of action in tort.

The classic case widely credited with paternity of the doctrine of strict products liability in tort for misrepresentation is *Baxter v. Ford Motor Co.*, 12 P.2d 409 (Wash. 1932). While the plaintiff was driving his Model A Ford, a pebble from a passing car struck his windshield, causing small pieces of glass to fly into his eye, which he lost as a result. The plaintiff sued Ford for misrepresenting the windshield's safety characteristics in its advertising catalogues:

> TRIPLEX SHATTER-PROOF GLASS WINDSHIELD. All of the new Ford cars have a Triplex shatter-proof glass windshield—so made that it will not fly or shatter under the hardest impact.... Its extra margin of safety is something that every motorist should look for in the purchase of a car—especially where there are women and children.

Ford defended on the basis that there could be no claim for "express warranty" in the absence of privity of contract, but the court rejected this argument, reasoning that a manufacturer should not be allowed to create demand for its products by false statements in mass advertising and then be permitted to hide behind the privity-of-contract defense when consumers, induced by the false statements to purchase the products, are injured as a result.

By holding that liability for misrepresentation was truly strict, like liability for express warranty, while ignoring the warranty law rules concerning privity of contract and other contractual limitations, *Baxter* in effect created a new tort, leading eventually to § 402B of the *Restatement (Second) of Torts*:

§ 402B. Misrepresentation by Seller of Chattels to Consumer

One engaged in the business of selling chattels who, by advertising, labels, or otherwise, makes to the public a misrepresentation of a material fact concerning the character or quality of a chattel sold by him is subject to liability for physical harm to a consumer of the chattel caused by justifiable reliance upon the misrepresentation, even though

(a) it is not made fraudulently or negligently, and

(b) the consumer has not bought the chattel from or entered into any contractual relation with the seller.

In part because it trespasses deeply into express warranty domain statutorily defined in UCC § 2–313, judicial support for § 402B has been weak. Most states have never adopted or applied the doctrine at all, and case authority for the doctrine in states in which the doctrine at one time or another has been discussed is generally sparse and often dated. Nevertheless, this section of the *Restatement (Second) of Torts* was reaffirmed by the *Restatement (Third) of Torts: Products Liability* § 9 with little fanfare, analysis, or debate, and the doctrine seems quite firmly established—even if infrequently used—in several jurisdictions (Cal., Pa., Tenn., Tex.), and decisions in a few others (e.g., Neb., N.J., Wyo.) have referred favorably to this doctrine.

Apart from the absence of seller fault, the elements of a § 402B cause of action for innocent misrepresentation closely track the elements of deceit, including proof that the seller made an affirmative representation, that the representation was one of fact, that it was material, that it was relied upon justifiably by the plaintiff (or someone acting on his or her behalf), and that it caused damage (personal injury or property damage, but not pure economic loss) to the plaintiff. Yet, unlike deceit, liability under § 402B is limited to (1) representations made to the public at large, as in labels and advertisements, and (2) physical harm, which excludes liability for pure economic loss.

CHAPTER 4

WARRANTY

Table of Sections

§ 4.1 Warranty—Generally.
§ 4.2 Express Warranty.
§ 4.3 Implied Warranty of Merchantability.
§ 4.4 Implied Warranty of Fitness for Particular
Purpose.
§ 4.5 Privity of Contract and Third-Party Beneficiaries.
§ 4.6 Notice of Breach.
§ 4.7 Disclaimers.
§ 4.8 Limitations of Remedy.
§ 4.9 Anti–Disclaimer and Other Warranty Reform
Legislation.

———

§ 4.1 WARRANTY—GENERALLY

Warranty law concerns the legal obligations arising from promises and other assertions connected
with transactions. In the products liability context,
the law of warranty prescribes the legal effect ac-
corded to assertions associated with the transfer of
a product for value, usually through a sale. Assertions about a product may be express, from a seller's affirmative communications about a product's
attributes, or they may be implied by the nature of
the sales transaction. For various reasons, such as a

statute of limitations (4 years from sale) that normally is longer than tort law (2 or 3 years from discovery), warranty claims are an important part of modern products liability litigation.

In contrast to most products liability law, which today is generally based in tort, the law of warranty ordinarily is conceived as part of the modern law of contract. Most states that never did adopt the doctrine of strict liability in tort for the sale of defective products (Del., Mass., Mich., N.C., Va.) have constructed their modern products liability jurisprudence on an implied warranty of quality. Yet much common-law "warranty" doctrine of such states has been patterned after the developed tort law jurisprudence of § 402A of the *Restatement (Second) of Torts* and so in essence (if not totally in doctrine) is part of the larger law of tort.

Warranty law governing the sale of chattels evolved in the common law and was first codified by the Sale of Goods Act of 1893 in Great Britain and by the Uniform Sales Act of 1906 in the United States. Article 2 (Sales) of the Uniform Commercial Code (UCC), promulgated in the 1950s and adopted in state legislatures during the late 1950s and the 1960s, supplanted the Uniform Sales Act. Thus, the modern American products liability law of warranty generally concerns the interpretation and application of various sections of UCC Article 2.

In 2002 and 2003, UCC Article 2 was revised by the National Conference of Commissioners on Uniform State Laws (NCCUSL) and the American Law

Institute (ALI). No state has adopted these amendments, and there appears little prospect that any state will adopt them any time soon, if ever at all. Even if some state legislatures begin to have a change of heart and adopt the revisions, widespread adoption will surely take a number of years, and courts in the meantime must continue to apply the current provisions of UCC Article 2 to products liability warranty cases. For a more thorough examination of warranty, see Owen, Products Liability Law ch. 4 (2d ed. 2008).

§ 4.2 EXPRESS WARRANTY

Express warranties are affirmative assertions, made by a seller in connection with a sales transaction, that a product possesses certain characteristics of quality, construction, performance capability, durability, or safety. This form of warranty springs from a seller's words or other form of affirmative communication rather than any inherent characteristic of the product itself. Hence, as with tortious misrepresentation, claims for breach of express warranty rest on the falsity of such asserted information rather than any deficiency in the product itself. Stated otherwise, a plaintiff need not prove that a product was "defective," or that the seller was at fault, to prove that the seller made and breached an express warranty. See *Forbes v. General Motors Corp.*, 935 So.2d 869 (Miss. 2006) (fault unnecessary to establish breach).

Manner of Communication

UCC § 2–313(a) provides that express warranties are created by "affirmations of fact" or "promises" relating to the goods that "become part of the basis of the bargain." There is no fixed manner by which an express warranty must be created, and such a warranty may arise from any affirmative means by which information is conveyed. Thus, an express warranty may arise from statements on a product's packaging or label, a seller's assurances to a buyer's pilots that a used plane is "ready to go," a sales clerk's assertion that a pressure cooker will not explode, a label on a can stating "Boned Chicken" and newspaper advertisements stating that the chicken contains "No Bones," or an "off" designation for a control handle on an electrical panel that is alive with current. Advertisements, catalogues, and circulars containing statements of fact may be interpreted as creating express warranties. *Descriptions* of goods, *samples*, and *models*, if they become part of the basis of the bargain, also may create express warranties.

Breach: Falsity and Interpretation

An express warranty is breached if the assertion is untrue. As in tortious misrepresentation, the truth or falsity of an assertion rests upon its fair interpretation in light of the context of the particular transaction. Questions of interpretation—as to whether or not a particular assertion amounted to an express warranty, its scope and meaning, and whether the assertion was true or false—are generally factual questions to be determined by the trier of fact.

Representations of Fact *vs.* Opinion ("Puffs")

To create an express warranty, a seller's affirmation ordinarily must be one of fact, meaning that such a statement must convey more information than simply the seller's opinion of the product's worth. In attempting to sell products to consumers, sellers often make exaggerated statements of opinion or "puffs" acclaiming their products' virtues—a form of salesmanship consumers are accustomed to treat as devoid of content. Reasonable buyers generally understand such puffs as merely sales pitch, designed to bend the buyer's will and encourage a sale. A representation is likely to be construed as fact, on the other hand, when it describes certain specific traits of quality, construction, performance capability, durability, or safety possessed by the product, information of a type likely to be known by a seller but not a buyer, which communicates a message of real value on which a prospective buyer may justifiably be expected to rely. See UCC § 2–313(2).

Seller representations that are specific and unambiguous, particularly if they concern the safety of a product, are likely to be construed as factual. Thus, express warranties have been found to be created by an advertisement that a skin cream was "safe"; a booklet stating that a steam vaporizer was safe to be used all night and featuring a picture of the appliance in use near a baby's crib, where a toddler was badly burned when the vaporizer overturned; representations that a tree hunting stand was "probably the safest one on the market" and "there is no way [one] can fall" from it, where the plaintiff did; and a nightclub server's statement that the club's special drink that night was "good," where plaintiffs were mistakenly served glasses of dish-washing liquid containing highly toxic lye.

In contrast to such specific factual assertions, a seller's vague and general representations that appear merely to express the seller's personal views on a product's characteristics, worth, or quality, do not ordinarily constitute material facts. So, statements that a Suzuki Samurai "never lets you down," has "fun written all over it," and is "nifty" are the kind of loose and general "sales talk" that should be viewed as puffing rather than as an affirmation of fact that the vehicle is not prone to roll over. See *Connick v. Suzuki Motor Co.*, 656 N.E.2d 170 (Ill. App. Ct. 1995). Other examples of statements held to be puffery rather than factual include claims that a truck, the roof of which collapsed after it fell nearly 30 feet, was "rock-solid" and its roof was "strong"; that an automotive manufacturer believed that "Quality is job one"; that a used car was in good shape; that a fondue pot, which tipped over and burned a young child caught in its cord, was the "finest product of its kind available" and was "engineered to give [an] extra measure of satisfaction"; that a bungee cord was of "premium quality"; and that "You meet the nicest people on a Honda" motorbike.

Basis of the Bargain; Reliance

In order for a seller's affirmation of fact to become an express warranty under UCC § 2–313(1), it must become "part of the basis of the bargain," a requirement that replaced "reliance" used in the Uniform Sales Act. Courts and commentators disagree on the meaning of this requirement. A "strong" interpretation of "basis of the bargain" assumes that the drafters of Article 2, in switching from "reliance" to "basis of the bargain," intended to make a major shift in warranty law—to redirect the focus away from the deal the buyer thought he or she was getting to the deal the seller's affirmations reasonably and objectively appeared to make. In pricing a product, a seller might fairly be expected to include as a reserved expense the cost of fulfilling its claims of product description, quality, and performance. So, whether or not a buyer relies on or even knows about a particular warranty, he or she arguably pays for it as part of the sales transaction. For these reasons and others, many courts have held that a plaintiff need not establish reliance in order to recover for breach of express warranty under § 2–313.

A second, "weak" interpretation of "basis of the bargain" postulates that reliance remains an important consideration, although its absence now must be proven by the seller. Adherents to this conception, pointing to the apparent unfairness of allowing a buyer to obtain redress for damage that in a real sense did not result from the seller's misstatement, have refused to abandon reliance as part of express warranty responsibility. On this view, a plaintiff's reliance is an implicit or explicit aspect of the "basis of the bargain" requirement under § 2–313.

§ 4.3 IMPLIED WARRANTY OF MERCHANTABILITY

The basic implied warranty of quality in the sale of goods, now called the implied warranty of "merchantability," developed in late Roman law nearly two thousand years ago. After a long period of stagnation, this warranty evolved in Anglo–American common law over the centuries, first in cases involving defective foodstuffs and much later (during the 19th century) as a broad repudiation of the long-entrenched doctrine of *caveat emptor*. The renewed doctrine of *caveat venditor* required a seller to take responsibility for damage caused by any latent defects in goods sold, on the theory that fair dealing implied a fundamental guarantee of fair quality into the sale of a product—that the product would conform to the general description under which it was sold. Fair quality received became a legal *quid pro quo* for a fair price paid. In the words of Lord Ellenborough: "The purchaser cannot be supposed to buy goods to lay them on a dunghill." *Gardiner v. Gray*, 171 E.R. 46, 47 (K.B. 1815).

Thus, the implied warranty of merchantability is an assurance, imposed by law upon the seller, that a product is reasonably suitable for the general uses for which it is purchased and sold. As the central warranty in Article 2 of the UCC, the implied warranty of merchantability can be a vital theory of liability in products liability litigation. Because liability is based merely upon a product's inadequate condition or malfunction without regard to the seller's fault, it truly is a form of "strict" liability. Generally, proof that a product is "defective" under strict liability in tort will establish that a product is not merchantable, and vice versa. In this respect, these two theories of products liability recovery are essentially coextensive.

UCC § 2–314—Fitness for Ordinary Purposes

Section 2–314(1) provides in pertinent part that, "[u]nless excluded or modified [§ 2–316], a warranty that the goods shall be merchantable is implied in a contract for their sale if the seller is a merchant with respect to goods of that kind." Section 2–314(2) provides a long and nonexclusive list of tests for the merchantability of a product, at the heart of which, in subsection (c), is that a seller impliedly represents that its products are "fit" for their "ordinary purposes."

For example, shoes may be expected to have their heels firmly attached so they will not fall off in normal use; a ladder may be expected not to collapse; hair lotion may be expected not to burn a user's scalp; a cookie may be expected to be free from foreign objects; and an SUV marketed for ordinary driving may be expected to be reasonably stable and not roll over in normal use.

But "fit" means *reasonably suitable* for the general purposes for which such an article is sold and used, which, in products liability cases, means *reasonably safe* for their ordinary uses. See *In re September 11 Litigation*, 265 F.Supp.2d 208 (S.D.N.Y. 2003). "Merchantability" and "fitness," in other words, do not imply perfection; they do not mean perfect, flawless, completely satisfactory, nor that a product will precisely fulfill every buyer's expectations. In other words, a product's fitness (safety) need not be absolute, and the warranty is met when an article is free of major imperfections, conforms to ordinary standards, and is of the average grade, quality, and value of similar goods sold commercially. See *Phillips v. Cricket Lighters*, 883 A.2d 439 (Pa. 2005).

Likewise, a product generally is not unfit for its ordinary purposes if it contains a characteristic that is "open and obvious," a risk apparent to the ordinary consumer. Section 2–316(3) treats obviousness as a kind of disclaimer, by providing that a buyer who examines (or refuses to examine) goods prior to purchase obtains "no implied warranty with regard to defects which an examination" would have revealed.

It is difficult to untangle "merchantability" in warranty from "defectiveness" in tort, and at least in products liability cases involving personal injuries, the two concepts appear largely, if not entirely,

congruent. See *Solo v. Trus Joist MacMillan*, 2004
WL 524898 (D. Minn. 2004) (merchantability warranty "breached when the product is defective to a
normal buyer making ordinary use of the product").
Indeed, amended § 2–314 explicitly adopts the latter view by defining "merchantability" in personal
injury cases by *tort* products liability law of the
state.

Requirement of a Sale

As with all warranty claims under UCC Article 2
(entitled "Sales"), breach of the implied warranty
of merchantability generally requires a "sale,"
though UCC Article 2A ("Leases") now applies the
implied warranty of merchantability to goods that
are *leased* rather than sold.

§ 4.4 IMPLIED WARRANTY OF FITNESS FOR PARTICULAR PURPOSE

The implied warranty of fitness for particular
purpose (often shortened to the "implied warranty
of fitness") is an implied promise by a seller that a
product will meet the buyer's *particular* needs. By
this warranty, a seller impliedly promises to exercise its special judgment or skills, on which it knows
the buyer relies, to select a particular product that
will satisfy the buyer's *special*, unusual uses—as
distinct from the *ordinary* uses to which such products normally are put (the suitability for which the
merchantability warranty is the implicit guarantee).

See *Crane v. Bagge & Son, Inc.*, 2005 WL 1576544, at *6 (Cal. Ct. App. 2005) ("A 'particular purpose' means something other than the ordinary purpose.... a specific use by the buyer which is peculiar to the nature of his business.").

UCC § 2–315 provides:

Where the seller at the time of contracting has reason to know any particular purpose for which the goods are required and that the buyer is relying on the seller's skill or judgment to select or furnish suitable goods, there is unless excluded or modified under the next section an implied warranty that the goods shall be fit for such purpose.

The fitness warranty typically arises in one-on-one dealing between a buyer and a seller that is calculated to create quite explicit expectations in the buyer that the product selected by the seller will safely and effectively perform the buyer's particular task. For example, a buyer may ask a hardware store salesman for a chain saw to cut out tree stumps below the level of the soil, requiring the saw to endure frequent encounters with dirt and rocks. If the salesman, after selecting a saw from several in stock, simply plunks it down on the counter saying, "That will be two hundred dollars," the implied warranty of fitness will likely have been made; and, if the saw's chain breaks from this particularly taxing use, the fitness warranty will possibly have been breached. If, as occurs more frequently in such face-to-face encounters, the salesman were to add, "Oh, sure; this one will work just fine," he will have made an express warranty as well. Thus, implied warranties of fitness often coexist with express warranties. See UCC § 2–317 (cumulation of warranties).

In *Klein v. Sears Roebuck and Co.*, 773 F.2d 1421 (4th Cir. 1985) (Md. Law), plaintiffs bought a particular model riding mower upon the recommendation of the defendant's salesman for use on their hilly property, subject to the salesman's inspection of the property to confirm that the mower was appropriate. When the salesman delivered the mower, he inspected the property and pronounced the mower suitable, provided it was driven vertically up the steepest hills. While the plaintiff husband was mowing vertically up one of the steeper slopes, the mower tipped over backwards, injuring him. On these facts, the court affirmed a verdict for the plaintiff husband for breach of an implied warranty of fitness (and breach of express warranty).

Two issues often predominate in products liability cases involving the fitness warranty: (1) the seller's knowledge, and (2) the buyer's reliance.

Seller's Knowledge

In order for the fitness warranty to arise, a seller must know (or have reason to know) that a buyer plans to put a product to some special use which is different from the ordinary uses for which the product usually is sold. The seller must further have reason to know that the buyer is relying on the seller's skill or judgment to select a product appropriate for this special purpose. Thus, the fitness warranty will not apply to the sale of a stove, if the distributor is unaware of the buyer's particular heating needs; or of retreaded tires for a pickup truck, if the seller is unaware of the special needs for the truck in the buyer's construction business; or of a truck cab chassis, if the manufacturer does not know it will be put to use as a tow truck. See *Ford Motor Co. v. General Accident Ins. Co.*, 779 A.2d 362 (Md. 2001).

Buyer's Reliance

If the buyer fails to rely on the seller's implicit assurances of special suitability, any harm suffered by the buyer cannot have resulted from the product's failure to conform to the assurances. A plaintiff's reliance or non-reliance on a seller's skill or judgment is sometimes very clear, such as where a beauty shop customer relies on a beautician to select an appropriate permanent wave solution, not one that will injure her scalp; or where purchasers of a casket and vault rely on a funeral home to select a casket that will fit in the vault. Sometimes evidence on the reliance issue points clearly the other way, revealing that the buyer made an *independent* decision to buy and put a product to a particular use.

§ 4.5 PRIVITY OF CONTRACT AND THIRD–PARTY BENEFICIARIES

In the early part of the twentieth century, the law of contracts quite firmly restricted the enforcement of contractual undertakings to the contracting parties themselves. Contractual rights extended to non-parties ("third-party beneficiaries") only in limited situations where the contracting parties clearly intended to confer benefits on such other persons "remote" from the contract. The logic is elemental that the absence of a contractual relationship (the absence of "privity of contract") is a significant obstacle to a breach of warranty or other contract claim.

The privity-of-contract problem may helpfully be divided into the separate notions of "vertical" and "horizontal" privity. The unifying question in both contexts involves the determination of the proper parties to breach of warranty actions: *What defendants are bound by warranties, and what plaintiffs obtain their benefits?*

"Vertical privity" refers to the contractual relationship between the parties up and down the chain of distribution, from suppliers of raw materials and component parts, at the top, to manufacturers, distributors, wholesalers, retailers, and, at the bottom of the chain, the purchasers of products. The vertical privity issue may be framed as: *Who can be sued?*

"Horizontal privity," on the other hand, concerns the reach of contractual protection to non-purchasers who may be harmed by a product and who seek to stand in the buyer's shoes to obtain the benefits of whatever warranties flowed to the buyer by virtue of his or her contract of purchase. Such non-purchasers, extending horizontally away from the buyer in diminishing order of affinity, include the buyer's family, members of the buyer's household and household guests, the buyer's employees, and others, often referred to as "bystanders." The horizontal privity issue may be framed as: *Who can sue?*

The first decisions to abolish outright the manufacturer's privity defense in personal injury cases were made at the turn of the twentieth century and involved defective foodstuffs. See *Mazetti v. Armour & Co.*, 135 P. 633 (Wash. 1913). By mid-century, the weakening of the privity defense in implied warranty cases began to spread to products for intimate bodily use such as soap, hair dye, and permanent wave solution. Then, in the late 1950s and early 1960s, several courts in rapid succession extended the idea to durable goods.

In 1960, in *Henningsen v. Bloomfield Motors, Inc.*, 161 A.2d 69 (N.J. 1960), the privity bar was emphatically repudiated in a landmark implied warranty case involving injuries from a defective automobile manufactured by defendant Chrysler Corporation, which sold it to a dealer, Bloomfield Motors, which sold it to Mr. Henningsen. The car had a steering defect, and Mr. Henningsen's wife was injured ten days after the purchase when the car went off the road. The court explained that the demise of the privity defense in food and drink cases compelled its demise in a case involving a defective car: "We see no rational doctrinal basis for differentiating between a fly in a bottle of beverage and a defective automobile. The unwholesome beverage may bring illness to one person, the defective car, with its great potentiality for harm to the driver, occupants, and others, demands even less adherence to the narrow barrier of privity."

Henningsen signaled the law's intolerance of the privity defense in products liability claims, leading to the so-called "fall of the citadel of privity." Prosser, *The Fall of the Citadel (Strict Liability to the Consumer)*, 50 Minn. L. Rev. 791, 791 (1966). In addition to the many state court decisions that abolished the vertical privity defense in various contexts involving warranty claims by purchasers against remote sellers, a few state legislatures (e.g., Va.) have expressly abolished it. Yet, a state's abolition of the *vertical* privity defense does not directly address the separate question of whether a non-purchaser who is injured can make a valid warranty claim against a product seller. This latter question involves the issue of *horizontal* privity, now addressed statutorily under the UCC.

Horizontal Privity—Third–Party Beneficiaries Under § 2–318

During the 1950s, the UCC addressed the issue of horizontal privity (and possibly vertical privity to some extent) in § 2–318, entitled "Third Party Beneficiaries of Warranties Express or Implied." By the mid–1960s, as the pro-consumer movement rapidly gained momentum in many states, substantial differences appeared in the development of the privity doctrine in the common law of the various states. Accordingly, in 1966, § 2–318 was amended and promulgated in three separate forms, allowing each state to choose whichever form best comported with its views on this fast-moving and controversial issue—the proper reach of strict products liability law in warranty.

Section § 2–318 provides, in *Alternative A*, that a warranty extends to "any natural person who is in the family or household of his buyer or who is a guest in his home if it is reasonable to expect that such person may use, consume or be affected by the goods and who is injured in person by breach of the warranty." *Alternative B* broadens the plaintiff group to "any natural person who may reasonably be expected to use, consume or be affected by the goods and who is injured in person by breach of the warranty." Broader still, *Alternative C* includes "any person who may reasonably be expected to use, consume or be affected by the goods and who is injured by breach of the warranty."

Each of the three alternatives to § 2–318 describes the extent to which warranty protection extends beyond the buyer in sales transactions. As stated in comment 2, the broad purpose of § 2–318 "is to give certain beneficiaries the benefit of the same warranty which the buyer received in the contract of sale, thereby freeing any such beneficiaries from any technical rules as to 'privity.' " Accordingly, "any beneficiary of a warranty may bring a direct action for breach of warranty against the seller whose warranty extends to him." The requirement of vertical privity had begun to crumble in the pre-Code law, as described above, and § 2–318 was directed principally at the horizontal privity question in implied warranty cases of what types of plaintiffs receive the benefit of warranties received by the purchaser.

Most American jurisdictions, including half the states, adopted Alternative A, or something similar. About 8 jurisdictions adopted Alternative B, or a close approximation, and about 13 adopted Alternative C, or a close equivalent. California omitted § 2–318 from its version of the UCC and requires privity in implied warranty cases as a matter of common law. Texas also leaves the matter to its courts, Louisiana never did adopt Article 2, and several states have nonuniform provisions on privity.

Alternative A Categories—Employees

Courts are split on whether an employee injured by a defective product purchased by his or her employer may maintain a warranty claim under Alternative A against the supplier of the defective product. Probably most courts preclude such claims, ruling that employees fit within none of the specifically designated categories, namely, the purchaser's "family," "household," and "guests in his home." Other courts, as in *Whitaker v. Lian Feng Machine Co.*, 509 N.E.2d 591 (Ill. App. Ct. 1987), reason that the categories of included beneficiaries are merely statutory *minima* which do not prevent a court from allowing other persons lacking privity to take the benefit of a seller's warranties to its buyers. The majority view seems quite clearly correct, since courts normally should not interpret a statute contrary to its plain meaning, here a listing of the *only* categories of non-privity plaintiffs entitled to the benefits of a buyer's warranties.

§ 4.6　NOTICE OF BREACH

After purchase and acceptance of a product, a buyer who is injured by breach of warranty—a defect in the goods or the falsity of a representation—must promptly notify the seller of the breach. A buyer's penalty for failing to promptly inform the seller is the loss of his or her right to recover damages for breach. Notice is required by UCC § 2–607(3)(a), which provides that:

> the buyer must within a reasonable time after he discovers or should have discovered any breach notify the seller of breach or be barred from any remedy. . . .

In *Buford v. Toys R' Us, Inc.*, 458 S.E.2d 373 (Ga. Ct. App. 1995), a boy was seriously injured when a defective weld caused the steer tube on his bicycle to separate from the front fork, throwing him to the pavement. His parents sued the retailer of the defective bicycle for strict liability in tort, negligence, and breach of the implied warranty of merchantability. The trial court granted summary judgment to the retailer on all three claims, which was affirmed on appeal. The appellate court ruled that there was no claim for strict liability in tort because the state products liability statute provided that such liability applied only to manufacturers, not retailers. Because the defective weld had been painted over during the course of manufacture, the retailer could not have been negligent in failing to discover it. As for the implied warranty of merchantability, which surely had been breached by the retailer's sale of a dangerously defective bike, the court ruled that the parents' failure to notify the seller of the claim until it filed a complaint two years after the accident was "unreasonable" as a matter of law, which barred the one claim against the retailer that surely would have succeeded on the merits.

Two states (Me., S.C.) amended their versions of the UCC to ban the notice requirement in personal injury cases, and amended UCC § 2–607(3)(a) relaxes the notice requirement by barring a claim only if and to the extent that the seller is *prejudiced* by the buyer's failure to give timely notice.

§ 4.7 DISCLAIMERS

In the interest of a free marketplace, but in recognition of the shortcomings of actual markets, Article 2 of the UCC establishes a framework for parties to structure their deals freely within certain guidelines, providing two principal means for sellers to avoid responsibility for the consequences of product defects and false representations:

- Disclaimers of warranties, in § 2–316, and

- Limitations on remedies for breach of warranty, in §§ 2–718 and 2–719.

Disclaimers and remedy limitations serve the same ultimate objective, but they operate independently and are conceptually distinct. An effective disclaimer under § 2–316 prevents a warranty from ever arising, so that there is nothing for the seller to breach. By contrast, §§ 2–718 and 2–719, which assume that a valid warranty exists and was breached, concern only the nature and extent of remedy for breach. A damages limitation under § 2–718 "liquidates" the buyer's damages at a predetermined, set amount; a limitation under § 2–719 typically limits the buyer's recovery for breach to repair or replacement of the product and allows no recovery for the buyer's incidental or consequential damages, including damages for personal injuries.

While § 2–316 provides that buyers and sellers may agree to shift the risk of loss arising from what would otherwise be a breach of warranty from the seller to the buyer, it further requires that such changes in the normal allocation of responsibility be made *apparent* to the buyer "to protect a buyer from unexpected and unbargained language of disclaimer by denying effect to such language when inconsistent with language of express warranty and permitting the exclusion of implied warranties only by conspicuous language or other circumstances which protect the buyer from surprise." Cmt. 1.

The Code's twin goals, therefore, are (1) to allow parties to sales transactions to make bargains that shift the normal allocation of risk, yet (2) to ensure that buyers know when such risk shifts occur (when products do not carry the kinds of warranties they normally bear). In this way, the Code mandates that sales transactions, as much as reasonably possible, reflect consensual "bargains" between the parties.

Disclaimers of Express Warranties

The very notion of a disclaimer of an *express* warranty appears unprincipled. Why should a seller be permitted to avoid responsibility for making a promise for which the buyer paid, on which the buyer relied, and which constituted part of the basis of the buyer's bargain? For this reason, one state (S.C.) simply prohibits the disclaimer of express warranties. Yet § 2–316(1) permits such "disclaimers" in a limited manner:

> Words or conduct relevant to the creation of an express warranty and words or conduct tending to negate or limit warranty shall be construed wherever reasonable as consistent with each other; but subject to the provisions of this Article on parol or extrinsic evidence [§ 2–202] negation or limitation is inoperative to the extent that such construction is unreasonable.

The first clause of § 2–316(1), which permits "consistent" express warranty limitations, is designed to permit sellers to *define* express warranties with specificity. All express warranties, of course, logically must have *some* definitional borders, some scope, for dividing product failures that fall within the warranty from those that fall without. So, a manufacturer of a new tire may expressly warrant it against "blowouts." But any such warranty will have some limitations to its scope—for time (3 years), mileage (36,000 miles), type of use (normal, non-commercial passenger car road and highway driving), and manner of use or hazard (no coverage for tires run flat or damaged from off-road driving, fire, collision, vandalism, misalignment, mechanical defects in the vehicle, or deliberate misuse).

If a disclaimer cannot reasonably be construed as consistent with an express warranty, the disclaimer is void. This is the basic purpose of the second clause in § 2–316(1), which invalidates attempts to limit or disclaim an express warranty where the disclaimer contradicts an essential aspect of the warranty, involving such basic features as a product's safety, or its express description as new, or the descriptions and pictures in advertisements and brochures.

Disclaimers of Implied Warranties

Implied warranties, obligations that arise merely from the sale of goods, are generally easier to disclaim than express warranties that a seller makes as part of a specific sales agreement. In the context of *commercial* transactions, the parties normally should be permitted to shape the nature of the deal as they desire. Yet, because of the inability of *con-*

sumers to evaluate and bargain over the content of warranties accompanying the sale of new products, permitting sellers to exclude the basic warranty of product quality and safety (merchantability) of new consumer goods seems singularly inappropriate.

For this reason, such disclaimers are restricted in a number of ways. UCC § 2–316 attaches certain requirements to such disclaimers, and a number of state statutes and the Magnuson–Moss Federal Warranty Act prohibit or substantially restrict the ability of manufacturers and other sellers to disclaim implied warranties or to limit damages for breach of warranty in sales of consumer products, as discussed below. Where state law permits the complete exclusion of implied warranties under § 2–316, as most states do, courts disfavor such disclaimers and interpret them narrowly in favor of consumers.

Notwithstanding the general oppressiveness of implied warranty disclaimers in sales of new consumer goods, however, most states long ago adopted the uniform version of § 2–316 that allows manufacturers and other sellers to disclaim completely both types of implied warranties. Accordingly, a disclaimer drafted to comport with the requirements of § 2–316 operates under the Code to prevent a consumer from recovering damages against a manufacturer or other seller even if the consumer is killed or seriously injured by a dangerously defective product.

For example, in *Ford Motor Co. v. Moulton*, 511 S.W.2d 690 (Tenn. 1974), the plaintiff was severely injured when a steering defect in his 14-month-old car caused it to veer off a bridge and fall to the street below. His 12–month/12,000–mile express warranty had expired, and the contract of sale disclaimed the implied warranty of merchantability in accordance with § 2–316(2). The plaintiff's tort law claims were barred by a one–year statute of limitations, and the court ruled that the properly drawn disclaimer barred his claim for breach of the warranty of merchantability.

Specific Disclaimer Techniques— "Safe–Harbor" Language

Subsection (2) disclaimers generally. Section 2–316(2) offers a pre-approved disclaimer method— a "safe harbor"—which ensures that a disclaimer will be effective:

> Subject to subsection (3), to exclude or modify the implied warranty of merchantability or any part of it the language must mention merchantability and in case of a writing must be conspicuous, and to exclude or modify any implied warranty of fitness the exclusion must be by a writing and conspicuous.

Thus, under this subsection, disclaimers of implied warranties of merchantability must

- Mention "merchantability," and

- Be conspicuous.

Conspicuousness generally. To be conspicuous, an exclusion of an implied warranty must be made to stand out from the rest of the sales contract, by some effective combination of:

- *Contrasting type*—larger, **bolder**, different color (such as red), or *style*;

- *Headings*—such as **DISCLAIMER OF IM-PLIED WARRANTIES**, which specifically call the buyer's attention to the fact of the disclaimer;

- *Location*—in a prominent place in the agreement, as immediately above the principal signature line for the buyer, or with a separate buyer signature or initial line accompanying the disclaimer and asserting that the buyer has read and understands the resulting forfeiture of rights; and

- *Any other means*—by which a buyer is protected from "unexpected and unbargained language of disclaimer." See § 1–201(10) and cmt. 1.

Back–side disclaimers. The conspicuousness of disclaimers that are located on the back side or an interior page of a standard-form sales contract are particularly suspect. Yet, a disclaimer located other than on the front page of a sales agreement is not invalid per se, provided that the buyer's attention is effectively directed to the clause and the clause is otherwise prominently displayed.

Disclaimers known to buyer. Courts are split on whether an inconspicuous disclaimer should be invalidated even if the buyer admits that he or she read or otherwise knew about it at the time of contracting.

Post–sale disclaimers. Sellers frequently include disclaimers in owners' manuals, postcards, and invoices; inside product packaging; on information delivered with a product; or otherwise in a manner inaccessible to buyers until after purchase. Such a post-sale disclaimer normally has no effect on a warranty claim by a consumer personally injured by a defective product.

General Disclaimer Approaches

In addition to § 2–316(2)'s *specific*, safe-harbor methods for communicating the absence of implied warranties, subsection (3) provides three *general*, alternative disclaimer approaches, "common factual situations in which the circumstances surrounding the transaction are in themselves sufficient to call the buyer's attention to the fact that no implied warranties are made or that a certain implied warranty is being excluded." Cmt. 6.

"As is" and similar language. First, § 2–316(3)(a) permits a seller to disclaim implied warranties by using an "as is" clause or similar language "which in common understanding calls the buyer's attention to the exclusion of warranties and makes plain that there is no implied warranty." A seller thus may exclude implied warranties by making it clear to the buyer, without using the magic language of "merchantability" and "fitness" required in subsection (2), that no such warranties accompany the sale and that the buyer takes the risk that a product may contain latent defects.

Prior inspection. Second, implied warranties may be disclaimed by:

- The buyer's inspection, or
- The seller's demand that the buyer conduct such an inspection

of a product prior to purchase. In the first situation, the buyer is deemed to discover any flaws in the product that an inspection would normally reveal and so to understand that there is no implied assurance that such flaws do not exist. As previously mentioned, *obvious dangers* are excluded from the scope of the condition warranted by the seller, whether the buyer actually discovers them or not. That is, the obvious nature of a danger effectively disclaims any implied promise that the danger does not exist. See § 4.3, above. In the second situation, by refusing a seller's demand, the buyer simply assumes the risk of such flaws. See cmt. 8.

Course of dealing. Third, a disclaimer may arise by "course of dealing or ... usage of trade," under § 2–316(3)(c)—a form of warranty exclusion rarely litigated in products liability cases.

Unconscionability

A question that has long vexed courts and commentators is whether a disclaimer drafted in compliance with § 2–316 can ever be struck down for being "unconscionable." More specifically, may a disclaimer of the implied warranty of merchantability, that is properly drafted under subsection (2) or (3) (by conspicuously mentioning merchantability, or conspicuously stating "as is") ever be invalidated as unconscionable under the Code? Those who reason that the Code's unconscionability principles *do* apply to disclaimers draw upon one or two sections of Article 2: (1) the general provision on unconscionability in § 2–302, and/or (2) the specific application of unconscionability doctrine to consequential damages limitations in § 2–719(3).

Section 2–302 authorizes courts to nullify unconscionable clauses in sales contracts. An important question is whether § 2–316 is entirely independent and self-contained, so that the validity of a disclaimer can be tested solely by whether it meets the requirements of this one section, which thus may be seen to "preempt" § 2–302. This might be called the "preemption" view. Alternatively, some courts and commentators take the position that disclaimers must jump through *two* separate validity hoops: (1) § 2–316's specific disclaimer requirements, *and* (2) § 2–302's general policing filter which requires that contract terms be conscionable. This might be called the "two-hoop" view.

Strong arguments support both views. Proponents of the preemption view argue, first, that § 2–

316 clearly and specifically authorizes disclaimers and nowhere, in the text or comments, makes any mention of unconscionability. By contrast, § 2–316's cousin section that addresses limitations of consequential damages, § 2–719(3), specifically conditions such limitations on their conscionability. Indeed, comment 3 to § 2–719 distinguishes that section from § 2–316 on the ground that, unlike § 2–719(3), "[t]he seller in *all* cases is free to disclaim warranties in the manner provided in Section 2–316." This suggests that § 2–316 contains within itself as much internal policing of the fairness of disclaimers as useful, such that it can do without assistance from the general policing provisions of § 2–302.

Proponents of the two-hoop view observe that § 2–302 by its terms applies to "*any* clause of the contract," and nowhere does it suggest that disclaimers under § 2–316 are somehow out of bounds. Moreover, seven of the ten illustrative cases in comment 1 to § 2–302 involve disclaimers denied full effect. And while § 2–316 may protect buyers from "surprise," it does not protect them from one-sided contractual "oppression" of the type the automotive industry imposed on consumers in *Henningsen*.

Like the commentators, the courts are split on whether § 2–316 disclaimers may be found unconscionable under § 2–302. And a couple of courts have even concluded that disclaimers may be ruled unconscionable under § 2–719(3), which is plainly incorrect in that comments to both § 2–316 and § 2–719 make crystal clear that § 2–316, which addresses whether a warranty's creation was nullified by a disclaimer, is totally independent of the entirely separate issue in § 2–719(3) of whether a seller may limit personal injury damages recoverable for breach of a warranty that has *not* been nullified under § 2–316.

Amended UCC § 2–316 improves consumer protection against unbargained-for disclaimers of implied warranties in a number of ways. Most importantly, amended § 2–316(2) provides that, to be entitled to safe-harbor protection, a disclaimer of the implied warranty of merchantability in a *consumer* contract must (1) be in writing, (2) be conspicuous, and (3) state "The seller undertakes no responsibility for the quality of the goods except as otherwise provided in this contract."

§ 4.8 LIMITATIONS OF REMEDY

As with any damages claim, a products liability action consists of two major components: (1) a breach of legal duty, and (2) resulting damage. In warranty law, a seller breaches a legal duty by making and breaching a warranty that has not been disclaimed. As previously discussed, a disclaimer is an explicit means by which a seller may contractually nullify warranties, particularly implied warranties, that otherwise may arise from the sale of a product. One might view disclaimers as a seller's "front-door" method for avoiding warranty responsibility for product accidents.

A second method by which a seller may sometimes contractually avoid some or all responsibility for breach of warranty is to exclude or limit a buyer's *remedies* for breach. In a world of perfect freedom of contract, a buyer and seller might agree to a sale in which (1) the product carries various (undisclaimed) express and implied warranties; but (2) the buyer's only remedy for breach, no matter how great the actual damages, would be one dollar. More plausibly, a dealer might sell a used car with a 30–day express warranty against mechanical defects but with an exclusion of damages for personal injuries and a limitation of the buyer's remedy to repair or replacement of defective parts.

If disclaimers are considered a seller's front-door approach to avoiding warranty liability, a limitation-of-remedy provision in a sales contract might be viewed as a seller's "back-door" method for avoiding substantial warranty responsibility for product accidents. Indeed, the Code suggests the tandem nature of disclaimers and remedy limitations, how they may interrelate in sales transactions. Thus, while operating independently, disclaimers and limitations form the "horse and buggy" of a product seller's responsibility-avoidance measures.

Section 2–719 allows and conditions the *alteration* of a buyer's remedies otherwise available under the general, default provisions on damages for personal injury, death, and property damage, §§ 2–714 and 2–715. Consistent with Article 2's objective of allowing parties to a sales transaction to shape their particular deals as they may agree, subject only to controls to help ensure that their decisions are informed and truly free, the purpose of § 2–719 is to allow sellers and buyers to frame the remedy provisions of their sales contracts consistent with informed free choice.

Limitation of Remedies Generally; Repair or Replacement

UCC § 2–719(1) generally allows a seller to limit a buyer's remedies to repair or replacement of the goods or defective parts, or otherwise to alter the types or amounts of damages normally available for breach, provided the contract makes clear that the limited or modified remedy is the *sole and exclusive remedy* available to the buyer. If the exclusivity of an attempted limitation-of-remedy provision is ambiguous, the remedy provided will be deemed to *supplement*, rather than displace, the Article 2 general remedy provisions. Thus, a contract that limits a seller's "warranties," "obligations," or "liability," rather than the buyer's "remedies," may be interpreted to be an invalid disclaimer of liability rather than a valid limitation of remedies.

Failure of Essential Purpose

Section 2–719(2) provides that "[w]here circumstances cause an exclusive or limited remedy to fail of its essential purpose, remedy may be had as

provided in this Act." Courts generally apply subsection (2)'s failure-of-essential-purpose provision to
cases involving products that are "lemons," not to
ordinary products liability claims for personal injuries. See *Pack v. Damon Corp.*, 434 F.3d 810 (6th
Cir. 2006) (Mich. law) (motor home out of service
for 162 days during first year of ownership; warranty likely failed of its essential purpose).

Personal Injury Damage Exclusions—
Unconscionability

Subsection (3) is far and away the most important aspect of § 2–719 for consumer products liability litigation involving personal injuries:

> Consequential damages may be limited or ex-
> cluded unless the limitation or exclusion is uncon-
> scionable. Limitation of consequential damages
> for injury to the person in the case of consumer
> goods is prima facie unconscionable but limitation
> of damages where the loss is commercial is not.

Because subsection (3) takes priority over subsection (1) (see preamble to § 2–719(1)), the second
sentence of § 2–719(3) means that sellers of consumer goods may not contractually limit damages
for personal injuries to repair or replacement or
otherwise, unless the seller can show that such a
limitation is not "unconscionable." At the very
least, such showings will be rare, and it is safe to
say that limitations on personal injury damages in
consumer goods cases will be held unconscionable
and void in almost every case. See *Ruzzo v. LaRose*

Enters., 748 A.2d 261 (R.I. 2000) (leased plumbing tool; UCC § 2A–719(3)).

One vital limitation on the scope of the unconscionability provision in § 2–719(3) bears special attention: it applies only to *consumer* goods. This restriction to consumer goods means that sellers of *commercial* products *may* exclude responsibility for consequential damages, including personal injuries to a buyer's workers, without such exclusions being held prima facie unconscionable under § 2–719(3). See *Blevins v. New Holland N. Am., Inc.*, 97 F.Supp.2d 747 (W.D. Va. 2000).

§ 4.9   ANTI-DISCLAIMER AND OTHER WARRANTY REFORM LEGISLATION

Disclaimers of warranties and limitations of remedies for personal injuries in sales transactions involving new consumer products are inherently perverse. Manufacturers and other sellers should not be permitted to shield themselves from warranty responsibility for personal injuries resulting from explicit or implicit misrepresentations concerning the essential quality and safety of new consumer products. A seller's effort to avoid such responsibility by fine-print legalese buried in standard form sales contracts should be considered contrary to public policy and void. See *Henningsen v. Bloomfield Motors, Inc.*, 161 A.2d 69 (N.J. 1960).

From the inception of Article 2, many commentators observed that its disclaimer provisions were unsatisfactory for consumer transactions. This should have come as no surprise, for Article 2 was based to a large extent on sales law principles of the 1800s, and, to some extent, even the 1700s. As interest in consumer rights spread across America during the 1960s and early 1970s, so too did criticisms of the Code's treatment of disclaimers. Although the Code claimed an interest in protecting buyers from unexpected and unbargained-for language of disclaimer, the safe-harbor disclaimer technique it provided for excluding the basic implied warranty, simply by using the legal jargon of "merchantability," virtually ensured that most consumers would be unexpectedly and grossly disappointed after a serious product accident to learn that they had "bargained" away their most important rights.

Targeting the specific problem of disclaimers in consumer sales transactions, some state legislatures and Congress eventually passed legislation that effectively curtailed the widespread manipulation of consumer warranty rights by product sellers.

State Anti–Disclaimer Statutes

At least fifteen states and the District of Columbia have legislation prohibiting or limiting disclaimers and/or limitations of remedies in sales transactions involving consumer products. Most states have achieved this result by amending their versions of UCC §§ 2–316 and/or 2–719. For example, Connecticut adds a fifth subsection to its version of § 2–316 which provides that "Any language, oral or written, used by a seller or manufacturer of consumer goods, which attempts to exclude or modify any implied warranties of merchantability and fitness for a particular purpose or to exclude or modify the consumer's remedies for breach of those warranties, shall be unenforceable." Several other states have accomplished the same goal in broader consumer protection statutes which, *inter alia*, limit disclaimers of implied warranties.

The Magnuson–Moss Federal Warranty Act

In an effort to improve the clarity, truth, and strength of consumer product warranties, Congress enacted the Magnuson–Moss Warranty—Federal Trade Commission Improvement Act of 1975, 15 U.S.C. § 2301 et seq. The Act does not require product sellers to issue warranties but imposes certain obligations on suppliers who choose to provide written warranties (or service contracts) for consumer products costing more than $10 or $15.

Under the Act, written warranties must be labeled either "full (statement of duration) warranty," requiring the warrantor to provide consumers with a designated spectrum of warranty rights, or "limited warranty." Written warranties for covered products must disclose fully, conspicuously, clearly, and without deception the warranty's terms and conditions; warranty terms must be disclosed to consumers before purchase; providers of full warranties must provide consumers with effective procedures for repairing or replacing defective products in a timely manner or provide a refund of the purchase price; and, as discussed below, disclaimers

of implied warranties under UCC § 2–316 are severely restricted.

Thus, the Magnuson–Moss Act is a consumer
protection statute designed to improve the truthful-
ness, strength, and comprehensibility of warranties
that accompany consumer products and to provide
consumers of products that carry "full" warranties
with effective mechanisms for resolving warranty
complaints. The Act does *not* provide new remedies
for injured plaintiffs to use in ordinary products
liability litigation.

Disclaimers

The Act contains one provision that profoundly
alters warranty responsibility for product accidents:
§ 108 of the Act outlaws implied warranty disclaimers in significant sales of consumer goods notwithstanding the fact that such disclaimers are authorized by state law. For consumer products costing
more than $10 for which a written warranty (or
service contract) is provided, the Act *nullifies* implied warranty disclaimers, despite their authoriza-
tion under UCC § 2–316. Under the Supremacy
Clause, Congress thus has rewritten state disclaimer law to this extent.

Although § 108 does not directly address products liability litigation, it does indirectly affect such
litigation in several important ways. Most importantly, § 108(a) nullifies complete disclaimers otherwise allowable under UCC § 2–316 in most substantial consumer product cases, thereby removing
the most deadly arrow from the product seller's

quiver of contractual defenses in products liability warranty litigation. It accomplishes this in two ways. First, subsection (b) prohibits *all* implied warranty limitations for products carrying "full" warranties. Second, it prohibits complete exclusions of implied warranties for sellers offering "limited" warranties, although it *permits* such suppliers to restrict the *duration* of implied warranties to the period of the written warranty, provided that such limitations on duration meet a rigorous fourfold test. Any such durational limitation must be:

- Reasonable;

- Conscionable;

- Set forth in clear and unmistakable language; and

- Prominently displayed on the face of the warranty.

Under § 108(c), a limitation that violates any of these requirements is void and of no effect.

CHAPTER 5

STRICT LIABILITY IN TORT

Table of Sections

§ 5.1   Strict Liability in Tort—Generally.
§ 5.2   The Path to Strict Liability in Tort.
§ 5.3   Restatement (Second) of Torts § 402A.
§ 5.4   Policies and Rationales.
§ 5.5   Liability Tests.
§ 5.6   The Consumer Expectations Test.
§ 5.7   The Risk–Utility Test.
§ 5.8   Alternative Tests.
§ 5.9   Comparison with Other Liability Theories.

------

§ 5.1   STRICT LIABILITY IN TORT—GENERALLY

The doctrine of strict liability in tort is widely considered the predominant theory of recovery in modern products liability law. Indeed, the development and growth of the doctrine of strict products liability in tort was the centerpiece around which the rest of modern products liability law was formed. This chapter describes the origins, evolution, nature, rationales, and tests for the doctrine of strict products liability in tort, particularly under § 402A of the *Restatement (Second) of Torts*. For a

126

more thorough examination of strict liability in tort, see Owen, Products Liability Law ch. 5 (2d ed. 2008).

§ 5.2   THE PATH TO STRICT LIABILITY IN TORT

The path to strict products liability in tort was long, tortured, and tortuous. This lengthy journey involved the intertwining of parts of tort and contract, each of which contributed a central feature to the development of strict manufacturer liability for harm caused by defective products, and they combined to contribute a third. Tort law's major contribution, launched by *MacPherson v. Buick Motor Co.*, 111 N.E. 1050 (N.Y. 1916), was its rejection of the privity-of-contract requirement in tort law claims. In so doing, tort law championed the view that manufacturers are obligated to "remote" consumers by a public duty, independent of any private contractual obligations that may exist between them. To this, contract law contributed the idea that liability should be "strict," contrary to the general tort law notion that breach of duty generally must rest on fault. Tort and contract law conjoined in warranty to generate the doctrine of strict manufacturer liability in tort. Though warranty today is perceived as part of the law of sales, a branch of the law of contracts, it developed from the tort action of deceit and remained a tort-type action, at least in food cases, until quite recently.

Escola

In the first edition of his celebrated tort law treatise in 1941, Dean William Prosser succinctly catalogued the variety of arguments favoring strict liability for injuries caused by remote sellers of defective products and why that liability should lie in tort. Three years later, in *Escola v. Coca Cola Bottling Co.*, 150 P.2d 436 (Cal. 1944), the Supreme Court of California upheld a *res ipsa* verdict for a waitress injured when a Coke bottle exploded in her hand. In perhaps the most renowned concurring opinion in all of American tort law, Justice Roger Traynor elegantly elaborated each of Dean Prosser's arguments for strict products liability in tort.

Justice Traynor concluded that "it should now be recognized that a manufacturer incurs an absolute liability when an article that he has placed on the market, knowing that it is to be used without inspection, proves to have a defect that causes injury to human beings." Regardless of fault, "public policy demands that responsibility be fixed wherever it will most effectively reduce the hazards to life and health inherent in defective products that reach the market." Manufacturers can test their products for defects in ways that consumers cannot, and the consequences of an injury from a defective product "may be an overwhelming misfortune to the person injured, and a needless one, for the risk of injury can be insured by the manufacturer and distributed among the public as a cost of doing business." Moreover, manufacturers rather than consumers are best situated to provide the most effective public protection against the "menace" of defective products. Id. at 440–41.

Further, Justice Traynor explained that a rule imposing strict liability without privity on manufacturers of defective products would result in judicial economies since manufacturers were already indirectly subject to strict liability to remote consumers for selling defective products—an injured consumer could sue the retailer for breach of the implied warranty of merchantability; the retailer could then recover against the wholesaler for selling an unmerchantable product; and the wholesaler could in turn recover back against the manufacturer. But such a tortuous path "is needlessly circuitous and engenders wasteful litigation. Much would be gained if the injured person could base his action directly on the manufacturer's warranty." Id. at 442.

Observing that manufacturers of defective foods are held to a warranty of quality running to remote consumers, and that the rights of such persons to legal protection do not depend "upon the intricacies of the law of sales," Justice Traynor asserted that the same protection should be extended to consumers of all types of defective products. Nor would courts have to resort to the kinds of fictions they created in food product cases to rationalize extending the manufacturer's warranty to remote consumers "if the warranty is severed from the contract of sale between the dealer and the consumer and based on the law of torts as a strict liability." Id. at 443.

Justice Traynor explained that a doctrine of strict products liability in tort was necessary to adapt the law to the vast changes in how products are manufactured and merchandised in the modern world. "As handicrafts have been replaced by mass production with its great markets and transportation facilities, the close relationship between the producer and consumer of a product has been altered." In marketing complex machines and chemicals, modern manufacturers urge remote consumers to trust in the safety of such products and to relinquish the consumer's historical self-protective role in evaluating a product's safety prior to purchase and use. For these many reasons, Justice Traynor concluded that manufacturers should be strictly responsible in tort to consumers for injuries caused by their defective products. Id.

Henningsen

During the 1950s, a number of courts expanded the "tort" food warranty to sales of dog and fish food, and to products for intimate bodily use; and scholars increasingly argued for strict manufacturer liability for defective products generally. Then, in *Henningsen v. Bloomfield Motors, Inc.*, 161 A.2d 69 (N.J. 1960), the court ruled that a manufacturer of a defective automobile was strictly liable to a consumer for injuries caused by defects in the car. Although the case was brought in contract for breach of an implied warranty of merchantability, the court stripped the warranty of its two most powerful contract law defenses—lack of privity, on the one hand, and disclaimer and remedy limitations, on the other—and imposed strict liability on the manufacturer.

"Assault on the Citadel"

Just a few weeks after *Henningsen* was handed down, Dean Prosser published *The Assault Upon the Citadel (Strict Liability to the Consumer)*, 69 Yale L.J. 1099 (1960), arguing for and predicting precisely such a result. Tracing the development of a manufacturer's warranty responsibility to consumers for injuries caused by defective products, Prosser related the variety of ingenious methods devised by courts to avoid contract law obstacles to recovery, such as privity, disclaimers, and the requirement that a buyer promptly notify the seller of a breach. Prosser argued that the "warranty" rule of strict liability should be extended, beyond cases of unwholesome food and other products for bodily use, to a general rule of strict liability for all products. In addition, he urged that the "warranty" label was wrong. "If there is to be strict liability in tort," contended Prosser, "let there be strict liability in tort, declared outright, without an illusory contract mask." Id. at 1134.

Greenman

It was a scant three years later, in 1963, that the California Supreme Court handed down the landmark case of *Greenman v. Yuba Power Products, Inc.*, 377 P.2d 897 (Cal. 1963). While using his combination power tool as a lathe, Mr. Greenman was injured when the tailstock of the lathe vibrated loose and the piece of wood he was shaping flew out and struck him on the head. He sued the manufacturer and retailer for negligence and breach of warranty, and he received a verdict and judgment against the manufacturer on his express warranty claim, which the manufacturer challenged on appeal, arguing that the plaintiff had failed to provide timely notice of breach.

Justice Traynor, who in 1944 had offered the eloquent, lone voice for strict products liability in *Escola*, authored an opinion in *Greenman*, too—but this time he spoke for a unanimous court. Affirming the plaintiff's judgment, the *Greenman* court ruled that the commercial code's requirement of prompt notice was inappropriate in cases involving injured consumers, such that even an untimely notice would not bar a consumer's express warranty claim. But Justice Traynor did not stop there. "Moreover, to impose strict liability on the manufacturer under the circumstances of this case, it was not necessary for plaintiff to establish an express warranty [under the commercial code]. A manufacturer is strictly liable in tort when an article he places on the market, knowing that it is to be used without inspection for defects, proves to have a defect that causes injury to a human being." Id. at 900.

Tracing the development of strict products liability doctrine under the *warranty* law umbrella—from the early food cases, through products for intimate bodily use, to durable products, such as the car in

Henningsen—Justice Traynor explained that the rejection of the requirement of privity of contract, "the recognition that the liability is not assumed by agreement but imposed by law, and the refusal to permit the manufacturer to define the scope of its own responsibility for defective products make clear that the liability is not one governed by the law of contract warranties but by the law of strict liability in tort." Id. at 901.

There was no reason to "recanvass the reasons for imposing strict liability on the manufacturer" which had already been "fully articulated," declared Traynor, citing his concurring opinion in *Escola*, Prosser's "*Assault Upon the Citadel*" article, and the Harper and James torts treatise. "The purpose of such liability is to insure that the costs of injuries resulting from defective products are borne by the manufacturers that put such products on the market rather than by the injured persons who are powerless to protect themselves. Sales warranties serve this purpose fitfully at best." Id.

For example, on the facts in *Greenman*, the plaintiff could rely on an express warranty only because he happened to have read and relied on representations of the Shopsmith's ruggedness in the manufacturer's brochure. "Implicit in the machine's presence on the market, however, was a representation that it would safely do the jobs for which it was built." Thus, "it should not be controlling whether plaintiff selected the machine because of the statements in the brochure, or because of the machine's

own appearance of excellence that belied the defect
lurking beneath the surface, or because he merely
assumed that it would safely do the jobs it was built
to do." Id.

In *Greenman*, the path to strict manufacturer
liability for defective products led home to the law
of tort.

§ 5.3 RESTATEMENT (SECOND) OF TORTS § 402A

The Progression of § 402A Drafts

In the 1950s and 1960s, the ALI was in the midst
of a quarter century revision of the *Restatement of
Torts*, originally published in the 1930s. In the late
1950s, prior to *Henningsen*, Dean Prosser began to
revise chapter 14 of the *First Restatement* which
covered rules of negligence law governing the liability of product suppliers. Revising the negligence
sections in conventional form, he then turned to the
special tort warranty that had been evolving in the
context of the sale of food. Crafting a special section, new § 402A, to serve as a vehicle for the
specialized development of "strict" tort liability for
the sale of food "in a dangerous condition to the
consumer," Prosser included the provision in a *Preliminary Draft* of the new *Restatement* in 1958, and
subsequently in a *Council Draft* in 1960. Section
402A was expanded to products "for intimate bodily
use" in the 1962 draft, and, once the California
Supreme Court decided *Greenman* (which involved
a power tool) in 1963, this section was extended to

include *all* products in the final draft approved by the ALI in 1964.

Section 402A was published the next year, 1965, in volume 2 of the *Restatement (Second) of Torts*. This section, which has been cited more frequently than any other section of any *Restatement*, provides as follows:

§ 402A. Special Liability of Seller of Product for Physical Harm to User or Consumer

(1) One who sells any product in a defective condition unreasonably dangerous to the user or consumer or to his property is subject to liability for physical harm thereby caused to the ultimate user or consumer, or to his property, if

(a) the seller is engaged in the business of selling such a product, and

(b) it is expected to and does reach the user or consumer without substantial change in the condition in which it is sold.

(2) The rule stated in Subsection (1) applies although

(a) the seller has exercised all possible care in the preparation and sale of his product, and

(b) the user or consumer has not bought the product from or entered into any contractual relation with the seller.

Stripped of its prolixity, the liability principle of § 402A is short and simple: manufacturers and other commercial suppliers are subject to strict liability in tort for harm to persons and property caused by defects in products they sell.

Nature of Strict Products Liability in Tort

"Strict" Liability

Liability is "strict" because a seller is liable even if it was not negligent, even if it exercised all due care. Yet, all courts agree that the doctrine of strict liability in tort is constrained by certain limitations—that a manufacturer or other seller is not an insurer of its product's safety and that a supplier is not required to provide only the very safest of products, nor those that represent only the "ultimate in safety." See *Barban v. Rheem Textile Sys., Inc.*, 2005 WL 387660, at *6 (E.D.N.Y. 2005) ("a manufacturer is not an insurer against injury, nor must the product be accident proof"). The obligation imposed on sellers under § 402A is to provide products that are not "unreasonably dangerous" or "defective," not to provide products that are perfectly safe.

Elements of a Strict Tort Claim

The basic rule in almost every state is that manufacturers are subject to liability in tort for injuries caused by defects in products they sell. Although the elements of this claim are variously expressed, all courts require a plaintiff to prove two core elements, which imply a third:

(1) That the defendant sold a defective product;

(2) That the product defect proximately caused the plaintiff's harm; and

(3) That the product was defective at the time of sale.

See *Rivera v. Philip Morris, Inc.*, 395 F.3d 1142 (9th Cir. 2005) (Nev. law).

While some courts interpret the prolix language of § 402A, "defective condition unreasonably dangerous," as implying two separate elements, there is widespread understanding that this bulky liability phraseology really means just one thing—that a product is more dangerous than it properly should be. Today, most courts capture that single concept in a single word: "defective."

Secondary Doctrine

Warranty law defenses. Since liability under § 402A is "purely one of tort," it is unaffected by warranty law defenses such as privity of contract or contractual disclaimers or limitations of remedy, which are simply null and void.

Plaintiffs. Section 402A applies explicitly to "users and consumers," but, since liability lies in tort, it also applies to bystanders, rescuers, and anyone else who is foreseeably put at risk by defects in a product.

Defendants. Strict products liability in tort applies to all parties in the commercial chain of a product's distribution, from suppliers of defective component parts to manufacturers, intermediate dealers, and retailers. While the strict liability rule generally applies to a commercial business that provides products incidental to its principal business (such as a movie theater that sells popcorn), it does not apply to the occasional private seller, such as a private individual who sells his or her used car.

Many cases have examined the suitability of the doctrine of strict liability in tort under § 402A for particular types of defendants engaged in a miscellany of sales and non-sales transactions involving a diversity of products. For example, courts have ruled on whether § 402A liability should be applied to raw material suppliers, bulk suppliers, repairers, successor corporations, employers, product lease transactions, bailments, licenses, franchises, services (including medical) in which products are provided incidentally, used products, electricity, real estate, publications of dangerous information, blood, and diseased or dangerous animals. Whether strict products liability is and should be allowed in each of these distinct situations is considered in chapters 15 and 16, below.

Damages. By its terms, § 402A provides that a seller of a defective product "is subject to liability for physical harm thereby caused to the ultimate user or consumer, or to his property.... " All courts thus allow recovery under this doctrine for personal *injury* and *death*, and the widely prevailing view is that recovery is allowable under strict products liability in tort for *property* damage alone.

Claims for an *increased risk* of disease generally have failed. Claims for *emotional distress* are often

allowed in strict tort, to both direct victims and
bystanders, under rules similar to those applied
under the law of negligence. With certain limitations, some courts have allowed recovery for fear of
cancer ("cancerphobia") or other disease from contact with a harmful substance—a special variety of
emotional distress claim.

Some courts have similarly allowed recovery for
lost consortium to spouses of victims killed or injured by defective products. A few courts have allowed recovery for *medical monitoring* of victims
exposed to some toxic substance or defective medical device, where future harm is possible but difficult to detect.

Since the inception of § 402A, a minor debate has
swirled around the issue of whether recovery in
strict liability in tort should be allowed for *pure
economic loss*, including damage a defective product
causes to itself. Spearheaded by *East River Steam-
ship Corp. v. Transamerica Delaval, Inc.*, 476 U.S.
858 (1986), a great majority of courts now apply the
"economic loss rule" to such cases, denying recovery in strict products liability (or negligence) for
pure economic loss. See *Kelleher v. Marvin Lumber
& Cedar Co.*, 891 A.2d 477, 495 (N.H. 2005) (no
recovery of "damages for purely economic loss in
tort or products liability claims").

Some courts, however, do allow a limited exception to the general bar of recovery for pure economic loss when such damages result from product
defects that present a hazard to property or human

safety. See *Lloyd v. General Motors Corp.*, 916 A.2d
257, 266 (Md. 2007) (class action for cost of repairing cars with dangerously defective seat backs;
recognizing and applying "increasingly popular" exception to general rule barring recovery for pure
economic loss when plaintiff alleges "facts that
demonstrate that the product at issue creates a
dangerous condition, one that gives rise to a *clear
danger of death or personal injury*") (emphasis in
original).

In a new form of class action litigation, courts in
recent years have been asked to allow recovery for
the *reduction in value of a product* because it contains a dangerous condition, such as a particular
type of tire likely to blow out or SUV likely to roll
over. The courts have been singularly unreceptive
to these "no-injury" claims, whether grounded in
strict liability in tort or other theory of recovery.
See *Frank v. DaimlerChrysler Corp.*, 741 N.Y.S.2d 9
(App. Div. 2002) (rejecting "no-injury" claims because of manifest unfairness in requiring manufacturer to become insurer of loss that might never
occur).

Punitive damages are widely recoverable on
claims for strict products liability in tort upon sufficient proof of recklessness or fraud. See ch. 18,
below.

Adoption of § 402A

Once the ALI approved § 402A in 1964 and published it in 1965, the bold new doctrine swept across

the face of America with a gusto unmatched in the annals of *Restatements of the Law*. Tort law has probably never witnessed such a rapid, widespread, and altogether explosive change in a rule and theory of legal responsibility.

Four states adopted § 402A principles in 1965 (Conn., Ill., Ky., N.J.). In 1966, four more states embraced the doctrine (Miss., Ohio, Pa., Tenn.), as did four more in 1967 (Minn., Or., Tex., Wis.). By the mid–1970s, over forty states had embraced the principle of strict manufacturer liability in tort for the sale of defective products. The last state to adopt the doctrine was Wyoming, in 1986, by which time a total of 45 states (and D.C., Puerto Rico, and the Virgin Islands) all embraced a doctrine of strict products liability in tort.

As of 2008, only five states (Del., Mass., Mich., N.C., Va.) still formally reject the doctrine of strict products liability in tort. Although these states still refuse to join the strict tort bandwagon, each applies the great bulk of developed § 402A jurisprudence, either through the law of warranty or the law of negligence, to sellers of defective products.

Variations on § 402A

Judicial Variations

Most states embraced the theory of strict products liability in tort by judicial "adoption" of § 402A. Since its initial adoption, however, the products liability jurisprudence of every state has moved far beyond the original formulation of the doctrine as described in § 402A and its comments, and variations in doctrine have developed among jurisdictions over time.

A number of states took a rather independent route from the start of modern products liability law, refusing simply to "adopt" § 402A yet adhering to the general principles of the developing jurisprudence on strict products liability in tort. For example, Oklahoma adopted an elaborate doctrine of strict products liability in tort, called "Manufacturers' Products Liability"; Alabama adopted its own "Alabama Extended Manufacturer's Liability Doctrine (AEMLD)"; and Louisiana, New York, and California also followed different drummers in adopting and developing their doctrines of strict products liability in tort.

Products Liability Reform Statutes

Several state legislatures enacted the doctrine of strict products liability in tort statutorily. Statutes enacted in several states (Ind., Me., Mont., Or., S.C.), at least initially, were nearly verbatim restatements of § 402A. A couple of others (Ark., Ga.) provided variations on the same theme. Other states (Conn., Ind., La., Miss., N.J., Ohio, Tex., Wash.) enacted products liability reform codes which quite comprehensively extended well beyond the provisions of § 402A, as by formulating in some detail the bases of recovery in different contexts, defenses, and various procedural aspects of such litigation.

Three products liability statutes (Ill., N.H., Ohio) were struck down as unconstitutional by their state supreme courts. North Carolina's statute, while expressly *rejecting* the doctrine of strict liability in tort, broadly adopts many of the secondary liability principles of modern products liability law.

Many other states have enacted products liability reform statutes covering a miscellany of topics, as by adopting "state-of-the-art" defenses, enacting statutes of repose, shielding manufacturers of guns, protecting retailers (entirely or conditionally) from strict liability, and by statutorily addressing a host of other secondary issues. These and many other topics are examined in subsequent chapters.

§ 5.4   POLICIES AND RATIONALES

Background

Conceptual explorations into strict manufacturer liability are discernable in the 1920s with one commentator's call for the seller's implied warranty, termed "insurer's liability," to be viewed in terms of "risk-bearing." The rationalization of such liability developed more fully in the 1930s, especially in writings by warranty law scholar Karl Llewellyn who argued that the law should impose strict liability on large manufacturers (and large retailers) who are "equipped to spread, and indeed to reduce, risks" to consumers from defective products that they sell.

Dean Prosser in 1941 catalogued the reasons for strict manufacturer liability in the first edition of his torts treatise, as previously discussed, and Judge Traynor elaborated upon those reasons in his famous concurring opinion in *Escola* in 1944. These were largely the same rationales relied upon by scholars in the 1950s as the march toward strict manufacturer liability accelerated, and drawn upon by commentators in the 1960s, to justify the doctrine that exploded upon the tort law landscape during that decade.

Comment *c* to *Restatement (Second) of Torts* § 402A summarized the rationales for strict products liability in tort: that manufacturers assume a "special responsibility" toward consumers who may be injured by their products; that consumers properly expect that reputable sellers will stand behind their goods; that the burden of injuries from product accidents should be borne by sellers and treated as a cost of production that may be widely spread by liability insurance; and that consumers are "entitled to the maximum of protection at the hands of someone, and the proper persons to afford it are those who market the products."

Rationales—In General

Early courts and commentators offered a variety of rationales for a manufacturer's strict products liability, generally predicating such liability on the increasing intricacy and danger of modern products comprised of complex mechanical and chemical substances. In contrast to simple products of previous generations, modern consumers often have no practical way to evaluate the safety of such products.

Consumer Expectations

Another major rationale for holding manufacturers strictly liable in tort to consumers was to protect the consumer's fair expectations of safety in the goods they buy. Through mass merchandising, manufacturers cultivate these expectations by suggesting that their goods are safe.

Probable Negligence

Some commentators reasoned that defective products usually result from a manufacturer's negligence, such that holding a manufacturer strictly liable serves as a proxy for the doctrine of *res ipsa* in the many cases where a manufacturer probably was negligent in making or selling a defective product but where proof of negligence is unavailable to the victim.

Judicial Efficiency

A judicial efficiency rationale reasoned that retailers were strictly liable to consumers anyway, *via* the implied warranty of merchantability; retailers held liable would obtain indemnity for their litigation losses from their suppliers; and those suppliers themselves would recover from the manufacturer. To avoid this type of wasteful circuitry of litigation, consumers injured by defective products should simply be allowed to skip over retailers (and other intermediate sellers) and maintain their actions directly against product manufacturers.

Cost Internalization

Early arguments for strict manufacturer liability to consumers centered on the propriety of relieving individual consumers of the economic consequences of injuries caused by defective products by shifting such losses to the enterprises that manufactured those products. Holding manufacturers liable for losses caused by defects in their products would force such firms to "internalize" these accident costs just as they must absorb other costs of production—materials, labor, and capital. Manufacturers would then "spread" these costs, as a kind of third-party insurer, by "passing them on" to those who benefitted from the enterprise—the owners (through lower profits) and consumers (through higher prices). An important additional aspect of this cost-internalization process is that it motivates manufacturers to eliminate defects in their products, in an effort to minimize accident costs which otherwise they must absorb, thus promoting public safety.

Deterrence and Risk–Spreading

Although courts and commentators offered a host of justifications for the doctrine of strict manufacturer liability in tort for harm caused by defective products both before and after the promulgation of § 402A, two rationales touched on above predominated:

- *Deterrence* (or "safety"), and

- *Risk-spreading* (or "cost-spreading," "loss distribution," or "insurance").

Some courts and commentators emphasized deterrence, and others emphasized risk-spreading, but both rationales were widely cited (and sometimes still are) in support of holding manufacturers of defective products strictly responsible for consumer injuries.

Deterrence

While there has been no shortage of skeptics, many courts and commentators are persuaded that raising the standard of liability for manufacturers from negligence to strict liability will improve product safety. To them, it has seemed self-evident that forcing producers to internalize the accident costs resulting from defects in their products will force them to take such costs into account and, hence, induce them to reduce or eliminate defects in their products as much as reasonably possible. Safety, so important to the public, should thereby be improved.

Risk–Spreading

The other major rationale, risk-spreading, presumes that manufacturers forced to absorb the costs of product accidents will pass along at least some portion of those costs to consumers through increased prices. In the process, manufacturers will relieve individual consumers of the possibly crushing financial burdens of personal injuries and, at the same time, spread such losses widely among the consuming public. Because modern science and technology benefit society as a whole, all consumers fairly can be asked to pay slightly higher prices as premiums for insurance against the risk of often random harm when science and technology go awry. By spreading the costs of product accidents in this manner, manufacturers thus provide all consumers, albeit indirectly, with mandatory accident insurance for harm from product defects. Moreover, because competition often prevents manufacturers from raising prices significantly, some portion of product accident costs are spread, not unfairly, to the owners (and operators) of enterprises that make and sell defective products.

Most courts and commentators in the 1960s and 1970s uncritically embraced deterrence, risk-spreading, and the other rationales for the doctrine of strict liability in tort for defective products, frequently overlooking the doctrine's important limitations. Even from the start, however, some judges and commentators found fault with the new strict products liability in tort doctrine and its underlying rationales, and, as the initial flush of excitement over the new strict liability doctrine subsided, commentators increasingly questioned the wisdom and logic of the doctrine's rationales. But the conventional justifications for strict manufacturer liability have not yet been consigned to the trash heap, and some courts and commentators still cling tenaciously, sometimes with a modern theoretical spin, to the traditional rationales.

§ 5.5 LIABILITY TESTS

"Strict" products liability in tort, indisputably, is *not* absolute liability. The doctrine of strict products liability in tort does not require manufacturers to ensure perfect product safety, except in the avoidance of production flaws. Since absolute safety is not to be the rule, courts must adopt liability "tests" to draw lines between degrees of safety—for deciding how to separate products that are unacceptably dangerous from those that are safe enough.

As liability under § 402A was beginning to be worked out in the 1960s and 1970s, courts and commentators generally sought a *unitary* liability standard or defect test—a single, general test that could determine defectiveness in every type of case. However, as products liability law and litigation matured in the 1980s and 1990s, and as its complexities were better understood, it became increasingly clear that liability standards should be contextually based—that a proper test of liability depended upon the particular manner in which a product was unsafe. Thus, in recent years, courts have moved toward using separate liability tests for (1) manufacturing defects, (2) design defects, and (3) warning defects. As discussed below, it has been the search for a proper definition of *design* defectiveness that has most confounded courts and commentators, and the evolution of strict tort liability tests has centered principally on judging the adequacy of a product's design.

The next three sections examine the progression of liability tests for strict products liability in tort. The various liability tests are contextually examined in the chapters on defective manufacture, design, and warning.

§ 5.6 THE CONSUMER EXPECTATIONS TEST

In attempting to ascertain the meaning of § 402A's liability standard—"defective condition unreasonably dangerous"—the first place courts looked for guidance was the Reporter's Comments that Dean Prosser wrote to that section of the *Restatement (Second) of Torts*. There, in comments *g* and *i*, lies the basis for the first important test for establishing strict products liability in tort, the "consumer expectations test." Comment *g* to § 402A states that *"defective condition"* means "a condition not contemplated by the ultimate consumer, which will be unreasonably dangerous to him." Comment *i* explains that *"unreasonably dangerous"* means that a product "must be dangerous to an extent beyond that which would be contemplated by the ordinary consumer who purchases it, with the ordinary knowledge common to the community as to its characteristics."

Because both halves of § 402A's "defective condition unreasonably dangerous" liability standard ultimately are defined in terms of *dangerous beyond a consumer's contemplations*, many courts interpreting § 402A in the 1960s and 1970s concluded that the full definitional phrase established a *single* test of liability based on a single standard of product safety measured by "consumer expectations."

Basis of the Test

Consumer expectation protection was a logical initial foundation for strict products liability under § 402A since modern products liability law evolved out of the law of warranty. One of the most basic goals of law in general, and the most fundamental pillar of contract law, is the protection of the expectations—the *reasonable* expectations—of the contracting parties. Warranty law is based on a manufacturer's explicit and implicit representations made to consumers in sales transactions, and the law reasonably protects consumer expectations predictably generated from such representations. Because the warranty law cases that paved the way for § 402A aimed to protect a consumer's ordinary or reasonable expectations, this was the natural liability test for the new tort doctrine.

Like most other standards of tort law, the consumer expectations test is an *objective* test: it is based on the average, normal, or "ordinary" expectations of a reasonable person. An objective standard is plainly necessary, because a manufacturer in its design decisions is bound to "legislate" an amount of safety that is optimal for all consumers as a class, and it cannot be expected to design products separately for every user's secret preferences.

An early example of a court adopting the consumer expectations test as the test of liability under § 402A was *Vincer v. Esther Williams All–Aluminum Swimming Pool Co.*, 230 N.W.2d 794 (Wis. 1975). There, a 2-year-old child climbed up the ladder of an above-ground swimming pool, fell in, and was brain-damaged in the water. In the strict tort claim against the manufacturer of the pool, the plaintiff claimed that the design of the pool was defective because the manufacturer failed to take the simple precaution of adding a self-closing and self-latching gate at the top of the ladder to prevent small children from entering the pool, but the trial court dismissed the claim. On appeal, the court affirmed, relying on comments *g* and *i* and reasoning that the safety expectations of an average consumer were plainly met, since such a person could not help but comprehend the danger to young children from the obvious absence of a self-latching gate.

The consumer expectations test was the dominant standard of defectiveness used by courts in the 1960s and 1970s, despite a growing number that rejected it as the sole or principal test of strict products liability. And despite the drawbacks of using consumer expectations as a liability standard, many courts continue to use this test either by itself or combined in some fashion with risk-utility. See *Calles v. Scripto–Tokai Corp.*, 864 N.E.2d 249, 256 (Ill. 2007) ("under the consumer expectations test, a plaintiff may prevail if he or she demonstrates that the product failed to perform as any ordinary consumer would expect").

Problems with the Test

Obvious Dangers

As *Vincer* illustrates, obvious product dangers are *ipso facto* "contemplated" by consumers. Put another way, because consumers' safety expectations are almost never frustrated by obvious product dangers, the expectancy test almost always precludes liability in such cases. See *Calles v. Scripto–Tokai Corp.*, 864 N.E.2d 249, 257 (Ill. 2007) (no recovery under consumer expectations test because utility lighter, which young child used to start fire, "performed as an ordinary consumer would expect"); *Crosswhite v. Jumpking, Inc.*, 411 F.Supp.2d 1228, 1231 (D. Or. 2006) ("There can be no dispute that an ordinary consumer buys and uses a trampoline to jump on it, and a design that allows for such activity is exactly that which is contemplated by an ordinary consumer or user of a trampoline.").

Whose Expectations?

Special problems arise in determining whose expectations to protect, particularly in the case of persons whose safety is protected by others, such as children, patients, and employees. The issue in such cases is whether the expectations of the ward (the child, patient, or employee) or those of the purchasing custodian (the parent, doctor, or employer) should govern. The user-bystander situation presents a similar problem.

Where the safety custodian, but not the ward, can best evaluate and control the risk (as often is the case with parents, doctors, users, and sometimes employers), courts generally have applied the expectations of the custodian, rather than the ward (whose safety expectations are usually vague or nonexistent). This often may be a proper result in such cases, since responsibility in tort is often best placed on those responsible for controlling risk. See *Bellotte v. Zayre Corp.*, 352 A.2d 723 (N.H. 1976) (expectations of parents controlled, not those of 5-year-old child burned when his cotton pajama top ignited while he was playing with matches).

Vagueness

An especially problematic aspect of the consumer expectations test lies in the vagueness of consumer expectations in many contexts. Particularly in considering the design adequacy of a complex product—such as an automobile, a pharmaceutical drug, or other chemical product—consumers have no idea how safely the product really ought to perform in various situations. How can an ordinary consumer possibly know the extent of protection fairly to be expected when an automobile crashes into a tree at 10, 20, or even 40 mph? Lurking at the very heart of the consumer expectations test, the vagueness problem undermines the test in most complex cases where a reliable standard of liability is needed most.

For these and other reasons, courts increasingly are abandoning the consumer expectations test as the sole or principal means for determining defectiveness in most products liability cases, as discussed below. Yet, while the consumer expectations test may be withering as the true, sole test for strict products liability in tort, it remains an important consideration in many products liability cases. In some states it remains the principal, or only, test of liability; in others, even if considered only as a factor in the risk-utility balance, it may be determinative in certain situations; and in a small set of special cases (such as those involving food and used products), it remains a central liability consideration.

§ 5.7   THE RISK–UTILITY TEST

In General

Many courts, dissatisfied with the consumer expectations test and unwilling to abandon the calculus-of-risk principles of negligence law, use some form of "risk-utility" ("risk-benefit" or "cost-benefit") test for strict products liability in tort. Borrowed from the law of negligence, this test was converted to the realm of strict liability in tort at an early date. For example, in *Helicoid Gage Div. of American Chain & Cable Co. v. Howell*, 511 S.W.2d 573 (Tex. Civ. App. 1974), a pressure gauge manufactured by the defendant burst, throwing a piece of the gauge lens into the plaintiff's eye. The jury rendered a verdict for the plaintiff, which the appellate court affirmed. "To determine whether a product is unreasonably dangerous," reasoned the court, "it is necessary to weigh the risk of harm against the utility of the product, considering whether safety devices would unreasonably raise the costs or diminish the utility of the product." The evidence supported liability because it revealed that shatterproof glass, which would have prevented the injury, would have increased the cost of each gauge by only $1 without reducing its utility at all. Id. at 577.

By the mid– to late–1970s, a number of products liability law scholars began to call for a shift away from § 402A's consumer expectations test toward a cost-benefit test, particularly in design defect cases. As more and more courts turned to some form of risk-benefit test in the 1980s and 1990s, and with the *Third Restatement*'s adoption of the risk-utility test for use in design and warning cases in 1998, cost-benefit analysis became the predominant liability test in products liability law.

Nature of the Risk–Utility Test

The basic risk-utility approach to products liability decisionmaking was explained in the context of negligence, above. This approach is fundamentally the same in the strict tort context, but it is worth restating here. The quality of a decision to act or refrain from acting in a particular way may be evaluated in terms of the balance of advantages (benefits) *vs.* disadvantages (costs) of the action to all foreseeably affected parties. The type and amount of safety required is generally a function of the type, likelihood, and amount of expected harm (together viewed as the magnitude of the risk) that precautions (of a particular cost) may be expected to prevent. If the risk posed by the sale and use of a product in a certain condition is great, substantial precautions must be taken (if feasible) to avert the risk; if the risk is small, precautions may be small as well.

As previously explained, if the risk at issue concerns the possible failure of an automobile's steering, brakes, or tires at highway speeds, or the possibility that a punch press ram may unexpectedly depress upon an operator's hand, the manufacturer must employ the utmost precautions to avert the risk. Yet, if the risk is relatively minimal, reasonably appearing to involve at most the risk of minor harm to person or property—scratches, stains, or the harmless malfunction of the product—then a manufacturer need apply only minimal precautions to reduce such risks. This principle of balance is sometimes called the "calculus of risk."

The "Hand Formula" in the Strict Liability Context

The most celebrated formulation of the risk-benefit test, albeit in the context of negligence rather than "strict" products liability, was provided by Judge Learned Hand in the case of *United States v. Carroll Towing Co.*, 159 F.2d 169 (2d Cir. 1947), discussed in § 2.2, above. In *Carroll Towing*, Judge Hand reasoned that a determination of the extent of precaution appropriate to an occasion generally reflects a calculus of three factors: the burden of taking precautions to avoid a risk of harm, on the one side, balanced against the likelihood that the actor's conduct will produce the harm multiplied by the seriousness of the harm, on the other. Under the "Hand formula," negligence is suggested if an actor fails to adopt a burden of precaution of less magnitude than the harm it is likely to prevent, to wit, if $B < P \times L \Rightarrow N$, where B is the burden or cost of avoiding accidental loss expected to result if B is not undertaken, P is the increase in the probability of loss if B is not undertaken, L is the probable magnitude (expected cost) of such loss if it does occur, and N is the implication of negligence.

By substituting "defect" for "negligence" (D for N), the Hand formula converts comfortably to the "strict" products liability task of determining defectiveness. So reformulated, the defectiveness "equation" looks like this:

$$B < P \times L \Rightarrow D$$

In cost-benefit terms, the formula states:

(Accident Prevention) Costs < (Safety) Benefits $\Rightarrow$ Defect

That is, a product defect is suggested if the safety benefits of an untaken safety precaution foreseeably exceed the resulting costs, including any diminished usefulness or diminished safety.

In sum, the risk-utility test demands that manufacturers adopt precautions proportionate to the magnitude of the expected risk. This simple yet fundamental principle of defectiveness, which ties the measure of precaution to the measure of risk, grounds the safety obligations of a manufacturer in strict liability as well as negligence. The virtual identity of the two doctrines in design and warning cases, in jurisdictions which rely upon the risk-utility test, is reexamined in § 5.9, below.

Problems with the Risk–Utility Test

The risk-utility balancing test is sometimes faulted for being too indeterminate to be of principled use. Other critics complain that risk-utility decisionmaking, based on stark economic efficiency, suffers from a lack of richness, humanism, and basic justice.

There is some truth to both of these challenges, but they fail to squarely hit the mark. Indeterminacy is a real problem for courts that try to balance a wide array of diverse factors. But the narrowly-focused cost-benefit formulation of the test outlined above escapes this problem to a large extent. Arguments that cost-benefit determinations lack humanism and justice miss a couple of important points as well. It is true that manufacturers are unable to bargain with consumers individually; if such individualization were possible, it would ideally permit each consumer to maximize (or optimize) his or her own preferences. Yet manufacturers are forced by circumstances to "legislate" safety decisions for consumers as a group, and a manufacturer that in good faith applies cost-benefit analysis to safety decisionmaking thereby necessarily respects the equality and safety rights of consumers as a group.

§ 5.8 ALTERNATIVE TESTS

Verbal Standards

While § 402A's "defective condition unreasonably
dangerous" standard appears to have two poles,
"defective condition" and "unreasonably dangerous," most courts eventually realized that the full
Restatement phrase signifies a unitary concept that
may be dubbed "defective"—convenient for general
discussion but unhelpful as a liability "test" for
ascertaining whether a particular product is or was
adequately safe. Yet, many courts (and some statutes) continue to employ the full *Restatement*
phrase, which unfortunately continues to lead some
courts (and probably some juries) to the false conclusion that the phrase must mean two things.

Courts from time to time have experimented with
a variety of other definitional phrases, such as "not
reasonably safe," "unduly unsafe," "not reasonably
fit, suitable and safe," and "dangerously defective."
In *Azzarello v. Black Bros. Co.*, 391 A.2d 1020 (Pa.
1978), the Pennsylvania Supreme Court announced
that a supplier of a product "is the guarantor of its
safety," a statement with frightening implications
that elsewhere has been soundly rejected as too
extreme and as running counter to the universally
accepted notion, even in Pennsylvania, that a manufacturer is not an "insurer" of the safety of its
products. Id. at 1027 n.12.

Combining Tests—Consumer Expectations and Risk–Utility

The discussion to this point of the consumer expectations and risk-utility tests has shown that both tests have much merit: the consumer expectancy test of contract law protects vital interests of buyers and sellers who strike private contractual bargains involving certain implied warranties of quality and safety, and the risk-utility test of tort law protects the general public by requiring product sellers to accord proper respect to the safety interests of persons foreseeably put at risk by defective products. Recognizing the validity of both of these goals and the dual origins of strict products liability in warranty law and tort, the Supreme Court of California embraced *both* such tests in an important decision, *Barker v. Lull Engineering Co.*, 573 P.2d 443 (Cal. 1978), discussed in chapter 8, below. Reasoning that a proper test of strict products liability should reflect its dual origins, the *Barker* court *combined* the consumer expectations and risk-utility tests into a single, two-pronged test, and shifted the burden of proof on risk-utility to the manufacturer.

A handful of courts have explicitly followed *Barker*'s two-pronged definition of product defect, but generally not its shift in the burden of proof, and at least a couple of courts have explicitly rejected the *Barker* test. Other courts follow a *de facto Barker* approach, sometimes applying one test, sometimes the other, usually without explanation. While these decisions might be faulted for failing clearly to specify when and how the two separate tests should be applied, much may be said for a liability regime which intelligibly blends, one way or another, both standards of liability.

Two other developments, also examined further in the design defect chapter, are also worthy of note here. First is the redefinition of consumer expectations in risk-utility terms, at least in certain types of cases, perhaps based on the idea that consumers should be able to expect manufacturers to make their products as safe as reasonably possible in view of the relevant costs and benefits. See *Potter v. Chicago Pneumatic Tool Co.*, 694 A.2d 1319 (Conn. 1997).

The second judicial development is the movement toward applying the *consumer expectations* test to cases involving the design of a *simple* mechanism, such as an unguarded fan, but applying a *risk-utility* test to a product with a *complex* design, such as a car. See *Soule v. General Motors Corp.*, 882 P.2d 298 (Cal. 1994).

Defect–Specific Tests

A major judicial development in connection with products liability defect tests in recent years is a trend toward separate tests for separate types of defect. There generally has been little need to define *manufacturing defects*, for the fact of "defectiveness" and the resulting violation of a consumer's expectations are both generally self-evident in such cases. Accordingly, the courts have rarely bothered to define this form of defect. Recently, however, a number of courts and state legislatures have begun defining manufacturing defects in terms of a deviation from the manufacturer's design.

Design defects formerly were widely defined in terms of consumer expectations, as discussed above, but many courts have been shifting to a risk-utility test for resolving design defectiveness, sometimes combining risk-utility with some form of consumer expectancy analysis.

Neither the consumer expectations nor risk-utility test is generally very helpful in determining whether a particular danger deserves a warning or whether a particular warning adequately conveys information about the risk. A product with an inadequate warning of danger quite obviously violates a consumer's expectations, and the safety benefits of adding a sufficient warning virtually always exceed its monetary costs. For this reason, the *warning defect* issue is generally posited merely in terms of the sufficiency or "adequacy" of the information provided and of the method by which it was conveyed. Most courts have turned to general negligence principles for such cases.

The trend toward separately defining the liability standard by type of defect was validated by the *Third Restatement* which, while defining design and warning defects in similar risk-utility terms, trifurcates defectiveness into the three separate types of defect, each with its own separate definition. The defect-specific definitions of liability are provided separate treatment below in the defect-specific chapters.

§ 5.9 COMPARISON WITH OTHER LIABILITY THEORIES

Strict Products Liability *vs.* Strict Liability for Abnormally Dangerous Activities

One might think that the two major strict liability in tort doctrines, one for selling a dangerously defective product and the other for conducting an abnormally dangerous activity, might have much in common. In fact, however, the two doctrines are fundamentally distinct. Strict *products* liability in tort concerns the responsibility of a supplier for making or selling a product containing an excessive and often unexpected danger (such as the manufacturer of a car with defective brakes) that injures the user or someone else. By contrast, strict liability for an *abnormally dangerous activity* involves the responsibility of an actor, such as a contractor who sets off a large charge of dynamite in a city, for the harmful consequences of introducing a substantial, unavoidable danger into a setting where the hazard is plainly out of place.

In the products liability context, strict liability follows the creation and sale of a product that is unreasonably dangerous because it was made improperly or bears insufficient warning of its dangers, such that the hazard could and reasonably should have been avoided—so that it should not have been *sold* in that condition at all. By contrast, strict liability for an abnormally dangerous activity arises out of an actor's *use* of a product or other activity whose dangers, though large, are reasonable when the activity is conducted in an appropriate location where the hazard may be properly contained. Such an actor is strictly liable for creating an unreasonable ("abnormal") danger by choosing to *use* (not sell) a product in a manner or context where the danger is substantial, unavoidable, and out of place.

With almost no exceptions, courts have steadfastly kept these two theories of strict tort liability separate and distinct.

Strict Liability *vs.* Negligence

In General

How strict liability differs from fault-based liability, and which is preferable, may be the most fundamental issue in all of tort law. It is elemental that the very basis of negligence liability, whether in products liability or other tort law context, is grounded on fault. In contrast, the very basis of strict products liability in tort is the supplier's responsibility for harm caused by product defects *regardless* of fault. Thus, *Restatement (Second) of Torts* § 402A "applies although ... the seller has exercised all possible care in the preparation and sale of his product." Liability is called "strict" because the responsibility for sellers of defective products is "no-fault" liability. In contrast to negligence, it is often said that strict products liability focuses on the *condition of the product* rather than on the *conduct of the manufacturer*. See *Calles v. Scripto–Tokai Corp.*, 864 N.E.2d 249 (Ill. 2007); *Shipler v. General Motors Corp.*, 710 N.W.2d 807 (Neb. 2006).

The fundamental divide between negligence and strict liability in tort is manifest in *manufacturing flaw* cases, where even the most careful supplier is subject to liability under § 402A for injuries caused by a stone in a can of peas, an air bubble in a tire, or a crossed wire in the electrical system of a punch press.

When the issue shifts away from manufacturing defects to dangers in a product's *design* or inadequate *warnings and instructions*, there can be little difference between negligence and strict liability because the plaintiff in each such case is required to show effectively the same thing—that the product contained a foreseeable danger that was *unreasonable*. If the question of whether a particular danger is unreasonable is determined by the consumer expectations test, the results may vary from a determination under principles of negligence. But as courts turn increasingly to the risk-utility test, which balances the costs and benefits of avoiding the danger, the method for determining "defect" or "unreasonable danger" is virtually identical to that for establishing the supplier's fault in negligence law, as discussed above.

Modern courts increasingly recognize that the basis of liability in both design and warning cases is nearly (or completely) equivalent in negligence and strict liability in tort. This recognition has finally reached the point that a few courts, usually indirectly but sometimes explicitly, have ruled that the equivalence of strict liability in tort and negligence in design and warning cases supports a single cause of action. But there remains a dwindling, yet stubborn, contingent of courts that cling tenaciously to the view that the doctrines of negligence and strict liability in tort are and must be kept conceptually distinct. See *Pennsylvania Dep't of Gen. Servs. v. U.S. Mineral Prods. Co.*, 898 A.2d 590, 602 (Pa. 2006) ("negligence concepts have no place in strict liability doctrine").

Juries, Strategy, and Inconsistent Verdicts

The near or complete equivalence of negligence and strict liability in tort in design and warning cases raises a couple of important trial considerations. One strategic issue concerns whether a plaintiff's lawyer should plead both theories, covering all bases, but risk confusing the jury which may, unless precisely guided by court and counsel, mistakenly believe that liability requires a finding of all the elements of both types of claims. If, on the other hand, the plaintiffs' counsel chooses to use a rifle shot approach by providing the jury with a single claim, which should it be, negligence or strict liability?

Common sense seems to suggest that a plaintiff's lawyer should simply abandon the negligence claim for the simpler and easier-to-prove claim of strict liability in tort, and that it would almost be mal-practice to assert a negligence claim alone. Yet seasoned plaintiff's counsel and an empirical study conclude that juries respond more favorably to plaintiffs—in both verdict likelihood and size of awards—on the "hot" rhetoric of negligence than the "cold" logic of strict liability. See Cupp & Polage, *The Rhetoric of Strict Products Liability Versus Negligence: An Empirical Analysis*, 77 N.Y.U. L. Rev. 874, 936–37 (2002) (in mock trials of the same case, 26% of jurors in strict liability trial awarded damages whereas 38% of jurors in negli-gence trial awarded damages; jurors on average awarded damages nearly twice as large in negli-gence than in strict liability).

Another issue arising from the closeness of the theories of negligence and strict liability concerns a thorny problem involving inconsistent jury verdicts. Suppose that a court submits a case to the jury on both negligence and strict liability in tort claims, and, by special interrogatories, the jury decides for the plaintiff on the negligence claim but for the defendant on the strict liability claim. The problem is that these two verdicts may be logically inconsis-tent. A strict liability ruling requires a finding that the product is defective; and a negligence ruling requires two implicit findings: (1) that the product was "bad" (defective), and (2) that the defendant was at fault in supplying the product in that condi-tion. A manufacturer or other supplier can hardly be faulted for supplying consumers with a "good" product, one that is *not* defective. So, a finding that a product is not defective for purposes of strict liability in tort logically precludes a finding that a manufacturer was negligent in making or selling it in that condition.

Despite a curiously large number of decisions to the contrary, most courts have convincingly reasoned that a negligence finding is necessarily inconsistent with a finding that a product was not defective. In such a case, a jury's rendering of two fatally inconsistent findings normally invalidates the verdict, requiring that the verdict be vacated and a new trial granted.

Strict Liability in Tort *vs.* Warranty

In General

As seen above, once the decisions in *Henningsen* and *Greenman* stripped the *implied warranty* claim of its traditional contract law defenses based on privity, disclaimers, and notice, what remained, in all its naked glory, was the doctrine of strict products liability in *tort*. Despite the different manner in which the tort and implied warranty of merchantability liability standards are phrased—"defective condition unreasonably dangerous" versus "fitness for ordinary purposes"—courts often recite the virtual or complete equivalence of the two standards of liability, holding that they require the same types of proof. Thus, most courts today view the notion of unmerchantability to be the equivalent of the defectiveness concept in both negligence and strict products liability in tort. See *Wright v. Brooke Group*

Ltd., 652 N.W.2d 159, 181 (Iowa 2002) ("a seller's warranty that goods are fit for the ordinary purposes for which such goods are used gives rise to the same obligation owed by manufacturers under tort law with respect to the avoidance of personal injury to others").

Inconsistent Jury Verdicts—Denny v. Ford Motor Co.

The virtual or complete identity between the concept of defectiveness under § 402A and the notion of unmerchantability under UCC § 2–314 has led some courts to hold that conflicting jury verdicts on the two theories must be irreconcilable and, hence, the basis for reversal. On such reasoning, for example, an extension cord found *not* to be defective can hardly also be found to be unmerchantable. Further, if the two claims are in fact redundant, a court may properly refuse to instruct a jury on both doctrines.

In *Denny v. Ford Motor Co.*, 662 N.E.2d 730 (N.Y. 1995), the New York Court of Appeals ruled that claims of strict products liability in tort and breach of implied warranty are *not* always coextensive. Nancy Denny was injured when she slammed on the brakes of her Ford Bronco II SUV to avoid hitting a deer and the vehicle rolled over. Ms. Denny sued Ford in federal court, challenging the vehicle's design for rolling over too easily due to its relatively narrow track width, high center of gravity, and short wheel base, and Ford's failure to warn of the vehicle's propensity to roll over. While the Bronco

II's design characteristics made it less stable for normal suburban highway driving, for which Ford marketed the car, they were necessary to make the vehicle useful for driving over irregular off-road terrain, an important purpose of such a "sport utility vehicle."

Plaintiff asserted the same design and failure to warn claims in separate counts of (1) strict liability in tort, for selling a product in a defective condition, and (2) breach of the implied warranty of merchantability, for marketing a car that was not fit for its ordinary purposes. Despite the defendant's objections that the claims were identical, the trial court submitted the case to the jury on both claims. Without objection, the court instructed the jury that the tort law claim required the plaintiff to prove that the vehicle was "defective" or "not reasonably safe," to be determined by a risk-utility evaluation of the costs and benefits of designing out the danger. The court further explained that the implied warranty claim required the plaintiff to prove that the vehicle was not "reasonably fit for the ordinary purposes for which it was intended." Id. at 732.

The jury returned a split verdict, concluding that (1) the Bronco was *not* "defective," so that Ford was not liable for strict products liability in tort, but that (2) Ford *had* breached an implied warranty of merchantability and so was liable on that basis for plaintiff's injuries. On defendant's appeal, the Second Circuit Court of Appeals certified certain questions to the New York high court, asking whether the two claims were identical, and, if not, whether the jury's finding of no defect was reconcilable with its finding of a breach of warranty. *Held*, the claims are *not* identical and, on the facts, the jury's findings *were* reconcilable: defectiveness in strict liability in tort contains a "negligence-like risk/benefit component," which rests on the manufacturer's unreasonableness in not adopting feasible alternative designs, whereas the implied warranty of merchantability rests on whether a product is "fit for ordinary purposes," measured by consumer expectations of how the product should operate in foreseeable situations. Id. at 736.

The court reasoned that the jury could reasonably have concluded that the Bronco II was not "defective" for tort law purposes, because its utility as an off-road vehicle outweighed the risk of rollovers, while also concluding that the vehicle was *not* safe under warranty law for the "ordinary purpose" of every-day on-road driving for which it was marketed and sold. Thus, the jury could have concluded simultaneously that the strict liability in tort claim failed but that the defendant had breached its implied warranty of merchantability of "fitness" for "ordinary purpose." The case was distinctive, thought the court, because the product was marketed and sold for two quite different uses. Id. at 738–39.

The commentators generally have been unkind to *Denny*, in part because it contravenes a strong majority rule, and it has been rejected by the Supreme Court of Texas and the ALI, both in the *Products Liability Restatement* and in its approval of amended Article 2 of the UCC, § 2–314 cmt. 7.

PART II
PRODUCT DEFECTIVENESS

CHAPTER 6
NATURE AND PROOF OF DEFECTIVENESS

Table of Sections

§ 6.1   Defectiveness—Generally.
§ 6.2   The Three Types of Defect.
§ 6.3   Proof of Defect—Expert Testimony.
§ 6.4   Proof of Defect—Recurring Issues.
§ 6.5   Restatement (Third) of Torts: Products Liability.

———

§ 6.1   DEFECTIVENESS—GENERALLY

Virtually every product, when put to certain uses, is dangerous in some manner and to some extent. But most such dangers are a simple fact of physics, chemistry, or biology which there is no reasonable way to avoid. For such natural risks of life, product users rather than product suppliers properly bear responsibility for avoiding and insuring against any injuries that may result. But some products carry excessive risk that users and consumers should not fairly be required to shoulder, either because the risks are unexpected or because they otherwise can be avoided more reasonably by manufacturers or other product suppliers. And so, before the law shifts a risk of loss to the seller, it properly requires that the type or level of danger in a product is *excessive*. The label the law attaches to products carrying such excessive risks is "defective."

At least implicitly, each of the three major causes of action in products liability law requires that the product be defective. Negligence claims are predicated on the defectiveness of a product, because its supplier ordinarily cannot be faulted for selling a product that is good (i.e., not defective). The implied warranty of merchantability is breached if a product is "unfit" for ordinary use, meaning virtually the same thing as "defective." And strict liability in tort, of course, explicitly rests on the sale of a defective product. The centrality of the concept of defectiveness to products liability law is reflected in the *Second* and *Third Restatements of Torts*, both of which ground liability on the notion of product defect. Quite simply, product defectiveness is the heart of products liability law. For a more thorough examination of product defectiveness, see Owen, Products Liability Law ch. 6 (2d ed. 2008).

§ 6.2   THE THREE TYPES OF DEFECT

The Distinctness of the Defect Concepts

When Dean Prosser crafted § 402A of the *Second Restatement* in the late 1950s and early 1960s, products liability law was in its infancy. At this very early stage in the development of this branch of law, the defect concept was only roughly understood and conceived of, quite naively, as a unitary concept: products were either too dangerous (defective) or safe enough (nondefective). As courts in the 1960s and 1970s applied the principles of § 402A to an ever-widening array of products in an ever-widening range of contexts, the disparities among the various forms of product dangers increasingly revealed themselves. Over time, courts and commentators came to understand the fundamental distinctions between the three very different forms of product defect:

(1) *Manufacturing flaws*—unintended physical irregularities in products that occur during the production process;

(2) *Design inadequacies*—hazards lurking in a product's engineering or scientific conception that can and reasonably should be avoided by a different design or formula; and

(3) *Insufficient warnings of danger or instructions on safe use*—the absence of information needed by users to avoid product hazards.

Misrepresentation, the fourth principal basis of products liability, is not generally classified as a product "defect." In the decades since § 402A first roughly sketched a general doctrine of strict products liability in tort, the need to accord separate treatment to the liability issues distinctive to each of these very different defect contexts has become a well-accepted axiom. Today, that the three separate types of defect create independent sets of obligations is a fundamental premise of American products liability law.

The Puzzle of Comment *j*

That the three types of defect beget distinct and largely independent obligations would seem to be so obvious as to be beyond dispute. Yet a sentence in one comment to § 402A, comment *j*, can be read quite literally to mean that a manufacturer who provides a warning—*any* type of warning, no matter how deficient—eludes altogether the separate duty of safe design.

Comment *j* basically sets forth, in a largely noncontroversial manner, a product seller's duty to warn of foreseeable hazards, but it concludes with this curious language:

Where warning is given, the seller may reasonably assume that it will be read and heeded; and a product bearing such a warning, which is safe for use if it is followed, is not in [a] defective condition, nor is it unreasonably dangerous.

This ambiguous language can be read literally, as several courts have done, to mean that *any* warning, no matter how inadequate, satisfies *every* duty of whatever type that a product seller has. Yet that would be quite preposterous, for it would allow a manufacturer of metal household fans to substitute a warning on the base of such a fan for the fan's protective cage.

The meaning of this curious sentence of comment *j* for decades lay shrouded in the mists of history. Yet, research has revealed that its actual meaning is far more limited than suggested above—that it really only means that sellers of inherently dangerous products like certain foods, alcohol, tobacco, and prescription drugs, in addition to supplying them free of impurities, need only warn consumers of any unavoidable, latent dangers such products foreseeably may contain. This narrow interpretation has been shown to be correct because of the purpose of comments *i*, *j*, and *k*, all of which were written by Dean Prosser to allay concerns that inherently hazardous but useful products like those just mentioned would give rise to liability for the harmful consequences of their unavoidable risks notwithstanding the inability of their manufacturers to design away such inherent hazards.

With the exception of a handful of misguided decisions that have misinterpreted comment *j* as negating the general duty of safe design, a great majority of courts, some explicitly rejecting comment *j* on this point, hold that the separate forms of defect give rise to separate obligations that may independently support a products liability claim. The *Products Liability Restatement* is in accord.

Thus, except in certain limited contexts, it is abundantly clear that a manufacturer is subject to liability for a product's *manufacturing* defects, no matter how clear the product's warnings or how perfect its design; for *warning* defects, no matter how perfect the product's manufacture or how impeccable its design; and for *design* defects, no matter the precision of its manufacture or the abundance of its warnings. This latter point may be the most significant because of the perverse effects of comment *j*'s long tentacles in a number of jurisdictions.

The courts have quite colorfully expressed this idea. See *Rogers v. Ingersoll–Rand Co.*, 144 F.3d 841 (D.C. Cir. 1998) (a manufacturer may not "merely slap a warning onto its dangerous product, and absolve itself of any obligation to do more"); *Glittenberg v. Doughboy Recreational Indus.*, 491 N.W.2d 208, 216 (Mich. 1992) ("A warning is not a Band–Aid to cover a gaping wound, and a product is not safe simply because it carries a warning."). More succinctly, warnings do not trump design.

Overlap of Safety Obligations

Proper Role of Warnings in Design Defect Determinations

While the three forms of defect generate independent safety obligations, such that the satisfaction of one obligation does not *ipso facto* satisfy the others, fulfilling one duty sometimes helps to satisfy another. This overlap of safety responsibilities is clearest in the areas of design and warnings. The safer a manufacturer *designs* its products, the fewer dangers there will be about which to *warn*. And, because warnings and instructions may in fact serve to reduce design hazards, at least to some extent, the provision of such information may have *some* bearing on design defectiveness. Just as the obviousness of a hazard reduces the likelihood of resulting harm, as discussed below, so too do warnings and instructions.

Thus, because warnings reduce the risk of injury from design hazards, the presence of a warning is one factor—sometimes an important one—to be balanced in the calculus of considerations involved in a determination of design defectiveness. That is, in balancing the risk factors relevant to design defectiveness, a trier of fact should consider, among other factors, whether the design hazard was obvious, warned about, or generally known.

Compatibility of Separate Defect Claims

While the three types of defect are conceptually distinct, separate claims for each often are compatible. Thus, in an appropriate case, the plaintiff may claim and attempt to prove that a product was defective according to two, or (albeit infrequently) all three different types of defect. Stated otherwise, the different types of defect claims are not mutually exclusive. For example, an SUV that rolls over too easily on particular steering maneuvers may be defective in design, because its center of gravity is too high and its track width too narrow, and it may also be defective because of the absence of a warning of this tendency. See *Bericochea–Cartagena v. Suzuki Motor Co.*, 7 F.Supp.2d 109 (D.P.R. 1998) (Suzuki Sidekick); *Purvis v. American Motors Corp.*, 538 So.2d 1015 (La. Ct. App. 1988) (Jeep CJ–5). And while manufacturing defect claims usually stand on their own, they may be combined with design and even warning claims on appropriate facts. So, if an occasional flashcube explodes when defectively manufactured, the seller may have a duty to warn of this tendency, see *Maybank v. S.S. Kresge Co.*, 266 S.E.2d 409 (N.C. Ct. App. 1980), and the explosions may also be attributable to some defect in design.

§ 6.3   PROOF OF DEFECT— EXPERT TESTIMONY

Understanding the various aspects of the design, manufacture, and labeling of products normally involves a host of complex, technical considerations requiring specialized expertise. Mechanical, chemical, and materials engineers; chemists; physicists; pharmacologists; epidemiologists; and other technical specialists are often necessary to help the fact finder comprehend how a product was made, how it was supposed to operate, whether and how it may have malfunctioned or otherwise caused an accident, and how it could have been made differently to avoid accidents of that type. Thus, involving as it does the inner workings of science and technology, products liability litigation often resolves into a "battle of the experts."

Qualifications and Sources of Expert Witnesses

To serve as an expert witness, an individual first must be *qualified*—"by knowledge, skill, experience, training, or education"—to offer opinions on the particular specialized matter before the court. Fed. R. Evid. 702. The bulk of qualified specialists in most fields of product design, manufacturing, and labeling are employed by private industry, often by the manufacturing enterprises who are defendants in products liability litigation. Thus, manufacturers typically have a ready source of experts to help defend products liability cases. Plaintiffs' lawyers, on the other hand, generally are limited to two principal resource pools for expert witness talent: universities and private consulting expert firms.

The Rise of the Professional Expert Witness— The Problem of "Junk Science"

As products liability litigation began to mushroom in the 1970s and 1980s, so too did the plaintiff's need for experts to battle a manufacturer's engineers over defectiveness and causation—in expert reports, depositions, and ultimately at trial. The resulting surge in demand for expert testimony spawned a whole new industry of "professional" expert engineers and other consulting specialists who mostly testified for the plaintiffs' bar. Many such experts were of course entirely competent to testify on the issues they agreed to evaluate. But others advertised a willingness to testify, for a fee, on the defectiveness (and even the appropriateness of punitive damages) of just about anything, from toys to airplanes.

The explosion of expert testimony in products liability litigation during the 1970s and 1980s, fueled by an expanding plaintiffs' bar fed by contingent fees, quite naturally led to a rather rapid increase of products liability lawsuits based on novel, untested, abstract, and occasionally quite fantastic theories of science and technology propounded by "experts" who sometimes were dubiously qualified to testify on issues on which they claimed expertise. As products liability litigation during this period marched along, courts and commentators, always skeptical of this form of witness, increasingly decried a perceived growth in abuses of expert testimony—of "junk science" run amok.

Early Limitations on Expert Testimony—*Frye*

The standard for admissibility of expert witness testimony long was set by *Frye v. United States*, 293 F. 1013, 1014 (D.C. Cir. 1923), in which the defendant in a murder case offered the results of an early polygraph test to show his innocence. In passing on the merits of a new form of science or technology, ruled the court, the test is whether it is "sufficiently established to have gained general acceptance in the particular field in which it belongs." The *Frye* "general acceptance" test tended to exclude testimony on cutting-edge science and technology since new ideas become accepted wisdom only over time.

In 1975, the Federal Rules of Evidence were adopted, including Rule 702, which provided for the admission of scientific and technical evidence by a qualified expert if such testimony will "assist the trier of fact"—if it is helpful to the jury, and Rule 703, which allows an expert to rely on facts and data "reasonably relied upon by experts" in the field. Rule 702 made no reference to the *Frye* general acceptance test and, during the 1980s and early 1990s, courts debated whether and to what extent *Frye* was consistent with Rule 702. During this period, courts struggled to find a balance between the need to open courtrooms to new science *vs.* the problems of allowing experts to propound bad science. Some courts began to shift the focus away from whether the expert's science was accepted by other scientists (*Frye*) to whether the expert's methodology, in reaching a conclusion, was acceptable to the court.

Daubert and Its Progeny

Daubert

In *Daubert v. Merrell Dow Pharmaceuticals*, 509 U.S. 579 (1993), the Supreme Court examined the admissibility of expert testimony on novel scientific theories and the relationship of the *Frye* test to Rule 702. *Daubert* involved the drug Bendectin, an anti-nausea medicine that, from 1956 until 1983, was widely prescribed to pregnant women for morning sickness. From the first Bendectin case filed in 1979, which claimed that the drug had caused the plaintiff's missing and malformed fingers, nearly

2000 cases eventually were filed claiming damages for birth defects from the drug. In *Daubert,* filed late in the life cycle of the litigation, the plaintiffs claimed that their birth defects were caused by Bendectin administered to their mothers during pregnancy. The defendant moved for summary judgment, arguing that there was no causal link between Bendectin and birth defects.

In affidavits from its expert scientists, Merrell Dow showed that *none* of the 38 epidemiological studies of Bendectin published by that time had found a causal connection between birth defects and the drug. In opposition, plaintiffs offered affidavits from 8 expert witnesses who concluded—on the basis of chemical structure analysis, *in vitro* (test tube) studies of animal cells, *in vivo* (live) animal studies, and a "reanalysis" of the previous epidemiological studies—that Bendectin can in fact cause birth defects. Concluding that the plaintiffs' proffered expert evidence did not meet *Frye*'s "general acceptance" standard of admissibility, the district court granted the defendant's summary judgment motion, and the Ninth Circuit affirmed.

In the Supreme Court, the plaintiffs argued that the *Frye* "general acceptance" standard had been superseded by the Federal Rules of Evidence. Vacating and remanding, the Supreme Court agreed that the Rules do not allow a court to use the degree of acceptance of a subject of scientific testimony as the sole determinant of admissibility. Because Rule 702 allows qualified experts to testify about "scientific

... knowledge," the Court reasoned that a trial judge must determine that proposed expert testimony is both "scientific" and "knowledge"—that the subject of the testimony is "ground[ed] in the methods and procedures of science," that it be "derived by the scientific method." An expert's proposed testimony must be "supported by appropriate validation—i.e., 'good grounds'...." That is, expert testimony must be *reliable*. Id. at 590.

In addition to requiring that expert testimony be *reliable*, the Court further reasoned that Rule 702 requires that such testimony be *relevant,* since the rule provides that expert scientific or technical testimony "assist the trier of fact to understand the evidence or to determine a fact in issue." This is the "helpfulness" requirement of Rule 702, requiring that expert testimony be sufficiently related to disputed facts to help the jury resolve facts or issues in dispute, a requirement the Court labeled "fit." Thus, when a party proffers expert scientific testimony, the trial court must make a preliminary determination of both the (1) *reliability* ("validity"), and (2) *relevance* ("fit") of the expert's reasoning or methodology underlying the testimony proposed. Id. at 591–93.

Among the factors a court may usefully employ in assessing the validity of an expert's proffered testimony on scientific evidence, the Court noted four or five (the Court unhelpfully lumped (2) and (3) together):

(1) **Testability**: whether the theory or technique is testable and has been tested—its ability to withstand objective, verifiable challenge and scientific trial;

(2) **Peer review**: whether it has been subjected to peer review and publication;

(3) **Error rate**: whether it has an acceptable known or potential rate of error;

(4) **Control standards**: whether its operation has been subjected to appropriate standards of control; and

(5) **General acceptance**: whether it is widely accepted in the relevant scientific community.

These are *Daubert*'s now-familiar reliability factors (reordered here).

In determining the admissibility of expert testimony under 702, the Court emphasized that the inquiry into pertinent reliability considerations should be flexible, and that the focus of inquiry "must be solely on principles and methodology, not on the conclusions that they generate." Because the lower courts had based their decisions in this case almost exclusively on *Frye*'s general acceptance standard, rather than on the broader reliability and fit requirements of Federal Rule of Evidence 702, the Supreme Court remanded the case to the Court of Appeals.

Supreme Court Progeny

Since *Daubert*, the Supreme Court has revisited the expert testimony issue a number of times. In *General Electric Co. v. Joiner*, 522 U.S. 136 (1997), it ruled that federal trial courts have wide discretion to exclude expert testimony, holding that such determinations are only subject to a permissive "abuse of discretion" standard of review.

Next came *Kumho Tire Co. v. Carmichael*, 526 U.S. 137 (1999), a tire blowout case in which the plaintiffs relied on testimony of an expert in tire failure analysis. The Court held that Rule 702's broad reference to expert testimony on "scientific, technical, or other specialized knowledge" means that the *Daubert* gatekeeping principles apply to *all* experts, including engineers and other technical specialists, not just "scientists."

The final Supreme Court decision to date on expert testimony is *Weisgram v. Marley Co.*, 528 U.S. 440 (2000), a wrongful death action against the manufacturer of a heater arising out of a house fire. The plaintiff won at trial, but the circuit court reversed, agreeing with defendant that plaintiffs' expert testimony offered mere speculation as to the heater's defectiveness, making it scientifically unsound. Rather than remanding for a retrial, the circuit court directed judgment for the defendant manufacturer, reasoning that plaintiffs had been given a fair opportunity to prove their claim and did not deserve a second chance. The Supreme Court affirmed. Rejecting an argument that a plaintiff might hold certain expert testimony in reserve to shore up the claim if the proffered expert testimony were found inadequate, the Court underscored *Daubert*'s basic message: parties have but one opportunity to present expert testimony rigorously grounded in good science and technology and relevant to the particular issues in the case.

Amendment to Federal Rule of Evidence 702

In 2000, the Supreme Court approved certain amendments to the Rules of Evidence on opinion evidence and expert testimony to conform them to the principles of *Daubert* and its progeny. In addition to minor changes in other rules, Rule 702 was amended to permit expert testimony only if such testimony is grounded on "sufficient facts and data" and is the result of "reliable principles and methods" that are themselves reliably applied to the facts of the case. The Advisory Committee's Note observes that this amendment requires only that the data, principles, and methods used by an expert are reliable and reliably applied, and that the quality of expert testimony is still largely to be tested by cross examination and the other safeguards of the adversary system.

The Advisory Committee's Note reiterates *Daubert*'s list of reliability factors set forth above and adds several more:

- Whether experts are "proposing to testify about matters growing naturally and directly out of research they have conducted independent of the litigation, or whether they have developed their opinions expressly for purposes of testifying";

- Whether the expert has unjustifiably extrapolated from an accepted premise to an unfounded conclusion;

- Whether the expert has adequately accounted for obvious alternative explanations;

- Whether the expert "is being as careful as he would be in his regular professional work outside his paid litigation consulting"; and

- Whether the field of expertise claimed by the expert is known to reach reliable results for the type of opinion the expert would give.

Daubert in the Lower Federal Courts

Daubert has had its intended effect of forcing courts to examine expert testimony more closely. Since *Daubert*, federal district courts, exercising their appointed "gatekeeper" function, have heightened their scrutiny of expert testimony, often holding rigorous pre-trial "*Daubert* hearings"—frequently outcome-determinative—to decide the admissibility of proffered expert testimony. The cases reveal that *Daubert* provides federal trial judges with a powerful operating manual for excluding expert testimony (usually presented by plaintiffs) that, in the court's sound discretion, does not meet current criteria for "good science."

But heightened judicial scrutiny of expert testimony does not mean that a court will necessarily exclude a plaintiff's expert even if his or her testimony is unusual. The circuit courts sometimes affirm plaintiff verdicts in novel contexts in which the traditional scientific indicia of defectiveness or causation is marginal at best, and they sometimes reverse district courts for excluding a plaintiff's expert testimony with excessive zeal. See *Sapping-ton v. Skyjack, Inc.*, 512 F.3d 440 (8th Cir. 2008).

Daubert in the State Courts

Because *Daubert* interprets Federal Rule of Evidence 702, it applies by its terms only to the federal courts. For this and other reasons, quite a few state courts, still trusting in *Frye* and other conventional rules governing the admissibility of expert testimony, have refused to adopt the *Daubert* principles. Yet, prior to the Supreme Court's decision in *Daubert* in 1993, many state courts had already adopted reliability principles quite similar to *Daubert*'s, and an increasing number of states have rejected *Frye* and swung over to the *Daubert* point of view.

In addition, a large majority of states have adopted codes of evidence patterned on the Federal Rules of Evidence, including Rule 702 on which *Daubert* is based. Moreover, to the extent that *Daubert*'s precepts are grounded in reasoned principles of logic and fair play for adjudicating disputes involving principles of science and technology, those precepts have a certain persuasive power that is difficult for state courts to ignore. For these reasons, a growing number of state courts, probably a majority, have now adopted the *Daubert* principles of reliability and relevance for expert testimony.

The Legacy of Daubert

In *Daubert* and its progeny, the Supreme Court attempted to bridge the yawning gap between how reality is perceived and described, and how problems are resolved, in science and the law. In particular, the Court has sought to improve the legitimacy of judicial determinations involving science and technology by forcing courts to rigorously scrutinize the foundations of an expert's scientific or technological opinions. Abandoning *Frye*'s "general acceptance" standard, which was based on the precept that courts should defer to scientific communities to decide for themselves whether a particular type of scientific approach should be recognized as useful, *Daubert* switched basic responsibility for making such decisions to the courts, which on balance may make good sense. It is hard to gainsay the Court's decision that trial judges should serve as "gatekeepers" for expert testimony, as preliminary decision-makers of whether an expert witness has devoted as much rigor, and has applied the same exacting methodologies, to the matter before the court as the expert devotes to his or her own professional projects. But courts must be cautious to apply the principles even-handedly—excluding expert testimony that is insufficiently grounded in sound methodology while allowing such testimony that reasonably, if boldly, reaches into uncharted waters of evolving knowledge.

By requiring experts to provide reasoned bases for their opinions, and by requiring that such opinions be grounded in reliable methodology and relevant to the legal issues in the case, *Daubert*'s principles, used properly, provide a firm foundation for the fair and rational resolution of the scientific and technological issues that lie at the heart of products liability adjudication.

§ 6.4 PROOF OF DEFECT—
RECURRING ISSUES

In most products liability cases, the plaintiff's basic claim is that a defect in a product sold by the defendant proximately caused the plaintiff's harm. The plaintiff has the burden of proof on each element of such a case, including the product's defectiveness. Sometimes, a plaintiff may introduce evidence that the product violated a safety standard—adopted by industry or the government—to establish the product defect and possibly the manufacturer's negligence. Or a defendant may rely on its *compliance* with such safety standards as evidence of its product's *non*defectiveness and possibly its non-negligence. Sometimes a plaintiff may seek to prove a product's defectiveness by proving similar failures of other similar products made by the defendant, and sometimes a defendant may prove the *absence* of similar accidents (the product's record of safe performance) to help prove the converse. Finally, a plaintiff may try to prove a product's defectiveness or the defendant's negligence by showing that the defendant itself acknowledged the problem by remedying the hazard after the product's sale or the plaintiff's injury. These are the recurring issues of proof covered below.

Safety Standards

Proof that a product violates or conforms to certain safety standards pertaining to the risk that caused the plaintiff's harm may be probative that the product was or was not defective. Such standards may be adopted by industry itself, perhaps through a standards-setting organization such as the American National Standards Institute (ANSI), the National Safety Council (NSC), or the Society of Automotive Engineers (SAE). Or safety standards may be promulgated by the government, by statute or regulatory standard of some governmental product safety agency, such as the federal food and drug agency (FDA) or the federal automotive safety agency (NHTSA).

In general, evidence that a products liability defendant violated or complied with an applicable safety standard is admissible on the issue of defectiveness. The role of such evidence in proving or disproving defectiveness derives from and parallels the law governing its use in proving and disproving negligence, a topic examined earlier.

Other Similar Accidents

A common, often quite persuasive, form of proof in products liability litigation is proof of other similar accidents. Plaintiffs commonly offer evidence of other similar accidents to help prove, circumstantially, a product's dangerous or defective condition, the defendant's notice of it, or that it caused the plaintiff's injury. Less commonly, defendants offer converse evidence of this type (the *absence* of other similar accidents) in an attempt to prove the contrary—that a product's condition was *not* especially dangerous. Plaintiffs' attorneys consider other-accident evidence to be an especially powerful form of proof, while defense attorneys often view it as largely, if not entirely, irrelevant and prejudicial to the fair and rational adjudication of a products liability case.

The most fundamental requirement of other-accident evidence is that the other accidents be "substantially similar" to the plaintiff's accident. First, of course, the *products* involved in the other accidents must be the same as, or similar to, the product claimed to have injured the plaintiff. But the relevance of such evidence also rests on a similarity in the principal *causative facts* and circumstances involved in the other accidents with those involved in the plaintiff's case. Evidence of other accidents generally is admissible if the plaintiff establishes their substantial similarity to the plaintiff's accident, and it will be excluded in the absence of such proof.

Subsequent Remedial Measures

The fact that a manufacturer has eliminated the very danger responsible for a plaintiff's injury can be powerful evidence that the particular safety enhancement was both practicable and otherwise reasonable at the time the safety change was made. So, by improving a product's design safety or by providing additional warnings or instructions, a manufacturer acknowledges the fact that, at that time, the benefits of the safety improvement exceeded their costs. Absent a technological breakthrough between the time the product is manufactured (or when the plaintiff is injured) and the time the product's safety is improved, evidence of such a product safety enhancement may well suggest that prior to its improvement the product was defective and possibly that the manufacturer was negligent. Normally, therefore, evidence that a manufacturer adopted a subsequent remedial measure is relevant to liability.

Common–Law Development of the Repair Doctrine

Although evidence that an actor cured a dangerous condition after it injured a plaintiff may be generally relevant to the condition's defectiveness and the actor's negligence, such evidence does not itself establish either, and it may unjustly punish persons for their care and prudence. Moreover, allowing subsequent repair evidence may serve to diminish safety by providing parties in control of dangerous conditions with a disincentive to reduce or cure such hazards for fear that their repairs may be used against them in subsequent litigation. For these reasons, courts at an early date developed a special rule of relevancy called the "repair doctrine" (also called the "subsequent repair," "subsequent remedial measure," and "post-accident corrective measure" rule or doctrine), barring evidence of a defendant's post-accident repairs to show the defendant's negligence.

Today, the rule barring evidence of subsequent remedial measures to prove negligence is the law in almost every state by common law or formal rule of evidence. The repair doctrine applies to products liability litigation, barring evidence of subsequent safety improvements to prove negligence and, in some jurisdictions, product defectiveness.

Federal Rule of Evidence 407

The general rule prohibiting evidence of post-accident repairs to prove negligence was adopted in Federal Rule of Evidence 407, "Subsequent Remedial Measures," which originally provided:

> When, after an event, measures are taken which, if taken previously, would have made the event less likely to occur, evidence of the subsequent measures is not admissible to prove negligence or culpable conduct in connection with the event. This rule does not require the exclusion of evidence of subsequent measures when offered for another purpose, such as proving ownership, control, or feasibility of precautionary measures, if controverted, or impeachment.

To resolve a couple of ambiguities, the first sentence of Rule 407 was amended in 1997 to read:

> When, after an injury or harm allegedly caused by an event, measures are taken that, if taken previously, would have made the injury or harm less likely to occur, evidence of the subsequent measures is not admissible to prove negligence, culpable conduct, a defect in a product, a defect in a product's design, or a need for a warning or instruction.

The revised rule thus makes clear that, in federal court, (1) the rule applies and so bars evidence of safety improvements in *strict* products liability as well as negligence, and that it applies to all three types of defect; and (2) the rule excludes only evidence of safety improvements adopted after the plaintiff's *injury*, leaving the admissibility of safety improvements made after manufacture but before the plaintiff's injury to the general rules of relevancy and prejudice.

Strict Liability Claims under State Law

While several states already have adopted the clarifications of the new federal rule, the evidence codes and common law of most states still track the repair doctrine's traditional formulation in terms of negligence and culpability. The states agree that the repair doctrine applies to products liability claims based on negligence, but they split on whether the rule should be limited to such claims or instead should be expanded to shield manufacturers against evidence of subsequent remedial measures in strict products liability claims.

The classic case allowing such evidence on a strict liability claim, with which many courts agree, is *Ault v. International Harvester Co.*, 528 P.2d 1148 (Cal. 1974), which reasoned that manufacturers will eliminate unnecessary hazards in their products as soon as possible, regardless of the evidentiary rule, to avoid the risk of a multitude of lawsuits and the bad publicity that might result if the product's hazard is left unrepaired. Many other states disagree, and so *exclude* evidence of subsequent remedial measures in strict liability cases as well as negligence. These courts reason that the policies for excluding such evidence in negligence cases—the questionable relevance of safety measures taken subsequent to a product's manufacture, the undesirability of discouraging safety improvements, and the risk of juror confusion—are as applicable to strict liability claims as those in negligence. See *Duchess v. Langston Corp.*, 769 A.2d 1131 (Pa. 2001) (5–2 decision).

Feasibility, Impeachment, and Other Limitations

The repair doctrine, which as a general rule excludes evidence of post-accident repair evidence, is subject to various exceptions that allow a plaintiff to present evidence of a manufacturer's subsequent remedial measures in certain situations. By its terms, the doctrine does not affect the admissibility of post-accident repair evidence "when offered for another purpose"—such as to prove "the feasibility of precautionary measures, if controverted," or to impeach a witness, exceptions that often overlap.

§ 6.5   RESTATEMENT (THIRD) OF TORTS: PRODUCTS LIABILITY

When the *Restatement (Second) of Torts* was about a quarter century old, the ALI decided to once again "restate" the law of Torts. Because tort law had grown so large and cumbersome, the ALI decided to subdivide the law on this topic into various components. Due to the explosive expansion of products liability law after the promulgation of

§ 402A of the *Second Restatement* in 1965, the ALI announced in 1991 that products liability would be the first of the new tort law *Restatements*. In 1992, Professor James Henderson and Professor Aaron Twerski were appointed Reporters for the project, and so began the process of converting a single section of the *Second Restatement,* § 402A, into an entire *Restatement* of its own. Over about 5 years, the Reporters issued a series of drafts critiqued by a number of Advisers (including a compulsive Editorial Adviser) and many other groups, and in 1997 the ALI voted to adopt a Proposed Final Draft, which it published in 1998 as the *Restatement (Third) of Torts: Products Liability.*

Basic Liability Provisions

Liability for Harm from Product Defects

Grounding the *Restatement,* § 1 provides the overarching general principle of modern products liability law—that commercial enterprises are liable for harm caused by defects in products that they sell:

> One engaged in the business of selling or otherwise distributing products who sells or distributes a defective product is subject to liability for harm to persons or property caused by the defect.

Defects Defined

Section 2, which contains the bulk of products liability doctrine, defines the three types of defect:

A product is defective when, at the time of sale or distribution, it contains a manufacturing defect, is defective in design, or is defective because of inadequate instructions or warnings. A product:

(a) contains a manufacturing defect when the product departs from its intended design even though all possible care was exercised in the preparation and marketing of the product;

(b) is defective in design when the foreseeable risks of harm posed by the product could have been reduced or avoided by the adoption of a reasonable alternative design by the seller or other distributor, or a predecessor in the commercial chain of distribution, and the omission of the alternative design renders the product not reasonably safe;

(c) is defective because of inadequate instructions or warnings when the foreseeable risks of harm posed by the product could have been reduced or avoided by the provision of reasonable instructions or warnings by the seller or other distributor, or a predecessor in the commercial chain of distribution, and the omission of the instructions or warnings renders the product not reasonably safe.

Malfunction Doctrine

Section 3 allows proof of defectiveness by circumstantial evidence when the specific kinds of proofs contemplated by the § 2 definitions are destroyed in the accident or are otherwise unavailable. This is the "malfunction doctrine," roughly adopted from *res ipsa loquitur*.

Government Safety Rules—Violation and Compliance

Section 4(a) provides that a product is defective if its design, warning, or instruction *violates* a product safety statute or safety regulation and a person is injured by the risk that the statute or regulation attempts to reduce. Section 4(b) provides that *compliance* with such safety provisions is merely some evidence that the product is not defective, such that a defectiveness determination is still possible in appropriate cases.

Special Types of Products

Component Parts and Raw Materials

Section 5 provides that a supplier of such products is liable (1) if the material or component is itself defective, or (2) if the component supplier so substantially participates in integrating the component into the assembled design of the integrated product that the supplier becomes in essence a co-designer of that final product.

Defective Drugs and Medical Devices

Section 6(a) provides that manufacturers of medical products are subject to true strict liability for manufacturing defects in their products, just as sellers of other types of products. But § 6(c) strictly limits design liability to cases where a drug is shown to have no net value for *any* class of patient.

Section 6(d) restates the "learned intermediary" doctrine for warning cases, which usually obligates prescription drug manufacturers to warn only the prescribing physician, not the patient. Section 6(e) provides that *pharmacists* and other retail sellers are subject only to negligence liability for selling such products containing design or warning defects.

Food

Section 7 adopts a "consumer expectations" test of liability for food cases.

Used Products

Section 8(a) provides that sellers of used products normally are liable only if they are *negligent*, with certain *exceptions*, when:

- consumers fairly *do* expect the same degree of safety as a new product (such as the buyer of an automobile used only for one week);

- products are sold as "remanufactured"; and

- a consumer's injuries are attributable to the seller's violation of statute or regulation.

Special Duty Issues

Misrepresentation

Section 9 provides that the general principles of tortious misrepresentation apply to products liability cases, including fraud, negligent misrepresentation, and strict liability for misrepresentation, and it explicitly endorses *Restatement (Second) of Torts* § 402B.

Post-Sale Duty to Warn

Section 10(a) imposes on suppliers a post-sale duty to warn when it is "reasonable" to so warn. Section 10(b) specifies when the duty to warn will arise in this context according to a balance of certain issues: the existence of a substantial danger of which the seller is or should be aware; the probability that consumers will be unaware of the danger; and the feasibility of identifying and providing warnings to persons who possess the product.

Post-Sale Duty to Recall

Section 11 provides that there is *no* duty to recall a product, even if defective, unless an administrative agency specifically requires the recall, as NHTSA (autos), the FDA (drugs), and the CPSC (consumer products) do from time to time. If for any reason a seller undertakes to recall its products, it must do so with reasonable care.

Liability of Successor Corporations

Section 12 provides that a successor company that merely purchases the assets of a predecessor (*vs.* merging or consolidating with it) is generally *not* liable for defects in products sold by the predecessor, subject to four conventional *exceptions*: (a) if it assumes such liability in the purchase agreement; (b) if the conveyance was a fraudulent attempt to escape such liability; (c) if the conveyance was a consolidation or merger with the predecessor; or (d) if the successor has become a continuation of the predecessor.

Successor's Own Post–Sale Duty to Warn

Section 13 provides that a successor, if it services its predecessor's products or otherwise undertakes some responsibility with respect to those products, must act with reasonable care to warn of the product's risks, particularized in the same manner as the general post-sale duty to warn, above.

Product Sponsorship

Section 14 adopts the principle of § 400 of the *Restatement (Second) of Torts* that sellers (such as large retailers) who market under their own names products manufactured by others are liable as if they were the manufacturer.

Causation

Causation—In General

Section 15 merely provides, in general terms, that causation between a product defect and the plaintiff's harm is an important element necessary to any products liability claim.

Causation of Additional Harm

Section 16 provides that a manufacturer may be liable for enhanced (in autos, "second-collision") injuries in certain situations.

Affirmative Defenses

Apportionment of Damages

Section 17 adopts damages apportionment principles for plaintiffs, defendants, and others according to their proportionate fault.

Contractual Disclaimers

Section 18 provides that contractual disclaimers and limitations of remedy have no affect on claims brought by plaintiffs injured in person by defective products.

Definitions

"Product"

Section 19 defines "product" to include most movable personal property, but to exclude services (such as a doctor's implantation of a defective pacemaker), blood, and human tissue.

Defendants

Section 20 applies the *Restatement* to manufacturers, wholesalers, retailers, and other commercial transferors of products for ultimate consumption, including commercial lessors (such as rental car companies) and commercial bailors (such as laundromats charging a fee for use of washing machines).

Economic Loss

Section 21 provides for the recovery of compensatory damages for personal injury, consortium losses to family members, property damage, and economic loss flowing therefrom, but not for pure economic loss.

CHAPTER 7

MANUFACTURING DEFECTS

Table of Sections

§ 7.1   Manufacturing Defects—Generally.
§ 7.2   Theories and Tests of Liability.
§ 7.3   Departure from Design Specifications.
§ 7.4   Product Malfunction.
§ 7.5   Food and Drink.

―――――

§ 7.1   MANUFACTURING DEFECTS— GENERALLY

Manufacturing defects—flaws or irregularities in products arising from errors in production—give rise to the most basic type of products liability claim. The law governing production errors is now quite settled, and it fairly may be viewed as the first pillar of modern products liability law. In general, manufacturers and other suppliers are liable for injuries caused by manufacturing defects in products that they sell.

The misalignment of a punch press may result in a jagged burr along a product's metal edge, the maladjustment of a nut on a bolt may interfere with a machine's operation, and the failure to prevent foreign matter from entering food or drink may cause its contamination. When the manufacturing process goes awry, the resulting products may fail to meet the manufacturer's own design specification standards. If such a product escapes the manufacturer's quality controls, its flawed condition may lead to its failure during use, to an accident, and possibly to an injury to the user or another.

Keeler v. Richards Mfg. Co., Inc., 817 F.2d 1197 (5th Cir. 1987) (Tex. law), which involved a surgical compression screw, is illustrative. The screw broke several months after a surgeon inserted it into the plaintiff's broken hip to assist the healing process. In the plaintiff's action against the manufacturer, her experts testified that the screw had four irregularities they considered manufacturing defects, any one of which could have caused the failure by increasing stress concentrations that could have led to fatigue failure in the screw:

- The screw's internal threads were longer (1.1875 inches) than the maximum length (1.125 inches) specified in the blueprint specifications;

- The screw contained excessive metal debris that could have interfered with the surgeon's ability to compress the screw properly;

- Its radius was smaller than an exemplar screw furnished by the manufacturer; and

- It failed to comply with the 35% ductility standard of the American Society of Testing Materials.

The jury concluded that the screw was defectively manufactured, and the court upheld this determination on appeal.

Manufacturing defect claims possess certain advantages for plaintiffs over claims involving design and warning defects. First, manufacturing defect claims are normally less expensive because they challenge only a single product unit rather than a company's entire line of products. In addition, quite unlike design and warning cases, the liability standards for manufacturing defects—departure from intended design and product malfunction—are truly "strict." Moreover, manufacturing defect claims may be immune from certain types of requirements, limitations, or defenses applicable to other types of claims.

A manufacturer may breach its duty to manufacture nondefective products in various ways. Raw materials or components used to construct the product may contain physical flaws, such as the defective wooden spoke of the car wheel in *MacPherson v. Buick Motor Co.*, 111 N.E. 1050 (N.Y. 1916). Or a product may become damaged or contaminated during construction, or a mistake may be made in how its components are assembled into final form. For example, a product's ingredients may deviate from their specified formulation; or its rivets, welds, screws, bolts, or nuts used to hold the components together may be improperly made, applied, inserted, or attached, weakening the product's structure. After assembly, an otherwise properly produced product may not be finished sufficiently, leaving its edges too rough, too sharp, or otherwise hazardous. Finally, a properly assembled and finished product may become defective because of a dangerous flaw in its package or container.

The quality control process is designed to catch such manufacturing mistakes, but sometimes it fails to do so. And while insufficient quality assurance may provide the basis for a claim of negligence, a manufacturer's failure to adequately inspect or test its products is not itself a strict products liability claim. For a more thorough examination of manufacturing defects, see Owen, Products Liability Law ch.7 (2d ed. 2008).

§ 7.2   THEORIES AND TESTS OF LIABILITY

Manufacturing defects may generate any number of products liability claims. For example, a manufacturer may misrepresent the purity of its products or a supplier of contaminated food or drink may be negligent per se for violating a pure food statute. More commonly, however, a seller of a defectively manufactured product is subject to liability under one or more of the three primary products liability theories of recovery—negligence, breach of implied warranty, and strict liability in tort.

Negligence

In earlier times, most products liability cases for manufacturing defects were brought in negligence, including *MacPherson v. Buick Motor Co.*, 111 N.E. 1050 (N.Y. 1916), discussed above. Indeed, until the development of the doctrine of strict products liability in tort in the 1960s, most products liability cases were manufacturing defect cases brought in negligence. Because negligence is much more difficult to prove than strict liability in manufacturing defect cases, negligence claims in such cases are less common today than formerly. Nevertheless, negligent manufacturing (including negligent testing and quality control) remains a viable basis of products liability recovery in almost every state.

Because of the difficulties in proving the specific manufacturing mistake that caused a production flaw in an accident product, together with the likelihood that any such mistake was the result of the manufacturer's negligence, courts commonly allow juries to infer negligence from proof of a manufacturing flaw alone. See *Jenkins v. General Motors Corp.*, 446 F.2d 377 (5th Cir. 1971) (Ga. law) (improper tightening of nut on bolt in rear suspension system).

Strict Liability

Even if manufacturers exercise due care, they generally are strictly liable—in warranty as well as tort—for injuries caused by production defects in products they make and sell.

Warranty

The earliest approach the modern law employed to enforce production quality, now in effect for about two centuries, was to *imply* into the exchange transaction a promise or warranty by the seller of the basic, uniform soundness—safety, in this context—of its goods. Today, the implied warranty of merchantability provides buyers a general guarantee, enforceable under UCC § 2–314, against manufacturing defects in the goods they buy. Less frequently, the sale of a defectively manufactured product may breach an express warranty or the implied warranty of fitness for particular purpose.

Strict Liability in Tort

The doctrine of strict liability in tort, which evolved out of warranty cases involving manufacturing defects, is particularly well-suited to claims for injuries caused by manufacturing defects. A majority of the earliest cases adopting § 402A of the *Restatement (Second) of Torts* in the mid–1960s involved manufacturing defects, and strict liability in tort remains the preferred basis of recovery in manufacturing defect cases generally and under § 2(a) of the *Restatement (Third) of Torts: Products Liability* in particular.

§ 7.3   DEPARTURE FROM DESIGN SPECIFICATIONS

For many years, courts and commentators considered the meaning of the "manufacturing defect" concept so self-evident as to be self-defining. A defect in manufacture simply meant that through some mistake in the production process the product was rendered "defective." Thus, until quite recently, judicial decisions involving this form of defect generally failed to provide a definitional "test" of liability for such defects. Even today, most courts simply do not bother to define the term. See *Bell v. T.R. Miller Mill Co.*, 768 So.2d 953 (Ala. 2000) (telephone pole made of rotten wood); *Sanders v. Hartville Milling Co.*, 14 S.W.3d 188 (Mo. Ct. App. 2000) (toxins in animal feed).

Products Liability Restatement § 2(a) provides that a product "contains a manufacturing defect when the product *departs from its intended design* even though all possible care was exercised in the preparation and marketing of the product," and an increasing number of courts have used some form of this standard for defining manufacturing defectiveness, some expressly relying on § 2(a). In addition, several states have enacted statutes defining manufacturing defects by some formulation of the *departure-from-design* theme. Mississippi's statute is the most concise, providing for liability if a product was "defective because it deviated in a material way from the manufacturer's specifications or from otherwise identical units manufactured to the same manufacturing specifications." Miss. Code Ann. § 11–1–63(a)(i)(1).

§ 7.4 PRODUCT MALFUNCTION

When a manufacturing defect causes a product accident, a plaintiff usually can prove the defect and its causal relation to the manufacturer and the accident largely by direct evidence—as by testimony from an expert that the accident product was manufactured by the defendant and contained an identifiable production flaw, deviating from design specifications, that caused the product to fail in a particular manner. Yet, sometimes the specific cause of a malfunction disappears in an accident, as when the product blows up, burns up, is otherwise severely damaged, or is thereafter lost. Other times, products simply malfunction, and mysteriously so, leaving no tangible trace of how or why they failed. In all such situations, where direct evidence is unavailable, most courts do *not* require proof of the specific defect causing the malfunction but, instead, allow proof of defect by circumstantial evidence.

In negligence law, if the specific cause of a product malfunction is unknown, the doctrine of *res ipsa loquitur* allows a jury to infer the manufacturer's negligence when the circumstances of the accident suggest that the product was negligently manufactured or designed. For strict liability cases, courts at an early date developed principles similar to those that underlie *res ipsa* into a separate doctrine for proving claims in strict products liability. Dubbed the "malfunction theory" (or "indeterminate" or "general" defect theory), these special principles of circumstantial evidence now provide a widely accepted means for proving defectiveness in cases where direct evidence of defectiveness is unavailable.

Under the *malfunction doctrine*, a plaintiff may establish a prima facie case of product defect by proving that the product failed in normal use under circumstances suggesting a product defect. Put otherwise, a product defect may be inferred by circumstantial evidence that:

- The product malfunctioned;
- The malfunction occurred during proper use; and
- The product had not been altered or misused in a manner that probably caused the malfunction.

Less formally, the malfunction doctrine holds that a plaintiff need not establish that a specific defect caused an accident if circumstantial evidence permits an inference that the product, in one way or another, probably was defective.

Applicability

The malfunction doctrine has been applied to malfunctions of a wide range of products, such as when a bottle of soda pop, glass baby bottle, transformer, gas grill, or propane fuel canister explodes; a bottle of ketchup, jar of peanuts, an automatic coffee maker's glass carafe, or a silicone breast implant breaks apart; a television, clothes dryer, dishwasher, portable heater, combine, refrigerator, or an electric blanket catches fire; a crutch, grain auger, football helmet, or ladder collapses; a crane drops its load; the blade guard of a power circular saw fails to close; a winch cable snaps; and many other situations in which products have inexplicably malfunctioned. This doctrine frequently is applied to cases involving automotive vehicles—such as when the brakes or steering suddenly fail; a vehicle inexplicably accelerates, changes gears, catches fire, or rolls over; a new tire explodes; or an airbag fails to deploy, deploys improperly, or spews acid on an occupant.

A good motor vehicle example is *Ducko v. Chrysler Motors Corp.*, 639 A.2d 1204 (Pa. Super. Ct. 1994), in which the plaintiff was driving a new Chrysler on a dry road at 55 mph when the car suddenly jerked to the right, the steering locked, and the brakes failed to respond. The car crashed, and the plaintiff broke her back. No specific defect could be found in the vehicle. The plaintiffs' expert concluded that the accident was caused by a transient malfunction of the power system for the steering and brakes, whereas Chrysler's expert postulated that the accident resulted from driver error. Because the plaintiff could not prove the specific defect that caused the crash, the trial court entered summary judgment for the defendant.

Based on the malfunction doctrine, the superior court reversed and remanded for trial, holding that a plaintiff need *not* establish a *specific* defect to prove a manufacturing defect but may establish a case-in-chief by proving: (1) that the product malfunctioned, and (2) the absence of likely causes other than product defect—which the court styled "abnormal use or reasonable, secondary causes for the malfunction." Because circumstantial evidence of this type would permit a jury to infer that the product probably was defective at the time of sale, the trial court's grant of summary judgment to Chrysler improperly kept the jury from determining the cause of the accident—whether driver error or, based on the plaintiff's testimony of steering and braking problems, some defect in the car.

Limitations

When a plaintiff successfully invokes the malfunction doctrine, a permissible inference arises that a defect caused the malfunction, an inference that the defendant has no obligation (and often has no evidence) to rebut. The plaintiff still has the burden of proving—by the *probabilities*, not just the possibilities—both defectiveness and causation; the doctrine merely provides a circumstantial method by which these elements may be proved in the limited class of cases in which direct evidence is unavailable for some good reason.

Acceptance

Having spread across the nation with little fanfare over the last half century, the malfunction doctrine has become a well-established precept of modern products liability law. A substantial and growing majority of American jurisdictions (usually *without* the "malfunction doctrine" label) now accept this principle of circumstantial evidence for proving defectiveness in strict products liability. Certifying its widespread acceptance, the *Products Liability Restatement* endorsed the principle in § 3. In a proper case (such as when a new appliance explodes or catches fire), it is difficult to see how any jurisdiction could reject some properly formulated version of this simple, well-established canon of circumstantial evidence.

§ 7.5 FOOD AND DRINK

Defective food and drink can kill or injure human beings in myriad ways. The types of defects in different foods span the gamut, from spoiled meat, particles of glass in ice cream; ptomaine poison in a can of pork and beans; a piece of metal in a meatball; arsenic in biscuit flour; tacks or wire in a loaf of bread; clam shells in a bowl of chowder or in fried clam strips; a crustaceous creature in a can of mackerel; strychnine in a box of candy; a metal screw in chewing gum; and glass, dead flies, worms, condoms, and mice in Coca–Cola and other soft drinks, not to mention contaminated water and soft drink bottles that explode. But the prize for the most repulsive "food" item sold to a consumer probably should be awarded for a can of chewing tobacco containing a human toe. See *Pillars v. R.J. Reynolds Tobacco Co.*, 78 So. 365 (Miss. 1918).

Theories of Recovery

Negligence

Often, the easiest way for a plaintiff to establish negligence in a bad food case is by proof of a violation of a pure food act, which in many states amounts to *negligence per se*. But without the assistance of a pure food act, a plaintiff may have difficulty proving the negligence of the purveyor of defective food. This is particularly true in the case of a food product retailer who purchases the food and then resells it in a sealed container, a situation that deprives the seller of any opportunity to inspect for defects. But, in other cases, the seller's fault is clear. See *Bullara v. Checker's Drive–In Rest., Inc.*, 736 So.2d 936 (La. Ct. App. 1999) (allowing cockroach to enter chili dog, failing to discover roach lurking in dog prior to sale, and making sale to customer of roach-infested dog); *Flagstar Enters., Inc. v. Davis*, 709 So.2d 1132 (Ala. 1997) (allowing blood from worker's unbandaged cut to spill into take-out order of biscuit and gravy).

Warranty

While the sealed-container doctrine, privity, and other sales law restrictions may sometimes limit the reach of warranty claims, courts have long and widely used warranty law to provide relief to persons injured by defective food and drink. See *Van Bracklin v. Fonda*, 12 Johns. 468 (N.Y. 1815) (diseased beef); Elliott v. Kraft Foods N. Am., Inc., 118 S.W.3d 50 (Tex. App. 2003) (rocks in Grape Nuts cereal); *CEF Enters., Inc. v. Betts*, 838 So.2d 999 (Miss. Ct. App. 2003) (insect in Burger King biscuit).

Strict Liability in Tort

While negligence and warranty claims are still frequently asserted in foodstuff cases, various advantages of strict liability in tort make this doctrine the preferred theory of recovery in most such cases.

See *Davila v. Goya Foods, Inc.*, 2007 WL 415147 (S.D.N.Y. 2007) (glass fragments in can of octopus); *Hickman v. William Wrigley, Jr. Co.*, 768 So.2d 812 (La. Ct. App. 2000) (metal screw in stick of chewing gum).

To recover for injuries from ingesting food or drink, a plaintiff must establish that the food contained some dangerous element that rendered it unwholesome or "defective." Thus, a food or beverage item generally is defective, and a seller generally is subject to liability if the food product's condition is dangerous in a manner neither intended by the seller nor expected by the consumer—that it was unwholesome, unfit for human consumption, adulterated, or contained a foreign or otherwise dangerous substance of a type that consumers generally do not expect.

The Foreign/Natural Doctrine

A number of older warranty cases applied strict liability, holding that food was unfit for human consumption, in cases involving foods contaminated with *foreign* substances such as glass, stones, wires, nails, or foods that were tainted, decayed, diseased, or infected. Yet, courts were reluctant to find foods unfit if they contained hazards that were *natural* to the food, such as a chicken pie with a chicken bone, a cherry pie with a cherry pit, or T-bone steaks or beef stew with bones "natural to the type of meat served." The idea was that consumers may fairly be held to anticipate and guard against such naturally occurring risks. This distinction developed into the "foreign/natural" test or doctrine. Yet the foreign/natural doctrine never was adopted in more than a handful of jurisdictions.

Shift to a Consumer Expectations Test

As criticism of the foreign/natural doctrine accelerated in recent decades, courts increasingly adopted a reasonable consumer expectations standard, often explicitly rejecting the foreign/natural doctrine, for determining the defectiveness of food. See *Kolarik v. Cory Int'l Corp.*, 721 N.W.2d 159 (Iowa 2006) (rejecting foreign/natural test and adopting reasonable expectations test endorsed by *Third Restatement*); Rest. (3d) § 7 (same).

CHAPTER 8

DESIGN DEFECTS

Table of Sections

§ 8.1   Design Defects—Generally.
§ 8.2   Theories and Tests of Liability.
§ 8.3   The Consumer Expectations Test.
§ 8.4   The Risk–Utility Test.
§ 8.5   Proof of a Reasonable Alternative Design.
§ 8.6   Combining Consumer Expectations and Risk–Utility.
§ 8.7   Constructive Knowledge—The Wade–Keeton Test.
§ 8.8   The Third Restatement.
§ 8.9   Optional Safety Devices.
§ 8.10 Prescription Drugs and Medical Devices.

———

§ 8.1 DESIGN DEFECTS—GENERALLY

The concept of design defectiveness is the heart of products liability law. Just as strict liability in tort is the dominant liability theory in major products liability litigation, design defectiveness is the dominant claim in most major products liability cases. Yet finding an acceptable definition for what constitutes a "defective" design is a difficult task.

A manufacturer's design determinations involve a multitude of safety-related choices, including decisions on the types and strengths of raw materials and component parts, the manner in which such materials and parts are combined, whether safety devices will be included, and the overall product concept. A frequent claim of design defectiveness is the absence of some type of adequate safety device, such as a housing surrounding a power lawnmower, a mechanical guard or electrical interlock cut-off device on a dangerous machine, or a "safety" on a gun. Much automotive products liability litigation challenges the design of motor vehicles, including the extent to which their designs are sufficiently "crashworthy" to provide their occupants adequate protection in the event of a crash. See ch. 17, below.

In addition to such typical design danger claims, numerous other forms of design hazards may give rise to claims of defectiveness—such as allergenic latex gloves, fabrics not treated with flame retardant chemicals, drain cleaners comprised of unnecessarily caustic chemicals, products whose moving parts are made of metal too soft to last throughout the product's useful life, tampons that are too absorbent, coffee that is too hot, raw asbestos comprised of toxic fibers, and tell-tale mechanical heart valves that emit excessive noise.

Early in the evolution of products liability law, observers recognized that determining how and why a design danger should or should not be characterized as "defective" was at once the most important and the most baffling problem in this entire field of law. For this reason, much of the search for a general definition of "product defect," examined under the "strict liability in tort" umbrella in chapter 5, above, was in fact a search for the meaning of defectiveness in design. Thus, the discussions there supplement the defect "test" discussions here.

Determining how to evaluate the acceptability or defectiveness of a product's design is difficult in part because a product's design is the essence of what the manufacturer decides to make and sell. A manufacturing defect is truly a mistake, one which results from some fault in the production process whereby a particular product deviates from the manufacturer's own "blueprint" specifications of the intended and correct design. Quite to the contrary, a charge that a product is defective in design challenges those very specifications on the ground that the design engineers, in their conceptual rendition of the product, failed to take safety into adequate account.

Challenging a product's design thus challenges the decision of the manufacturer's engineers and managers to develop and sell a product containing a particular type and level of danger. Unlike a manufacturing defect claim, which implicates merely a single product unit, a design defect claim challenges the integrity of the entire product line and so pierces to the very core of the manufacturer's enterprise. For this reason, design defect claims are of greatest concern to manufacturers, since a judicial declaration that the design of a particular product is "defective" condemns the entire product line. For a more thorough examination of design defects, see Owen, Products Liability Law ch. 8 (2d ed. 2008).

§ 8.2   THEORIES AND TESTS OF LIABILITY

Manufacturers and other sellers are subject to liability for defective design under each of the major theories of liability. Thus, as is true with respect to other types of defects, product suppliers are subject to liability in negligence, for negligently making and selling products that are defectively designed; in implied warranty, for selling products that are not fit for their ordinary purposes (and hence "unmerchantable") because they are defectively designed; and in strict liability in tort for simply selling products that are defective in design.

§ 8.3 THE CONSUMER EXPECTATIONS TEST

Prior to the development of strict products liability in tort, courts applying strict liability in *warranty* drew from the law of contracts, which protects a purchaser's expectations predictably generated by a product's appearance and a manufacturer's representations, express and implied. When Dean Prosser (Reporter for the *Restatement (Second) of Torts*) searched for a foundation for the new doctrine of strict liability in *tort*, it was only natural that he would turn to the same consumer expectations basis of the warranty law cases that provided the sole authority (except for *Greenman*) for the new tort doctrine.

It was also natural for the courts, in beginning to apply § 402A to design defect cases, to adopt the warranty-based definition of liability provided in that section's comments. As seen in § 5.6, above, the comments to § 402A define "defective condition" and "unreasonably dangerous" as *dangerous beyond a consumer's contemplations.* Accordingly, most courts applying § 402A in the 1960s and 1970s concluded that design defectiveness under § 402A should be tested according to a standard of product safety gauged by "consumer expectations."

One of the few cases applying the consumer expectations standard to *allow* a design defect claim is *Jarke v. Jackson Products*, 631 N.E.2d 233 (Ill. App. Ct. 1994), which involved a welder's claim against the manufacturer of a welding mask for injuries from molten metal that spilled from the mask into his ear. The plaintiff was injured while squatting beneath an object he was welding overhead, with his head cocked to one side, when some molten metal dropped from above onto his mask, rolled down to the mask's side rim, which channeled it into his ear. The complaint alleged that the mask was defectively designed (1) because it did not provide ear guards to protect a user's ears; and (2) because the mask's overall configuration, including its side rim, could channel molten metal into a user's ears. Reasoning that the danger to a user's ears was obvious, the trial court granted the defendant manufacturer's motion for summary judgment, and the plaintiff appealed. Although the appellate court agreed that the obvious absence of an ear guard precluded a finding of design defectiveness under the consumer expectations test on that particular ground, it reversed and remanded on the issue of whether an ordinary person would understand that the mask's design itself created the means for molten slag to be channeled into a user's ear.

Problems

Though the consumer expectations standard was conventionally viewed as more protective to plaintiffs than the risk-utility standard, courts have used the consumer expectations test most frequently to *deny* recovery to plaintiffs in cases involving obvious design hazards. Obvious dangers—such as the risk to human limbs from an unguarded power mower or industrial machine—are virtually always contemplated or expected by the user or consumer who thereby is necessarily unprotected by the consumer expectations test, no matter how probable or severe the likely danger or how easy and cheap the means of avoiding it. In such cases, the buyer got what he or she paid for, or the user engaged a danger that he or she expected, so that the risk of injury shifts to the buyer or user who chose to accept it, or to a third-party victim who had no say in the matter at all. The failure of the consumer expectations test to deal adequately with the obvious danger problem profoundly weakens the usefulness of the test as the sole basis for determining defects in design.

Another significant limitation on the usefulness of consumer expectations as a liability standard in design cases is the problem of identifying whose expectations should control in cases where the buyer or user controls the safety of other persons, such as children, patients, or employees. Finally is the problem of vagueness in a consumer's expectations concerning most complex designs. All these problems are discussed in § 5.6, above, and the vagueness problem is further explored in § 8.6, below.

Current Role

Although the consumer expectations test is now considerably weakened, it is far from dead. Even in a risk-utility regime, consumer expectations may be considered together with the other evaluative factors and occasionally can even be conclusive of design defect determinations. In addition, the consumer expectations standard is still widely accepted as the most appropriate test for food and used product cases. The consumer expectations test still plays some role as a liability standard for design defectiveness in roughly half the states by common law (e.g., Conn., N.H., Wis.) or statute (e.g., N.D., Ohio, Tenn.), and a related standard, at least in name, exists in Europe. See Kysar, *The Expectations of Consumers*, 103 Colum. L. Rev. 1700 (2003); Phillips, *Consumer Expectations*, 53 S.C. L. Rev. 1047 (2002).

§ 8.4 THE RISK–UTILITY TEST

While liability for design defects was more commonly based on the consumer expectations test in the 1960s and early 1970s, even during these early years some courts saw the wisdom of assessing design defectiveness according to whether the safety benefits of remedying a design danger were worth the costs. As numbers of courts over the decades have turned away from the consumer expectations test in design danger cases, they have substituted some form of cost-benefit ("risk-utility," "risk-benefit," or "benefit-risk") standard of liability. At the start of the new millennium, despite the tenacity of consumer expectations in a decreasing (yet surprisingly large) number of jurisdictions, the risk-utility test appears to have become America's preferred test for design defectiveness.

The risk-utility test is often determinative of design defectiveness under all three theories of recovery—negligence, strict liability in tort, and even implied warranty—because the balance of cost, safety, and utility of precautions is fundamental to the sufficiency of a product's design.

Cost–Benefit Analysis and the Hand Formula

The fundamentals of the risk-utility test were examined earlier, in the discussions of negligence and strict liability in tort, but they should be reviewed here, too. An analytical technique explicitly relied upon by Benjamin Franklin and Oliver Wendell Holmes, cost-benefit analysis is as old as rational thought. All deliberative decisions involve a weighing of the advantages (benefits) and disadvantages (costs) of a contemplated course of action.

Whether a particular *design* danger is "unreasonable" (that is, "defective") involves "a balancing of the probability and seriousness of harm against the costs of taking precautions. Relevant factors to be considered include the availability of alternative designs, the cost and feasibility of adopting alternative designs, and the frequency or infrequency of injury resulting from the design." *Raney v. Honeywell, Inc.*, 540 F.2d 932, 935 (8th Cir. 1976) (Iowa law). The frequency of injury often is affected by whether the danger is hidden from and thereby unexpected by consumers or whether it is instead open and obvious, warned about, or commonly known.

A product's design is "defective" under a risk-utility (cost-benefit) test if the costs of avoiding a particular hazard are foreseeably less than the resulting safety benefits. In other words, if the *safety benefits* from preventing the danger that harmed the plaintiff were foreseeably greater than its *precaution costs*, the product's design is defective under a cost-benefit standard of liability.

The cost-benefit test, in balancing the safety benefits of avoiding a particular risk against the avoidance costs ("burdens"), is especially well suited to establishing the safety or defectiveness of a product design. The type and degree of design safety required in any situation depends on the type, likelihood, and amount of harm (viewed together as the magnitude of the risk) that a particular burden of precaution (of a particular cost) may be expected to prevent. If the risk posed by the design of a product in a certain manner is great, greater precautions must be taken to avert the risk; if the risk is small, less precaution is required. This principle of balance, inherent in tort law generally, is sometimes referred to as the "calculus of risk."

The most celebrated formulation of the risk-benefit test was provided by Judge Learned Hand in *United States v. Carroll Towing Co.*, 159 F.2d 169 (2d Cir. 1947), previously discussed. Applied to design defectiveness, the strict liability version of the Hand formula, as discussed in § 5.7, above, may be stated:

$$\mathbf{B < P \times L \ \Rightarrow \ D}$$

In cost-benefit terms, the formula states:

(Accident Prevention) Costs < (Safety) Benefits ⇒ Defect

In short, a product's design defectiveness is suggested if the safety benefits of an untaken design precaution foreseeably exceed its costs.

Most appellate courts formulate the risk-utility test more broadly in terms of whether a *product*'s risks are greater than its benefits or utility. While such a formulation may appear harmless at first glance, it is logically misleading and in fact conflicts with how the law is actually applied. As discussed in § 8.5, below, the proper issue that is almost always litigated in trial courtrooms is the narrow "*micro-*

balance" of pros and cons of a manufacturer's failure to adopt some alternative design *feature* that
would have prevented the plaintiff's harm—that is,
whether the costs of changing the design in some
particular ("micro") manner would have been
worth the resulting safety benefits.

In designing products, manufacturers properly
consider such factors as usefulness, cost, and profit-
ability. What the cost-benefit formula requires is
that manufacturers also consider risks of injury to
consumers and bystanders and weigh the interests
of those parties equally to its own interest in maximizing profits. That is, the risk-utility formula
ensures that manufacturers, in legislating for consumers the proper mix of a product's costs and
benefits, include in the balance a proportionate
consideration of the various hazards in the product's particular design. Tying the measure of precaution to the measure of risk, the risk-utility test
demands only that a manufacturer adopt design
precautions proportionate to the magnitude of the
expected risk. In this manner, the risk-utility test
succinctly captures the commonsense idea that a
product's design is unacceptably dangerous if it
contains a danger that may cost-effectively (and
practicably) be removed.

Burdens, Benefits, and Utility;
the Wade Factors

Over-broad formulations of risk-utility analysis
for design defect decisionmaking are traceable to a
widely quoted set of liability factors proposed in an

early, influential article by John Wade, *On the Nature of Strict Tort Liability for Products*, 44 Miss. L.J. 825, 837–38 (1973), which proposed that courts consider a broad list of factors:

(1) The product's "usefulness and desirability";

(2) Its "safety aspects";

(3) The "availability of a substitute product";

(4) Whether a particular danger can be eliminated inexpensively and without impairing the product's utility;

(5) Whether users can avoid the danger by careful use;

(6) Whether the danger is obvious, warned of, or commonly known; and

(7) The feasibility of loss-spreading by insurance and pricing.

The Wade factors are problematic for a variety of reasons, and modern design defect jurisprudence has moved well beyond the place it was when Dean Wade conceived it at the time § 402A was getting off the ground. Indeed, modern courts rarely do little more than pay lip service to the Wade factors, which are simply past their prime. Typically, courts recite the factors and then move on to a narrow cost-benefit analysis of some particular design feature the plaintiff offered as a safer alternative design. See *Nunnally v. R.J. Reynolds Tobacco Co.*, 869 So.2d 373 (Miss. 2004); *Irion v. Sun Lighting, Inc.*, 2004 WL 746823 (Tenn. Ct. App. 2004); *In re*

September 11 Litigation, 265 F.Supp.2d 208 (S.D.N.Y. 2003).

§ 8.5 PROOF OF A REASONABLE ALTERNATIVE DESIGN

Just as design defectiveness lies at the center of products liability law, cost-benefit analysis of an *alternative design* lies at the heart of design defectiveness. As just discussed, the purpose of risk-utility analysis is to determine "whether the risk of injury might have been reduced or avoided if the manufacturer had used a feasible alternative design." *McCarthy v. Olin Corp.*, 119 F.3d 148, 155 (2d Cir. 1997) (N.Y. law). Indeed, "one simply cannot talk meaningfully about a risk-benefit defect until and unless one has identified some design alternative (including any design omission) that can serve as the basis for a risk-benefit analysis." G. Schwartz, *Foreword: Understanding Products Liability*, 67 Cal. L. Rev. 435, 468 (1979).

Examples

The great majority of design defect cases have involved proof by the plaintiff of a feasible alternative design—proof of some practicable, cost-effective, untaken design precaution that would have prevented the plaintiff's harm, such as:

- A commercial coffee urn that exploded, where the explosion could have been prevented by a simple reducing valve;

- A tractor steering wheel made of rubber and fiber that broke in the hands of the driver, causing him to fall under the tractor, where wood or metal would not have broken;

- A vaporizer that overheated and caught fire when the water boiled away, where a simple cut-off device would have prevented the fire;

- A moving metal mechanism under the arm-rest of a lawn chair that amputated a user's finger, where a simple housing would have shielded the mechanism;

- A drain cleaner comprised of chemicals that were highly corrosive to human skin, where an altered formulation would have been safer and better at cleaning drains;

- A Dalkon Shield IUD that had a multifilament tail string, facilitating migration of bacteria into the uterus, where a single filament would have minimized the risk;

- An industrial machine with a sharp edge that cut a worker, where the sharp edge served no purpose and could easily have been rounded smooth;

- A small Playskool play block that asphyxiated a baby, where a slightly larger size would have been too big to swallow; and

- A truck liftgate equipped with a single hydraulic cylinder that was prone to collapse, causing the liftgate to fall where a second cylinder would have eliminated the risk.

Without affirmative proof of a feasible design alternative, a plaintiff usually cannot establish that a product's design is defective. Put otherwise, there typically is nothing wrong with a product that simply possesses inherent dangers that cannot feasibly be designed away.

Recognizing the central role of an alternative design to design defectiveness, many courts, perhaps most, hold that proof of a feasible design alternative is generally, or always, a necessary element of design defectiveness. See *General Motors Corp. v. Edwards*, 482 So.2d 1176, 1191 (Ala. 1985) ("In order to prove defectiveness, the plaintiff must prove that a safer, practical, alternative design was available to the manufacturer."). Yet, some jurisdictions (e.g., Colo., Conn, Kan., Neb., N.H., Or.)— sometimes noting the value of proof of a feasible alternative design, other times observing how difficult and costly a requirement of such proof would be for plaintiffs—explicitly reject any idea that proof of an alternative design is a necessary element of a plaintiff's design defect case. See *Smith v. Brown & Williamson Tobacco Corp.*, 2007 WL 2175034 (Mo. Ct. App. 2007); *Potter v. Ford Motor Co.*, 213 S.W.3d 264 (Tenn. Ct. App. 2006).

Risk–Utility Analysis of an Alternative Design

Although the risk-utility issue in design defect cases is frequently framed vaguely in terms of a balance between the risks and benefits of the "product," as mentioned earlier and discussed further below, the true cost-benefit issue litigated in almost every case is much narrower—whether the safety benefits of altering the product's design in a particular manner would foreseeably have exceeded the costs of the alteration. Risk-utility analysis is focused, in other words, on the costs and benefits of the specific alternative design feature proposed by the plaintiff. The relevant *benefits* of a proposed alternative design are limited to the aggregate *safety* benefits to people suffering injury and property damage in accidents of a similar type to that which harmed the plaintiff. But the *costs* of an alternative design feature more diversely may include: (1) the monetary costs of adopting the alternative design for all such products; (2) any loss of usefulness in the product that the design alteration may cause; and (3) any new dangers that the design feature may introduce.

Dollar Costs

The risk-utility (cost-benefit) issue often is conceptually quite simple: whether the aggregate dollar costs of adding some safety feature proposed by the plaintiff is or is not outweighed by the aggregate benefit of preventing foreseeable accidents like that which injured the plaintiff. So, if a proposed alternative safety feature would be expensive to adopt, and if it would be unlikely to produce substantial safety benefits, it is not required. But a manufacturer will fail the risk-utility test if it does not adopt a relatively inexpensive safety feature that could appreciably improve a product's safety, as by incorporating a child-resistant feature in a utility lighter for less than 5¢ per lighter; installing a $2.50 shield made of shatterproof glass over a pressure gauge to protect a person's eyes; or installing a $3 shield over the rear of a power mower. And even if adding a child-proof device to a disposable butane cigarette lighter increases its cost by as much as 60%–75%, raising its price to that extent may be worth the benefit of substantially reducing the massive losses regularly caused by children playing with lighters not equipped with such a device. See *Griggs v. BIC Corp.*, 981 F.2d 1429 (3d Cir. 1992) (Pa. law).

Utility Costs

Risk-utility analysis of a plaintiff's proposed alternative design requires consideration of another significant cost—any reduction in the product's usefulness. Adding a guard to a punch press may help to keep out hands, but it may preclude the operator from feeding large sheets of metal into the press and may slow down production. Child-proofing tops of medicines and household cleansers will reduce the number of small children poisoned by such products, but childproof designs make such products useless to older persons whose hands are weakened by arthritis. Adding flame repellant chemicals to fabrics used for clothing will protect against fabric fire injuries, but such chemicals may decrease a fabric's comfort and durability, may make it more difficult to wash out odors, and may make the fabric more prone to wrinkle and more difficult to dry. Many hazards are serious enough that sacrificing a little product usefulness in exchange for greater safety makes good sense. But people buy and use products to help them with their labors and to give them satisfaction, so that sacrifices in a product's utility are important costs that must be carefully evaluated in balancing the costs and benefits of a proposed alternative design.

Safety Costs

Another important (though less common) cost in the risk-utility evaluation of a plaintiff's proposed alternative design is the possibility that it may introduce *new* dangers into the product. For example, airbags of various designs protect adults in certain collisions, but they may kill or injure small children in other situations—possibly causing more harm than good. Any new dangers that a proposed alternative design is likely to create are important costs which must be balanced against the alternative design's safety benefits, such that the ultimate safety function in the calculus becomes the overall (net) safety *improvement* from the alternative design.

The "Feasibility" of the Alternative Design

An "alternative" design implies a reasonable choice between available designs. A safety feature that a plaintiff claims a product should have carried can fairly be considered a design "alternative" only if there was a practical means by which a manufacturer reasonably could have adopted such a safety feature at the time the product was designed and sold. Thus, the plaintiff must prove that an alternative design, offered to show that the manufacturer's chosen design was defective, was "feasible."

Because the feasibility of an alternative design suggests that the design feature proposed by the plaintiff was technologically and commercially practicable, feasibility is often bound up in the issue of "state of the art." Feasibility requires at least technological capability, but it normally is viewed more broadly to include cost, commercial practicability (including practicable availability of materials and components), and even the likelihood of consumer acceptance. Viewed in this expanded fashion, "feasibility" really means "reasonableness," as reflected in the *Products Liability Restatement* § 2(b) definition of a design defect in terms of the availability of a "reasonable alternative design."

§ 8.6   COMBINING CONSUMER EXPECTATIONS AND RISK–UTILITY

Evolving separately from the law of warranty and the law of negligence, the consumer expectations and risk-utility tests of design defectiveness developed largely as rival theories of design defect liability. More recently, however, reflecting the combined warranty–tort heritage of products liability law, and because of inadequacies in consumer expectations as an exclusive standard, many courts have begun to blend the two tests in one way or another.

The two principal approaches for blending the two standards are: (1) defining one test in terms of the other; or (2) establishing each as separate liability "prongs," either one of which may independently support a design defect finding. Some jurisdictions which embrace the two-pronged approach have recently begun to narrow the applicability of the consumer expectations prong to product designs viewed as "simple."

Defining One Test in Terms of the Other— The *Potter* Approach

Potter v. Chicago Pneumatic Tool Co., 694 A.2d 1319, 1333 (Conn. 1997), was a case brought by workers at a shipyard against the manufacturers of pneumatic hand tools for injuries the workers claimed were caused by excessive vibration of the tools. Although the consumer expectations test was well established in Connecticut, the court was nevertheless troubled by the vagueness problem in consumer expectations concerning the safety of complex designs. Following jurisdictions like Washington "that have modified their formulation of the consumer expectation test by incorporating risk-utility factors into the ordinary consumer expectation analysis," the *Potter* court reformulated its consumer expectations test in risk-utility terms. That is, particularly with complex products, consumers reasonably expect manufacturers to make fair and reasonable risk-utility decisions in designing their products. Other courts (e.g., Kan., N.H., Or.) have adopted similar "blended" approaches.

Two Liability "Prongs"—The *Barker* Approach

A more forthright and intelligible approach for accommodating the warranty and tort law foundations of strict manufacturer liability, which acknowledges the separate value of each, holds a manufacturer accountable for breaching its duties under either one by recognizing two independent bases or "prongs" of liability. By such a "two-pronged" approach to design defectiveness, a plaintiff injured by a product may establish a design defect if it fails *either* (1) the consumer expectations test, *or* (2) the risk-utility test. This approach has logical appeal because it protects the essential interests furthered by each test: contract law's protection of the expectations of buyers and sellers in their private bargains, and tort law's protection of the public welfare by requiring sellers to accord due respect to the interests of persons foreseeably endangered by defective products.

Barker v. Lull Engineering Co., 573 P.2d 443 (Cal. 1978), was the first judicial formulation of an explicitly two-pronged definition of design defectiveness. While operating a high-lift loader manufactured by the defendant, the plaintiff was struck by a piece of lumber when he leaped from the vehicle as his load began to shift. Plaintiff's strict liability in tort claim alleged that the loader's design was deficient because it was not equipped with stabilizing outriggers, a seatbelt, a roll bar, or an automatic locking device on the leveling lever. The jury found for the defendant, and plaintiff appealed. Reversing because of defects in the design defect jury instruction, the court ruled that a product may be defective in design:

(1) If the plaintiff demonstrates that the product failed to perform as safely as an ordinary consumer would expect when used in an intended or reasonably foreseeable manner, or

(2) If the plaintiff proves that the product's design proximately caused his injury and the defendant fails to prove, in light of the relevant factors, that on balance the benefits of the challenged design outweigh the risk of danger inherent in such design.

Among other factors relevant to the risk-utility prong of this test, the court listed the likelihood and gravity of danger posed by the challenged design, "the mechanical feasibility of a safer alternative design, the financial cost of an improved design, and the adverse consequences to the product and to the consumer that would result from an alternative design." Id. at 455.

As for the burden of proof, the *Barker* court left it on the plaintiff for the consumer expectations prong but shifted it to the manufacturer for the risk-utility prong. Observing that the doctrine of strict manufacturer liability in tort was designed to relieve injured plaintiffs of the evidentiary difficulties of proving a manufacturer's negligence, the court explained the shift in the burden of proof by noting that most risk-benefit evidence on the feasibility and cost of alternative designs involves "technical matters peculiarly within the knowledge of the manufacturer." Id.

A handful of states (Alaska, Ariz., Haw., Ill., Ohio, Tenn., Wash.) have explicitly followed *Barker*'s two-pronged definition of product defect. A few courts have danced around the issue, seemingly adopting the *Barker* two-pronged approach, but without saying so explicitly. A number of jurisdictions follow a *de facto Barker* approach, variously applying the consumer expectations and risk-utility tests in different cases, generally without explanation as to why one test is applied in one situation and the other test in another.

Yet most courts adopting *Barker*'s two-pronged approach, agreeing with most commentators, have rejected the shift in burden of proof as too radical a departure from the plaintiff's traditional responsibility to persuade the trier of fact of the merits of the case. Such jurisdictions thus continue to require the *plaintiff* to prove the feasibility and cost-effectiveness of an alternative design, together with other components of the risk-utility analysis.

Complex Designs—The *Soule* Approach

By the 1990s, it had become quite clear that the consumer expectations test was a poor gauge for ascertaining the adequacy of complex designs. In *Soule v. General Motors Corp.*, 882 P.2d 298 (Cal. 1994), the California Supreme Court squarely confronted the vagueness problem inherent in *Barker*'s consumer expectations prong. The plaintiff's ankles were fractured when the Chevrolet Camaro she was driving collided with another vehicle at a closing speed of 50–60 mph. She sued the manufacturer, asserting that the design of her automobile was defective because the left front wheel broke free, collapsed rearward, and smashed the toe pan and floorboard into her feet. In particular, she claimed that the configuration of the car's frame, and the bracket attaching the wheel assembly to it, were defectively designed because they did not limit the wheel's rearward travel in the event the bracket should fail.

At trial, the parties disagreed on the angle and force of the impact and the extent to which the toe pan had actually deformed. Design defectiveness and causation were addressed by numerous experts on biomechanics, metallurgy, orthopedics, design engineering, crash-test simulation, and other matters. The plaintiff's experts, relying on crash tests, metallurgical analysis, and other evidence, explained how the damage to her car would have been minimized had it been properly designed. The defendant's experts attempted to refute these claims by explaining how the plaintiff's ankle injuries were caused by the force of the collision and her failure to wear a seatbelt rather than any defect in the car. The trial court instructed the jury on the consumer expectations test, and the jury returned a verdict for the plaintiff.

On appeal, the Supreme Court reversed, holding that the trial court erred in instructing the jury on the consumer expectations test on the facts of the case. The court noted that a proper evaluation of the costs, benefits, and practicality inherent in complex designs normally requires risk-utility balancing rather than attempting to gauge consumer expectations. Cases involving simple design safety issues—such as whether a bus should be equipped with a "grab bar" in easy reach of passenger seats—are distinguishable because both consumers and jurors share an understanding of widely accepted minimum safety expectations for such products. Yet cases involving complex products often involve risks of injury that do not intelligibly engage the reasonable minimum safety expectations of consumers.

In automotive crashworthiness situations, consumers typically have "no idea" how safely their vehicles should have performed in the particular circumstances of the crash. In such cases, "the jury must consider the manufacturer's evidence of competing design considerations, and the issue of design defect cannot fairly be resolved by standardless reference to the 'expectations' of an 'ordinary consumer.' " Because safety expectations in such cases are vague, and because safety mechanisms are complex, juries must turn to "the balancing of risks and benefits required by the second prong of *Barker*." The *Soule* court thus concluded that the jury should *not* have been instructed on the consumer expectations test because the plaintiff's design defect theory involved complex technical and mechanical issues. Id. at 308–09.

Several other courts have adopted *Soule*'s approach of choosing a design defect test based on the complexity of the product's design, sometimes citing *Soule*, sometimes not. *Potter* effectively adopted the *Soule* approach, ruling that the true ("ordinary") consumer expectations test should be reserved for simple design cases, whereas the blended risk-utility version of the test should be used in complex design danger cases.

§ 8.7 CONSTRUCTIVE KNOWLEDGE— THE WADE–KEETON TEST

In the 1960s, products liability scholars began to search for a way to define strict liability in design (and warning) cases in a manner that distinguished the strict liability standard from mere negligence. As modern products liability law was just beginning to emerge in the 1960s, Deans Page Keeton of Texas and John Wade of Vanderbilt, both advisors to the ALI's *Restatement (Second) of Torts*, offered separate versions of a similar definition of product defectiveness that fundamentally distinguished negligence-based responsibility from liability called "strict." The test they developed, which in time became known as the "Wade–Keeton" test, quite simply was a negligence test stripped of its *scienter*.

Both Deans Wade and Keeton proposed defining defectiveness in terms of whether a manufacturer or other seller with full knowledge of its product's dangerous condition would be negligent in selling it in that condition. By requiring a seller to know its product's risks, commensurately relieving an injured plaintiff of the burden of proving the *foreseeability* of those risks, this test imposes on the seller "constructive knowledge" of any dangers its products may possess.

A number of courts, themselves searching for a basis by which to distinguish strict liability design (and warning) claims from those in negligence, adopted the Wade–Keeton hindsight test (sometimes referred to as the "prudent-manufacturer test"). For example, in *Phillips v. Kimwood Machine Co.*, 525 P.2d 1033, 1036 (Or. 1974), the court formulated the test as follows:

> A dangerously defective article would be one which a reasonable person would not put into the stream of commerce *if he had knowledge of its harmful character*. The test, therefore, is whether the seller would be negligent if he sold the article *knowing of the risk involved*. Strict liability imposes what amounts to constructive knowledge of the condition of the product.

By the 1980s, however, courts and commentators began to question the fairness and logic of imposing strict liability for design defectiveness, and the only other truly strict test of products liability, the consumer expectations test, had already begun its decline. Recognizing the problems in forcing truly strict liability on manufacturers for dangers in design, Deans Wade and Keeton, in the early 1980s, both repudiated the test that bore their names.

Despite the rejection of the Wade–Keeton test by the scholars who gave it birth, courts continued to adopt the test after its "official" demise in the early 1980s (e.g., N.Y.), and some have continued rotely to restate the test, and even proudly to reaffirm allegiance to it while knowing it has died (e.g., Ariz.). While one state legislature (Or.) reversed the judicial adoption of the Wade–Keeton test, another (Tenn.) appears to have affirmatively adopted it, and one wonders at its staying power in scattered decisions across the nation.

§ 8.8 THE THIRD RESTATEMENT

Products Liability Restatement § 1 provides that one who sells "a defective product is subject to liability for harm to persons or property caused by the defect." Section 2(b) explains that a product is "defective in design" if:

the foreseeable risks of harm posed by the product could have been reduced or avoided by the adoption of a reasonable alternative design by the seller or other distributor, or a predecessor in the commercial chain of distribution, and the omission of the alternative design renders the product not reasonably safe.

Paraphrased, § 2(b) says:

A product is defective in design if the seller failed to reduce the foreseeable risk that harmed the plaintiff by adopting a reasonable alternative design, the omission of which renders the product not reasonably safe.

By requiring that an alternative design be "reasonable," and basing a manufacturer's liability on its failure to adopt such an alternative design only if it renders the product "not reasonably safe," the *Third Restatement* rejects absolute safety in favor of optimality: "Society does not benefit from products that are excessively safe ... any more than it benefits from products that are too risky. Society benefits most when the right, or optimal, amount of product safety is achieved." Cmt. *a*. The risk-utility balance prescribed in § 2(b) for design defectiveness determinations ordinarily resolves into a negligence-style evaluation of the foreseeable costs and benefits of the manufacturer's decision to forego an alternative design:

> Subsection (b) adopts a reasonableness ("risk-utility balancing") test as the standard for judging the defectiveness of product designs. More specifically, the test is whether a reasonable alternative design would, at reasonable cost, have reduced the foreseeable risks of harm posed by the product and, if so, whether [its] omission ... rendered the product not reasonably safe. Cmt. *d*.

In making the relevant cost-benefit assessment, "[a] broad range of factors may be considered [balanced] in determining whether an alternative design is reasonable and whether its omission renders a product not reasonably safe," including the foreseeable risks of harm, consumer expectations, usefulness, cost, longevity, responsibility for maintenance, aesthetics, marketability, and other advantages and disadvantages of the chosen and alternative designs. Cmt. *f*.

A judge or jury must evaluate these factors with respect to both the accident product as designed and the alternative design feature put forward by the plaintiff. A product's design is "not reasonably safe," and hence is "defective," if a comparison between the accident product *without* the plaintiff's proposed safety feature and the alternative product *with* the proposed safety feature demonstrates that the balance of costs and benefits of the alternative design is better than the balance of these same factors in the chosen design that resulted in the accident. And the converse is also true: if the balance of competing design considerations in the accident product without the proposed safety feature was as good as or better than the balance in the proposed alternative design, then the accident product's design will be deemed "reasonably safe" and "nondefective."

"[T]he requirement of Subsection (b) that a product is defective in design if the foreseeable risks of harm could have been reduced by a reasonable alternative design is based on the commonsense notion that liability for harm caused by product designs should attach only when harm is reasonably preventable." Cmt. *f*.

Consumer Expectations

One of the most controversial aspects of the *Third Restatement*'s definition of design defectiveness concerns the elimination of consumer expectations as an *independent* test of liability, and the relegation of those expectations to mere "factor" status in the list of risk-utility considerations. Section § 2 cmt. *g* declares: "Under Subsection (b), consumer expectations do not constitute an independent standard for judging the defectiveness of product designs." Yet, "although consumer expectations do not constitute an independent standard for judging the defectiveness of product designs, they may substantially influence or even be ultimately determinative on risk-utility balancing in judging whether the omission of a proposed alternative design renders the product not reasonably safe." *Id.* Moreover, the *Restatement* makes clear that manufacturers and other sellers may not use consumer expectations as a defense when a product contains substantial hazards, even if obvious, which may easily be designed away.

§ 8.9 OPTIONAL SAFETY DEVICES

Sometimes manufacturers offer safety devices only as optional add-ons to their products rather than installing them as mandatory features of every product unit sold. For example, a manufacturer may sell a chain saw with an optional, rather than a mandatory, chain brake; a radial arm saw with an optional, non-mandatory lower blade guard; a forklift or tractor with an optional rather than mandatory overhead guard; a truck chassis and cab, forklift, or bus with an optional back-up alarm; or a motorcycle, with or without leg-protective crash bars at the option of the buyer.

If a purchaser rejects an optional safety device, and the purchaser, user, or a third party is subsequently injured in a manner that the safety device would have prevented, the accident victim may seek recovery against the manufacturer for failing to incorporate the safety device as a standard feature of the product. Whether such a claim may lie is a question that has confounded courts and commentators.

The problem is this: safety features that are feasible, cost-effective, and vitally important in some contexts may be unnecessary, inconvenient, and even dangerous in others. Just as consumers want and need vehicles and other products that come in varying size, shape, power, and even color, depending on their special needs and preferences, the type and amount of safety individual consumers may need and want also varies according to their special needs and preferences. One safety size, in short, may not fit all.

It often is asserted that there are two lines of conflicting authority on the optional safety device issue. The first one derives from *Bexiga v. Havir Mfg. Corp.*, 290 A.2d 281 (N.J. 1972), an early case where the plaintiff's hand was crushed while he was adjusting a piece of metal beneath the ram of an unguarded punch press when he mistakenly depressed the foot control. The trial and intermediate appellate courts held that the plaintiff could not

maintain a design defect claim against the manufacturer of the press for failing to equip the machine
with guards because, by custom and state statute,
responsibility for guarding industrial machinery lay
with the employer-purchasers of such machinery
rather than with the manufacturer. Reversing, the
New Jersey Supreme Court ruled that the manufacturer was in a better position than the employer to
install feasible safety devices on industrial machinery. The court reasoned that manufacturers can
make the best decisions about what types of safety
devices are reasonably necessary on such machinery, and that the law should place responsibility for
such devices on manufacturers rather than leaving
such critical decisions about design safety to "the
haphazard conduct" of buyers.

Bexiga did not directly involve the issue of optional safety devices, but its holding that manufacturers
may not *delegate* design safety decisions to purchasers lay the foundation for the optional safety device
debate. Quickly becoming a landmark for the "non-
delegable duty doctrine," *Bexiga* provided a beacon
for the view that manufacturers, even if they have a
reasonable basis for believing that purchasers normally will add appropriate safety devices to their
products, should nevertheless bear ultimate responsibility for harm caused by a buyer's failure to add
such design features as may be necessary to make
the product reasonably safe.

Six years after *Bexiga*, a couple of cases were
decided quite the other way, shielding manufactur-

ers from liability for delegating the choice of appropriate safety devices to purchasers down the chain of distribution. In one, *Verge v. Ford Motor Co.*, 581 F.2d 384 (3d Cir. 1978) (V.I. law), a garbage truck without a back-up buzzer backed into and squashed a garbage man against a garbage can. The garbage truck had been assembled by a company that installed a compactor unit on a multi-purpose flat-bed truck cab and chassis it had purchased from Ford Motor Company. In an action against Ford and the garbage truck assembler for failing to equip the vehicle with a back-up buzzer, the jury ruled for the plaintiff. Reversing, the circuit court ruled that Ford had no duty to install the alarm. The court reasoned that (1) trade custom, (2) the relative expertise of the parties, and (3) feasibility mandated that the assembler alone should bear responsibility for the selection and installation of appropriate safety equipment on the final truck. Compare *Biss v. Tenneco, Inc.*, 409 N.Y.S.2d 874 (App. Div. 1978) (manufacturer's only duty is to see that appropriate safety devices are made known and available to purchasers who are better equipped to make such safety decisions).

For a variety of reasons, the optional safety device issue is more complex than the stark contrast suggested by *Bexiga* and *Verge*, and the optional safety device issue remains one of the most elusive problems in products liability law.

§ 8.10   PRESCRIPTION DRUGS
AND MEDICAL DEVICES

Prescription drugs are paradoxical: as one of the greatest triumphs of the twentieth century, their powerful chemicals and biologics save many millions of humans from suffering and death; yet, these same chemicals also *cause* great suffering and death. All prescription drugs, that is, possess substantial costs as well as benefits. This is because most drug hazards are inherent and unavoidable. Normally, these dangers simply cannot be removed: the same chemical properties in drugs that can cause great harm are usually the very properties that are therapeutic. Put another way, if a drug's chemical structure were altered to avoid some adverse health effect, that same change would often also reduce or eliminate the drug's beneficial health effects. Thus, a drug's "design" normally cannot be changed to improve its safety.

Penicillin may be the classic example of a drug that, while highly beneficial to most people, can be hazardous, indeed lethal, to others. Accutane is a good modern example of a drug that combines great benefits with great risks of harm: it is highly effective in treating the most severe cases of acne; yet, it is a virulent teratogen that can cause birth defects when given to pregnant women. Surely the most impelling example is thalidomide, another teratogen, prescribed widely as a sedative and morning sickness drug throughout much of the world (but not the U.S.) during the 1950s and 1960s. Despite the enormous toll of birth defects this drug wreaked around the globe, the FDA approved thalidomide in 1998 for fighting leprosy. These are only 3 examples, and the list of unavoidably unsafe drugs goes on and on.

The Restatements and the Courts

The Second Restatement—Comment k

Comment *k*, a controversial comment to § 402A, provides that manufacturers are *not* subject to strict liability in tort for harm caused by certain "unavoidably unsafe" but useful products, notably prescription drugs, solely on the basis of their inherent hazards that cannot feasibly be designed away:

> The argument that industries producing potentially dangerous products should make good the harm, distribute it by liability insurance, and add the cost to the price of the product, encounters reason for pause, when we consider that two of the greatest medical boons to the human race, penicillin and cortisone, both have their dangerous side effects, and that drug companies might well have been deterred from producing and selling them.

Prosser on Torts § 99 (4th ed. 1971). Drugs, in short, are different.

Most courts agree that comment *k* properly exempts useful prescription drugs that are unavoidably unsafe from strict products liability, assuming always that they are properly prepared and carry adequate warnings. And while design hazards in medical devices often can be designed away, some courts have nevertheless extended comment *k*'s exemption from design defect liability to cases involving prescription medical devices.

Yet courts and commentators disagree on a number of other, important aspects of comment *k*, including whether its application is confined to a limited class of drugs properly characterized as "unavoidably unsafe," or whether it applies to *all* prescription drugs. On this issue, most courts have taken a case-by-case approach, reluctant to surrender judicial oversight of a drug manufacturer's responsibility for safety in design. See *Hill v. Wyeth, Inc.*, 2007 WL 674251 (E.D. Mo. 2007); *Bryant v. Hoffmann–La Roche, Inc.*, 585 S.E.2d 723 (Ga. Ct. App. 2003).

The Third Restatement

Products Liability Restatement § 6(c) provides:

A prescription drug or medical device is not reasonably safe due to defective design if the foreseeable risks of harm posed by the drug or medical device are sufficiently great in relation to its foreseeable therapeutic benefits that reasonable health-care providers, knowing of such foreseeable risks and therapeutic benefits, would not prescribe the drug or medical device for any class of patients.

The most important thing to note about this novel liability standard is that it leaves a very small window for design defect claims for prescription drugs, a window so tiny that almost no drug claim could fit through it. Even thalidomide would not be captured by the *Third Restatement* test, because of its value in treating leprosy.

But thalidomide may prove the virtue of this test, rather than its folly, for lepers should not be deprived of beneficial drug therapy because some doctors improperly give the drug to child-bearing women. In such a case, the defect, it would seem, would lie in the doctor rather than the drug. While not minimizing the tragedy of a child born deformed to a woman who was prescribed the drug improperly, perhaps tort (and possibly criminal) remedies against the prescribing doctor would be a better way to address the consequences, rather than forcing the manufacturer and lepers to suffer from an untoward misuse of a pharmaceutical that is highly beneficial to at least one class of patients.

Pointing to the weaknesses in the FDA and health care delivery systems, the profit motivations of drug manufacturers to scrimp on research and design, a patent system that artificially protects manufacturers from competition, and the industry's temptation to overpromote its products, some courts and commentators reject the *Third Restatement*'s narrow definition of design defectiveness for drugs. See *Bryant v. Hoffmann–La Roche, Inc.*, 585 S.E.2d 723 (Ga. Ct. App. 2003); Conk, *Is There a Design Defect in the Restatement (Third) of Torts: Products Liability?*, 109 Yale L.J. 1087 (2000).

The argument for rejecting § 6(c) is the belief that drug designs should be subject to challenge on some basis or another—either by means of a normal risk-utility test (on proof of a safer alternative design) or a macro-balance test (on proof that a drug caused all patients of every type more harm than good). Yet neither approach works well in most drug cases. The first simply does not work for most drugs that cannot be redesigned because their hazards are inherent. As for the second test, it is true that any product that causes more harm than good is truly bad ("defective") from a utilitarian point of view. And, if there were an effective way to identify such products, their manufacturers might fairly be required to pay for all the harm they cause, and the products normally should be banned. Yet, particular classes of patients (like lepers) deserve therapy from drugs, even if doctors sometimes do misuse those drugs on other classes of patients. Moreover, there is a devil residing in the process of distinguishing which drugs, on balance, have net value from those that produce net harm—and in the threat of repeated litigation over the ultimate social value of any type of drug that causes someone harm, because it did not suit that patient.

Empowering Warning Claims

If a drug's adverse effects are not reasonably foreseeable, the manufacturer should not be responsible for reasons examined in § 10.4, below. If a manufacturer properly performing its research and development obligations in fact should reasonably discover a drug's adverse effects, then the manufacturer has a duty to warn doctors of those effects.

And if a doctor fails to provide this information to his or her patients—fails to provide them with the basis for informed consent to drug therapy—then a medical malpractice claim would seem the proper remedy, not a claim against the manufacturer for a supposed defect in the drug's design.

So the *Third Restatement*'s test for defective drug designs, though very narrow, and incomplete in failing to identify important exceptions, seems basically correct. That is, by putting most drugs beyond the reach of design defect litigation (under any liability theory), the *Third Restatement* properly pours most litigation concerning hazardous drugs into the defectiveness of their warnings and instructions.

Thus, most prescription drug litigation properly is based on the adequacy of warnings and instructions provided to the doctor about the drug, because the best place to locate a drug manufacturer's responsibility is in the information it provides to doctors—information that must be clear, complete, and properly conveyed. And in the great majority of deserving cases, a challenge to a drug's design can easily be reformulated as a defect in a warning or instruction. Yet, as a counterweight to relieving manufacturers from judicial scrutiny of their drug designs, courts should robustly review the adequacy of drug warnings. Thus, litigation over injuries from prescription drugs normally lies in the sufficiency of their warnings and instructions, not in the sufficiency of their designs.

CHAPTER 9

WARNING DEFECTS

Table of Sections

§ 9.1   Warning Defects—Generally.
§ 9.2   Theories and Tests of Liability.
§ 9.3   Adequacy.
§ 9.4   Persons to Be Warned.
§ 9.5   Sophisticated Users and Bulk Suppliers.
§ 9.6   Prescription Drugs and Medical Devices.

---

§ 9.1   WARNING DEFECTS— GENERALLY

Manufacturers and other sellers have a duty to provide consumers with warnings of hidden product dangers and instructions on how their products may be safely used. Products that fail to carry sufficient informational "software" of this type are deemed "defective." If a user or consumer is injured as a result of a warning defect ("marketing defect," in Texas), because such danger or safety information was not provided, the manufacturer is subject to liability for the harm.

The "duty to warn" is an umbrella term for describing a manufacturer's informational obli-

261

gations to those who purchase and use its products. This duty actually is comprised of two quite separate obligations: the duty to *warn*—to inform buyers and users of hidden dangers in a product; and the duty to *instruct*—to inform buyers on how to avoid those dangers in order to use the product safely. Together, these duties require that important information on product hazards and product safety are transferred from manufacturers, who possess the information, to buyers and users of products, who need it.

From a manufacturer's perspective, it usually is less costly to warn of a danger than to improve quality assurance or to design the problem entirely out of the product. Courts sometimes assume that supplying warnings and instructions is an easy and inexpensive way for manufacturers to fulfill their obligation to make their products reasonably safe. And injured plaintiffs often reinforce this view, frequently adding warning defect claims indiscriminately to cases where they have no business, since proving that a warning is "defective" is often a far easier (and less expensive) task than successfully attacking a product's design. Yet many courts look skeptically at warning claims and do not lightly impose a duty to warn on manufacturers. See *Killeen v. Harmon Grain Products, Inc.*, 413 N.E.2d 767 (Mass. App. Ct. 1980) (manufacturer of cinnamon-flavored toothpicks had no duty to warn of danger to child falling during play while holding one in mouth: duty to warn not imposed as "a mindless ritual").

Purposes of Duty to Warn

Probably the most generally accepted goal of products liability law is deterrence—risk reduction—predicated on the view that a consumer informed about product dangers and methods of safe use will use that information for self-protection. And deterrence rests on the more complex goal of economic efficiency, which seeks to maximize social resources by minimizing wasteful injuries. Yet, while the direct economic costs of providing warnings and instructions typically are minimal, less obvious costs raise subtle and important issues. One is the danger of providing too *much* information—the risk of over-warning or "warnings pollution."

Another reason for requiring warnings and instructions, grounded in a more fundamental human value, is the promotion of individual autonomy—by shifting cost-benefit decisionmaking on product hazards from manufacturers to individual consumers. A consumer who is fully informed of a product's dangers and how to avoid them may choose to use the product in a particular, safer manner. Or the informed consumer may choose not to buy or use the product at all. Unlike the risk-reduction rationale, which reflects a utilitarian perspective rooted in economic efficiency, this kind of informed consent value focuses on protecting a user's individual rights—specifically, the user's right of self-determination, the right "to determine his own fate." The idea here is "that the user or consumer is entitled to make his own choice as to whether the product's utility or benefits justify exposing himself to the risks of harm. Thus, a true choice situation arises, and a duty to warn attaches, whenever a reasonable man would want to be informed of the risk in order to decide whether to expose himself to it." *Borel v. Fibreboard Paper Prods. Corp.*, 493 F.2d 1076, 1089 (5th Cir. 1973) (Tex. law) (asbestos insulation worker, not warned of risks, contracted asbestosis and mesothelioma). On the obverse side of individual freedom lies the value of personal responsibility, and with it issues of paternalism.

The Paradox of the Duty to Warn

Lurking within the duty to warn lies a paradox: The duty to warn is at once the most important, yet least effective, duty in the law of products liability. Its importance lies in its respect for the autonomy of consumers, as discussed above, together with its promotion of utility by helping to reduce the level of unnecessary product accidents. Its ineffectiveness springs from how easy it is to assert a warnings claim, even if unjustified; how elusive such claims are to rationally adjudicate; and what little impact warnings have on product safety—since mounting studies reveal that they often are ignored. If this latter point be true, if most warnings and instructions truly are ignored, then a manufacturer's duty to warn and instruct may be mostly sound and fury, signifying little. So, warnings are powerful because they transfer important safety information and decisionmaking to consumers, yet they are trivial because consumers often fail to process safety information rationally. This is the paradox of the duty to warn.

Relationship Between Duty to Warn and Duty of Safe Design

A fundamental aspect of the duty to warn is its relationship to the duty of safe design. The duty to warn is undoubtedly linked to a product's design, in that a warning or instruction provides information about hazards that are inherent in a product's design and how those design hazards may be avoided. Yet, while design defect and warning defect claims often go hand in hand, almost all jurisdictions view the duty to warn and the duty of safe design as largely distinct, independent obligations. Thus, even if a product's design is as safe as it can be, the manufacturer still has a duty to warn of hidden dangers in the product. And if a substantial danger can be designed out of a product practicably and at little cost, all but a few courts hold that even an "adequate" warning does not insulate a manufacturer who fails to employ the safer design. For a more thorough examination of warning defects, see Owen, Products Liability Law ch. 9 (2d ed. 2008).

§ 9.2   THEORIES AND TESTS OF LIABILITY

Warning defect claims may be brought in most jurisdictions on the basis of negligence, breach of the implied warranty of merchantability, and strict liability in tort. While plaintiffs often plead two or all three causes of action to support a warnings claim in modern products liability litigation, the negligence cause of action traditionally has been viewed as the most natural basis for such claims. To "apprise a party of a danger of which he is not aware, and thus enable him to protect himself against it," *Jonescue v. Jewel Home Shopping Serv.*, 306 N.E.2d 312, 316 (Ill. App. Ct. 1973), due care may require a manufacturer "to speak out if the product is capable of harm and does not itself carry a message of danger." Dillard & Hart, *Product Liability: Directions for Use and the Duty to Warn*, 41 Va. L. Rev. 145, 147 (1955).

Strict liability in tort is the most common cause of action for defective warning claims. A product with inadequate information about product dangers and how to avoid them is "defective," plain and simple. See *Simonetta v. Viad Corp.*, 151 P.3d 1019 (Wash. Ct. App. 2007) (inadequate warning of the inherent dangers of asbestos); *Leary v. Syracuse Model Neighborhood Corp.*, 799 N.Y.S.2d 867 (Sup. Ct. 2005) (inadequate warning that stove could tip); *Lewis v. Sea Ray Boats, Inc.*, 65 P.3d 245 (Nev. 2003) (warnings of carbon monoxide in engine exhaust from using boat's heater may not have adequately warned of such risk from using air conditioner run by generator).

The Duty to Warn "Test"

It will be recalled that the two principal liability tests for design defectiveness in strict liability in tort are the consumer expectations test and the risk-utility test. These tests may sometimes helpfully be employed to test the defectiveness of a product alleged to contain insufficient information on a product's danger. Yet neither test is especially helpful for distinguishing between dangers that should be warned about and those which should not, or for determining whether a given warning adequately conveys information about a risk. If a product fails to have adequate warning of a hidden danger, it plainly violates a consumer's expectations, as the implied warranty discussion explains; and the safety benefits of adding a sufficient warning virtually always exceed its monetary costs, as noted in the negligence discussion.

Thus, when applied to warning cases, both design defect tests point toward liability in every case in which a manufacturer fails to provide meaningful warnings of material hidden risks in its products. Not surprisingly, but without explanation, this is precisely the standard that courts apply in judging warning defects: if a latent hazard is foreseeable to the manufacturer, if it is material to and hidden from consumers, and if there is a reasonable means to inform users and consumers about the risk to users, a product is defective if the manufacturer fails to provide them with such information. More concisely, a manufacturer has a duty to provide adequate warnings of all foreseeable risks that are material, and a manufacturer is subject to strict liability in tort for failing to supply adequate warnings and instructions with the products that it sells.

Thus, the duty to warn in negligence, implied warranty, and strict liability in tort, under § 2(c) of the *Third Restatement*, and under state products liability reform statutes, centers on one central issue: whether "adequate" warnings and instructions were provided with a product—if so, the product supplier has fulfilled its duty to warn; if not, it has breached its duty and is subject to liability. In short, the liability test for warnings claims, regardless of the theory of liability, is "adequacy."

§ 9.3 ADEQUACY

At the center of the duty to warn lies "adequacy." Each theory of liability supporting a warnings claim is premised on the defendant's failure to provide users and consumers adequate information about a product danger, or how to avoid it, as just discussed. Unless a plaintiff can prove that a warning was "inadequate," a defective warning claim will fail. See *Austin v. Will–Burt Co.*, 361 F.3d 862 (5th Cir. 2004) (Miss. law) (dismissing inadequate warnings claim for electrocution of news van worker killed when van's telescoping mast hit power lines; yellow labels on mast, with red and black lettering, stated: DANGER! PLEASE READ INSTRUCTIONS BEFORE RAISING!—DANGER. WATCH FOR WIRES. YOU CAN BE KILLED IF THIS PRODUCT COMES NEAR ELECTRICAL POWER LINES).

Many courts have stated what makes a warning "adequate." One frequently cited formulation is from *Pavlides v. Galveston Yacht Basin, Inc.*, 727 F.2d 330, 338 (5th Cir. 1984), where the court explained that, to be adequate, a warning "must provide 'a complete disclosure of the existence and extent of the risk involved,' " meaning:

A warning must (1) be designed so it can reasonably be expected to catch the attention of the consumer; (2) be comprehensible and give a fair indication of the specific risks involved with the product; and (3) be of an intensity justified by the magnitude of the risk.

Another court remarked:

To be legally adequate, the warning should (1) attract the attention of those that the product could harm; (2) explain the mechanism and mode of injury; and (3) provide instructions on ways to safely use the product to avoid injury.

Gray v. Badger Mining Corp., 676 N.W.2d 268, 274 (Minn. 2004). The *Products Liability Restatement* notes that determining a warning's adequacy requires focusing on its "content and comprehensibility, intensity of expression, and the characteristics of expected user groups." The adequacy of a warning is often bound up with the issue of who should be warned, so that a warning ordinarily will not be adequate unless it warns persons foreseeably threatened by a product hazard or others in the best position—such as parents, employers, and doctors—to act on warnings to protect persons subject to the hazard.

More concisely, it might be said that a warning is adequate if it provides a reasonable amount and type of information about a product's material risks and how to avoid them in a manner calculated to reach and be understood by those likely to need the information.

Content—"Substantive Adequacy"

Nature and Degree of Specific Risk

To be adequate, a warning must clearly and comprehensibly describe the nature and degree of a product's specific risks. This formulation conflates at least three ideas:

- *Clarity.* Warnings must be expressed in *terms that are clear and comprehensible*, meaning that they use language that effectively communicates information about a product's hazards. If warning language is confusing and unclear, such that users cannot understand its meaning, then the warning is inadequate;

- *Specificity.* A warning should describe, with reasonable precision, the particular way in which a product is dangerous, *the specific risks* from using or misusing it in different ways. A warning that describes these risks vaguely and too generally, or that describes a different risk from the one which harms a plaintiff, will likely be inadequate; and

- *Intensity.* A warning must effectively communicate *the degree of risk*, the likelihood and severity of injury the risk may cause. If serious

injury of a particular type, or death, may be a
consequence, those potential consequences
should be described—with an intensity proportionate to the risk—or the warning will be
inadequate.

Form—"Procedural Adequacy"

For a warning or instruction to be adequate, it
must be conveyed in such a form that is likely to
reach and be comprehended by those who buy and
use the product. Because it deals with physical
methods for delivering substantive information, this
type of *conveyance adequacy* may be referred to as
"procedural," to distinguish it from the information's substantive content. Procedural adequacy has
various dimensions, from the conspicuousness of
written warnings, including their placement in
prominent locations, to the use of foreign language
or nonverbal warnings when fairly called for in the
circumstances.

Conspicuousness

The most significant procedural adequacy issue in
this context, conspicuousness, typically depends on
the type size, its style or font, its color, whether it
contrasts with other messages nearby, and whether
it has a heading such as "WARNING!" or "CAU-
TION." If a warning is written in yellow or red
letters that are large and bold, and preceded by a
large "**WARNING!**" heading, it is more likely to be
conspicuous than if the warning is black and white,
small, and has no heading.

Location

An important feature of conspicuousness is location. When warnings are set apart, and located in a prominent position—such as the front of a label or booklet (*vs.* deep inside an instruction manual), or on the particular part of the product that is hazardous—they are most likely to be observed and absorbed. Warnings normally can quite easily be located on a container's label, on a warning plate attached near the ram of a press or other danger point of a machine, etched into the body of the product, or printed on a tag attached somewhere likely to be seen. Depending on the circumstances, however, a warning may still be adequate even if it is provided off the product in a manual or other writing.

Foreign Language Warnings

With the increasingly global marketplace for products manufactured in this nation, and with Spanish spoken on our southern borders, French spoken on our northeastern borders, and Oriental languages increasingly spoken in the West, one must wonder whether product warnings can possibly be adequate when they are limited to English. If manufacturers market their products heavily in southern portions of Florida, Texas, New Mexico, Arizona, and California, or in Northern Vermont and Maine (adjacent to Québec) the question is whether the law should require them to warn in Spanish, French, or Japanese as well as English. There has been surprisingly little debate on this important issue, perhaps reflecting the deep English-only tradition that has long prevailed in America, which is geographically isolated from most other cultures. But the world is rapidly going global, as is the law of products liability, and the various branches of American government increasingly will need to address the multi-lingual question.

Only a handful of judicial decisions in America have examined whether a warning must be made in a foreign language to be adequate. Two decisions have ruled that a warning is not inadequate because it is written in English only, that is, there is in general no duty to warn in Spanish or other foreign language—even if the product is advertised in Spanish or sold in Puerto Rico. See *Torres–Rios v. LPS Labs.*, 152 F.3d 11 (1st Cir. 1998) (P.R. law) (no duty to warn in Spanish of explosion risk to workers welding near 55–gallon chemical drum). See also *Ramirez v. Plough, Inc.*, 863 P.2d 167 (Cal. 1993) (no duty to warn in Spanish on St. Joseph's Aspirin for Children that infant could contract Reye's Syndrome from product). But a couple of other decisions appear to disagree and suggest that foreign-language warnings sometimes may be necessary to make a warning adequate. See *Fuentes v. Shin Caterpillar Mitsubishi*, Ltd., 2003 WL 22205665 (Cal. Ct. App. 2003); *Stanley Industries, Inc. v. W. M. Barr & Co.*, 784 F.Supp. 1570 (S.D. Fla. 1992).

Nonverbal Warnings—Pictures, Symbols, Bells, and Smells

Symbols

For children and foreigners, symbols may be the only way to provide warnings directly to potential victims. Empirical evidence suggests that warnings to such groups may be quite effective. See *Strothkamp v. Chesebrough–Pond's, Inc.*, 1993 WL 79239 (Mo. Ct. App. 1993) (5-year-old child who injured his ear with a Q–Tip from box that did not have Mr. Yuk sticker testified that he would not touch anything marked with a Mr. Yuk sticker). Yet very few cases address whether danger symbols may sometimes be required to warn adequately of a hazard. One early case involved two Spanish-speaking farm workers who died from inhaling insecticide dust from bags that warned against inhalation of the dust in English only. The court held that a jury could find the English-only warnings inadequate because it was foreseeable that the insecticide would be used by illiterate farm workers who would need a skull and crossbones or other danger symbol on the bags. *Hubbard–Hall Chemical Co. v. Silverman*, 340 F.2d 402 (1st Cir. 1965) (Mass. law).

Other Nonverbal Warning Methods

Apart from pictorial warnings, danger information may be communicated to users in other nonverbal ways—even in non-visual ways, relying on other senses. A *gauge* or *warning light* may helpfully inform an operator that a crane is about to tip, that the fuel is low, that a parking brake is engaged, or that a rear mounted aircraft engine has stopped operating. A *buzzer, bell, rear-view mirror*, or *rear camera* (with a viewing screen inside the cabin) may warn operators or potential victims of the risks from operating bulky vehicles in reverse. *Color* may be added to a dangerous, clear, chemical fluid to distinguish it from water, and *odor* may be added to propane gas to give notice of its presence. And warnings may rely on the sense of touch, such as *vibration* in the seat of a crane about to tip over. There simply is no end to the kinds of creative ways warnings may be improved.

Nullifying Warnings with Safety Assurances— "Overpromotion"

An otherwise adequate warning may be nullified by assurances of safety. The classic case on this issue is *Maize v. Atlantic Refining Co.*, 41 A.2d 850 (Pa. 1945), where a woman died from inhaling tetrachloride fumes in a cleaning fluid she used to clean her rugs. The label on the can twice stated, "CAUTION: Do not inhale fumes. Use only in a well ventilated place." However, in letters that were several times larger, the cleaner's name—"Safety-Kleen"—was emblazoned around the container. *Held*, that the jury properly could find that the "Safety-Kleen" statements cancelled out the warnings. A small number of other decisions have applied the "overpromotion" principle to nullify a manufacturer's product warnings, including one in which warnings and instructions provided by the manufacturer of a jet boat were cancelled out by a salesman's demonstration of the boat in ways contrary to those warnings. See *Levey v. Yamaha Motor Corp.*, 825 A.2d 554 (N.J. Super. App. Div. 2003).

Overwarning—"Warnings Pollution"

Cutting across the ideal formulations of adequacy, both substantive and procedural, is an important real-world limitation—"warnings pollution." As noted above, warnings, to be adequate, ideally should provide precise information about all specific dangers from all foreseeable uses, and this information ideally should be conveyed to users in a form most likely to catch their attention and help them understand the true nature and degree of risk. The background assumptions are that, since warnings are good, more warnings are better; and that, since the cost of warnings is close to zero, warnings should be extremely thorough and complete. What this overlooks, of course, is the real-world cost to consumers—in terms of time and trouble—of having to read, consider, and act upon the many long lists of warnings and instructions they confront every day, which causes consumers in many situations simply to ignore such information altogether.

In the last couple of decades, courts have begun to appreciate the warnings pollution problem—that there is such a thing as *too much* information—that information, like everything, can be an evil in excess. This simple idea is that product warnings ideally should contain *optimal* types and levels of danger and safety information, not maximum information. See *Cotton v. Buckeye Gas Products Co.*, 840 F.2d 935 (D.C. Cir. 1988) ("flammable" warnings on propane cylinders were not inadequate for failing to warn that they could be "explosive";

keying warnings to every particular type of risk is *not* "cost free," because of costs of time and effort necessary to grasp the message: each extra item included "dilutes the punch of every other item. Given short attention spans, items crowd each other out; they get lost in fine print.").

The best way to capture the warnings pollution problem may be to recognize that warnings need not be perfect to be "adequate," just *reasonable*. See *General Motors Corp. v. Saenz*, 873 S.W.2d 353 (Tex. 1993).

§ 9.4 PERSONS TO BE WARNED

The duty to warn supposes that the warning will reach, be read by, and protect the safety of certain types of persons. Deciding what categories of persons should be warned raises important questions of duty and adequacy. The selection of the proper groups to warn is part of a lexical series of questions following a determination that a warning is appropriate:

(1) Whom the warning should protect;

(2) Who can best accomplish that protection; and

(3) What type of warning will do it best.

The last question is one of adequacy, the factual question just examined. Although the first two questions sometimes mix law and fact, they involve basic duty issues for a court.

Normally, people quite obviously can best protect themselves, assuming that they recognize a hazard and can control it. Thus, even when a manufacturer sells its products to intermediaries, it normally should provide warnings and instructions about product hazards directly to users and consumers if there is a reasonable way to do so. One iteration of the warn-consumers-directly principle is the manufacturer's duty, previously discussed, to place warnings directly on the product, if feasible. The principle rests on reason, rather than being absolute, because some products come in a form that precludes warnings on the body of the product, such as products that are very small or liquid sold in bulk. The bulk-supplier doctrine, discussed below, addresses the latter point.

In other situations, where users and consumers rely on others for protection, warnings should be given to those other persons in addition to or, if appropriate, in substitution for warnings provided to users and consumers:

- Young children depend on *parents* to make informed safety decisions about their food, clothing, and toys;

- Workers depend on *supervisors* to make informed safety decisions on what types of machinery to purchase and on safe procedures for operating and maintaining those machines; and

- Patients depend on *doctors* to make informed decisions on prescription drugs.

These and other special categories of persons charged with protecting others often can make better use of product safety information than the ultimate users and consumers, as discussed in later sections. Two special categories of persons treated briefly here are bystanders and persons who are allergic to certain products, both of whom need special warnings.

Bystanders

Warnings play two different roles in protecting bystanders. Bystanders may well be placed at risk when products are used dangerously by other people, as when a crane operator uses a crane in a dangerous manner that threatens workers underneath the load. In such cases, warnings necessary to the safe operation of the crane protect persons foreseeably placed at risk, including the operator's fellow workers ("bystanders") who may be standing beneath the crane. The manufacturer of such a crane has a duty to warn the operator and others foreseeably placed at risk, including bystanders, for the benefit of them all. So, also, although the manufacturer of a car or plane normally has a duty to provide warnings and instructions concerning operational hazards only to the operator, not to passengers, the breach of the duty to warn the operator will violate the safety rights of passengers and other bystanders injured as a result of the operator's failure to have such safety information. This is the normal type of bystander case in which a manufacturer's duty to bystanders is governed by ordinary principles of reasonable foreseeability, in tort, and by third-party beneficiary principles, in warranty.

In addition to this form of indirect benefit from a manufacturer's provision of warnings and instructions to product users, bystanders sometimes are entitled to warnings directly to themselves. For example, cranes sometimes must move in reverse, and a crane cab may make it impossible for the operator to see directly behind the crane. In this type of situation, the crane normally would need to be equipped with a horn or buzzer, and also perhaps with flashing lights, to warn bystanders behind the crane that it is being run in reverse by an operator with diminished visibility. Surely rear-view mirrors also would be required, to increase the operator's range of vision as much as possible and, depending on the risk and feasibility, possibly a rear camera with a viewing screen inside the cab.

Allergic Persons

Some foods, drugs, cleansers, and lotions that are useful and entirely safe to the great majority of people can cause serious allergic reactions in other persons. Peanuts, aspirin, strawberries, penicillin, oysters, monosodium glutamate, and latex gloves are examples of products that many people enjoy or need but which cause some people to get very sick and even die. The defect in such situations might be seen to lie in the persons who incur idiosyncratic reactions, rather than in the product. The question in these situations is whether the producer has a duty to warn that its product may cause allergic reactions.

If the population of allergic users is foreseeably quite large, and if such users are not generally aware of the risk, then the manufacturer must provide adequate warnings of a product's allergenic tendencies. If the group of allergic persons is small, the courts are split on whether the manufacturer has a duty to warn. Most courts require the manufacturer to warn only if it can foresee a risk of serious allergy to a *substantial* (or "appreciable") number of persons. This was the position of the *Second Torts Restatement*, and it is followed by the *Third Restatement* which notes that the "substantial number" concept logically should decrease as the risk of harm increases. Section 2 cmt. *k*. Another line of cases rejects a strict no-duty approach for "insignificant" or "insubstantial" numbers of allergy victims and, instead, imposes a duty to warn of *any* foreseeable allergy that may be serious.

§ 9.5   SOPHISTICATED USERS AND BULK SUPPLIERS

Two doctrines that exempt manufacturers from their normal obligation to provide end-users and consumers with warnings of product hazards are the "sophisticated user doctrine" and the "bulk supplier doctrine." Both doctrines relieve an upstream seller of the duty to warn a downstream purchaser or user in circumstances where the purchaser already knows about the risk. Because both doctrines rest on hazard information possessed by downstream purchasers, the two doctrines sometimes are blended together into a single doctrine. Yet, while they often overlap, most courts view them as legal doctrines that are related but quite distinct. See *Gray v. Badger Mining Corp.*, 676 N.W.2d 268 (Minn. 2004) (examining both doctrines).

Sophisticated User Doctrine

The sophisticated user doctrine may arise if there is no *need* to warn, because of the expertise of the buyer or user. A product supplier has no duty, under this doctrine, to warn employees of knowledgeable commercial buyers about product hazards of which such buyers are aware, since the purpose of warnings is to provide information to people about hazards and safety information they do not know about. So, a supplier of sheet metal has no duty to warn a building contractor that its metal may be slippery, or to warn about the dangers of working with metal at heights; and a seller of diving platforms has no duty to warn a high school purchasing them that they are dangerous if used for diving in shallow water. More typically, the doctrine shields a silica sand supplier of a duty to warn foundry workers that they can contract silicosis from breathing silica dust, if the supplier has reason to believe that the foundry which purchases the sand, being a "sophisticated user," already fully knows this risk and how to avoid it. See *Haase v. Badger Mining Corp.*, 669 N.W.2d 737 (Wis. Ct. App. 2003), aff'd on other grounds (Wis. 2004).

Bulk Supplier Doctrine

The bulk supplier doctrine may arise if there is no *way* to warn, because of the nature of the product and the form in which it is sold. This doctrine normally applies to liquids, sand, and other products provided in bulk to commercial purchasers by railroad car or tanker truck. Such purchasers may repackage the chemical or other product in drums or other containers for subsequent transport and distribution to users or consumers or may simply use it as it arrives in bulk for some manufacturing process. The difficulty with imposing a duty to warn on such bulk suppliers is that there normally is no practical way to place a warning on such a product to alert end-users of its dangers. Thus, if the purchaser knows of the product's hazards, the bulk supplier normally will have no duty to provide additional warnings to the ultimate user or consumer. See *Genereux v. American Beryllia Corp.*, 518 F.Supp.2d 306 (D. Mass. 2007).

Thus, upstream manufacturers sometimes may properly rely on downstream distributors to perform the warning function, provided there is a reasonable basis for the supplier to believe that the purchasing distributors will pass along appropriate warnings to its vendees. However, if the bulk supplier knows more about a product hazard or how to avoid it than its purchasers, it has a duty to provide this additional safety information to the purchaser of its materials, if there is some reasonable way to do so. See *Gray v. Badger Mining Corp.*, 676

N.W.2d 268 (Minn. 2004). And if the bulk supplier
has reason to expect that its purchasers will not
pass along important warnings to end-users, it may
have a duty to use reasonable means to get the
warnings to those persons.

The Restatements

Both the bulk supplier and sophisticated user
doctrines are offshoots of a general principle expressed in *Restatement (Second) of Torts* § 388, the
basic provision on a chattel supplier's duty to warn
under the law of negligence. Addressing a seller's
duty to warn when it sells a product to an intermediate supplier, comment *n* to § 388 provides that a
seller may rely on the intermediary to provide
warnings to the end-user if that reliance is reasonable in the circumstances. Such reliance is reasonable only if the seller has reason to believe that the
intermediary will faithfully discharge this obligation
and, even then, the seller may have a duty to warn
end users of particularly serious hazards if a feasible means of communication exists. Section 388
often is relied on for the principle that a manufacturer may *not* always rely on an intermediary to
pass along warnings of a product hazard, but the
other side of this coin—that a manufacturer *may*
properly rely on an intermediary if there is a reasonable basis for such reliance—provides the basis
for the exemption from the duty to warn for both
the sophisticated user and bulk supplier doctrines.
While § 388 of the *Restatement (Second) of Torts*
addresses the obligations of a supplier to warn in

the law of negligence, most courts also apply its principles to the duty to warn in strict products liability.

Providing some amount of danger information to an intermediate buyer may not be enough if a reasonable supplier would supply the buyer with more or better information, or would provide it directly to the ultimate users, considering the overall balance of costs and benefits, including the reliability of the intermediary, the magnitude of the hazard, and the feasibility of providing better warnings, a principle well summarized in *Restatement (Third) of Torts: Products Liability* § 2 cmt. *i. But see* § 5 cmt. *c* (raw material suppliers do not have a duty to warn end users).

§ 9.6 PRESCRIPTION DRUGS AND MEDICAL DEVICES

Warning and instruction claims dominate prescription drug and medical device litigation, unlike most other types of products liability cases. Whether a warning or instruction about a drug or medical device is "adequate" is usually the principal issue in this type of litigation.

Theory of Liability

Courts widely apply all three theories of liability to cases of this type—negligence, breach of the implied warranty of merchantability, and strict liability in tort—as well as special warning liability provisions of state products liability statutes. As earlier discussed, courts have been drawn to negligence principles in warnings cases more than in cases involving other types of defects. This has been especially true where prescription drugs and medical devices are involved. Except for cases of contamination, drugs (as food) were largely exempted from strict liability in tort from the very start of modern products liability law in comments *j* and *k* to § 402A of the *Restatement (Second) of Torts*, and courts have continued to apply negligence principles—and to reject true strict liability principles—in landmark prescription drug and medical device cases over the years. See *Brown v. Superior Court*, 751 P.2d 470 (Cal. 1988); *Feldman v. Lederle Labs.*, 479 A.2d 374 (N.J. 1984) (in warnings cases, negligence and strict liability are "functional equivalents").

The reasons for preferring negligence principles to true strict liability in this context include:

- Banning foreseeability from the liability calculus—the principal way in which strict liability distinguishes itself from negligence—does violence to basic principles of justice and fair play;

- The extra deterrent effect of strict liability is needed less for products whose warnings must be specifically approved prior to marketing by a federal agency, the FDA; and

- The risk of too *much* deterrence, discouraging pharmaceutical manufacturers from investing in new prescription drugs and medical devices, already extremely expensive to develop and bring to market, for fear of financial ruin if the new product possesses unexpected problems.

For these and other reasons, while most courts in this context continue to apply "strict" liability by name to warnings cases, the principles that most of them in fact apply are nothing more than negligence. Section 6(d) of the *Third Restatement* follows this approach in limiting a manufacturer's warning responsibility in prescription drug and medical device cases to a duty to provide "reasonable instructions or warnings regarding foreseeable risks of harm."

Regulation by the FDA

In addition to ensuring that prescription drugs are safe and effective before they are sold in interstate commerce, the FDA approves all information a manufacturer plans to provide physicians on a drug's recommended use, contraindications, risks, and side effects. Underlying the regulatory scheme are two assumptions reflecting the special types of dangers that inhere in drugs classified as prescription pharmaceuticals. First is the belief that the risks in many drugs are so complex and dangerous that the FDA must determine their safety and effectiveness before they can be marketed at all. The second premise is that the potential risks of improperly using many drugs are so substantial as to require professional medical judgment and supervision by doctors and nurse practitioners, rendering such products available to consumers only through prescriptions written by such health professionals.

Who Must Be Warned—The "Learned Intermediary Doctrine"

In General

In addition to the required pre-market approval by the FDA, a prescription drug's warnings and instructions must be provided to health professionals—doctors and nurse practitioners—rather than directly to patients. Such "learned intermediaries" stand between the drug manufacturer and the patient, dispensing what medications and information they deem best. Thus, like the sophisticated user and bulk supplier doctrines previously examined, the learned intermediary doctrine is an exception to the general requirement that manufacturers take all reasonable steps to provide warnings directly to a product's ultimate user or consumer. That is, under the "learned intermediary doctrine," the prescription drug manufacturer's duty to inform consumers runs only indirectly through physicians, rather than directly to consumers.

The basic rationale for the learned intermediary doctrine is quite powerful: medical professionals, and only medical professionals, have the requisite knowledge, training, and judgment to properly match particular drugs with distinctive benefits and dangers to particular patients with distinctive constitutions and medical conditions, and to properly monitor the results thereafter. If manufacturers fulfill their obligations to provide full and fair information to health care professionals, those professionals should be able to make intelligent, reasonably safe, and effective treatment decisions. In turn, a prescribing doctor is obliged under the law of torts to inform the patient of a drug's benefits and dangers (as well as the benefits and dangers of no treatment and alternative treatments), and to monitor how the drug affects the patient. See *Larkin v. Pfizer, Inc.*, 153 S.W.3d 758 (Ky. 2004) (summarizing rationales).

Sprouting in the 1960s, and becoming firmly planted in the early 1970s, the learned intermediary doctrine is an established fixture in American products liability law, adopted now in almost every state. In addition to prescription drugs, the learned intermediary doctrine has been applied to a various medical devices, but *not* to extended-wear contact lenses fitted by an optometrist. While efforts to apply the doctrine outside the medical field have largely failed, some courts, misled by the generality of the doctrine's name, have used the "learned intermediary" label when applying principles of the "sophisticated user doctrine" to other types of products. The rule was explicitly endorsed by § 6(d) of the *Third Restatement*.

Exceptions

If a prescription drug is dispensed under circumstances where a health professional does not render the type of individualized balancing of risks and benefits contemplated by the learned intermediary doctrine, warnings may have to be provided directly to the patient. That is, when the rationale for the learned intermediary doctrine falls away, the general rule requiring manufacturers to warn consumers directly reappears. This commonsense principle has spawned three exceptions, only one of which has much support.

Mass immunization programs. The most established exception to the learned intermediary rule is for mass immunization programs where no health professional mediates information about drug risks for the benefit of the patient. As an exception to the learned intermediary rule, which itself is an exception to the manufacturer's general obligation to warn consumers directly, the mass immunization doctrine restores the manufacturer's duty to provide warnings directly to recipients of the vaccine.

Birth control pills. *MacDonald v. Ortho Pharmaceutical Corp.*, 475 N.E.2d 65, 70 (Mass. 1985), made an exception to the learned intermediary doctrine for birth control pills, reasoning that oral contraceptives "stand apart" from other types of prescription medications because of the "heightened participation of patients in decisions relating to use of 'the pill'; the substantial risks affiliated with the product's use; the feasibility of direct warnings by the manufacturer to the user; the limited participation of the physician (annual prescriptions); and the possibility that oral communications between physicians and consumers may be insufficient or too scanty standing alone to apprise consumers fully of the product's dangers at the time the initial selection of a contraceptive method is made and at subsequent points when alternative methods may be considered." For these reasons, the court concluded that birth control pill manufacturers must provide warnings directly to ultimate users on the nature, gravity, and likelihood of foreseeable side effects.

The dissenting justice, observing that manufacturers of prescription pharmaceuticals have a duty to provide full information on all material risks to prescribing physicians who, in turn, have a duty (under the informed consent doctrine, redressable in a malpractice action) to provide full information on all material risks to patients for whom they prescribe the drug, argued that this traditional division of responsibility best allocates risks and responsibilities among the parties. While *MacDonald* frequently is cited as creating a new common-law exception to the learned intermediary rule for birth control pills, only a couple of federal judges followed it, and other courts uniformly reject it and continue to apply the learned intermediary doctrine to birth control pills as other types of prescription pharmaceuticals.

Direct–to–consumer advertising. *Perez v. Wyeth Labs.*, 734 A.2d 1245 (N.J. 1999), ruled that the learned intermediary doctrine should no longer insulate prescription drug manufacturers from a duty to warn consumers directly if manufacturers seek to influence their choice of drugs through mass-marketing. The court reasoned that the learned intermediary doctrine was based on outmoded images of health care from a time when doctors made house calls, charged small sums for their advice, and prescribed medicines compounded by neighborhood pharmacists. Sadly, this picture is radically different from the health care world that presently exists. Today, managed health care organizations are mammoth businesses, dispensing medical care and prescriptions impersonally; and medicines are manufactured in distant places, sold over the Internet and in supermarket pharmacy departments, and often paid for by third-party providers. Against this back-drop, modern manufacturers of prescription drugs mass-market their wares directly to consumers by radio, television, the Internet, billboards on public transportation, and in magazines. The court observed that the problems in these advertising practices are manifest, permitting manufacturers and advertisers to manipulate information on safety and effectiveness that, at best, presents a diluted picture of a product's risks.

Since *Perez*, several other courts have reconsidered the learned intermediary doctrine in light of direct-to-consumer advertising, the sale of prescription pharmaceuticals over the Internet from abroad, and the general depersonalization of health care delivery in the modern world. For eight years, all courts considering the issue rejected *Perez* and continued to apply the learned intermediary doctrine. But in 2007, the West Virginia Supreme Court of Appeals, as a matter of first impression, refused to adopt the learned intermediary doctrine in *State v. Karl*, 647 S.E.2d 899, 900, 919 (W. Va. 2007). While acknowledging that most states have adopted the doctrine, and that many lower court decisions have applied it, the majority opinion lists 21 states whose high courts have *not* adopted this special drug exception to the ordinary duty of manufacturers to provide warnings directly to consumers. Agreeing with *Perez* that the learned intermediary doctrine is outmoded in the modern medical world, the *Karl* majority held that "manufacturers of prescription drugs are subject to the same duty to warn consumers about the risks of their products as other manufacturers." Concurring, Justice Maynard observed that "[p]atients can read the labels, instructions and warnings, and if the manufacturer makes them clear enough, then patients can be proactive in working with their doctors to receive the best care."

Now that *Perez* is accompanied by *Karl*, it may well be that other jurisdictions will begin to rethink the logic of applying a rigid, paternalistic doctrine that developed under very different circumstances than exist today. But two decisions do not make a trend, and it is still too early to know when other courts may begin to recognize the wisdom of broadening the duty of pharmaceutical manufacturers to share vital information about drug risks directly with consumers.

Of these three exceptions, note that only the mass immunization program exception is generally accepted, and even it is applied infrequently. Nonetheless, *Products Liability Restatement* § 6(d) provides a general exception wide enough to accommodate all three exceptions.

Adequacy of Warnings

The principles of adequacy applicable to warnings generally, discussed above, apply as well to prescription drugs and medical devices. All material information on possible risks must be conveyed to the doctor, comprehensible to the general practitioner as well as to the specialist, or to consumers, comprehensible to them, if the circumstances warrant. For a drug or medical device warning to be "adequate," it must describe the scope of the danger; the effects of misuse, including the failure to follow instructions; and the physical aspects of the warning, and broader method of conveyance, must be likely to alert recipients to the danger. Other aspects of a warning's adequacy discussed above apply as well to prescription drugs and medical devices, including whether warnings should be made in foreign languages, and the effect of "overpromotion."

The Products Liability Restatement

The *Third Restatement* defines a manufacturer's responsibility for warning defects in drugs and medical devices in conventional negligence terms that give no cause to cavil. In § 6(d), the *Third Restatement* provides that "[a] prescription drug or medical device is not reasonably safe due to inadequate instructions or warnings if reasonable instructions or warnings regarding foreseeable risks of harm are not provided to" health care providers or patients, depending on the applicability of the learned intermediary doctrine, as discussed above. Principles of adequacy are embraced by the requirement that warnings and instructions be "reasonable," and the limitation on responsibility to "foreseeable" risks reflects the now well-established principle that the law should not hold manufacturers of drugs, medical devices, or any other type of product responsible for harm that is unforeseeable or otherwise unavoidable under the prevailing state of the art.

The Pharmacist's Duty to Warn

Because pharmacists are more in the nature of service providers, like doctors, than retail merchants, like hatters, they are subject to liability for selling prescription drugs only in negligence, not strict liability. See *Madison v. American Home Products Corp.*, 595 S.E.2d 493 (S.C. 2004) (pharmacy not subject to strict liability for filling prescription in accordance with doctor's orders). In filling prescriptions, pharmacists are held to the highest standard of care, such that a pharmacist who makes a mistake in filling a prescription is almost certainly responsible for any resulting harm. But pharmacists long have been held to have no duty other than to dispense drugs accurately according to the terms of a valid prescription.

In particular, pharmacists simply have no general duty to warn patients—not even to pass along package inserts (intended for physicians) containing detailed warnings—of hazards or side effects in prescription drugs that they dispense. See *Deed v. Walgreen Co.*, 927 A.2d 1001 (Conn. Super. Ct. 2007) (pharmacy customer died from acute toxicity resulting from 149 prescriptions filled according to physician directions in the year prior to her death; pharmacy had no duty to warn); *Schaerrer v. Stewart's Plaza Pharmacy*, 79 P.3d 922 (Utah 2003) (pharmacist compounded and sold phen-fen without warning of risks); *Moore v. Memorial Hosp. of Gulfport*, 825 So.2d 658 (Miss. 2002) (pharmacist did not warn pregnant woman that Diovan was contraindicated for pregnancy, and child suffered kidney failure as a result).

The pharmacist's immunity from a general duty to warn patients has been justified on a number of grounds, including:

- The learned intermediary doctrine's placement of warning responsibilities solely on doctors and nurse practitioners who theoretically are aware of a patient's treatment needs as well as the benefits and dangers of particular prescription drugs;
- The burdens on pharmacists of having to second-guess decisions of prescribing doctors;
- The confusion of patients receiving conflicting information from their doctors and pharmacists; and
- An assumption that doctors are simply better skilled than pharmacists at evaluating the possible consequences of prescription medications.

But cracks are beginning to appear in the pharmacist's general immunity from a duty to warn, reflecting legislative requirements that pharmacists monitor and counsel their clients about prescription drugs, a development that has stimulated increased education and professionalism in this field. In a number of cases, courts have held that pharmacists may have a duty of reasonable care to warn in certain circumstances, as where there is a clear error on the face of the prescription, such as when the medication's maximum dosage is not denoted; or if the pharmacist knows a drug is contraindicated for the customer, as when a pharmacist knows a customer is an alcoholic, has an allergy, or is taking another, incompatible drug. In addition, if a pharmacist *undertakes* to collect data on a client's allergies, to monitor its clients prescriptions for drug interactions, or, perhaps, to warn of side effects, it normally will be bound to perform that undertaking with reasonable care. In such situations where a pharmacist has special knowledge of a risk to a particular client, courts have sometimes broken through the traditional immunity and held that pharmacists *do* have a duty of reasonable care to warn of the risk of addiction, potential drug interactions, and other adverse effects of prescription drugs.

How far these small cracks in the pharmacist's no-duty-to-warn wall eventually may propagate is impossible to say. There clearly is no stampede to break down the pharmacist's virtual immunity from a warning obligation. Yet the pharmacy profession is changing in ways that suggest that these strategically positioned experts in prescription pharmaceuticals might properly be required to bear a greater responsibility for warning patients of the hazards of such medications.

CHAPTER 10

LIMITATIONS ON DEFECTIVENESS

Table of Sections

§ 10.1　Limitations on Defectiveness—Generally.
§ 10.2　Obvious Dangers.
§ 10.3　Inherent Product Hazards.
§ 10.4　State of the Art.
§ 10.5　Prenatal Harm.
§ 10.6　Deterioration.
§ 10.7　Disposal and Salvage.
§ 10.8　Post–Sale Duties to Warn, Repair, or Recall.

———

§ 10.1　LIMITATIONS ON DEFECTIVENESS— GENERALLY

The inquiry to this point has focused on when and why manufacturers *should* be held accountable for accidental harm caused by defective products. In this chapter, the focus reverses direction to a consideration of arguments and doctrine that *deny* a manufacturer's responsibility for harm from product accidents. While the underlying justifications for assigning responsibility in such cases remain largely the same—feasibility, economic efficiency, manufacturer accountability, consumer choice, personal responsibility, and judicial competency—the issues explored here (as in the remaining chapters) look past the preliminary conditions and justifications for imposing liability to factors that tend to *limit* a manufacturer's duty for harm from product hazards. For a more thorough examination of limitations on defectiveness, see Owen, Products Liability Law ch. 10 (2d ed. 2008).

§ 10.2   OBVIOUS DANGERS

Design Defects

Prior to the 1970s, victims of accidents from obvious design dangers were broadly barred from recovery under the "patent-danger doctrine." The classic case was *Campo v. Scofield*, 95 N.E.2d 802 (N.Y. 1950) (Fuld, J.). The plaintiff, working on his son's farm, was dumping a crate of onions into an "onion topping" machine when his hands were caught and injured in its revolving steel rollers. In his suit against the manufacturers of the machine for negligently failing to equip it with a guard or stopping device, the trial court denied the defendants' motion to dismiss, but the Appellate Division reversed. On appeal, *held,* affirmed: the plaintiff's failure to allege that the danger was latent or unknown was fatal to the complaint:

> If a manufacturer does everything necessary to make the machine function properly for the purpose for which it is designed, if the machine is

without any latent defect, and if its functioning creates no danger or peril that is not known to the user, then the manufacturer has satisfied the law's demands.

Id. at 804. A manufacturer simply has no duty to protect people against "a patent peril or from a source manifestly dangerous." Otherwise, the manufacturer of an axe, buzz saw, or airplane with an exposed propeller would be subject to liability to a user cut by the blade or propeller. But a "manufacturer has the right to expect that such persons will do everything necessary to avoid such contact, for the very nature of the article gives notice and warning of the consequences to be expected." In short, manufacturers have no duty to design out dangers that are "obvious and patent to all."

Campo was not the first case so holding, but it anchored the patent-danger doctrine like a rock. During the 1950s and 1960s, many other courts adopted or reaffirmed the *Campo* obvious-danger rule. For example, in *Bartkewich v. Billinger*, 247 A.2d 603 (Pa. 1968), the hand of a glass-breaking machine operator was crushed when he reached into the machine to free a piece of glass that was jamming it. Addressing the worker's design defect claim against the manufacturer for failing to provide guards or strategically located cut-off switches, the court held that the manufacturer had no such duty: "If he thought the machine was being damaged, what did he think would happen to his hand?"

But not all courts were unsympathetic to the plight of workers and others injured by obvious product dangers, and as the consumer protectionist perspectives of § 402A swept across America in the late 1960s, adherence to the patent-danger rule began to soften. Some courts, persuaded by the safety, representational, and risk-spreading rationales behind the new strict tort doctrine, began to ignore defendants' pleas to apply the patent-danger doctrine. And, by 1970, some courts began expressly to reject the obvious-danger rule as outmoded and wrong-headed. See *Palmer v. Massey–Ferguson, Inc.*, 476 P.2d 713, 719 (Wash. Ct. App. 1970) (The patent-danger rule "is somewhat anomalous. The manufacturer of the obviously defective product ought not to escape because the product was obviously a bad one. The law, we think, ought to discourage misdesign rather than encouraging it in its obvious form.").

As the decade of the 1970s progressed, more and more courts rejected the patent-danger doctrine in design defect cases, holding that the obviousness of a danger is merely one factor in assessing the negligence or defectiveness of a design, not an absolute bar to liability. The landmark case repudiating the obvious-danger doctrine was decided by the same court that had provided the doctrine's bedrock *Campo* decision. In *Micallef v. Miehle Co.*, 348 N.E.2d 571 (N.Y. 1976), the New York court repudiated *Campo*'s patent-danger rule, observing that it had suffered a "sustained attack" by courts and commentators and was little more than an assumption of risk defense as a matter of law. While the obviousness of a product danger might reduce the likelihood of accidents, and so factor into the calculus of risk, and while a danger's obviousness might affect the issues of contributory negligence and assumption of risk, "the patent-danger doctrine should not, in and of itself, prevent a plaintiff from establishing his case."

Once the *Campo* patent-danger doctrine was repudiated in its own home state, the rule proceeded to collapse around the nation. One court after another, usually for claims in both negligence and strict liability in tort, abandoned the rule's absolute no-duty power and reduced the obviousness of danger to mere "factor" status in the cost-benefit evaluation of the safety of a product's design. Some states continued the obvious-danger rule into the 1980s, and a few lingering offshoots of the doctrine persisted in five or six states even into the 1990s. Perhaps the doctrine's last real stronghold was the state of Georgia, and the Supreme Court of that state finally surrendered in 1998. See *Ogletree v. Navistar Int'l Trans. Corp.*, 500 S.E.2d 570 (Ga. 1998).

Despite the formal collapse of the patent-danger doctrine in recent decades, it is important to note that the obviousness of a product's risk still serves as a *total* bar to liability in some jurisdictions in special situations and in other states under the guise of the consumer expectations test or a misreading of § 402A's comment *j*. That said, the rise and fall of the patent-danger rule in design defect cases during the last half of the twentieth century is one of the fascinating tales of products liability law. Now entirely discredited as an absolute limitation on a manufacturer's duties of design in virtually every state, the patent-danger doctrine as an independent no-duty rule in design defect cases essentially is dead.

Warning Defects

In contrast to design cases, modern courts widely hold that there simply is no duty to *warn* of dangers that are obvious. While two courts (Colo., Mont.) still hold that the *Micallef* only-one-factor principle applies to warning cases too, the great majority of courts hold, and statutes in several states provide, that manufacturers and other sellers have no duty to warn of dangers that are open, obvious, or commonly known. See *Johnson v. American Standard, Inc.*, 179 P.3d 905 (Cal. 2008); Ohio Rev. Code Ann. § 2307.76(B) (no duty to warn of risk that is open and obvious or a matter of common knowledge).

A warning of a *hidden* danger provides users with useful information that enables them to act so as to reduce or avoid the risk, but courts frequently observe that it is senseless to require warning of dangers that are *obvious*. If a product's danger is evident for all to see, it carries the warning of danger on its face, so to speak, such that adding a formal warning of the danger would duplicate information users already possess. Indeed, requiring such warnings trivializes warnings generally, which may lead to an increase in product injuries rather than the other way around.

Thus, courts have ruled that there is no duty to warn about the obvious and generally known risks of spilling hot coffee; shooting a BB gun at a person's eye; riding a motorcycle with the kickstand down; jump-starting a bulldozer while kneeling on its track; operating a forklift without an overhead guard; allowing a 3-year-old child to ride on the running board of a tractor over bumpy ground; driving into the side of a moving train; suffering electrocution from a frayed extension cord, or from striking a power line with a CB antenna, an aluminum sailboat mast, mop handle, ladder, or possibly a crane; sticking a limb into a potato chopper, a drill press, under a power lawn mower, or into the propeller of an outboard motor; playing with a loaded pistol; diving headfirst into a shallow above-ground swimming pool; leaving a butane cigarette lighter in the reach of young children; flying a private plane without locking the seat to prevent it from slipping back, depriving the pilot of control; smoking cigarettes; lighting a cigarette minutes after being soaked with gasoline at the pump; falling from a ladder; colliding head-on with another vehicle at speeds in excess of 100 mph; or driving a car after drinking too much beer.

Defining "Obvious"

A danger is "obvious" if it would be apparent to an ordinary or reasonable user or consumer of the type of product involved in the accident. Rest. (2d)

§ 343A cmt. *b*. Many courts logically widen the notion to include hazards which may be classified as being widely, generally, or commonly known and recognized. See *Glittenberg v. Doughboy Recreational Indus.*, 491 N.W.2d 208, 213 (Mich. 1992) (if the hazard "is fully apparent, widely known, commonly recognized, and anticipated by the ordinary user or consumer"). Thus, the issue requires an *objective* determination of whether the risk is evident to ordinary or reasonable persons in the plaintiff's position—*not* whether the risk is perceived by the particular plaintiff.

§ 10.3 INHERENT PRODUCT HAZARDS

A small handful of courts and a number of commentators have taken the position that a product can fail a risk-utility test applied to a product considered *as a whole,* as distinguished from the normal risk-utility test that balances the costs and benefits of *a particular untaken precaution*, the absence of which the plaintiff asserts rendered the product's design defective. In some cases, the argument goes, even though there is no practicable way to design away the product's inherent danger, a product may be adjudged defective at a global level if it fails a "macro-balance" of its social costs and benefits—if, on balance and in the aggregate, the product is simply "bad." Yet the vast majority of courts have been markedly unreceptive to such arguments, decisively refusing to displace markets, legislatures, and governmental agencies by decreeing whole categories of products to be "outlaws." See *Rose v. Brown & Williamson Tobacco Corp.*, 855 N.Y.S.2d 119, 125 (App. Div. 2008) (courts should not effectively outlaw cigarettes that have "long been consciously tolerated—and taxed and regulated—by the political branches of government"); *Parish v. Jumpking*, 719 N.W.2d 540 (Iowa 2006) (trampoline); *Jones v. Amazing Prods., Inc.*, 231 F.Supp.2d 1228, 1250 (N.D. Ga. 2002) (drain cleaner containing 97% sulfuric acid not defectively designed where CPSC had found sulfuric acid no more dangerous than other drain cleaner chemicals: "Traditionally, legislatures and regulatory bodies, not juries, make policy decisions concerning whether a given product is too inherently dangerous to be marketed in any form.").

Both the *Second* and *Third Restatements* endorse this highly restrained judicial approach. The *Second Restatement* addresses unavoidably dangerous products—such as food, alcohol, cigarettes, and drugs—in comments *i, j,* and *k* to § 402A. These comments make clear that a manufacturer of such unavoidably dangerous products must avoid manufacturing defects (such as contamination) and must warn of hidden dangers. But the central message of the comments to § 402A, responding to the central concern at the time (the early 1960s) over the potentially broad scope of the new strict liability doctrine, is that a manufacturer of useful but unavoidably dangerous products is *not* liable for making them available to a public who desires them despite knowing of their inherent risks. See *Myers v. Philip Morris Cos.*, 50 P.3d 751 (Cal. 2002).

The *Third Restatement* emphatically adheres to the principle that entire categories of products commonly understood to be inherently dangerous (there illustrated as alcoholic beverages, firearms, and above-ground swimming pools, but *not* cigarettes) cannot be judicially classified as "defective" in *design*. That is, the *Third Restatement* takes the position that plaintiffs in design defect cases generally must establish that the manufacturer failed to adopt some reasonable method for designing out the danger—an impossible task, of course, if a product's inherent risks are, by hypothesis, unavoidable.

Yet the *Third Restatement* recognizes that some courts have quite reasonably retained wiggle room for rare cases to conclude that an "egregiously unacceptable" product may be of "manifestly unreasonable design," even if there is no reasonable way to design the danger away—cases where "the extremely high degree of danger posed by its use or consumption so substantially outweighs its negligible social utility that no rational, reasonable person, fully aware of the relevant facts, would choose to use, or to allow children to use, the product." § 2 cmt. *e*. Yet the list of such products must properly be short, including only products—such as toy guns that shoot hard pellets at high velocity, exploding novelty cigars, lawn darts, and clothing made of highly flammable fabrics—that courts can confidently declare possess far greater risk than utility, such that they probably should not be sold at all. Moreover, courts should be wary of allowing most of these claims to go to the jury and so normally should bar such claims as a matter of law. See *Jones*, above (97% sulfuric acid drain cleaner).

Alcohol, *cigarettes*, and, most recently, *fast food* may be singled out as prototypical products containing inherent risks that victims sometimes seek to shift judicially to manufacturers. Rarely do courts in such cases explicitly address the underlying social welfare question of whether courts and juries should characterize such products as defective (in design) because their global injury costs exceed their global social benefits. Occasionally, however, courts do address issues of personal autonomy that lie close to the heart of these cases—concepts of free choice and individual responsibility—concepts which support the idea that consumers who choose to accept the benefits of an obviously and unavoidably dangerous product must accept responsibility for the product's risks as well. Sometimes this powerful ideal finds doctrinal expression in the consumer expectations test of product defectiveness, or in rules on assumption of risk or no duty to warn of commonly known dangers, but frequently it lies hidden below discussions of unrelated legal doctrines. Embedded in various rules of products liability law, the value of personal responsibility assuredly is the reason why plaintiffs have had such little success in convincing courts and juries that cigarette manufacturers should pay for the hundreds of thousands of American smokers who die each year.

§ 10.4 STATE OF THE ART

In products liability law, "state of the art" is an unrefined concept whose meaning and proper role still continue to evolve. Nevertheless, emerging from the cases and statutes is a common theme: reluctance to impose liability on manufacturers for dangers that were unknowable, or unpreventable, at the time their products were sold—reluctance to hold producers responsible for risks they cannot control.

State-of-the-art issues may be conveniently classified according to whether an asserted defect is one of warning or design. In *warning* cases, the state-of-the-art issue raises the question of whether a manufacturer has a duty to warn of *unforeseeable* dangers. This issue often arises in cases involving pharmaceutical drugs, chemicals, and other substances, such as asbestos, that may be discovered to have toxic effects only after such products are marketed and harm consumers, sometimes generations later. In *design* cases, the state-of-the-art issue raises the question of whether a manufacturer has a duty to design away *unavoidable* dangers. The question in these types of cases, usually involving durable products like lawn mowers and punch presses, is not whether the *risks* are known or knowable, for the hazards are well known, but whether the means of *avoiding* the risks, by designing them away, are known or reasonably knowable and feasible under the existing state of science and technology.

Changes in Science and Technology

As science and technology evolve over time, and as new and improved methods for discovering and eliminating product hazards are developed, public attitudes toward risk and responsibility also evolve. In the twenty-first century, people expect much more safety in machine guarding, automotive crash protection, and fabric flammability than they did in 1900, or even in 1950. "A consumer would not expect a Model T to have the safety features which are incorporated in automobiles made today." *Bruce v. Martin–Marietta Corp.*, 544 F.2d 442, 447 (10th Cir. 1976) (Md. law). Whether manufacturers should be liable for failing to avert product-caused injuries that happen today, but which were unforeseeable or unpreventable (literally or practicably) at the time a product was designed and sold, raises difficult and important questions of logic, fairness, social policy, and legal doctrine. Penetrating to the heart of the notions of defectiveness and "strict" liability, the state-of-the-art issue forces a reexamination of the goals of products liability law.

Definitions

As products liability law has developed, the terms "undiscoverable," "unknowable," "unavoidable," and "state of the art" have often been interchanged indiscriminately by courts and commentators attempting to describe certain kinds of risks that manufacturers and other sellers are unable to control. Increasingly, however, issues of this type are collected under the latter phrase, as in "state-of-the-art evidence" and "state-of-the-art defense." Neither courts nor legislatures have agreed on a definition of the term. Thus, "state of the art" means quite different things to different persons. To many manufacturers and some courts, the phrase refers to customary practice in the industry. To many plaintiffs' counsel and some courts, it means the ultimate in existing technology, including all knowledge pertinent to a problem existing at the time, regardless of its location or source, regardless of whether possessed by or accessible from industrial, governmental, or academic institutions, or even from the defendant's competitors.

Neither of these extreme views of state of the art is a helpful definition for products liability law. Most judicial opinions and statutes define the state-of-the-art idea more moderately in terms of feasible safety: Nebraska's act defines state of the art as "the best technology reasonably available at the time," Missouri's statute states that the phrase "means that the dangerous nature of the product was not known and could not reasonably be discovered at the time the product was placed into the stream of commerce," and Arizona's statute provides that the term means "the technical, mechanical and scientific knowledge of manufacturing, designing, testing or labeling the same or similar products which was in existence and reasonably feasible for use at the time of manufacture."

Thus, "state of the art" definitions vary considerably, some leaning more toward industry custom, others leaning more toward theoretical scientific or technological capability, and the best ones lying somewhere in between.

Applicability to Different Types of Claims

Negligence

Negligence claims are predicated on a manufacturer's ability to foresee and prevent product accidents. In a negligent *warning* case, if a risk is "unknowable," it is "unforeseeable" and so lies outside the manufacturer's duty to avoid. In a negligent *design* case, if the manufacturer had no practical ability to eliminate a danger, then the burden on the manufacturer to avoid an injury outweighs virtually any risk of harm. Perhaps all courts thus hold that state-of-the-art evidence is especially relevant to products liability claims brought in negligence.

Strict Liability

The relevance of the state-of-the-art issue to *strict* liability claims is more problematic. "Strict" liability implies that liability is imposed merely for selling a product that is too dangerous, according to some standard of excessive danger, *not* whether the manufacturer or other seller should be faulted for selling the product. Indeed, "strict liability" is often labeled "no-fault" liability. If fault indeed is irrelevant to this form of liability, the state-of-the-art issue might appear to be irrelevant to whether a manufacturer is strictly liable for selling a defective product.

This was the court's thinking in *Johnson v. Raybestos–Manhattan, Inc.*, 740 P.2d 548 (Haw. 1987), an asbestos case in which the court ruled that state-of-the-art evidence on the foreseeability of risk was not relevant to a "strict" tort claim that considers the condition of the product, not the conduct of the manufacturer. A small handful of older decisions agree, and at least a couple of courts more recently have reaffirmed their commitment to a truly "strict" products liability doctrine uncontaminated by principles of foreseeability, fault, negligence, or state of the art. See *Townsend v. Sears, Roebuck & Co.*, 879 N.E.2d 893 (Ill. 2007) (dictum); *Golonka v. General Motors Corp.*, 65 P.3d 956 (Ariz. Ct. App. 2003); *Green v. Smith & Nephew AHP, Inc.*, 629 N.W.2d 727 (Wis. 2001).

From a strictly doctrinal perspective, barring state-of-the-art evidence is logical under a pure consumer expectations test for defectiveness because a manufacturer's knowledge of a danger or ability to eliminate it might well seem irrelevant to the degree of safety consumers actually expect. Nevertheless, some courts allow state-of-the-art evidence even under the consumer expectations test, reasoning that such evidence helps to determine the safety expectations of ordinary consumers, which tend to increase over time. See *Bruce v. Martin–Marietta Corp.*, 544 F.2d 442 (10th Cir. 1976) (Okla. law).

The Wade–Keeton constructive knowledge test of liability, which imputes knowledge of all a product's dangers to the manufacturer, compels rejection of the state-of-the-art defense, at least in cases involving a failure to warn. By its nature, this test evaluates the safety of a product with the hindsight available at the time of trial and so leaves no room for evidence, much less a defense, based on the state of knowledge prevailing at the time the product was made and sold.

However, as the risk-utility test of design defectiveness has increasingly displaced the consumer expectations standard around the nation, and as the Wade–Keeton constructive knowledge test has fallen into desuetude, the relevance of state-of-the-art evidence in *design* defect cases has become increasingly clear. In balancing the costs and benefits of a design feature that would have prevented the plaintiff's injury, the risk-utility test rests on (1) the foreseeability of the risk, and (2) the availability of a *feasible* alternative design. Consequently, in the increasing number of jurisdictions that employ some form of risk-utility test for design defectiveness, courts widely hold that state-of-the-art evidence is admissible on the issue of the defectiveness of a product's design. See *Folsom v. Kawasaki Motors Corp. U.S.A.*, 509 F.Supp.2d 1364 (M.D. Ga. 2007) ("the state of the art at the time the product is manufactured" is one factor in the risk-utility analysis); *Falada v. Trinity Indus.*, 642 N.W.2d 247 (Iowa 2002) (statutory defense); *LaBelle v. Philip Morris Inc.*, 243 F.Supp.2d 508 (D.S.C. 2001) (Pa.

law) (no design defect if plaintiff unable to prove availability of technology to make safer cigarette); *Potter v. Chicago Pneumatic Tool Co.*, 694 A.2d 1319, 1347 (Conn. 1997) (such evidence is "relevant and assists the jury in determining whether a product is defective and unreasonably dangerous").

In *warning* defect cases involving "unknowable" risks of harm, state-of-the-art evidence plays a critical role, regardless of the liability test employed. Notwithstanding the approach of a few decisions (such as the *Johnson* asbestos case discussed above), almost all courts allow state-of-the-art evidence in such cases to defeat strict liability claims. Otherwise stated, and as examined below, the vast majority of courts today refuse to impose a duty on manufacturers to warn of unknowable risks—and, hence, refuse to enforce a liability standard that is truly "strict."

Unknowable Dangers—Duty to Warn of Unknowable Risks

Truly unknowable risks are a rarity in products liability law. Cases involving genuinely unforeseeable hazards surely must represent less than one in a hundred products liability cases, and probably less than one in a thousand. Manufacturers of *durable products* virtually always can foresee the harmful consequences of their products: that a punch press may crush a hand, that a defective electrical appliance may start a fire, or that a car may crush inward or roll over in an accident. Claims of unknowable risks are far more common in cases involving *toxic substances*—pharmaceutical drugs, other chemical products, and certain natural substances such as asbestos and tobacco, all of which may cause cancer or other untoward harm. Even in such toxic substance cases, however, if manufacturers have conducted proper testing and laboratory analysis, truly unforeseeable dangers are very unusual.

Notwithstanding the rarity of legitimate claims that a product hazard was unknowable at the time of marketing, this issue does sometimes arise. And when it does, the question of whether a manufacturer has a duty to warn of unknowable dangers presents the starkest and most intriguing state-of-the-art issue of all.

Prior to § 402A, the few courts considering the state-of-the-art issue, in both negligence and warranty, had mostly held that a manufacturer only had to warn of risks of which the manufacturer knew or reasonably should have known. Beginning in 1965, § 402A seemed to change all this, because it defined strict liability explicitly in no-fault form, so that the new liability standard on its face appeared to banish any possible defense based upon a manufacturer's best efforts to make its products safe. Such a definition seemed to preclude any possibility of a ''state of the art'' defense based on the unforeseeability of a product risk.

Comments j and k

Yet another aspect of § 402A suggests the opposite—that manufacturers should *not* have a duty to warn of unknowable risks. Notwithstanding the general "strictness" prescribed by § 402A's black-letter liability standard, two comments to that section, comments *j* and *k*, address the duty to warn in *negligence* terms and effectively provide that the duty to warn under § 402A is limited to *foreseeable* risks. Comment *j* provides that a seller must warn of significant latent risks "if he has knowledge, or by the application of reasonable, developed human skill and foresight should have knowledge, of the presence of the ingredient and the danger." Comment *k* states that a seller of an unavoidably dangerous product, such as a new or experimental drug or vaccine, "is not to be held to strict liability for unfortunate consequences attending their use, merely because he has undertaken to supply the public with an apparently useful and desirable product, attended with a known but apparently reasonable risk." Together, though they generally are read too widely, see § 6.2, above, these two comments may suggest that sellers are immunized from liability for failing to warn of unknowable product risks.

The "Wade–Keeton" Test

Comments *j* and *k* probably would have effectively squelched any notion of a duty to warn of unknowable hazards were it not for the development of the "Wade–Keeton" hindsight or constructive knowledge test, discussed in § 8.7, above. In the 1960s and early 1970s, both scholars reasoned that the law should base strict liability on *hindsight*, by imputing "constructive knowledge" to manufacturers of all subsequently discovered product dangers. Strict liability thus depended on whether a manufacturer would be negligent in selling a product if it had known of the risks the product actually possessed. The sole distinction between the Wade–Keeton test and ordinary negligence was that the constructive knowledge aspect of the standard eliminated the requirement of the law of negligence that the risk of harm be foreseeable.

As products liability litigation began to spread around the nation, courts increasingly adopted the Wade–Keeton constructive knowledge test for defining strict products liability in tort. At the same time, however, courts continued to turn to comments *j* and *k* for guidance on the scope of a manufacturer's duty to warn. Yet courts for quite awhile studiously avoided a head-on collision of these two inconsistent standards.

The New Jersey Experience—Beshada and Feldman

Apart from *Henningsen* and *Greenman*, the two most important judicial decisions in modern products liability history may well be *Beshada v. Johns–Manville Products Corp.*, 447 A.2d 539 (N.J. 1982), and *Feldman v. Lederle Labs.*, 479 A.2d 374 (N.J. 1984), for they present a microcosm of the rise and fall of strict products liability in this nation. *Beshada* was the first significant case in the United States applying the Wade–Keeton test and other principles of strict products liability to a warning claim defended on the ground that the risk was

unforeseeable. That is, this was the first state supreme court decision squarely confronting the question of whether there should be a duty on manufacturers to warn of unknowable product risks.

Beshada was an asbestos case brought by insulation workers who suffered asbestosis and mesothelioma from working with asbestos insulation products over many years. The workers claimed that the
manufacturers breached their strict liability duty to
warn of these dangers, and the defendants asserted
a state-of-the-art defense, claiming that no one at
the time knew or could have known that asbestos
was so dangerous to insulation workers. Reaffirm-
ing the Wade–Keeton constructive knowledge test,
the New Jersey Supreme Court unanimously ruled
that a defendant's compliance with the state-of-the-
art is *not* a defense to a strict liability failure to
warn claim. The court likened the defendants'
state-of-the-art position to an argument that they
were not at fault. "But in strict liability cases," the
court explained, "culpability is irrelevant." That
the product "was unsafe because of the state of
technology does not change the fact that it was
unsafe. Strict liability focuses on the product, not
the fault of the manufacturer."

In addition to a doctrinal explication, the *Beshada* court explained the policy rationales for holding
manufacturers responsible for failing to warn of
undiscoverable dangers:

  • ***Risk spreading***—Costs of product injuries are
  better placed on manufacturers, who may spread

them widely, than on "the innocent victims who suffer illnesses and disability from defective products. This basic normative premise is at the center of our strict liability rules. It is unchanged by the state of scientific knowledge at the time of manufacture."

• *Deterrence*—The defendants' argument, that manufacturers cannot protect against risks they cannot foresee, missed the point: a manufacturer's knowledge that it must absorb the costs of all harm caused by its products, foreseeable or not, will spur its investment in safety research, advance the state-of-the-art of product safety, and thus deter product accidents. "By imposing on manufacturers the costs of failure to discover hazards, we create an incentive for them to invest more actively in safety research."

• *Simplifying trials*—Denying a state-of-the-art defense avoids the "vast confusion" in ascertaining the state of the art in particular cases. Proving when particular scientific knowledge was scientifically discoverable with more or better research would require costly, confusing, and time-consuming expert testimony on "the history of science and technology to speculate as to what knowledge was feasible in a given year." And juries might not "be capable of even understanding the concept of scientific knowability, much less be able to resolve such a complex issue."

Beshada unleashed an immediate and powerful storm of academic protest. The commentators complained that, by imposing a duty on manufacturers to warn of unknowable dangers, the court had adopted an unfair standard that was impossible to meet; that it would lead to inefficient corporate behavior that might encourage strategic and unnecessary declarations of bankruptcy; that the decision reflected a lack of understanding of how liability rules affect corporate behavior; and that the decision applied anachronistic strict liability rationales that had become discredited over time. See *Symposium: The Passage of Time: The Implications for Product Liability*, 58 N.Y.U. L. Rev. 733 (1983). At least in part because of *Beshada*, but also because the test had "not worn well with time," Dean Wade repudiated his half of the Wade–Keeton standard in a 1983 journal article, and Dean Keeton repudiated the other half in his tort law treatise the following year.

A scant two years after rendering *Beshada*, the New Jersey Supreme Court in 1984 had an opportunity to reconsider this now-battered decision in another products liability case, *Feldman v. Lederle Labs.*, 479 A.2d 374 (N.J. 1984), which involved a claim against a pharmaceutical manufacturer for a possibly unforeseeable risk that a tetracycline drug could discolor an infant's teeth. In one of the most striking reversals in the history of the law of torts, a unanimous court in *Feldman* effectively overruled *Beshada*, holding that "drug manufacturers have a duty to warn [only] of dangers of which they know or should have known on the basis of reasonably obtainable or available knowledge." *Feldman*

(1) endorsed comment *j*'s restriction of the warning duty to foreseeable risks, and (2) applied to the "strict" liability context the traditional *negligence* definition of "constructive knowledge"—what the defendant knew or should have known in view of knowledge available at the time—which the defendants had argued and that the court had explicitly rejected in *Beshada*.

Feldman thus turned *Beshada* completely on its head, ruling not only that state of the art was a good defense to a warning claim but also substantially equating strict liability and negligence in this context. The court correctly realized that its redefinition of the knowledge for which a defendant is responsible in negligence terms folds "strict liability" right back into the arms of negligence, reducing the two theories of liability essentially to one. Finally, reasoning that information on the knowability of risks in a particular field is more accessible to manufacturers than to plaintiffs, the court placed on manufacturers the burden of proving that information on a risk was unavailable at the time a product was made and sold.

In dramatic fashion, the *Beshada–Feldman* duo marks the rise and fall of the duty to warn of unknowable hazards—and, more broadly, of the doctrine of strict manufacturer liability for warning (and indirectly design) dangers—in American products liability law. For a time, *Beshada* had reigned supreme as the first major decision in the nation to apply a truly strict manufacturer liability rule in a warning or design context, where the difference between strict liability and negligence really mattered. But *Beshada*'s moment in the sun was brief, and its fall from glory was spectacular and complete.

The Triumph of the State-of-the-Art Defense

After *Feldman*, several important decisions certified that its use of the state-of-the-art defense in failure to warn cases was correct:

• ***Brown v. Superior Court***, 751 P.2d 470 (Cal. 1988), involved the duty of manufacturers to warn of the possibly unforeseeable risk that a drug, DES, administered to pregnant women could cause certain birth defects in their unborn children. Following *Feldman* and the principles of comments *j* and *k*, the court held that manufacturers of the drug were *not* liable for failing to warn of risks that were not scientifically knowable when the drug was distributed.

• ***Anderson v. Owens–Corning Fiberglas Corp.***, 810 P.2d 549 (Cal. 1991), was an asbestos case in which the California court completed the loop by extending its holding in *Brown* beyond pharmaceutical drug products to products generally. *Anderson* adopted "the requirement, as propounded by the *Restatement Second of Torts* and acknowledged by ... the majority of jurisdictions, that knowledge or knowability is a component of strict liability for failure to warn."

• ***Vassallo v. Baxter Healthcare Corp.***, 696 N.E.2d 909 (Mass. 1998), was an action for atypical autoimmune disease allegedly caused by silicone breast implants, in which the court reevaluated its adherence to the Wade–Keeton strict liability (in warranty) duty-to-warn rule which "presumes that a manufacturer was fully informed of all risks associated with the product at issue, regardless of the state of the art at the time of the sale." The court recognized that it was "among a distinct minority of States that applies a hindsight analysis to the duty to warn"; that most states follow the foreseeability limitation in § 402A cmt. *j* of the *Second Restatement*; that § 2(c) of the *Third Restatement* similarly limits the duty to warn to foreseeable risks; that product safety is not advanced by a rule which requires the impossible; that the minority approach "has received substantial criticism in the literature"; and that an important pillar of its original decision to adopt the hindsight approach, *Beshada*, had crumbled. For all these reasons, the *Vassallo* court decided that a defendant should *not* be strictly liable for failing to warn or instruct on risks that were not reasonably foreseeable or discoverable at the time of sale.

Yet, as noted in *Vassallo*, a small number of states continue to rule that manufacturers *should* be strictly liable for failing to warn of unforeseeable product risks and, thus, still cling to the idea that strict liability imputes constructive knowledge to manufacturers of all product dangers, even risks that are entirely unknowable. See *Johnson v. Raybestos–Manhattan, Inc.*, 740 P.2d 548 (Haw. 1987) (asbestos); *Brooks v. Beech Aircraft Corp.*, 902

P.2d 54, 63 (N.M. 1995) ("in those hypothetical instances in which technology known at the time of trial and technology knowable at the time of distribution differ—and outside of academic rationale we find little to suggest the existence in practice of unknowable design considerations—it is more fair that the manufacturers and suppliers who have profited from the sale of the product bear the risk of loss"); Sternhagen v. Dow Co., 935 P.2d 1139 (Mont. 1997) (herbicide 2,4–D); *Green v. Smith and Nephew AHP, Inc.*, 629 N.W.2d 727 (Wis. 2001) (latex gloves). See also *Townsend v. Sears, Roebuck & Co.*, 879 N.E.2d 893 (Ill. 2007) (lawn tractor) (dictum).

But for a few rogue jurisdictions, American courts no longer hold manufacturers responsible for unknowable product risks. The rise and fall of the duty to warn of unforeseeable hazards has played a decisive role in the more general rise and fall of "strict" products liability in America, a broader development examined previously. See ch. 5, above.

Statutory Reform

Eight states (Ariz., Iowa, La., Mich., Miss., Mo., Neb., N.H.) have adopted "true" state-of-the-art statutes that either (1) condition liability on a defendant's ability to conform to the state of the art, or (2) create a state-of-the-art affirmative defense, which places the burden of proof on the defendant. Statutes in three states (Colo., Ind., Ky.) provide rebuttable presumptions of nondefectiveness and non-negligence if a product conforms to the state of the art. And nine states (Ariz., Colo., Fla., Idaho, Kan., Mich., S.D., Tenn., Wash.) provide that a defendant may introduce evidence of the prevailing scientific knowledge or technology at the time of manufacture or sale, or that a claimant may not introduce evidence of improved science or technology developed thereafter. In addition, statutes in several states (La., Miss., N.J., N.C., Tex., and maybe Wash.) require proof in design cases of a feasible alternative design.

The Products Liability Restatement

The *Restatement (Third) of Torts: Products Liability* avoids the state-of-the-art definitional problem by neither defining nor otherwise using the term. Accepting the premise that manufacturers should only be held to a standard of responsibility they reasonably can achieve, the *Third Restatement* employs the precept of *reasonableness*, based on *foreseeability* and other principles of negligence, to define the nature and scope of design and warning responsibility. "Sections 2(b) and 2(c) rely on a reasonableness test traditionally used in determining whether an actor has been negligent." § 1 cmt. *a*. In this way, the *Products Liability Restatement* rejects any notion that there might be a duty to warn of (or design against) unknowable product risks, or to employ safer design approaches that are not reasonably available at the time of manufacture.

Because the state-of-the-art components—foreseeability of risk; and the feasibility, availability, and practicality of an alternative design—are included in the liability definitions, they are part of the plaintiff's case in chief, such that the plaintiff has the burden of pleading and proof on these issues.

Foreign Law

The spread of the state-of-the-art defense across America is mirrored by its widespread acceptance in other industrial nations. The European Community's *Directive on Liability for Defective Products* provides manufacturers with a state-of-the-art defense, referred to in Europe as the "development risk" defense, applicable to most European nations. Article 7(e) provides a defense for a manufacturer who proves "that the state of scientific and technical knowledge at the time when he put the product into circulation was not such as to enable the existence of the defect to be discovered." Japan's products liability law, patterned in many respects after the EC *Directive*, adopts an identical principle in Article 4.

§ 10.5   PRENATAL HARM

If a pregnant woman comes in contact with a toxic drug or other chemical that directly harms the fetus, the normal principles of recovery for foreseeably inflicted harm apply to products liability as to other types of cases involving prenatal harm. So, if the plaintiff in such a case can overcome the sometimes daunting problems of proving causation, there is no special reason why recovery should not be available against a manufacturer or other seller for harm caused by prenatal exposure to a pesticide, fungicide, drug, or other toxic substance.

More difficult are the *preconception* cases, where a plaintiff's mother (or father) is exposed to a toxic substance even before the plaintiff is conceived. Perhaps the first preconception products liability case was *Jorgensen v. Meade Johnson Labs., Inc.*, 483 F.2d 237 (10th Cir. 1973) (Okla. law), an action against the manufacturer of birth control pills for the Down Syndrome suffered by twin girls born to a woman who took the pills for several months before she became pregnant. Allowing the strict liability in tort claim, the court ruled that the preconception nature of the tortious conduct was no reason to bar a claim for foreseeable harm to plaintiffs born thereafter.

In the few preconception products liability cases to follow *Jorgensen*, courts have been less hospitable to claims by plaintiffs who themselves were not exposed, even *in utero*, to the defendant's product. This issue most pointedly arose in three cases involving the prescription drug, DES, prescribed to pregnant women to prevent miscarriage from the late 1940s into the 1960s. In each case, the plaintiffs ("DES grandchildren") were children of daughters of women to whom DES was given. The plaintiffs claimed that their mothers' reproductive systems were harmed *in utero* when the plaintiffs' grandmothers took the drug, eventually injuring the plaintiffs when their mothers became pregnant and, unable to carry their children to term, delivered them prematurely. The premature births caused the plaintiffs to suffer cerebral palsy and other disabilities. In each case, a split appellate court ruled that recovery should be denied for such intergenerational harm on grounds of duty, proximate cause, the remoteness of the harm, and the "rippling effects of DES exposure [that] may extend for generations." See *Grover v. Eli Lilly & Co.*, 591 N.E.2d 696, 699 (Ohio 1992) (4–3 decision).

§ 10.6 DETERIORATION

Nothing stays the same. Like lawyers and law students (who may one day become lawyers, if they study hard), even the very best of products age and eventually wear out. This simple truth generates a simple principle: "There is no duty upon a manufacturer to furnish a machine that will not wear out." *Auld v. Sears, Roebuck & Co.*, 25 N.Y.S.2d 491, 493 (App. Div. 1941), aff'd (N.Y. 1942). Appended to this basic principle are several corollary principles, such as that responsibility for accident prevention shifts incrementally as products age, from manufacturers to users, whose increasing responsibility eventually replaces that of the manufacturer altogether.

No matter how many years pass from the time a product is made and sold, the basic liability principle remains the same: if a plaintiff's injury was foreseeable and probably was caused by a defect that existed at the time of sale, the manufacturer is liable; but, if the defect probably is attributable to other causes, the manufacturer is not responsible. In *Mickle v. Blackmon*, 166 S.E.2d 173 (S.C. 1969), a passenger in a car accident was thrown upon the gearshift lever, shattering the protective knob and becoming impaled on the lever. The court concluded that passage of time alone did not shield Ford from responsibility if its negligence—in selecting a material that it knew would weaken over time from exposure to ultraviolet rays—was what caused the knob to fail. Thus, the mere passage of time, even over several decades, does not relieve manufacturers of responsibility for defects present in products when they are sold, including the failure to warn how a product may unexpectedly become dangerous as it ages.

§ 10.7   DISPOSAL AND SALVAGE

After a product wears out, it must be dismantled, recycled, disposed of, or destroyed. In the process, "junked" products pose hazards to the community. The largest safety problems surround the disposal of toxic waste. In recent years, courts and commentators have begun to consider whether manufacturers of toxic chemicals, and products that contain toxic chemicals, should be subject to liability under products liability principles. The issue, for example, is whether manufacturers of the acid used in automotive batteries and the polychlorinated biphenyls (PCBs) used in electrical transformers, and the manufacturers of the batteries and transformers themselves, should be strictly liable for injuries from the chemicals when such products are dismantled and disposed of by their users.

Several cases have examined the liability issues arising out of injuries to salvage workers and other damage from the release of PCBs from electrical transformers sold as junk. The transformers contained copper coils immersed in PCBs, and salvage workers became exposed to the PCBs by transporting the transformers, dismantling them to recover valuable components, or burning the fluid during the winter for warmth or cooking. Each of the courts refused to apply strict liability in tort to the transformer manufacturer, reasoning that the dismantling of a junked product was not an *intended* use, or not a *foreseeable* use, of the product; that the injuries resulted not from the original product but from a *substantial alteration* of the product; and that such an alteration amounted to an independent *intervening cause*. See *Monsanto Co. v. Reed*, 950 S.W.2d 811 (Ky. 1997) (disallowing products liability claims against manufacturers of both the PCBs and the transformer in which they were used).

Courts in other contexts have agreed that the rules of strict products liability generally do not support claims against manufacturers for injuries from dismantling products at the end of their useful lives—reasoning that dismantling and destroying products are not foreseeable product "uses," and that persons who do so are neither "users" nor "consumers." More recent decisions cast the issues more in terms of duty and superseding causation but agree that manufacturers of junked products are not *strictly* liable for injuries from disposal or dismantling.

But at least a couple of decisions (one reversed) have allowed *negligence* claims to proceed against manufacturers of products containing unreasonable risks to persons endangered by their disposal or destruction, and also against direct suppliers of dangerous junked materials. See *High v. Westinghouse Electric Corp.*, 610 So.2d 1259 (Fla. 1992) (once hazard was discovered, manufacturer of electrical transformers had duty of reasonable care to warn purchasing electric companies of PCB dangers); *Jones v. United Metal Recyclers*, 825 F.Supp. 1288 (W.D. Mich. 1993) (manufacturer/seller could be found negligent in selling scrap aluminum in wet condition causing it to explode in furnace).

§ 10.8   POST–SALE DUTIES TO WARN, REPAIR, OR RECALL

A manufacturer's post-sale discovery that its products, believed to be reasonably safe when first sold, are in fact dangerously defective may give rise to a post-sale duty: (1) to *warn* consumers, so they can avoid the risk; *or* (2) to *repair* ("retrofit") or *recall* the product, to reduce or eliminate the risk. While a good many jurisdictions recognize a post-sale duty to warn in some circumstances, only a small handful of cases have recognized a common-law duty to repair or recall.

Post–Sale Duty to Warn

The seminal case on the post-sale duty to warn was *Comstock v. General Motors Corp.*, 99 N.W.2d 627 (Mich. 1959), where plaintiff was injured due to a defect in a car's power braking system. The court held that General Motors had a duty, once it discovered the braking problem after marketing the vehicle, "to take all reasonable means" to warn purchasers promptly of the hazard. Thereafter, scattered decisions in the 1970s and 1980s began to recognize some form of post-sale duty to warn, particularly in cases involving hazardous drugs. By the 1990s, courts and legislatures had begun to impose a post-sale duty to warn with some frequency, often rejecting the "continuing" duty to warn nomenclature of earlier decisions in favor of the more accurate "post-sale" characterization of the duty. The momentum in favor of this duty in the mid–1990s was such that the *Products Liability Restatement* adopted the duty unequivocally in § 10(a), which provides that a product seller has a post-sale duty to warn when a reasonable seller in the circumstances would do so.

While a fair number of states still refuse to accept the post-sale duty to warn, a majority of states now agree with at least the general proposition of the *Third Restatement* that manufacturers (and possibly other sellers) have a post-sale duty of reasonable care to provide warning of newly-discovered, serious hazards to those persons who can best avoid the danger, assuming there is a practicable and cost-effective means to distribute such information. See *Ostendorf v. Clark Equip. Co.*, 122 S.W.3d 530 (Ky. 2003) ("Numerous cases impose a duty to warn of later discovered defects.") (dictum); *Hiner v. Deere & Co.*, 340 F.3d 1190 (10th Cir. 2003) (Kan. law) ("even when it may be infeasible for a manufacturer to issue post-sale warnings to consumers, there may still be a duty to issue warnings to retailers").

Post–Sale Duty to Retrofit or Recall

Apart from post-sale warning to consumers, a more aggressive (and expensive) way for a manufacturer to remedy dangerous conditions discovered in its products after their sale is to physically eliminate or reduce the danger by some form of repair, upgrade, or "retrofit," which may require a "recall."

Congress has empowered several product safety agencies to order recalls (notably the CPSC and NHSTA), the violation of which may give rise to liability. At common law, however, there is no general duty to recall defective products. A couple of early cases did suggest that manufacturers might have a duty to recall and repair hazardous conditions discovered after sale, and several more recent decisions have suggested that there may be a duty to retrofit a product if it was defective when originally sold, or if the manufacturer has a special continuing relationship with the buyer based on the manufacturer's post-sale undertaking to maintain or even recall the product, and in various other situations.

Yet most decisions, reasoning that governmental regulatory agencies are better suited than courts to forge such complex and onerous duties that might discourage manufacturers from developing new safety technologies, emphatically refuse to impose a common-law duty on manufacturers to recall their products or retrofit them with newly developed safety devices, especially if the product was not defective when sold. See *Hammes v. Yamaha Motor Corp., U.S.A.*, 2006 WL 1195907 (D. Minn. 2006); *Ostendorf v. Clark Equip. Co.*, 122 S.W.3d 530 (Ky. 2003); Rest. (3d) § 11 (no duty to recall; liability only for violating agency recall orders or for negligently performing recall voluntarily undertaken).

*

PART III
CAUSATION

CHAPTER 11
CAUSE IN FACT

Table of Sections

§ 11.1   Cause in Fact—Generally.
§ 11.2   Tests and Proof of Causation.
§ 11.3   Multiple Defendants.
§ 11.4   Warning Cases—Special Causation Issues.

---

§ 11.1   CAUSE IN FACT—GENERALLY

Causation (sometimes referred to as "proximate causation") is comprised of two distinct issues: (1) cause in fact, and (2) proximate cause. "Cause in fact" (or "factual cause") is the actual connection between a product defect, or the defendant's negligence, and the plaintiff's harm. Though this physical (or metaphysical) nexus is not controverted in most cases, a plaintiff must always establish this kind of actual link between his or her injury or disease and a defect in a product that the defendant sold—and, in negligence cases, to the defendant's negligence. ("Proximate cause" refers to the *close-ness* of whatever actual causal connection is proven to exist.) To satisfy the burden of proof on factual causation, a plaintiff must introduce evidence that establishes, more likely than not, that the defendant's negligence, or a defective condition in the defendant's product, was a cause of the plaintiff's harm. For a more thorough examination of cause in fact, see Owen, Products Liability Law ch. 11 (2d ed. 2008).

§ 11.2   TESTS AND PROOF OF CAUSATION

To establish causation, a plaintiff normally must prove two things: (1) that the defendant is the source of the challenged product—that is, that the product most likely was manufactured or sold by the defendant, not by someone else; and (2) that some defective condition in the product (or the defendant's negligence) most likely caused the harm. A plaintiff's causation evidence on the latter point must satisfy the "but-for" or "substantial-factor" tests for factual causation.

Defendant Identification

The first step in establishing causation is to show that the challenged product was manufactured or sold by the defendant. Usually, establishing the identity of the manufacturer of a toaster, a punch press, an SUV, or a butane lighter is a simple task, and the issue is not disputed. Yet, after a serious accident, sometimes butane lighters and other products disappear, and memories fade. Many kinds of products—like cleaning solvents, dish towels, and industrial chemicals—may come from sources not remembered or quite unknown. And so a plaintiff must connect the defendant to the product that caused the plaintiff's harm by establishing that the subject product was manufactured or sold by the defendant.

In *Moore v. Mississippi Valley Gas Co.*, 863 So.2d 43 (Miss. 2003), plaintiff was one year old when she was scalded by hot water in a bath tub. Two years later, the heater was discarded. Four years after that, the plaintiff's mother sued the manufacturer of the brand of hot water heater she believed was in her apartment complex at the time, although the landlord at the time of suit had no record identifying the manufacturer of the heater. In these circumstances, the court upheld summary judgment for the defendant manufacturer. See also *Waters v. NMC–Wollard, Inc.*, 2007 WL 2668008 (E.D. Pa. 2007) (plaintiff unable to identify manufacturer of defective airline luggage belt loader where "four different companies manufactured two different models of belt loaders under the 'Wollard' name for over two decades").

Even if the product is lost, however, a plaintiff may be able to establish the product's identity by circumstantial evidence, such as proof that the product bore the defendant's name on a label or decal. The memory of the plaintiff or purchaser as

to the product's name may suffice, as may the
retailer's records that it had purchased the product
from a particular supplier. And other evidence may
point toward the defendant, such as the product's
color, composition, or method of construction (like a
garment's stitching) that is unique to the defendant.

Tests of Cause in Fact

The "But–For" Test

The standard method for establishing factual causation is the "but-for" test. By this test, a manufacturer or other defendant may be found causally
responsible for a plaintiff's harm if it would not
have occurred but for a defect in the product or the
defendant's negligence. That is, a product defect
may be a cause in fact of the plaintiff's injury if the
defect was a *sine qua non* of the injury—a necessary
antecedent without which the injury would not have
occurred.

The but-for issue arises quite clearly in some
cases. If, against doctor's orders, a patient walks on
a surgical pin implanted in his broken leg before it
heals, breaking the pin, any manufacturing defects
in the pin are *not* a cause in fact of resulting
complications if the pin was designed only to hold
the fractured bones together (not to support a person), such that even a nondefective pin would have
broken under the plaintiff's weight. And if a driver
crashes into a traffic warning sign whose flashing
arrow is not working, injuring the plaintiff, recov-

ery will be barred if the driver would not have seen a flashing arrow because he was asleep.

The "Substantial–Factor" Test

Most courts reserve the substantial-factor test for *multiple cause* situations in which some question exists as to the materiality of the plaintiff's contribution to the harm. In such situations, usually toxic substance cases, the substantial-factor test normally works quite well. See *Verret v. American Biltrite, Inc.*, 2006 WL 2507318 (Tex. App. 2006) (La. law) (asbestos); *Bockrath v. Aldrich Chem. Co.*, 980 P.2d 398 (Cal. 1999) (worker could maintain cancer claims against 55 manufacturers of chemicals under substantial-factor test).

While some courts (e.g., Cal.) use the substantial-factor test more broadly to establish factual causation in any context, most courts use the but-for test as the principal (usually exclusive) test for factual causation in ordinary products liability contexts involving single, durable products. The *Third Restatement* follows this general approach, providing a general definition of factual causation in but-for terms and providing a separate standard for multiple causation cases. Compare Restatement (Third) of Torts: Liability for Physical Harm § 26 ("Conduct is a factual cause of harm when the harm would not have occurred absent the conduct."), with § 27 (if multiple sufficient causes, each is a cause of harm).

It is axiomatic that a plaintiff must establish that a product defect or the defendant's negligent conduct was *a* cause of the plaintiff's harm, not that it was *the* cause of the harm. Every harmful effect has an infinite number of causes, and some number of those causes often are significant. In addition to the substantial-factor test, principles of concurring, multiple causation help plaintiffs establish causation in such cases.

Proving Causation—In General

Plaintiffs frequently lose products liability cases because they provide insufficient evidence, by experts or otherwise, establishing that a defect in the defendant's product caused their harm. See *Menz v. New Holland N. Am., Inc.*, 507 F.3d 1107 (8th Cir. 2007) (Mo. law) (plaintiff's expert testified that warning of tractor's propensity to roll over would not have changed plaintiff's behavior, and jury otherwise lacked experience and knowledge to determine causation on the warning claim); *438 Main Street v. Easy Heat, Inc.*, 99 P.3d 801 (Utah 2004) (insufficient proof that deicing cable caused fire).

Yet, causation need not be proved with certainty, and a plaintiff may establish causation by circumstantial evidence that demonstrates that a defect in the defendant's product most likely caused the harm. The fire cases illustrate this point. Fires may be started by defective products, but they may be started by cigarettes and other things as well. Conflicting experts often provide conflicting theories of a fire's origin from burn patterns and other circumstantial evidence, and the trier of fact must weigh the conflicting inferences to determine whether the evidence on balance traces the fire to a defect in the defendant's product.

Proving Causation—Toxic Substance Litigation

In General

Tracing injuries and illnesses to asbestos fibers, drugs, and other kinds of chemicals involves perplexing causation problems both in science and the law, and the substantial-factor test previously mentioned helps plaintiffs in only limited ways. While the but-for test remains at the center of the causal inquiry, courts in toxic substance cases necessarily draw from scientific notions of causation to help make determinations of legal causation. Yet causation is established very differently in science than in law, which often causes a clash between these disciplines when toxic substance causation issues arise in products liability cases. Because the causal issues in such litigation are so arcane, expert testimony is almost always necessary and sits at the center of most toxic substance disputes.

A toxic substance case typically arises when a person is diagnosed with some illness or injury, such as cancer, that his or her doctor may (or may not) believe was caused by a cell phone; or by a toxic substance, such as asbestos or silicone gel in a breast implant; or by some drug or other chemical. The doctor may suspect that a particular agent caused the illness, yet most physicians are trained principally to diagnose and treat a disease, not to determine its etiology. For a products liability claim to lie, a person suffering from an illness that may have been caused by a toxic agent will have to assemble proof that the substance probably caused the harm. Such proof, for a number of reasons, may be difficult to obtain, and proving that any particular toxic agent caused a particular person's injury or illness can be a daunting task.

Proof of causation in toxic substance cases always involves, at least implicitly, two separate forms of causal proof: (1) general causation, and (2) specific causation.

General Causation

"General causation" is the capacity of a particular agent to cause an injury or illness of a particular type. For example, a plaintiff who seeks to prove that a cell phone caused his brain cancer, or that a drug she took during pregnancy caused birth defects in her child, first must establish that the suspect agent in fact is capable of causing the type of injury or illness the plaintiff suffers. General causation is sometimes so well established (that asbestos can cause asbestosis and mesothelioma), or its markers so self-evident (DES), that little or no proof of general causation is necessary. Ordinarily, however a plaintiff must affirmatively establish general causation, as by controlled human studies, epidemiological studies of population groups, animal experiments, laboratory studies of the chemistry of an agent and disease, or some combination of these forms of evidence.

Specific Causation

"Specific causation" is the actual connection between a person's exposure to a substance and a particular illness that person suffers. Establishing specific causation first requires proof of *exposure*—that the plaintiff was exposed to the defendant's product—normally not a problem in prescription drug litigation, but sometimes a problem in cases where the suspect agent is some chemical or a particular defendant's asbestos. Particularly in asbestos litigation, a plaintiff may have worked for many years with and around asbestos products produced by many manufacturers. In such cases, proving whether any particular manufacturer's asbestos product truly "caused" the plaintiff's asbestos disease is difficult if not impossible. To address this problem, the court in *Lohrmann v. Pittsburgh Corning Corp.*, 782 F.2d 1156 (4th Cir. 1986) (Md. law), crafted a variant of the substantial-factor test—today called the "frequency, regularity, and proximity test"—for this particular type of litigation. Now widely applied in asbestos litigation, this test allows a causal conclusion—linking a particular asbestos product to the plaintiff's asbestos disease—if the plaintiff produces "evidence of exposure to a specific product on a regular basis over some extended period of time in proximity to where the plaintiff actually worked." Id. at 1162–63.

Other, more particularized forms of proof are often useful in establishing specific causation. One well-established, if somewhat controversial, scientific method for proving (or helping prove) specific causation is commonly referred to as "differential diagnosis." By this approach, a physician attempts to determine the cause of a malady by considering the range of its plausible causes, and *ruling them out*, one by one, until just one remains. Assuming that a physician applies this technique properly, it can be a particularly useful tool to help prove a specific causal link between a defendant's toxic substance and the plaintiff's injury or disease.

§ 11.3 MULTIPLE DEFENDANTS

Most causation problems involving multiple products liability defendants concern toxic substances, and methods for establishing causation in that type of litigation were just examined. Yet problems from a multiplicity of actual or possible causal agencies extend beyond toxic substance litigation, so that multiple defendant causation issues arise more generally.

Concurrent Causation

A manufacturer or other seller may be responsible, at least in part, for causing a plaintiff's injuries no matter how many other causes may combine with it to cause the harm. If a product defect (or the defendant's negligence) played a material role in causing the plaintiff's injuries, then the defect or conduct was a cause of the harm. This is the principle of concurrent causation, and the substantial-factor test was devised to address just this type of multiple cause situation, as discussed above. So, if a defendant's asbestos, chemical, or tobacco product plays a substantial role in causing a plaintiff's disease, the defendant may be held to have caused that disease, at least in part, even if it was also caused by similar products of other manufacturers.

It is often difficult to determine which portions of a plaintiff's injuries are attributable to each of two or more responsible parties. If the trier of fact, on some reasonable basis, is able to determine which aspects of the plaintiff's loss are attributable to which defendant, then damages ordinarily must be apportioned on that basis. But where no fair and practicable method for apportioning the loss is available, then, at common law, each defendant whose breach of duty was a substantial factor in producing the damage is held jointly and severally responsible for the total loss.

In recent years, the doctrine of joint and several liability has been widely altered in many jurisdictions (and abolished altogether in a few states) due to the rise of comparative fault and apportionment, spurred by tort reform. While the general approach of the reform statutes is to apportion damages to a defendant proportionate to that defendant's fault or responsibility in causing the plaintiff's harm, variations between the statutes are significant, and a lawyer must look to the statutory and other law of the applicable jurisdiction.

A special difficulty exists if a plaintiff can trace his or her injuries to a single type of product manufactured by A, B, or C but is unable to identify which one manufactured the offending product. Since the plaintiff has the burden of proof on causation, the plaintiff's case in this type of situation normally will fail. See *Garcia v. Joseph Vince Co.*, 148 Cal.Rptr. 843 (Ct. App. 1978) ("*Hamlet II*").

Multiple Defendants—Theories of Collective Liability

Ordinarily, the law properly requires that a plaintiff identify the manufacturer of the specific product that caused his or her harm, the fundamental causal identification requirement examined earlier. Sometimes a plaintiff can trace his or her injuries to a specific type of drug, chemical, or asbestos product, yet, if the substance has left no identifying traces, the plaintiff may be unable to identify the product's manufacturer. When such products undoubtedly are defective—like asbestos products sold without warning of their serious health hazards, or defective generic drugs like DES—plaintiffs and courts alike have sought to find an equitable way to shift the resulting losses to some or all members of the industry that profited from their sale.

The most prominent theory of this type is "market share liability," but plaintiffs have also turned to other collective liability theories, including "alternative liability," "enterprise liability" (sometimes called "industry-wide liability"), "concert of action," and "civil conspiracy." None of these theories has proved particularly helpful in most situations, but a lawyer needs to be aware of their possible existence as well as their benefits and limitations.

Market Share Liability

Sindell v. Abbott Labs., 607 P.2d 924 (Cal. 1980), gave judicial birth to "market share liability." The case involved class actions brought by women for injuries they suffered from taking a synthetic form of the hormone estrogen, diethylstilbesterol, called DES. During the late 1940s, doctors began to prescribe DES to help prevent miscarriages, and eventually the drug was manufactured generically and sold for this purpose by some 300 pharmaceutical companies. In 1971, the FDA banned the drug when researchers discovered that it could cause a form of vaginal cancer, and precancerous growths in the vagina and cervix, in daughters of women who took it during pregnancy.

Although DES pills came in all different shapes and colors, each pill was chemically identical, and pharmacists typically filled prescriptions from whatever stock they had on hand. Thus, most women taking the pills had no idea who manufactured them, and by the time their daughters realized they had been injured by the drug (the reproductive tract injuries did not manifest themselves until puberty), it often was impossible to identify the manufacturer. Unable to identify the manufacturer of the DES taken by her mother, the named plaintiff in *Sindell* sought recovery against several major manufacturers of the drug. Because of her failure to identify the particular manufacturer that made the precise drug ingested by her mother, the trial court dismissed the action.

Adopting a theory of "market share liability," the California Supreme Court reversed. Because DES manufacturers chose to sell a drug generically that could cause harm long after its sale, allowing them to cover their tracks with the winds of time, the court reasoned that they should be responsible for the share of total harm for which they were statistically responsible. Expanding upon its earlier alternative-liability decision in *Summers v. Tice*, 199 P.2d 1 (Cal. 1948), the celebrated quail hunter case in which a pellet from the shotgun of one of two negligent hunters injured the plaintiff's eye, the *Sindell* court reasoned that the burden of proof on causation should be shifted to the defendants, provided that the plaintiff joined the manufacturers of a "substantial share" of the DES her mother may have taken. Unless a manufacturer could prove that it did not manufacture the drug taken by the plaintiff's mother, each would be severally liable for the share of the plaintiff's injuries represented by the share of the DES market it supplied.

It is difficult to quarrel with the fairness and logic of market share liability: if manufacturers benefit from selling a generic product with unduly harmful consequences that they know cannot be traced to them, they may be fairly held responsible for the share of harm properly assigned to each. For this reason, variations of market share liability, sometimes under other names, were adopted by the high courts of several states (Fla., Haw., Mich., N.Y., Wash., Wis.) together with a handful of lower state and federal courts. Each of these decisions altered the operational specifics of the market share theory somewhat, and each (except Hawaii) applied the doctrine to DES.

But the market share liability theory confronted two major obstacles, one practical and the other doctrinal. The *practical* objection is the enormous difficulty in ascertaining reasonably accurate market shares for individual manufacturers. Regardless of how one resolves the significant issue of whether to designate the "market" as the plaintiff's pharmacy (or pharmacies), neighborhood, town, city, county, state, region, nation, or the entire world, other difficulties in locating detailed distribution records from the various manufacturers and retail pharmacies decades after sale may be colossal, to say the least. The *doctrinal* objection to market share liability is that it simply does too much violence to the fundamental tort law element of factual causation—in particular, to the fundamental requirement that a plaintiff identify the specific product, manufactured by the specific defendant before the court, that probably caused the injuries for which recovery is sought.

Largely because of these two obstacles, market share liability has been rejected by a large majority of courts. See *Sutowski v. Eli Lilly & Co.*, 696 N.E.2d 187 (Ohio 1998). A small number of decisions from market share states have allowed such claims outside of DES litigation, but most courts have rejected efforts to extend it to such contexts as lead paint, asbestos, breast implants, guns, blood, tire rims, and a miscellany of other types of products.

Other Theories of Collective Liability

In addition to market share liability, courts have fashioned a number of other collective liability theories in an attempt to provide compensation to plaintiffs who are unable to identify the manufacturers of the specific products that caused their injuries, sometimes (as in the asbestos context) to fix responsibility on members of an industry who still are solvent.

Alternative liability. *Sindell* is an outgrowth of the theory that has become known as alternative liability, illustrated by *Summers v. Tice*, above, which shifts the burden of proof on causation to two or more defendants when their tortious but independent actions cause harm to the plaintiff who cannot establish which particular defendant caused the harm. Both the *Second* and *Third Restatements* adopt this principle.

A very few courts have applied some form of alternative liability to certain multiple-defendant products liability situations. But the alternative liability theory presumes that there are only two or a small number of defendants who are all before the court, and that the defendants are likely to know who among them caused the harm, conditions which reduce the unfairness of shifting to the defendants the burden of establishing causation. Because these conditions normally are not present in litigation on DES and many other products, the alternative liability theory was rejected by the California Supreme Court in *Sindell*, as it has been rejected by many other courts in various contexts in products liability litigation.

Enterprise liability. "Enterprise liability," also referred to as "industry-wide liability," was the first collective theory of liability devised for products liability litigation, initially put forth in *Hall v. E.I. Du Pont De Nemours & Co.*, 345 F.Supp. 353 (E.D.N.Y. 1972) (Weinstein, J.). *Hall* and another case involved the liability of the blasting cap industry arising out of injuries to 18 children across the nation who could not identify the manufacturers of the blasting caps that injured them because the caps blew themselves to smithereens in each incident. The defendants in *Hall* were the six blasting cap manufacturers (the entire American industry) and their trade association. Each manufacturer had acted independently, but each adhered to industry-wide safety standards, and they all delegated to their trade association certain safety responsibilities, including labeling standards and investigation. Liability was premised on the defendants' failure to place warnings on individual caps and to design the caps to make them more difficult for children to detonate.

On motions to dismiss, Judge Weinstein ruled that each member of the industry could be held jointly liable only if the plaintiffs established that the defendants (1) were all aware of the risks, and (2) jointly controlled those risks. Recognizing that enterprise liability could not fairly be applied to industries that are large and decentralized, Judge Weinstein limited its application to small industries of five to ten producers. The enterprise liability theory has not caught on, and other courts (including the California court in *Sindell*) have uniformly refused to apply this not illogical but clearly radical departure from the basic causal requirement of product identification.

Concert of action. The "concert of action" theory of liability results in collective liability when, under a common plan or scheme, a party assists, participates with, or actively encourages one or more wrongdoers who tortiously harm the plaintiff. The classic concert of action cases involved drag races, where one car hit the plaintiff and the driver of the other car was also held liable for tortiously helping create the risk that harmed the plaintiff. Thus, concert of action turns on an actor's participation in and furtherance of a group activity that the actor knows to be tortious toward the plaintiff, a kind of "aiding and abetting" of another who actively and unlawfully causes the plaintiff's harm. The *Second Restatement* expresses the concert of action principle in § 876, a section on which courts and commentators frequently rely.

A couple of courts, on summary judgment motions in cases where plaintiffs were unable to identify the makers of their drugs, have allowed concert of action claims, holding that "conscious parallelism" by the manufacturers to suppress warnings of side effects, or to sell without warnings a drug they knew to be ineffective and dangerous, might render them subject to liability to plaintiffs injured by the drugs. And the court in at least one cigarette case allowed the plaintiff to proceed on such a claim. But the great majority of decisions hold to the contrary, agreeing with the *Sindell* court's conclusion that applying the concert of action theory to industry-wide sharing of information and techniques in most situations stretches this joint-liability theory beyond its proper scope "and would render virtually any manufacturer liable for the defective products of an entire industry, even if it could be demonstrated that the product which caused the injury was not made by the defendant." *Sindell*, 607 P.2d at 933.

Civil conspiracy. A "civil conspiracy" is a combination of two or more persons for the purpose of accomplishing by concerted action an unlawful purpose or a lawful purpose by unlawful means. A civil conspiracy is not a tort in and of itself, and a plaintiff alleging civil conspiracy must plead and prove an underlying tort (often fraud) or other unlawful act on which the conspiracy claim may rest. Like concert of action, to which it is closely related, a civil conspiracy finding provides a basis for extending liability beyond an active tortfeasor to others who worked together to effectuate the unlawful result, rendering each member of the conspiracy jointly liable for all consequences ensuing from the wrong.

While civil conspiracy claims occasionally survive motions to dismiss and motions for summary judgment, such claims routinely are found wanting in products liability litigation, particularly when based on a defendant's participation in a *trade association*. Not only is such an association not *unlawful*, it may well be constitutionally protected under the First Amendment, particularly if the association's activities involve lobbying for governmental standards. But the First Amendment is not a teflon defense in every case of civil conspiracy, and it provides no shield for manufacturers who conspire to violate the law. See *Lewis v. Lead Ind. Ass'n, Inc.*, 793 N.E.2d 869 (Ill. App. Ct. 2003) (lead paint; reinstating plaintiffs' civil conspiracy claim against defendants).

§ 11.4   WARNING CASES— SPECIAL CAUSATION ISSUES

As with other types of products liability claims, factual causation is a necessary element of a warning defect claim. No matter how dangerous a defective warning may make a product, the plaintiff must prove that the absence of that safety information caused the plaintiff's injury. In warning cases, like most others, the plaintiff ordinarily must prove causation by the but-for test—that the accident probably would not have occurred but for the absence of adequate warning. If the provision of an

adequate warning would have made no difference—
if the plaintiff probably would have been injured
anyway—then a warning claim will fail on causation grounds.

The causal connection between a warning or instruction defect and the plaintiff's harm is sometimes clear. If given proper information about serious hazards under their control, people naturally
seek to avoid those dangers. It thus is likely that
the user of a propane heater, if warned that it
might cause asphyxiation if used inside a tent,
would use some other means to warm the tent; that
a user of a telescope, if instructed on how properly
to install a sun filter, would install it with utmost
care; and that the user of a spermicide contraceptive, if warned that it might cause birth defects if
conception does occur, would use a different form of
contraceptive. In none of these instances is it certain that proper warnings and instructions would
have averted harm, but in all of them it is quite
probable, which satisfies the but-for test.

Sometimes warning information clearly would
have made no difference, in which case causation
plainly cannot be established. No causal link exists
when the warning claim concerns a risk of which
the plaintiff *already* was aware, for such a user is
unlikely to change his or her behavior from receiving information he or she already has. A worker
who knows the danger of unjamming a machine
without cutting off its power cannot prove that the
manufacturer's failure to affix to the machine a

warning of that very risk would have caused him to turn it off. And a driver of a car with a high center of gravity, even if warned that it might roll over if the steering wheel were sharply turned, will probably instinctively turn the wheel sharply to avoid a high-speed collision with a concrete rail, despite the driver's awareness of the risk of rolling over. And without causation, a warning claim will fail.

Special Causal Problems in Warning Claims

Warning cases present certain *special* causation problems. Unlike the causal examples just provided, where causation appears quite clearly present or quite clearly absent, the causal connection between a warning defect and the plaintiff's injury is usually quite uncertain. Proving that an adequate warning would have prevented the plaintiff's harm depends on the vagaries of human psychology, requiring speculation on whether the user would have read and followed the warning had it in fact been provided. It is difficult, to say the least, to posit that a teenager, who ignores extensive warnings and instructions on how to use a trampoline, will heed additional, more specific warnings of the dangers; or that an adult, warned that a baby left unstrapped in a high chair might get strangled in attempting to slide out, would always remember to strap the child in.

The point is not that adequate warning in such cases would have made no difference, only that determining whether they would have averted harm rests on an uncomfortably slender reed. The most typical form of evidence used to prove causation in a warning case is the user's own testimony that he or she would have read and heeded an adequate warning or instruction if one had been provided. This forces the user into an awkward position of having to swear, in response to a hypothetical question, that a good warning would have caused him to change his behavior in some manner to prevent an accident. For the legal system to require plaintiffs to provide such highly speculative, self-serving testimony provides the most shallow basis for a finding of causation.

The "Heeding Presumption"

Beginning in the early 1970s, courts began adopting a "heeding presumption" to help plaintiffs surmount the inherent difficulties, just described, in proving causation in warning cases. This is a presumption, drawn obliquely from comment *j* to § 402A, that a plaintiff would have read and heeded adequate warnings and instructions, had they been provided. A heeding presumption relieves a plaintiff of the necessity of having to testify affirmatively on this issue and thus provides a basis for a finding of causation where the plaintiff is killed in the accident or otherwise dies before he or she is able to provide testimony in the case.

The presumption is *rebuttable*, so that a defendant may establish that a plaintiff most likely would *not* have read or heeded an adequate warning in the particular circumstances of the case. For example, a manufacturer may rebut the presumption by showing that the user was blind, illiterate, intoxicated, irresponsible, had bad judgment, or for some other reason probably would have ignored the warning.

Courts in more than half the states have now adopted the heeding presumption, at least in some types of cases, to help a plaintiff prove causation with warning claims. See *Bass v. Air Prods. & Chems., Inc.*, 2006 WL 1419375 (N.J. Super. Ct. App. Div. 2006); *Golonka v. General Motors Corp.*, 65 P.3d 956 (Ariz. Ct. App. 2003).

CHAPTER 12

PROXIMATE CAUSE

Table of Sections

§ 12.1 Proximate Cause—Generally.
§ 12.2 Foreseeability and Other "Tests."
§ 12.3 Intervening and Superseding Causes.

---

§ 12.1 PROXIMATE CAUSE— GENERALLY

Proximate cause, though linked to factual causation, is a separate element unto itself. Presupposing some factual connection between a defendant's breach of duty and the plaintiff's injury, proximate cause addresses instead the question of whether in fairness, policy, and practicality the defendant ought to be held legally accountable for the plaintiff's harm which in some manner is "remote" from the defendant's breach.

Proximate cause might thus be defined, if somewhat tautologically, as a reasonably close connection between the plaintiff's injury and a defendant's wrong, a connection that is not "remote." More broadly, proximate cause is a doctrine that serves to limit a tortfeasor's responsibility to the conse-

361

quences of risks viewed fairly as arising from the wrong. Because "[i]t is always to be determined on the facts of each case upon mixed considerations of logic, common sense, justice, policy and precedent," 1 Street, Foundations of Legal Liability 110 (1906), proximate cause is an "elusive butterfly" that e'er evades a net of rules. See *Accordini v. Security Cen., Inc.*, 320 S.E.2d 713, 714 (S.C. Ct. App. 1984).

Quite like duty, proximate cause provides a broad cauldron into which many factual and legal issues are thrown and mixed together. Yet, while traditionally referred to as "legal cause" (in an effort to distinguish it from factual cause), proximate cause is an issue of "fact" for resolution by a jury on the facts of a particular case. In an effort to reduce terminological confusion, the *Restatement (Third) of Torts* renames the proximate cause concept "scope of liability."

By whatever name, proximate cause is an elemental requirement of every products liability claim. In applying proximate cause "principles," products liability law draws from the law of negligence. In the early days of modern products liability law, in an effort to distinguish the then new doctrine of strict products liability in tort from negligence, some courts and commentators sought to eliminate the proximate cause limitations of negligence law (principally, the limitation of responsibility to foreseeable risks) from the strict tort doctrine. In time, however, this effort proved futile, and proximate cause (with its foreseeability limitations) is alive and well today as an element of claims for negligence, breach of warranty, strict products liability in tort, and even fraud. For a more thorough examination of proximate cause, see Owen, Products Liability Law ch. 12 (2d ed. 2008).

§ 12.2 FORESEEABILITY AND OTHER "TESTS"

Because proximate cause is often little more than a swirling maelstrom of policy, practicality, and case-specific fairness considerations—rather than a meaningful set of rules or even principles—it would seem incapable of being subjected to rational "testing." Yet, lawyers, courts, and juries need some guidance in unraveling the mysteries of this perplexing doctrine, which has led courts and commentators on an eternal search for a proper "test" for deciding whether a plaintiff's injury in any particular case was a proximate result of the defendant's wrong.

Foreseeability as the Dominant Test

The central notion of proximate cause, often loosely referred to as its "test," is that an actor's responsibility for the consequences of wrongful action is limited by principles of reasonable "foreseeability." As some courts aptly put it, foreseeability is the "touchstone" or "cornerstone" of proximate cause. This outer boundary of tortious responsibility ensures that actors are not held liable for consequences that fall outside the scope of their wrongdoing, consequences beyond their moral accountability. Because there is little moral connection between a person's chosen actions and the *un*foreseeable consequences of those actions, only *foreseeable* consequences of an actor's choices may ordinarily be considered in evaluating those choices. This is a moral justification for bounding responsibility in tort by the foreseeable scope of risk.

Thus, the safety obligations of manufacturers and other sellers in products liability law are limited by principles of reasonable foreseeability. More specifically, in making design and warning choices, a manufacturer must contemplate and fairly evaluate only such risks to such persons as are reasonably foreseeable. The range of risks and persons to be foreseen include how a product may be used, how it may be misused, and the ways in which these risks may endanger users and other persons.

This limiting principle may be stated in terms of the *"scope" of a product's foreseeable risks*. Viewed this way, the central question of proximate cause in a products liability case is whether the risks that caused the plaintiff's harm were among the foreseeable risks which made the defendant negligent or its product defective.

Other Tests

Direct Consequences; Natural and Probable Consequences

Simple "foreseeability" for many years has been crowding out other competing "tests" for proximate cause, most of which have a quaint appearance of times gone by. Yet other proximate cause tests that long have challenged foreseeability in the law of negligence compete as well in the products liability arena. So, courts still sometimes use the "direct consequences" test of *Polemis* fame, by which proximate cause is defined as a cause which, in natural and continuous sequence, unbroken by any efficient, intervening cause, produces the plaintiff's harm. See *In re Polemis*, 3 K.B. 560 (1921). A variation on this formulation is the "natural and probable consequences" test, also occasionally referred to in products liability decisions.

The Third Restatement

Drawing from a wealth of judicial and academic support, and rejecting "proximate cause" phraseology as too confusing, the *Restatement (Third) of Torts: Liability for Physical and Emotional Harm* adopts a "scope of risk" ("harm-within-the-risk") test for proximate causation in § 29:

> An actor's liability is limited to those physical harms that result from the risks that made the actor's conduct tortious.

This kind of "scope of foreseeable risk" formulation well describes the essential concept, nebulous though it may be, of proximate causation.

Foreseeability and Bizarre Consequences

Perhaps the most intuitively appealing type of case for applying some proximate cause limitation on the harmful consequences of a tortious action is where the consequences appear totally bizarre, even in retrospect, "too cockeyed and far-fetched." Prosser, *Palsgraf Revisited*, 52 Mich. L. Rev. 1, 19 (1953). If the plaintiff is injured by slipping on the vomit of a friend nauseated by the defendant's smelly plate of shrimp, the consequences may simply seem too far outside the foreseeable risks of serving foul food to hold the restaurateur responsible for the plaintiff's injury. See *Crankshaw v. Piedmont Driving Club*, 156 S.E.2d 208 (Ga. Ct. App. 1967). And other products liability claims have been rejected on the ground that the consequences are simply too bizarre.

But courts allow juries to decide the proximate cause issue in some quite extraordinary situations. In one case, for example, the plaintiff was driving at 45–50 mph when he hit a horse that suddenly appeared in front of his car. The horse was thrown into the air and fell upon the roof, collapsing the roof rail (called the "header") on the passenger side of the car, which instantly killed the plaintiff's wife. Rejecting the defendant car manufacturer's argument that the accident was "freak and bizarre," the court upheld a verdict for the plaintiff. See *Green v. Denney*, 742 P.2d 639 (Or. Ct. App. 1987).

Another case involved a boating accident that began when an outboard motor stalled due to a defective fuel system. While the husband attempted to restart the engine, the anchor line became entangled in the propeller and, as he tried to cut the line, he was pulled into the water. While his wife tried to rescue him, an onrush of water washed her below deck. The boat capsized, and the wife, trapped beneath, drowned. Despite this bizarre set of freak occurrences, the court ruled that foreseeability was properly for the jury. See *Greenfield v. Suzuki Motor Co.*, 776 F.Supp. 698 (E.D.N.Y. 1991). And courts in many other cases quite unusual have allowed juries to find a plaintiff's injuries proximately connected to a product defect.

Foreseeability as a Powerful *Veil*

An unsettling aspect of foreseeability, even when helpfully modified as *reasonable* foreseeability, is that it, like other "tests" for proximate cause, provides so little guidance that a court or jury can hide behind it all sorts of biases and ideologies that have no proper place in such decisions. Foreseeability, that is, and proximate cause more generally, both serve too often as a *veil* that shrouds the motivating reasons for allowing or, more typically, disallowing recovery in products liability as in other tort law cases. Compare *Winnett v. Winnett*, 310 N.E.2d 1 (Ill. 1974), with *Richelman v. Kewanee Machinery & Conveyor Co.*, 375 N.E.2d 885 (Ill. App. Ct. 1978).

Often noted (and usually decried), the malleability and opaqueness of the foreseeability "test" for proximate cause has significant implications for lawyers litigating products liability as other tort law cases. Foreseeability becomes a vessel into which a lawyer—in arguing either to a jury or the judge—can pour any number of equitable considerations present in the case but which really have no doctrinal home. In this respect, the doctrine of proximate cause, defined in terms of foreseeable risk, can be an especially powerful arrow in a lawyer's quiver of legal tools.

Foreseeability of Product *Use*

An important limitation on the scope of a manufacturer's responsibility for product accidents lies in the foreseeability of a product's *use*. While liability is no longer limited to product uses that a manufacturer *intends*, a manufacturer's accountability still is limited to consequences from uses of its products that it reasonably can *foresee*.

So, because a product's *use* must be foreseeable, a manufacturer is *not* liable when a defective elevator stalls six feet short of the floor and a passenger is injured in trying to jump out; the foot of an intoxicated person, who falls asleep or passes out in his car with the engine running, presses the accelerator and causes the exhaust system to overheat and ignite; a person attempts to commit suicide by closing herself in a car trunk without an inside release latch, changes her mind, and is trapped inside for nine days thereafter; a grocery shopper, who trips, hopes that a shopping cart does not scoot away when he grabs for it to save himself from falling; the owner of a riding lawn mower attaches a wooden "dog box" to the mower and places a 2-year-old child in the box who falls out and is run over by the mower; a teenage boy hangs himself with a rope on a swing set as a joke to impress the girls; or a young boy, riding a canister vacuum cleaner like a toy car, is injured when his penis slips through an opening into the cleaner's fan.

While the product uses in these cases all were deemed unforeseeable, courts in many other cases, involving other kinds of uses beyond those normally expected, have ruled quite the other way. Because of the inherent elasticity of "foreseeability," no prudent lawyer would attempt to predict how a jury might rule on the foreseeability of any particular product use that seems unusual.

Conventional Foreseeability *Categories*

Foreseeability is the controlling issue around which various *categories* of proximate cause cases cluster. Three categories of foreseeability are conventionally compared, the foreseeability of:

- The *extent* of harm;

- The *manner* of its occurrence; and

- The *type* of risk or harm.

See Rest. (2d) § 435. Conventional doctrine provides that a manufacturer or other tort defendant remains subject to liability even if it cannot foresee the *extent* of a plaintiff's harm, or the particular *manner* in which that harm occurs. But, under scope of (foreseeable) risk reasoning, a defendant is *not* responsible if it cannot foresee the *type* of *risk* that harms the plaintiff.

§ 12.3 INTERVENING AND SUPERSEDING CAUSES

The connection between a defendant's breach of duty and the plaintiff's harm may appear tenuous or "remote" because of the intervention of some person or force other than the plaintiff or defendant. Some third party may use the product abusively, or may ignore its warnings or instructions, in a manner that might give rise to a contributory or comparative negligence, assumption of risk, or misuse defense had the misconduct been the plaintiff's. Such misconduct by third parties, that combines somehow with a product defect (or its consequences) in a manner that harms the plaintiff, raises a question of how the conduct should affect the responsibility of the manufacturer or other seller, if at all.

The question in such cases is whether the third party's conduct, intervening upon a set of risks created by the defendant's sale of a defective product, distances the seller from the plaintiff's harm so much that the product defect and the seller's conduct become legally "remote" and, hence, no longer a "proximate" cause of the plaintiff's harm. Stated another way, the issue in products liability cases of this type is whether the third party's conduct is so significant in comparison to the product defect as to trivialize the role of the defect in causing the plaintiff's harm, so that the manufacturer or other seller fairly should be relieved of all responsibility.

Intervening Causes

The first question in such cases is whether some third party's conduct, which came into existence after the defendant's sale of a defective product, combined in some manner with the product's defective condition so as to cause the plaintiff's injury. If so, the third party's actions are viewed as an "intervening" force or cause. So characterizing the third party's conduct means little more than that it was a "concurring cause," together with the product defect, which may make the third party concurrently liable with the seller for the plaintiff's injury.

While, traditionally, concurrent tortfeasors were jointly and severally liable for a plaintiff's entire harm, they now in most jurisdictions may be responsible only for some equitable portion of the plaintiff's damages under principles of comparative fault and apportionment. Even in such apportionment regimes, however, each concurrent tortfeasor may be responsible for at least some portion of the plaintiff's damages. Thus, a third party whose tortious conduct joins with a product defect to cause the plaintiff's injuries is normally subject to liability to the plaintiff anyway, under joint and several liability or comparative fault principles of apportionment, which makes the "intervening cause" classification superfluous unless something else is added to the mix.

Superseding Causes

That something else is whether the intervening party's conduct is so significant that it "breaks the chain" of proximate causation, insulating the seller from *all* responsibility for the plaintiff's harm. When an intervening cause has such significance that a product seller's responsibility is severed altogether, the intervening cause is denominated "superseding":

> A superseding cause is an act of a third person or other force which by its intervention prevents the actor from being liable for harm to another which his antecedent negligence is a substantial factor in bringing about.

Rest. (2d) § 440.

An intervening cause, which arises after a defendant's tortious conduct and is sufficient in itself to cause the plaintiff's injury, may become a superseding cause if it is an independent force that operates upon, but is neither triggered by nor flows from, the defendant's wrongdoing. It is important to note that these common statements characterizing superseding cause merely state the legal consequence of classifying an intervening cause as "superseding." What they do not do is provide a test for determining *whether* an intervening cause or force should be so classified. In other words, the "superseding cause" term is just a label, not a recipe.

Foreseeability as a "Test" of Superseding Cause

For a recipe, almost every case turns principally or exclusively on a single test—*foreseeability*. While courts and commentators sometimes elaborate upon foreseeability, explaining how it operates in varying contexts, the underlying analysis remains essentially the same. And, as with proximate cause more generally, commentators continue to object to the vagueness prison from which foreseeability cannot escape, often arguing that courts should apply a richer, *scope of (foreseeable) risk* approach to superseding cause determinations. But this is what courts in fact do, if often they do not say so, and there is little debate about the appropriateness of foreseeability as the test for superseding cause.

Courts, at least, seem perfectly content with using foreseeability as the polestar for determining whether a third party's misconduct should sever the responsibility of a manufacturer or other seller of a defective product. "For an intervening force to be a superseding cause that relieves an actor from liability, the intervening cause must be a cause that could not have been reasonably foreseen or anticipated." *Small v. Pioneer Mach., Inc.*, 494 S.E.2d 835, 844 (S.C. Ct. App. 1997). And the converse is also true: "A third party's acts of negligence do not break the causal chain if the acts are foreseeable." Id.

Some courts enrich the foreseeability inquiry in this context by focusing on several helpful perspectives on the intervening force in § 442 of the *Second Restatement*:

- **Unforseeable Hazard.** Whether the intervention brought about a harm different in kind from that risked by the defendant's tortious behavior;

- **Retrospectively Bizarre.** Whether the operation or consequences of the intervention appear, *after* the event, "extraordinary";

- **Independent *vs.* Normal Result.** Whether the intervention operated "independently" or was a "normal result" of the actor's negligence; and

- **Seriousness of Wrong.** Whether the intervening cause was a human wrongdoer and, if so, the degree of that wrongdoing.

All of the foregoing principles and perspectives, it should be noted, although originating in the law of negligence, apply equally to claims in strict products liability.

Types of Third Parties

Parents

Most courts consider parental neglect—and the resulting wandering and mischief of curious youngsters—part of the "foreseeable environment of use" of products in the home. Because negligent supervision is passive misconduct, it generally is not viewed as superseding. Yet courts are also loathe to attach a superseding label to a parent's active misbehavior, such as knocking over a bottle of liquid drain cleaner onto the child, or falling asleep at the wheel of a car in which the child is riding.

Doctors

A common failing of doctors that quite often leads to serious harm is the failure to pass along to a patient drug warnings and instructions the manufacturer provided to the doctor. *Kirk v. Michael Reese Hosp. & Medical Center*, 513 N.E.2d 387 (Ill. 1987), was such a case. A passenger was injured when the driver of a car lost control of the vehicle and crashed into a tree. Earlier in the day, when the driver was discharged from a psychiatric hospital, his doctors prescribed two drugs, Thorazine and Prolixin, but failed to warn him of the dangers of mixing alcohol with the drugs. After leaving the hospital, he consumed an alcoholic drink that may have interacted with the drugs to cause the loss of control later in the day. The court held that the drug manufacturers could not reasonably foresee that doctors would dispense the drugs without passing on the warnings the companies had furnished to physicians. Nor must a manufacturer foresee that a doctor will use a drug contrary to its express warnings, nor must a manufacturer warn doctors of the risks of prescribing a drug for an off-label use.

Employers

Warnings. If the manufacturer of an industrial machine has a duty to provide warnings and instructions directly to a buyer's employees, yet warns only the employer (in a safety sheet or technical manual) and not the employees (by a label on the product's container or warning plate on a machine), the employer's failure to pass along the warning to its employees generally will *not* supersede the manufacturer's duty to warn them directly.

Maintenance. Courts often hold that an employer's improper maintenance of a machine is unforeseeable.

Alteration—"substantial change." Courts often examine product *alterations* by employers—such as altering or removing a machine's guard—in terms of whether the product was "substantially changed" after it left the manufacturer. This derives from *Restatement (Second) of Torts* § 402A(b) which provides for liability only if a product "is expected to and does reach the user or consumer without substantial change in the condition in which it is sold." While some courts shield manufacturers from responsibility for injuries caused by an employer's alteration of safety devices on "substantial change" grounds, other courts refuse to relieve the manufacturer from liability unless the change is deemed *unforeseeable*. In addition, courts sometimes bar recovery in alteration cases on grounds of unforeseeable *misuse*.

Statutory reform. Several state reform acts make product alteration a defense to products liability suits. Kentucky's statute, for example, shields manufacturers from liability for injuries caused by "product alteration or modification [which] shall include failure to observe routine care and maintenance, but shall not include ordinary wear and tear." Ky. Rev. Stat. § 411.320(1). Other reform statutes (Or., Tenn.) expressly limit the defense of alteration to those that are unforeseeable.

Intentional and Criminal Misconduct

Most courts hold that the intentionally harmful, criminal misconduct of an intervening party is unforeseeable, and that, accordingly, it is a superseding cause that severs the chain of proximate causation. But courts in several cases have ruled the other way, allowing such cases to proceed if the risk of harm was deemed foreseeable in the circumstances. Foreseeability, whether the intervening conduct fell within the foreseeable risk that rendered the product defective, is the purported "test" of superseding cause in cases of this type. But the decisions are difficult to reconcile.

Criminal Behavior

If a defect in a product designed for the particular purpose of self-protection (like a burglar alarm or mace) causes the product to malfunction, allowing a criminal to steal from or assault the plaintiff, then the resulting criminal act would appear to fall quite clearly within the foreseeable risk of a product malfunction. But when this envelope is stretched a bit, the foreseeable risk approach begins to waffle. Thus, a locksmith was held not liable for the rape of a woman in an apartment building supposedly protected by one of his locks. In another case, *Williams v. RCA Corp.*, 376 N.E.2d 37 (Ill. Ct. App. 1978), a security service guard was injured during a robbery attempt at a restaurant he was guarding. He used his transmitter-receiver manufactured by the defendant to call other security patrols for backup assistance, but the transmitter malfunctioned, and he was shot by the robber while trying to make an arrest himself. Because the receiver was designed for communication, not the prevention of criminal attack, the court ruled that the criminal intervening cause was unforeseeable as a matter of law.

In *Stahlecker v. Ford Motor Corp.*, 667 N.W.2d 244, 250 (Neb. 2003), a young woman was stranded in a remote area while driving her Ford Explorer when one of its Firestone radial tires failed. She was found alone by an assailant who assaulted and murdered her. Her parents sued Ford and Firestone, alleging that they had long known of the tires' propensity to unexpectedly blow out "causing wide-ranging results that included stranding and rollovers." The Stahleckers alleged that while their daughter's particular assault and murder may not have been foreseeable, "the potential for similar dangerous situations arising as a result of a breakdown of a Ford Explorer and/or its tires resulting in danger to its consumers and users from criminal activity, adverse weather conditions, inability to communicate with others or any combination thereof, were known and/or should have been known to Defendants Ford and Firestone." Relying on *Williams*, the court affirmed summary judgment for the defendants. Yet, it might be argued that an apartment lock, a security officer's transmitter, and a young woman's car are similar to burglar alarms and mace in that an important purpose of all five types of products is to help the user avoid dangerous situations.

Many other decisions similarly hold deliberate assaults to be unforeseeable. See *Sanders v. Acclaim Entm't, Inc.*, 188 F.Supp.2d 1264, 1276 (D. Colo. 2002) (unforeseeable that video game would cause shooting incident at Columbine; superseding causes relieve defendants of liability when "the harm is intentionally caused by a third person and is not within the scope of the risk created by the actor's conduct"); *James v. Meow Media, Inc.*, 90 F.Supp.2d 798 (W.D. Ky. 2000) (unforeseeable that assailant who watched violent video games would shoot girls as a result), aff'd (6th Cir. 2002); *Briscoe v. Amazing Prods., Inc.*, 23 S.W.3d 228 (Ky. Ct. App. 2000) (unforeseeable that man would throw defendant's drain cleaning product at plaintiff during altercation); *Bellotte v. Zayre Corp.*, 531 F.2d 1100 (1st Cir. 1976) (N.H. law) (unforeseeable that 12-year-old boy would throw match on 5-year-old brother causing his pajamas to ignite; such a deliberate act was an "absolute defense").

Yet some courts rule the other way in assault cases, holding the risk to be foreseeable. For example, the plaintiff's decedent and 27 others perished in a hotel fire set by an arsonist. The court refused to protect the manufacturer of excessively flammable acrylic fiber used in the carpeting, ruling that the risk of a hotel fire if the carpet ignited was foreseeable. See also Price v. Blaine Kern Artista, Inc., 893 P.2d 367 (Nev. 1995) (foreseeable that entertainer at Harrah's Club in Reno, wearing large caricature mask of George Bush ("41") not equipped with safety harness, might be pushed by patron and injure his neck).

Terrorist Attacks

A case arising out of the September 11, 2001 terrorist attacks on the World Trade Center places more weight on "foreseeability" than it fairly should be asked to bear. *In re September 11 Litig.*, 280 F.Supp.2d 279, 293, 309 (S.D.N.Y. 2003) (Pa. and Va. law), involved a motion to dismiss the claims of about 70 plaintiffs for injuries and deaths for Boeing's failure to design the cockpit doors of two aircraft—American Flight 77 that crashed into the Pentagon, and United Flight 93 that crashed in rural Pennsylvania—strongly enough to prevent entry by the terrorist hijackers. Boeing argued that, even if the cockpit doors could be found to have been defectively designed, the acts of the terrorists constituted a superseding cause that defeated proximate cause as a matter of law. In particular, Boeing argued that "the criminal acts of the terrorists in hijacking the airplanes and using the airplanes as weapons of mass destruction constituted an 'efficient intervening cause' which broke the 'natural and continuous sequence' of events flowing from Boeing's allegedly inadequate design." The plaintiffs argued that terrorist acts, including airplane hijackings, were "reasonably foreseeable"; that passengers, crew, and people on the ground were foreseeably endangered; and that, "[g]iven the critical nature of the cockpit area, and the inherent danger of crash when a plane is in flight," a jury might find that Boeing reasonably should have foreseen the risks of a feeble cockpit door. Ruling that a jury could agree with the plaintiffs, the court denied the motion to dismiss.

The court addressed three other cases, *Port Authority of N.Y. & N.J. v. Arcadian Corp.*, 189 F.3d

305 (3d Cir. 1999) (N.J. law), *Gaines-Tabb v. ICI Explosives USA, Inc.*, 160 F.3d 613 (10th Cir. 1998) (Okla. law), and *Korean Air Lines Disaster of September 1, 1983*, 1985 WL 9447 (D.D.C. 1985), each of which held that an unprovoked terrorist or military attack was an unforeseeable superseding cause as a matter of law. The first two cases involved claims of warning defects against the manufacturers of explosive grade fertilizer used to make the bombs employed in terrorist attacks against the New York World Trade Center, in 1993, and the Oklahoma City Murrah Federal Building, in 1995. The third case was brought against Boeing on behalf of passengers killed in Korean Airlines Flight 007 which, due to an alleged defect in the plane's navigation systems, flew off course over a sensitive Russian military zone and was shot down by Russian fighter planes. The *September 11* court valiantly attempted to distinguish each case on foreseeability grounds, concluding (with little reasoning) that, unlike the September 11 attacks, the fertilizer manufacturers and aircraft manufacturer could not foresee such unprovoked attacks.

It is difficult not to notice how little decisional power "foreseeability" has in these superseding cause cases, even when the standard is expanded to the scope of reasonably foreseeable risk. Any of these cases might be decided either way, and courts and lawyers in cases of this type are left with no alternative but to spin foreseeability arguments that shift, and turn, and jump about like the elusive butterfly that is proximate cause.

Superseding Cause in a Comparative Fault World

Some commentators argue that superseding cause is outmoded in a comparative fault world. Because the superseding cause doctrine is so blunt, allowing manufacturers and other sellers to escape liability altogether even if a product defect is partially responsible for a plaintiff's injuries, it is seen to conflict with the basic principles of equitable damages apportionment that control comparative fault. Moreover, the basic proximate cause principle limiting responsibility to the scope of risks that may foreseeably be expected to arise from a tortious act—risks that make the act tortious—sufficiently embraces the concept of superseding cause without complicating proximate cause doctrine. These arguments have some power, and they have been accepted by some courts. See *Barry v. Quality Steel Prods., Inc.*, 820 A.2d 258 (Conn. 2003).

That these few rumblings of discontent with the "doctrine" of superseding cause are well founded is demonstrated by the inconsistency and lack of meaningful reasoning in the cases previously discussed. Over time, other courts may also begin to rethink the role of superseding cause in a comparative fault world, a development that may prove beneficial. It is quite unlikely, however, that courts will soon stampede to abolish the intriguing subdoctrine of superseding cause in the law of proximate cause.

PART IV
DEFENSES

CHAPTER 13
USER MISCONDUCT DEFENSES

Table of Sections

§ 13.1   User Misconduct Defenses—Generally.
§ 13.2   Contributory Negligence.
§ 13.3   Comparative Fault.
§ 13.4   Assumption of Risk.
§ 13.5   Misuse.
§ 13.6   Defenses to Warranty Claims.
§ 13.7   Defenses to Misrepresentation Claims.

---

§ 13.1   USER MISCONDUCT DEFENSES—GENERALLY

Product accidents result more often from consumer misconduct than from product defects. In the words of a former chairman of the Consumer Product Safety Commission:

> [O]ver ⅔ of all injuries related to consumer products have nothing to do with the design or the performance of the product. They relate to the misuse or abuse of the product.

Fisk, An Interview with John Byington, Trial Magazine 25 (Feb. 1978).

If a product accident is caused in whole or in part by a user's behavior that is by some measure improper, or that is informed and voluntary, the manufacturer or other seller of a defective (or misrepresented) product may avoid responsibility for some or all of the resulting harm. Product sellers are fairly responsible for injuries proximately caused by dangerously defective conditions in their products, not for injuries caused by a user's improper or deliberately risky use of the product. It would be unfair to a manufacturer's shareholders, and to other more careful consumers forced to pay higher prices for a product, to require them to subsidize users who choose to use a product in a dangerous manner or for an improper purpose and are injured as a consequence. In such cases, the law protects manufacturers and other sellers through user misconduct defenses.

The classic misconduct defenses to products liability negligence claims are *contributory negligence* and *assumption of risk*. With the advent of the modern doctrine of strict products liability in tort during the 1960s and 1970s, most jurisdictions added the new "defense" of product *misuse*.

While contributory negligence has remained the basic defense to products liability claims grounded in negligence, most jurisdictions in the latter part of the twentieth century renamed the doctrine "comparative negligence" (or "comparative fault") and changed its effect from barring a plaintiff's claim altogether to reducing the plaintiff's damages proportionate to his or her fault. In addition, comparative fault principles now define the role of assumption of risk in many jurisdictions and of product misuse in a few. Nevertheless, the traditional user misconduct defenses still apply to products liability claims in states that continue to reject the doctrine of comparative fault. Moreover, much of the traditional doctrine surrounding contributory negligence, assumption of risk, and product misuse has survived the conversion to comparative fault.

When a plaintiff acts carelessly or adventurously in a manner that causes or contributes to a product accident, that conduct may give rise to two or all three traditional misconduct defenses. See *Jett v. Ford Motor Co.*, 84 P.3d 219 (Or. Ct. App. 2004) (unreasonable use, misuse, and assumption of risk). Thus, subject to applicable principles of comparative fault, a practitioner representing a defendant seller in a case involving plaintiff misconduct should almost always consider the possible availability of two or all three of the traditional misconduct defenses. For a more thorough examination of user misconduct defenses, see Owen, Products Liability Law ch. 13 (2d ed. 2008).

Reform Legislation

Many states have enacted comparative fault and/or products liability reform statutes that specifically address the definition, scope, and effect of various defenses based on a plaintiff's misconduct.

Such statutes variously reduce damages or bar recovery if a product accident is caused by a plaintiff's unreasonable behavior or contributory fault, assumption of risk, misuse of the product, or sometimes specifically designated types of plaintiff misbehavior, such as drug or alcohol intoxication.

§ 13.2 CONTRIBUTORY NEGLIGENCE

Contributory negligence is the conventional common-law defense to products liability negligence claims. In the products liability context as in others, contributory negligence is defined as conduct of a plaintiff which falls below the standard of reasonable behavior required for a person's own protection that proximately contributes, together with a defendant's negligence or other breach of duty, to cause the plaintiff's harm.

Contributory negligence operates in much the same manner in products liability cases as in other types of negligence cases. So, unless comparative fault principles dictate to the contrary, a finding that a plaintiff was contributorily negligent will bar the plaintiff altogether from recovering damages from a negligent defendant. Yet, if the defendant's misconduct is not merely negligent but rises to the level of reckless, willful, or wanton misbehavior, a plaintiff's recovery will not be barred by his or her contributory negligence, although it will be barred if the plaintiff is contributorily reckless.

In most respects, contributory negligence is the mirror image of negligence. Thus, though there is some debate on whether people properly may be said to have a "duty" to act with reasonable care to protect themselves, courts widely hold that the classic elements of negligence—duty, breach, cause in fact, proximate cause, and damage—comprise contributory negligence as well. So, whereas negligence is the failure to exercise due care toward the safety of others, contributory negligence is the failure to exercise due care toward the safety of oneself. In the products liability setting, contributory negligence includes the unreasonable use of a product contrary to adequate warnings and instructions, the unreasonable use of a product known to be defective, or the use of a product in an unreasonable manner.

For example, a user may drive an automobile at excessive speed or in an intoxicated condition; carelessly push a piece of meat into a meat slicing machine; stand on a slippery substance dangerously close to the exposed moving parts of a machine; fail to wear a mask while operating a spray-painting machine; improperly use a condom; walk too fast on a slippery floor; or carelessly light a cigarette with a disposable lighter near one's "big hair" bouffant hairdo held in place with excessive hair spray, the fumes of which ignite. In short, persons using products sometimes fail to exercise reasonable care to avoid injuring themselves.

Warning Cases

Contributory negligence doctrine operates under a special limitation in cases involving products with inadequate warning of hidden dangers or instructions on safe use. If a warning or instruction is substantively inadequate in failing to inform users of the nature or seriousness of a hidden danger or reason for a particular instructed method of use, then a user who has not otherwise discovered the risk ordinarily will not be contributorily negligent for using the product in disregard of the danger. However, to be contributorily negligent for exposing oneself to a hazard, a user generally needs only to be aware of the *general* nature and magnitude of a risk, not the particular chemical or physical attributes of the product and how they specifically may harm the user's body. This was the holding in *Parris v. M.A. Bruder & Sons, Inc.*, 261 F.Supp. 406 (E.D. Pa. 1966), where a spray painter of more than twenty years claimed that the manufacturer of an epoxy product had failed to warn him that inhaling the epoxy fumes could cause asthma. Because the plaintiff knew generally of the substantial danger of inhaling paint fumes, even if he was not aware of the specific risk of contracting asthma, the court held that the jury properly could find that he was contributorily negligent for frequently failing to wear a mask furnished by his employer.

As a Defense to Strict Liability in Tort

A plaintiff's ordinary contributory negligence is *not* a defense to a claim for strict liability in tort. Comment *n* to *Restatement (Second) of Torts* § 402A provides that "simple" or "ordinary" contributory negligence—conduct that is merely careless and that does not also amount to a voluntary assumption of risk—does *not* bar liability under § 402A for harm caused by a defective product:

> ... Contributory negligence of the plaintiff is not a defense when such negligence consists merely in a failure to discover the defect in the product, or to guard against the possibility of its existence. [Yet] the form of contributory negligence which consists in voluntarily and unreasonably proceeding to encounter a known danger, and commonly passes under the name of assumption of risk, is a defense under [§ 402A] as in other cases of strict liability. If the user or consumer discovers the defect and is aware of the danger, and nevertheless proceeds unreasonably to make use of the product and is injured by it, he is barred from recovery.

Courts widely adopted comment *n*'s abandonment of simple contributory negligence as a bar to strict products liability in tort because this doctrine is premised on the thought that suppliers of defective products impliedly represent that their products are safe and should be required to internalize the costs of accidents if their products prove dangerously defective.

§ 13.3 COMPARATIVE FAULT

From the late 1960s through the early 1990s, the doctrine of comparative fault swept across America. Its rapid and widespread adoption sprang from the evident unfairness of the all-or-nothing rule of contributory negligence that barred a plaintiff from all recovery against a tortfeasor if the plaintiff was at fault in any way in connection with the accident. The law of comparative fault (otherwise known as "comparative negligence," "comparative responsibility," or "apportionment"), which reduces an accident victim's damages proportionate to his or her fault rather than barring recovery altogether, is now so extensive that it has its own *Restatement (Third) of Torts: Apportionment* (2000) and a new uniform law, *Uniform Apportionment of Tort Responsibility Act* (2002, revised 2003).

Now law in all but 4 states (Ala., Md., N.C., Va.), the comparative fault doctrine significantly affects modern products liability litigation where it provides a giant umbrella over the traditional misconduct defenses of contributory negligence, in almost every state; assumption of risk, in many states; and product misuse, in some states. While comparative fault most typically affects claims for negligence and strict liability in tort, its principles of apportionment may also affect claims for breach of warranty and tortious misrepresentation.

It is important to note that the widespread adoption of comparative fault still leaves some room for the traditional all-or-nothing misconduct defenses to operate. Traditional misconduct defenses, operating as a total bar to recovery, continue to govern products actions in the few states that still reject comparative fault apportionment. Moreover, in most states, a plaintiff's misconduct remains a *total* bar to recovery if the plaintiff's fault equals (or, in some states, exceeds) that of the defendant. In addition, some courts refuse to apply comparative fault principles to assumption of risk, or do so only to a limited extent, and almost all still consider the plaintiff's unforeseeable misuse to be a total defense. Finally, in claims for breach of warranty and misrepresentation, a buyer's or user's misconduct often goes to issues—such as scope of warranty, justifiable reliance, and proximate cause—that are part of the plaintiff's case in chief, making the absence of such misconduct essential to the plaintiff's underlying claim.

What all this means, of course, is that comparative fault has not beaten the traditional misconduct defenses completely into the ground. Defendants sometimes still put traditional all-or-nothing misconduct defenses effectively to use as gladiators against misbehaving plaintiffs despite the modern urge to purge clear judgments of right and wrong from legal outcomes by fixing responsibility, like Solomon, by division.

Yet, while comparative fault still has competition, let no one doubt its power. This section outlines how comparative fault operates in products liability litigation in general and, more particularly, how it affects claims based on strict liability in tort. The specific effects of comparative fault on other defenses is addressed in sections on those doctrines.

Types and Examples of Comparative Fault
"Pure" and "Modified"

Comparative fault systems applicable to products liability cases come in two basic forms: "pure" and "modified." A comparative fault system is "pure" if the plaintiff may recover damages from a tortfeasor, reduced proportionately by those attributable to the plaintiff's fault, regardless of how great the plaintiff's proportion of total fault may be. For example, if a plaintiff's fault is 90% and the defendant's fault is only 10%, the plaintiff in a pure comparative fault jurisdiction may still recover the 10% of damages attributable to the defendant. See *Thornton v. Gray Auto. Parts Co.*, 62 S.W.3d 575 (Mo. Ct. App. 2001) (mechanic, 95% at fault for improperly using jack that slipped out from beneath vehicle, could recover against manufacturer of jack who was 5% at fault for not equipping it with safety feature).

A large majority of states, including most that adopted the doctrine legislatively, use some "modified" version of comparative fault. Modified comparative fault systems reduce recoverable damages proportionate to a plaintiff's fault, just as under the pure approach, but they continue to bar recovery completely (as under traditional contributory negligence) if the plaintiff's fault *exceeds* the defendant's fault, known as the "New Hampshire system," or, under the "Georgia system," if the plaintiff's fault *equals or exceeds* the defendant's fault. So, under either type of modified system, a plaintiff 30% at fault may recover the 70% of damages apportioned to the defendant, but a plaintiff 60% at fault is entitled to no recovery. A plaintiff who is 50% at fault may recover half of his or her damages under the New Hampshire system but nothing whatsoever under the Georgia system. To leave plaintiffs with some recovery in the occasional cases where fault is apportioned 50–50 between plaintiffs and defendants, a number of states have switched to the New Hampshire system, as have two states (Ill., Iowa) that had been pure.

Pure comparative fault now exists in 16 American jurisdictions (Alaska, Ariz., Cal., Conn., Fla., Haw. [for strict liability in tort and warranty, but not negligence], Ky., La., Mich., Miss., Mo., N.M., N.Y., R.I., Wash., P.R.). As for the *modified* versions, only 11 states remain in the Georgia camp (Ark., Colo., Ga., Idaho, Kan., Me., Neb., N.D., Tenn., Utah, W. Va.), whereas 20 states now follow the increasingly popular New Hampshire approach that *allows* a 50% at-fault plaintiff to recover (Del., Haw. [negligence claims only], Ill., Ind., Iowa, Mass., Minn., Mont., Nev., N.H., N.J., Ohio, Okla., Or., Pa., S.C., Tex., Vt., Wis., Wyo.).

Examples of Comparative Fault

Product accidents occur in myriad ways, resulting in myriad divisions of fault between manufacturers and product users. For example, when a defect in a car's steering column caused the steering to lock, after which the plaintiff neglected to apply the brakes, responsibility for the resulting crash was divided 85% to the manufacturer and 15% to the driver; a manufacturer of an aluminum ladder sold without warning of the risk from hitting power lines was 2% responsible for a painter's electrocution, the company that rented the ladder to the painting crew was 3% responsible, and the painter himself, who failed to have the power lines de-energized before painting in their vicinity and failed to use a wooden or fiberglass ladder, was 95% responsible; the manufacturer of a car with a defective door latch, which allowed the door to open when it collided with another car, was 75% responsible, and the plaintiff's responsibility for speeding was 25%; the manufacturer of a potato chip cooker kettle was 52% responsible for a kettle shaft that popped out of place, and the injured Frito Lay employee who attempted to repair the shaft was 48% at fault for conducting the repairs while standing on a board across a kettle of hot oil, and for slipping in; a pharmacy was 51% responsible for failing properly to warn a customer that an anti-depression drug could cause permanent impotency, whereas the customer was 49% at fault for failing for 30 hours to seek medical attention for an erection; and the divisions of responsibility for product accidents go on and on.

Strict Liability in Tort

Applicability of Comparative Fault

As one state after another adopted comparative fault in the latter decades of the twentieth century, courts had to decide whether to apply this new form of damages apportionment to claims based on strict liability in tort. In most states, courts have had to interpret statutes requiring the comparison of the parties' "negligence" or "fault" without explicitly defining those terms. The courts have split on whether such statutory language covers claims for strict products liability in tort.

Courts with leeway to decide whether or not to apportion damages in strict liability actions, rejecting "apples-and-oranges" arguments to the contrary, have opted for the apparent justice of making each party to an accident bear responsibility for the losses attributable to that party's breach of good behavior. See *Daly v. General Motors Corp.*, 575 P.2d 1162 (Cal. 1978) (classic case applying comparative fault to strict products liability in tort as a matter of common law).

Negligent Failure to Discover a Product Defect

Comment *n* to § 402A, as seen above, takes the position that a plaintiff's "simple" or "ordinary" contributory negligence in failing to discover a defect, or in failing to guard against the possibility of its existence, should not shield a manufacturer from responsibility for its harmful consequences. But this special category of plaintiff protection arose in the 1960s, before the advent of comparative fault, when the effect of the misconduct defenses was to bar a plaintiff's claim completely. Once most courts and legislatures abandoned the all-or-nothing effect of contributory negligence in the 1970s and 1980s, one might think they would have reconsidered the role of such simple contributory negligence in products liability actions and thrown it back into the well for consideration with all other types of fault. Yet, almost every court that has considered the matter has chosen to shield consumers from all responsibility for their failure to watch for product defects by holding that a plaintiff's careless failure to *discover* that a product is defective lies outside the realm of damages apportionment. See *Jett v. Ford Motor Co.*, 84 P.3d 219 (Or. Ct. App. 2004); *General Motors Corp. v. Sanchez*, 997 S.W.2d 584 (Tex. 1999) (but plaintiff's conduct in parking truck, which shifted from Park to Reverse, was more than a mere failure to discover shift's defect).

§ 13.4   ASSUMPTION OF RISK

Assumption of risk is a classic defense in products liability litigation, even to claims for strict products liability in tort, and it remains a total bar to liability in a fair number of states. Its underlying idea is that a user has fully consented to incur a risk that he or she fully comprehends. By choosing voluntarily to incur the risk, the user thus implicitly agrees to accept responsibility for any harmful consequences that may result from the encounter and so relieves the person who created the risk from responsibility. In other words, *volenti non fit injuria* ("to a willing person, no injury is done").

Thus, a person may assume the risk of injury if he uses his hand instead of a metal stomper to push meat into a grinder; reaches from outside a forklift between horizontal cross bars to engage the throttle that lowers a cross bar on his arm; walks on top of a tanker truck covered with oil that he knows is "real slick"; jump-starts a tractor he knows may lurch forward when it starts; leaves a power mower's blades spinning when moving an obstacle from the mower's path; or entangles his pants in a machine that he knows could injure him if he gets too close.

For a product user to assume responsibility for a risk to the exclusion of the defendant, his or her decision must be based on an understanding of the nature of the risk, and it must be a choice that is freely made—a person cannot "consent" to what he does not know nor to what is forced upon him. For this reason, assumption of risk arises only when a user's encounter with a risk is both "informed" and "voluntary." These two basic requirements are reflected in the definition, or statement of elements, of the assumption of risk doctrine:

- The plaintiff must *know* and *understand* the risk; and,

- The plaintiff's choice to encounter the risk must be free and *voluntary*.

Knowledge and Appreciation

Knowledge, it is said, is the "watchword" of assumption of risk. A plaintiff's vague and general understanding that a product may be dangerous if not carefully used is neither "knowledge" nor "appreciation" of a particular risk of harm. If the plaintiff does not know just *how* a product may be hazardous, then the plaintiff cannot assume the risk that he may be injured by that hazard. Particularly in jurisdictions that do not separately require that the risk be "appreciated," courts sometimes require that the plaintiff know of the *specific* risk. This means the plaintiff must understand with some particularity how the product may cause an injury, so that he or she is able to evaluate the likelihood and seriousness of potential injury and thereby make an informed decision on whether or not to engage the risk.

But most courts hold that appreciation may be established even if a plaintiff does not understand the precise nature and operation of the mechanical, chemical, or biological mechanisms that may result in harm nor the precise manner in which a product is legally "defective." See *Bowen v. Cochran*, 556 S.E.2d 530 (Ga. Ct. App. 2001) (plaintiff knew and appreciated that gas grill might explode if he failed to light and vent it properly, even if he did not understand exactly where and how the unlighted gas might pool).

If a product is defective because the manufacturer has not *warned* of a hidden risk, then a plaintiff unaware of that risk cannot be barred by the doctrine of assumption of risk. But a plaintiff's knowledge may come from any source, and assumption of risk may be one reason (the other is causation) to bar a claim that a manufacturer failed to provide an adequate warning of a risk that the plaintiff already knows about and understands.

Voluntary Encounter

A plaintiff's decision to encounter a risk must also be "free and voluntary." The notion of consent suggests that a plaintiff makes a true and meaningful *choice* to engage a particular risk. If a plaintiff's only (or best) "choice" is to encounter a known risk—if he or she has no *reasonable options* to avoid it—then the encounter is not "voluntary." A plaintiff confronted with a choice between two evils is subjected to a "species of duress," a dilemma that destroys the very idea of choice and consent. But, if a plaintiff has a perfectly reasonable way to avoid a danger created by the defendant, yet knowingly chooses to encounter it anyway, then he cannot complain that he was compelled to take this path, for such a choice is free and voluntary.

Courts have been especially open to challenges to the voluntariness of risk encounters in two situations: *rescues* and *workplace* accidents. In the rescue situation, as with the contributory negligence defense, a number of courts have held that a rescuer of a person endangered by a defective product may not be barred by the defense of assumption of risk. See *Dillard v. Pittway Corp.*, 719 So.2d 188 (Ala. 1998). In the workplace situation, courts sometimes reason that encounters with dangerous substances and machinery in the workplace often are not truly "voluntary." Indeed, the Supreme Court of Ohio has abolished the assumption of risk defense in the workplace setting on the ground that workers often are effectively trapped into performing dangerous activities, a situation that destroys any voluntariness in many such job-related risk encounters. See *Cremeans v. Willmar Henderson Mfg. Co.*, 566 N.E.2d 1203 (Ohio 1991).

Yet other courts continue to treat the voluntariness of encounters in the workplace like any other encounter, concluding that assumption of risk bars recovery even in this setting when workers make entirely deliberate decisions exposing themselves to risks they fully understand to be unreasonable. See *Karim v. Tanabe Mach., Ltd.*, 322 F.Supp.2d 578 (E.D. Pa. 2004) (machine operator grabbed control box near moving chain and sprocket that caught his hand).

As a Defense to Strict Liability in Tort

While assumption of risk as classically defined is a standard defense to products liability claims brought in negligence, many jurisdictions alter its definition—and a couple alter its availability and effect—in claims for strict liability in tort. Comment *n* to § 402A, examined above in § 13.2, provides:

> [T]he form of contributory negligence which consists in voluntarily and unreasonably proceeding to encounter a known danger, and commonly passes under the name of assumption of risk, is a defense under this Section as in other cases of strict liability. If the user or consumer discovers the defect and is aware of the danger, and nevertheless proceeds unreasonably to make use of the product and is injured by it, he is barred from recovery.

A few states ignored comment *n* and continued applying the traditional elements of assumption of risk even for claims brought in strict products liability in tort. Yet many jurisdictions adopted comment *n*'s approach of restricting the availability of the assumption of risk defense in strict products liability in tort to cases of *unreasonable* ("negligent") assumption of risk. In effect, such jurisdictions engraft an additional element—unreasonableness—onto the traditional assumption of risk elements. So altered, the assumption of risk defense to claims for strict products liability in tort requires that a plaintiff:

(1) Know and appreciate the risk;

(2) Voluntarily encounter it; *and*

(3) Be unreasonable in deciding to encounter the risk.

As with voluntariness, some courts have ruled that workplace decisions to encounter risk may be found not to be "unreasonable" if the practical demands of the job sabotage an opportunity for truly consensual decisionmaking about such encounters.

Reform

Assumption of risk is on the run. Plainly problematic, the doctrine may unfairly place responsibility for injuries upon a victim whose only fault lay in making a choice, perhaps correctly, that was forced improperly upon him by a tortfeasor. To the extent that a plaintiff truly is at fault in encountering a risk, the doctrines of (no) duty, contributory (and comparative) negligence, and (sole) proximate causation would appear to cover virtually every case where assumption of risk bars recovery. The assumption of risk defense thus has long been roundly criticized and is being abolished, partially or completely, by an increasing number of courts and legislatures. With the widespread adoption of comparative fault, other courts and legislatures have done what amounts to the same thing by "merging" assumption of risk into comparative fault. Now that the new *Restatement of Apportionment* takes the position that assumption of risk as a separate doctrine should be abolished, the trend toward abolishing the doctrine and merging it into comparative fault appears inexorable. No doubt assumption of risk will linger on in some jurisdictions for some time, yet it clearly is a doctrine that is doomed.

§ 13.5 MISUSE

A user's "misuse" of a product may bar recovery in a products liability action. Though a few jurisdictions (Ariz., Ind., N.D., Tex.) have merged misuse into their comparative fault systems, so that some or all forms of product misuse only reduce a plaintiff's damages, a user's *unforeseeable* misuse is widely considered an absolute bar to recovery. While product misuse is a common-law doctrine, reform statutes in several states provide that a plaintiff's misuse reduces damages (Idaho, Mo.) or bars liability (Ariz., Ind., Mich., Mont., Tenn.).

The basic idea of the misuse doctrine is that products are necessarily designed to do certain limited tasks, within certain limited environments of use, and that no product can be made safe for every purpose, manner, or extent of use. Consumers know that products may be used safely only for certain limited purposes; that they should be used properly and within the manufacturer's warnings and instructions; and that using products beyond their capabilities may cause them to break, overheat, or otherwise fail in a possibly dangerous way. If a user chooses to put a product to a type or manner of use the product cannot fairly be expected to withstand, and the user is injured as a result, he or she cannot reasonably demand that the manufacturer (and, indirectly, other consumers) shoulder the economic consequences of the loss. "We cannot charge the manufacturer of a knife when it is used as a toothpick and the user complains because the sharp edge cuts." *General Motors Corp. v. Hopkins*, 548 S.W.2d 344, 349 (Tex. 1977).

Through much of the 1960s, 1970s, and even into the 1980s, as the role of product misuse evolved and began to come into focus, three different concepts and terms—"intended use," "abnormal use," and "misuse"—shared an uncomfortable coexistence. By the 1980s and 1990s, however, courts and commentators had worked out a generally accepted definition of the "misuse" doctrine. The misuse doctrine is difficult to apply in a principled manner, as discussed below, but it is quite easy to state: manufacturers and other sellers are subject to responsibility for harm from product uses that are reasonably foreseeable, but they are not liable for harm from unforeseeable product use. See *Ricci v. AB Volvo*, 2004 WL 1686936 (9th Cir. 2004) (Nev. law).

Theory of Liability

The correlative ideas of restricting a seller's responsibility to normal or expectable product uses, on the one hand, and making users responsible for their injuries caused by particularly unusual product uses, on the other hand, have been central pillars of products liability law for many years. The *Restatement (Second) of Torts* limits a manufacturer's liability in negligence to intended and probable uses. In warranty law, Article 2 of the UCC treats improper use as lying outside the scope of a warranty. And in strict liability in tort, an original premise of manufacturer liability was that the injury arose out of the *proper* use of the product, as Judge Traynor explained in *Greenman*, 377 P.2d at 901:

> Implicit in the machine's presence on the market ... was a representation that it would safely do *the jobs for which it was built*.... To establish the manufacturer's liability it was sufficient that plaintiff proved that he was injured while using the Shopsmith *in a way it was intended to be used* as a result of a defect in design and manufacture of which plaintiff was not aware that made the Shopsmith unsafe *for its intended use*.

In § 402A of the *Restatement (Second) of Torts*, the scope of strict products liability in tort is limited to injuries from proper product uses: products safe for "normal handling" are not defective, and product sellers are shielded from strict liability for injuries resulting from "mishandling," "over-consumption," "excessive use," "abnormal" use, and a failure to read and heed an adequate warning. Cmts. *g*, *h*, *i*, and *j*. The *Third Restatement* succinctly limits responsibility in black-letter definitions of both design and warning defects to "the foreseeable risks of harm posed by the product," and a Reporters' Note makes clear that design defect claims are barred "[w]hen a product is put to an unforeseeable use."

Whether Misuse Is a "Defense"; Burden of Pleading and Proof

While many lawyers speak loosely of a product misuse "defense," the common-law principle of product misuse is more accurately viewed as a liability-limiting principle concerning the scope of a defendant's duty that involves the issues of negligence, product defect, scope of warranty, and proximate causation. As part of the plaintiff's prima facie products liability case in most states, the plaintiff must at least theoretically plead and prove that the accident arose out of a reasonably foreseeable product use, which suggests that the plaintiff's unforeseeable misuse cannot be an affirmative defense. This seems to be the better view accepted by most courts. Yet, all but one of the several states that have enacted *statutory* reform provisions on misuse define it as an affirmative defense.

The Foreseeability Limitation

"The ways in which a product might be misused are, like the stars, an endless number." *Goodman v. Stalfort, Inc.*, 411 F.Supp. 889, 894 (D.N.J. 1976) (plaintiff burned by flashback when he poured charcoal fluid on grill after enlarging can's opening with tine of garden tool to increase its flow). To protect product sellers from liability for an endless number of accidents caused by adventurous product uses, courts in recent years have almost universally limited responsibility to "foreseeable" product uses. Yet, defining a principle that supposedly is one of limitation in such an amorphous manner creates enormous problems of application, which is a major reason why the misuse defense is so much easier to state than to apply.

The best the courts have been able to do, in placing at least the appearance of some halter on the foreseeability concept, is to modify it with the word "reasonable," thus limiting a manufacturer's responsibility to accidents resulting from uses that are "reasonably foreseeable." Surely such a definition of the standard may be faulted for providing no further touchstone for deciding cases, but a reasonableness modification of foreseeability is plainly better than leaving it stark naked. So modifying foreseeability usefully reminds courts and juries that there are indeed reasonable limits to the kinds of uses a manufacturer fairly must consider when making design and warning decisions.

The decisions are all over the map on the foreseeability of misuse issue, and a prudent judge will
almost always recognize product misuse as a question of fact for a jury to decide. Accordingly, a
prudent lawyer should hesitate to predict whether a
judge or jury would find that a manufacturer reasonably should foresee that a young boy will hurl a
beer bottle against a telephone pole; a teenage girl
will scent a candle by pouring cologne upon it below
the flame; a woman wearing a cotton flannelette
nightgown inside out, with its pockets protruding,
will lean over the burner of a stove, causing a
pocket to come in contact with a flame; a person
will insist on buying shoes that are too small for her
feet, on buying automobile tires too large for his
rims, on sitting in a chair or an exercise bicycle too
frail for one's weight (300 and 500 pounds, respectively); a car will be driven at 115 mph, go out of
control, and injure a third party; a car's emergency
brake will be left on undetected at highway speeds
long enough to vaporize the hydraulic brake fluid,
causing the brakes to fail; "burning alcohol," sold
only for professional dental use, will be drunk by
penal farm inmate dental assistants who then go
blind; a doctor will transplant synthetic fibers, normally used for wigs and hairpieces, into a patient's
scalp as a treatment for baldness, causing irritation
and infection; a youth will tilt or rock a soft-drink
vending machine, to dispense a can without pay-
ment, causing the machine to fall upon and kill
him; a youth, thinking the safety is on, will point a
BB gun at his friend's head and pull the trigger; a

child will open and stand on an oven door to see what is cooking on the stove, causing the stove and a pot of boiling water to topple over; or that terrorists will use fertilizer or airplanes to blow up the World Trade Center.

Whether one views the misuse issue in terms of the foreseeability of the plaintiff's use, the presence or absence of a defect, or the presence or absence of proximate cause, the result in each case depends ultimately upon the reasonable foreseeability—or just plain fairness—of the plaintiff's particular use. If the manufacturer or other product seller reasonably should have contemplated and guarded against the risk, the defendant is subject to liability for the harm; if the plaintiff put the product to a use that was "unforeseeable" (unfair), the defendant simply is not liable.

Failure to Follow Warnings and Instructions

A user's failure to follow a manufacturer's warnings of danger or instructions on safe use provides a special form of misuse which ordinarily should bar recovery whenever the danger from noncompliance is evident, the noncompliance is a substantial cause of the plaintiff's harm, and there is no simple way or apparent reason for the manufacturer to design the danger out of the product. Accordingly, many courts and a couple statutes (Ariz., N.C.) bar recovery for injuries from ignoring warnings and instructions. See also Rest. (2d) § 402A cmt. *j*.

Comparative Fault

Whether, and to what extent, "product misuse" should be merged into a jurisdiction's system of comparative fault, and so be treated as a damage-reducing factor rather than as a total bar, is a vexing problem that has yet to be carefully addressed by most courts and legislatures. Viewing misuse merely as another plaintiff misconduct "defense," a few courts and legislatures have simply merged it into their comparative fault schemes. In those states, misuse reduces but does not bar a plaintiff's recovery, unless, in modified comparative fault states, the plaintiff's fault is found to exceed that of the defendant. While at least a couple of courts have ruled mysteriously that a plaintiff's *un*foreseeable misuse is somehow subject to comparison with the defendant's conduct or a product defect, it seems more logical to view *unforeseeable* misuse as lying entirely outside the scope of responsibility of manufacturers and other sellers—and, hence, outside the ambit of comparative fault. If a seller has no duty to guard against unforeseeable product risks, there can be no seller fault or product defect to compare.

§ 13.6   DEFENSES TO WARRANTY CLAIMS

How a plaintiff's misconduct affects liability in warranty is one of the most confused issues in all of products liability law. The issue examined here is what the effect should be on a claim for breach of express or implied warranty against a product seller if a plaintiff carelessly uses a product, ignores warnings and instructions, deliberately and unreasonably engages a product danger, or puts a product to an unforeseeably dangerous use. While the developing warranty law on these questions in some states roughly parallels the law applied in strict products liability in tort, the law on warranty misconduct defenses teeters on the edge of chaos.

Contributory Negligence; Assumption of Risk

Some early cases held that contributory negligence bars recovery in warranty, and occasional decisions still so hold. See *Nicholson v. American Safety Util. Corp.*, 488 S.E.2d 240 (N.C. 1997). But many courts long have held that a consumer's "simple" contributory negligence should be irrelevant to warranty claims. See *Jones v. Ford Motor Co.*, 559 S.E.2d 592 (Va. 2002). In warranty cases today, many courts require the kind of knowingly unreasonable misconduct described in § 402A comment *n*, discussed above, to bar recovery. See *Velleca v. Uniroyal Tire Co.*, 630 N.E.2d 297 (Mass. App. Ct. 1994).

Misuse

Many courts have applied a misuse defense to warranty claims quite similarly to how they apply it to products liability claims based in tort. Thus, early warranty cases denied recovery if the injury arose out of a product use not *intended* by the manufacturer. More recently, courts have limited the implied warranty of merchantability, which requires that products be "fit" for their "ordinary purposes," to uses that are reasonably *foreseeable*. See *Patterson v. Central Mills, Inc.*, 2003 WL 2007941 (6th Cir. 2003) (Ohio law) (jury properly could find that child wearing adult T-shirt unforeseeably misused shirt by climbing onto kitchen counter and reaching for ketchup in cupboard over lit burner on stove); *Venezia v. Miller Brewing Co.*, 626 F.2d 188 (1st Cir. 1980) (Mass. law) (plaintiff's intentionally smashing empty beer bottle against telephone pole, causing broken glass to injure his eye, is unforeseeable and, hence, not bottle's "ordinary purpose").

UCC Article 2

Three black-letter UCC Article 2 Sections—§§ 2–314(2)(c), 2–316(3)(b), and 2–715(2)(b)—obliquely address the role in warranty litigation of a buyer's misconduct in terms of the scope of warranty, based respectively, on:

- Whether a use is *ordinary*;
- Whether a defect was *discoverable*; or
- Whether an injury is a *proximate* result of the defect or the user's misconduct.

In contrast to the obscure manner in which buyer misconduct is treated in the Official Text, the Official Comments specifically address the effect of both a buyer's carelessness and behavior that implies risk acceptance, framing the issue in terms of whether a buyer's loss is "proximately caused" by a product defect or, alternatively, by the buyer's choice or conduct. For example, comment 5 to UCC § 2–715 states that there is no proximate cause, and hence no damages for breach of warranty, if a buyer either (1) unreasonably fails to inspect a product for defects, or (2) uses a product after discovery of a defect, whether such use was unreasonable or not. Yet, only rarely do courts in consumer misconduct cases refer to any of these provisions.

Comparative Fault

Whether consumer misconduct should be considered a matter of comparative fault for damages apportionment on a *warranty* claim depends upon the scope of each particular jurisdiction's comparative fault system and/or products liability reform legislation. In states that have enacted "comparative *negligence*" legislation, courts have been properly hesitant to compare a user's misconduct with a defendant's *breach of warranty*. Yet statutes in some states apply damages apportionment more broadly in a manner that includes breach of warranty as a form of defendant conduct to be apportioned.

§ 13.7 DEFENSES TO MISREPRESENTATION CLAIMS

The basic misconduct "defense" asserted in tortious misrepresentation actions is that the plaintiff's reliance, if any, was not "justifiable." Indeed, the justifiability of reliance, sometimes referred to as "reasonable reliance" or the "right to rely," has long been a central element of all three forms of tortious misrepresentation: fraud, negligent misrepresentation, and strict products liability in tort for misrepresentation under *Restatement (Second) Torts* § 402B and the *Restatement (Third) of Torts: Products Liability* § 9. As an essential element of all three causes of action for tortious misrepresentation, the non-justifiability of the plaintiff's reliance cannot be characterized as an affirmative defense because the plaintiff in all such cases has the burden, as with each element of such claims, to plead and prove the justifiability of his or her reliance upon the defendant's misrepresentation.

When is Reliance Justifiable?

Whether a plaintiff's reliance is justifiable depends on the nature of the representation and all of the circumstances of the particular transaction. So, a court or jury may conclude that a person may reasonably believe explicit assurances that a golfing practice device is "completely safe" and that the "ball will not hit player," or that a mace weapon sold for self defense "disables as effectively as a gun" and will "subdue" an attacker "instantly." However, a person, ignoring widespread publicity about the evils of drinking and smoking, may *not* justifiably base personal beer or cigarette consumption decisions on advertisements that glorify drinking or smoking and that somehow convey the idea that the prolonged and excessive consumption of such products is not harmful or addictive.

Contributory and Comparative Negligence; Assumption of Risk; Misuse

Because a plaintiff must prove the justifiability of his or her reliance for any tortious misrepresentation claim, the traditional products liability misconduct defenses are simply out of place. Of the few decisions that have addressed this issue, the better reasoned ones have exhibited little tolerance for attempts by defense lawyers to get two bites at the misconduct apple by arguing, first, that the plaintiff's reliance upon the representation was unjustified, and, second, that, even if the reliance in fact was justified, the plaintiff was negligent, assumed the risk, or misused the product. These decisions persuasively conclude that the justifiability (or reasonableness) of a plaintiff's reliance encompasses all forms of plaintiff misconduct addressed by the traditional misconduct defenses, although a few courts disagree. If a statute does not compel a contrary result, little would be lost, except confusion, if the courts would clearly rule that none of the traditional misconduct defenses apply to common-law tortious misrepresentation claims in products liability litigation.

CHAPTER 14

SPECIAL DEFENSES

Table of Sections

§ 14.1   Special Defenses—Generally.
§ 14.2   Compliance with Contract Specifications;
         Government Contractors.
§ 14.3   Compliance with Statutes and Regulations.
§ 14.4   Federal Preemption.
§ 14.5   Statutes of Limitations and Repose.

---

§ 14.1   SPECIAL DEFENSES— GENERALLY

Products liability defenses may be broadly divided into three categories: (1) *user-misconduct* defenses, examined in the previous chapter; (2) *no-duty* defenses, considered in chapter 10 and scattered throughout other chapters; and (3) other, *"special,"* defenses, treated here. For a more thorough examination of special defenses, see Owen, Products Liability Law ch. 14 (2d ed. 2008).

§ 14.2   COMPLIANCE WITH CONTRACT SPECIFICATIONS; GOVERNMENT CONTRACTORS

Two important products liability defenses are based on the idea that a manufacturer, relying entirely on the purchaser's own design specifications, did not originate the design defect—a general defense, based on the manufacturer's fabrication of a product according to a buyer's precise, contractual terms, and a specific one, where the buyer is the government.

For example, General Motors may contract with a punch press manufacturer to construct a press for making hubcaps, according to precise design specifications GM provides to the press manufacturer. If the press design specifications include no guards and a GM worker is injured as a result, should the worker have a claim against the press manufacturer for making and selling a defectively designed machine? Or, suppose that Wal–Mart designs a toaster with a dangerously defective heating element, and contracts out production of the toaster to a small appliance manufacturer. Should the toaster manufacturer be liable for harm that results from a fire caused by the toaster when it overheats due to a defect in Wal–Mart's design? Finally, if the US Army contracts with Chrysler to produce a fleet of Jeeps without roll bars according to a design provided or approved by an Army procurement official, should Chrysler be subject to a design defect claim to a soldier injured in a rollover accident involving such a vehicle?

Normally manufacturers are responsible for the harmful consequences of design defects in products they make and sell, but this is because a manufacturer's own engineers normally develop the designs used to make those products. When a manufacturer simply follows the design requirements specified by a purchaser, the design and manufacturing functions are separated. If a manufacturer's role is reduced to merely "fabricating" the product, the fairness and logic of holding the manufacturer liable for a dangerous design are called into question.

The Contract Specifications Defense

The contract specifications defense shields a manufacturer from liability for injuries caused by a design defect in products it manufactures pursuant to plans and specifications supplied by the purchaser, unless the design is *obviously* defective. An independent contractor "is not required to sit in judgment on the plans and specifications or the materials provided by his employer" and is not liable for their insufficiency unless the design specified "is so obviously bad that a competent contractor would realize that there was a grave chance that his product would be dangerously unsafe." Rest. (2d) § 404 cmt. *a*.

The courts have split over whether this defense, developed in negligence law, should also apply to products liability claims based on *strict* liability. But many modern courts hold that the defense *should* be applied to such claims, and a number of states (Ariz., Ga., Idaho, N.J., Wash.) have enacted statutes adopting some form of this defense.

The Government Contractor Defense

A special "government contractor" defense applies only to manufacturers who build products according to specifications provided or approved by the government. This defense gained prominence in the 1980s after the Supreme Court decided *Boyle v. United Technologies Corp.*, 487 U.S. 500 (1988), which involved the copilot of a Marine Corps helicopter who was killed during a training exercise when his helicopter crashed in the ocean. As the helicopter sank in the water, Boyle was unable to escape and drowned. His representatives sued the helicopter's manufacturer, the Sikorsky Division of United Technologies, claiming that the escape hatch was defectively designed because (1) it opened out rather than in, precluding it from opening in a submerged craft because of water pressure; and (2) the position of various instruments blocked access to the escape hatch handle. Sikorsky defended on the basis of the "military contractor defense," and the Supreme Court adopted a three-part government contractor defense that shields military contractors from design defect liability when:

   (1) A government agency approves reasonably precise specifications;

(2) The product conforms to those specifications; and

(3) The manufacturer informs the agency of any hidden dangers it knows about.

"Stripped of its essentials," in the words of one court, "the government contractor defense arises when the defendant can prove that 'the government made me do it.' " The defense does not apply if the government merely "rubber stamps" a contractor's design, yet the government need not participate in developing the design so long as it genuinely evaluates it. Courts are split on whether the defense applies to:

- Manufacturers of non-military equipment;
- Warning and/or manufacturing defects; or
- Claims for negligence.

The *Boyle* government contractor defense is a federal common-law rule, and some state courts have refused to apply a similar defense to state and local government contractors. See *Conner v. Quality Coach, Inc.*, 750 A.2d 823 (Pa. 2000). Yet some states do, and others (Ind., Kan., Mich.) have enacted statutes that protect government contractors who comply with mandatory government contract specifications.

§ 14.3 COMPLIANCE WITH STATUTES AND REGULATIONS

Manufacturers of many types of products are subject to two (or even three) different forms of safety regulation—by federal (and possibly state) administrative agencies, *ex ante*, and by the judicial products liability system, *ex post*. For example, manufacturers of industrial machines must conform to safety standards of a federal agency (OSHA), to the standards of each state's industrial safety department, and, finally, to a state's judicial standards of "defectiveness" if the product causes harm and ends up as the subject of a products liability case in court. Manufacturers question the logic and fairness of having to conform to safety regulations imposed by the government's executive/administrative branch before marketing a product only to have the government's judicial branch declare the conforming product illegal thereafter.

A government standards (or "regulatory compliance") defense, that would bar a products liability action if the accident product complied with all relevant governmental safety standards at the time it was sold, has an appearance of fair play and common sense. However, arguments favoring the defense are more than offset by a large number of problems: statutes (and sometimes regulations) tend to be abstract, vague, limited in scope, and incapable of adequately addressing the myriad factual situations that may arise in individual cases; conversely, regulations may be so narrow and specific that they fail to capture related matters at the margins of the regulation, leaving large categories of similar matters unregulated; statutes and regulations are difficult to amend to reflect changes over time, and those dealing with science and technology quickly become obsolete; statutes and regulations both may be shaped more by lobbyists for the regulated parties than by detached and objective decisionmakers neutrally balancing all affected interests in pursuit of optimal safety; and, unlike the inherent flexibility of the common law, the rigidity of regulatory safety standards tends to stifle creativity and innovation.

For these and other reasons, the courts have never seen fit to create a common-law regulatory compliance defense to products liability actions, whether based on negligence, warranty, or strict liability in tort. Compliance with a relevant governmental safety standard is some evidence of a product's nondefectiveness and a manufacturer's nonnegligence, but it is not conclusive on those issues. See Rest. (3d) § 4(b). Only in the rarest of situations has a court chosen to adopt a regulatory standard as a matter of law. See *Ramirez v. Plough, Inc.*, 863 P.2d 167 (Cal. 1993) (infant contracted Reye's Syndrome when his Spanish-speaking mother gave him St. Joseph's Aspirin for Children for cold; label warned of risk only in English, pursuant to FDA's English-only labeling policy).

Statutes in about a dozen states variously address regulatory compliance, typically creating a rebuttable presumption that a product is not defective—or not defective *and* that the manufacturer or seller is not negligent—if a product complies with applicable state or federal safety statutes or agency regulations.

§ 14.4 FEDERAL PREEMPTION

Federal preemption is an affirmative defense that arises, and a products liability claim is foreclosed, when the claim somehow conflicts with a federal product safety statute or regulation specifying design, marketing, or manufacturing standards.

When enacting product safety legislation, Congress normally vests regulatory authority over the matter in a federal administrative agency, often specifying in a "preemption clause" that state law may not interfere with safety standards or "requirements" in the statute itself or, more typically, as promulgated by the federal agency. In some statutes, Congress includes a "savings clause" providing that compliance with the statute does *not* exempt a person from liability at common law. In any event, state law that *in fact* interferes with the operation of a federal statute or regulation thereunder contravenes the Supremacy Clause of the United States Constitution.

State statutes and administrative regulations are of course governed by the Supremacy Clause, but so too are products liability actions that can interfere, if less directly, with the administration of a federal safety statute. In determining whether a products liability claim conflicts with federal law, courts must interpret the statute to ascertain its aims. Congressional intent, divined by statutory construction, is thus the cornerstone of preemption analysis.

Types of Preemption

Federal preemption of state law may be "express" or "implied." That is, preemption "is compelled whether Congress's command is explicitly stated in the statute's language or implicitly contained in its structure and purpose." *Jones v. Rath Packing Co.*, 430 U.S. 519, 525 (1977). So, Congress may *expressly* preempt state law in a preemption clause that explicitly states the statute's preemptive scope—the extent to which it precludes state law. Yet, even if a federal statute is silent with respect to the preemption issue, a products liability claim may be foreclosed by one of two types of *implied* preemption:

- **Implied *field* preemption**, which arises when *federal regulation* of the field is *so complete* and pervasive that no room is left for state regulation, or the *federal interest* in the field is *so dominant* that state law should be excluded; and

- **Implied *conflict* preemption**, which arises when federal and state provisions *directly conflict*, so that it is impossible for a person to comply with both, or the state law *obstructs the purposes* of the federal statute.

Specific Federal Safety Statutes

Rooted in statutory construction, the federal preemption defense rests on a determination that Congress in a particular statute intended to preclude particular products liability claims. The preemption issue thus is both *statute*-specific and *claim*-specific, meaning that the resolution of this issue is governed in any given case by an interpretation of the relevant provisions of the particular federal statute in relation to the particular claims involved. While preemption analysis in every case will therefore turn on the meaning and purposes of a specific statute—as revealed by its express provisions, its structure, and its legislative history—the basic issue in every case remains the same: whether Congress intended, expressly or implicitly, to prohibit the type of products liability claims asserted by the plaintiff.

Cigarettes—Cipollone

In *Cipollone v. Liggett Group, Inc.*, 505 U.S. 504 (1992), the Supreme Court for the first time applied federal preemption doctrine to a products liability case. *Cipollone* was an action against certain cigarette manufacturers on behalf of Rose Cipollone who died of lung cancer after smoking their cigarettes for over 40 years. At issue was the preemptive effect of cigarette labeling statutes passed in 1965 and 1969.

Holding that the narrower 1965 Act did not preempt state law damages actions, the Supreme Court ruled that the broader 1969 Act—which precluded states from imposing "requirements" or "prohibitions" in advertising or on labels—*did* bar some products liability claims because the latter statute was based on an agreement imposing stiffer warning requirements on cigarette manufacturers in exchange for explicit limitations on lawsuits.

Reasoning that a products liability claim is a "requirement" or "prohibition" under the Act, and
that the plaintiff's inadequate warning claim effectively asserted that the manufacturers' post–1969
advertising should have included better warnings,
the Court ruled that the 1969 Act expressly
preempted the plaintiff's warning claim—but not
the claims for breach of express warranty or fraud.

Automotive Airbags—Geier

The Supreme Court subsequently examined the
preemptive effect of other product safety statutes in
a number of cases, including *Geier v. American
Honda Motor, Co.*, 529 U.S. 861 (2000). *Geier* involved the preemptive effect of Federal Motor Vehicle Safety Standard 208, a NHTSA regulation that,
between 1975 and 1997, offered manufacturers an
evolving menu of passive restraint options, including airbags or various combinations of passive restraints, shoulder harnesses, lapbelts, and warning
systems. Beginning in the late 1980s, an increasing
number of products liability claims were based on
the failure of auto manufacturers to equip their
cars with airbags during the transitional period
before NHTSA required such devices in all cars.
Courts divided on the preemption issue.

The plaintiffs in *Geier* claimed that the 1987
Honda Accord was defectively designed because it
was not equipped with a driver's-side airbag, to
which Honda replied that such a no-airbag claim
was preempted by Standard 208, which at the time
permitted manufacturers to choose between seat-

belts and airbags. The district court granted summary judgment for Honda, ruling that the plaintiffs' no-airbag claims were *expressly* preempted, and the court of appeals affirmed on the basis that such claims were *impliedly* preempted because they conflicted with the objectives of federal Standard 208.

The Supreme Court affirmed, agreeing with the court of appeals. Since the plaintiffs' claim was that the car was defectively designed because the manufacturer *failed* to equip it with an airbag, while FMVSS 208 *permitted* manufacturers at the time to choose between airbags and alternative passive restraints, the no-airbag claims actually conflicted with the federal standard and so were impliedly preempted.

The Supreme Court also has examined (or soon will examine), the preemptive effect of statutes and regulations governing the safety of:

- **Truck Braking Systems.** See *Freightliner Corp. v. Myrick*, 514 U.S. 280 (1995), holding that the National Traffic and Motor Vehicle Safety Act of 1966 and safety standards issued by NHTSA do not preempt products liability claims;

- **Drugs.** See *Wyeth v. Levine*, 128 S.Ct. 1118 (2008) (granting *certiorari*), which will consider whether FDA drug labeling requirements preempt state law products liability claims alleging that different labeling was necessary for reasonably safe use;

- **"Light" Cigarettes**. See *Altria Group, Inc. v. Good*, 128 S.Ct. 1119 (2008) (granting *certiorari*), which will consider whether statements regarding tar and nicotine yields in cigarette advertising approved by the Federal Trade Commission preempt state law claims;

- **Medical Devices—Express Preemption.** See *Riegel v. Medtronic, Inc.*, 128 S.Ct. 999 (2008), holding that FDA device specific requirements under the "premarket approval" (PMA) process expressly preempt state law claims; *Medtronic, Inc. v. Lohr*, 518 U.S. 470 (1996), holding that the Medical Device Amendments of 1976 (MDA) do not expressly preempt products liability claims;

- **Medical Devices—Implied Preemption**. See *Buckman Co. v. Plaintiffs' Legal Committee*, 531 U.S. 341 (2001), holding that fraud-on-the-FDA claims conflict with federal law and are impliedly preempted. See also *Warner-Lambert Co., LLC v. Kent*, 128 S.Ct. 1168 (2008), a split decision without opinion, and hence of no precedential value;

- **Recreational Boats.** See *Sprietsma v. Mercury Marine*, 537 U.S. 51 (2002), holding that the Boat Safety Act neither expressly nor impliedly preempts common-law products liability claims; and

- **Pesticides and Insecticides.** See *Bates v. Dow Agrosciences LLC*, 544 U.S. 431 (2005), holding that the Federal Insecticide, Fungicide and Rodenticide Act (FIFRA) neither expressly nor impliedly preempts state law tort claims.

Concluding Thoughts on Federal Preemption

Federal preemption is an important issue that products liability lawyers need to keep constantly in mind. The first thing a lawyer should do in any particular case is to determine if the courts have addressed the preemptive effect of a regulatory statute that might concern the pertinent product. If the courts have not yet spoken, the lawyer must ascertain whether the pertinent products liability claims would contravene either an express preemption clause or the purposes of the particular act of Congress. This is often a daunting task, but it is assisted by a growing body of jurisprudence specific to particular product safety statutes and specific products liability claims.

§ 14.5 STATUTES OF LIMITATIONS AND REPOSE

Time-limitation statutes impose maximum time limits on products liability claims, cutting off a plaintiff's rights after a particular period of time. If a plaintiff files a products liability claim after the statutory period has run, the time-limitation statute simply bars the claim.

Time-limitation statutes come in a variety of forms, the two basic types of which are:

- Statutes of *limitations*; and
- Statutes of *repose*.

Statutes of limitations and repose provide a potent defense to products liability actions that a plaintiff's lawyer must seek to avoid and a defendant's lawyer must be sure not to overlook.

Both forms of statute cut off a defendant's products liability exposure after a period of time, but they operate quite differently. The time periods of statutes of limitations are shorter—from 1 to 6 years (typically 2 or 3), depending on the jurisdiction—than those of statutes of repose, which run from 5 to 20 years (typically 8, 10, or 12). In addition, statutes of limitations begin to run at the time an injury occurs or is discovered (actually or constructively), whereas statutes of repose generally begin to run when a product is sold; and statutes of limitations normally may be delayed or "tolled" by certain equitable circumstances, such as a plaintiff's infancy or failure to discover an injury, whereas statutes of repose ordinarily may not.

Statutes of *limitations* come in various forms. All states have statutes of limitations applicable to personal injury torts and for wrongful death. In the absence of a more specific statute (addressing products liability claims), these general statutes of limitations govern products liability claims for both negligence and strict liability in tort. In addition, most states adhere to the uniform statute of limitations for breach of warranty claims in UCC § 2–725, which is 4 years from the date of sale. An increasing number of states, now a slight majority, have special statutes of limitations specifically applicable to products liability claims.

Statutes of *repose* also come in a number of forms. The most basic form of repose statute per-tains to products liability claims generally, though sometimes making exception for particular types of products, such as asbestos. A quite different form of repose statute, called a "useful-life" statute, bars a plaintiff's claim at the expiration of the product's useful life rather than after a set period of time. In addition, some states apply repose statutes governing improvements to realty to cases involving products attached to land, such as large grain silos or overhead cranes. Finally, a federal statute of repose—the General Aviation Revitalization Act of 1994 ("GARA")—provides an 18–year statute of repose for manufacturers of private planes and their component parts.

By imposing an absolute cut-off to products liability claims after a set period of time, statutes of repose sometimes extinguish claims before they are discovered, and sometimes even before injuries occur and claims exist at all. For this reason, several courts have struck down repose statutes as unconstitutional, typically for violating the Due Process or Equal Protection clauses of the state or federal constitution, or the open courts or similar provision of a state constitution. Yet most courts have upheld products liability statutes of repose against these and a variety of other constitutional challenges. Similarly, while some realty improvement statutes of repose have been held unconstitutional, most have withstood constitutional scrutiny. To date, GARA has proved immune to successful constitutional challenge.

PART V

SPECIAL ISSUES

CHAPTER 15

SPECIAL TYPES OF DEFENDANTS

Table of Sections

§ 15.1 Special Types of Defendants—Generally.
§ 15.2 Retailers and Other Non-Manufacturing Sellers.
§ 15.3 Raw Material and Component Part Suppliers.
§ 15.4 Parent and Apparent Manufacturers;
         Franchisers.
§ 15.5 Successor Corporations.
§ 15.6 Employers as Manufacturers.
§ 15.7 Miscellaneous Marketing Participants.

§ 15.1 SPECIAL TYPES OF DEFENDANTS—GENERALLY

In most products liability cases, the only or principal defendant is the manufacturer that designed, manufactured, and marketed the product which injured the plaintiff. Thus, most discussion in this book concerns the responsibility of such manufacturing enterprises. Yet parties in the product distri-

431

bution chain other than ordinary manufacturers, notably retail sellers, often profit from moving products from factories to consumers and so may bear some responsibility when product hazards injure consumers.

Sometimes the varying roles of special defendants call for liability principles differing from those applied to principal manufacturers, but often the rules remain the same. The most recurring issue in such cases is the applicability of the doctrine of strict liability in tort. Yet negligence, breach of warranty, tortious misrepresentation, and other theories of liability (such as negligent entrustment, in the case of retailers) can also be important claims in cases brought against the type of special defendants examined here. For a more thorough examination of the special types of defendants, see Owen, Products Liability Law ch. 15 (2d ed. 2008).

§ 15.2 RETAILERS AND OTHER NON–MANUFACTURING SELLERS

Negligence in General

Like other product suppliers, retail sellers have a duty to exercise reasonable care, in supplying products, not to injure their customers or others. Unlike manufacturers, however, who typically design, manufacturer, package, and affirmatively market their products, most retailers ordinarily have little or no knowledge of, or control over, whether the products they sell may be dangerously defective. Thus, in the absence of some reason to believe that a product may be defective, a retailer normally is not negligent in merely passing it along to the consumer. See *Sanns v. Butterfield Ford*, 94 P.3d 301 (Utah Ct. App. 2004) (auto dealership, as passive retailer, had no duty in negligence law to warn customers of manufacturing defect of which it was unaware); *Bren–Tex Tractor Co. v. Massey–Ferguson, Inc.*, 97 S.W.3d 155 (Tex. App. 2002) (retailer had no duty in negligence to warn customer of danger from tractor not being equipped with rollover protection system).

Some states have a common-law or statutory principle that shields retail sellers and other distributors from liability for negligence when selling goods in their original, sealed containers or packages, variously known as the "sealed-container" or "original-package" doctrine or defense. Yet, if a retail seller acts affirmatively to prepare, assemble, install, repair, test, or inspect a product, it no longer acts merely as a conduit and will have a duty to exercise reasonable care in its actions. And some courts find an exception to the retailer no-duty rule for sellers of *used* goods, especially automobiles, holding that such sellers have a duty of reasonable care to test or inspect, while other courts apply the general no-duty rules to such dealers.

Negligent Entrustment

Retailers may be liable for selling dangerous products to children or other persons likely to use them dangerously under the theory of negligent entrustment. So, if a retail dealer sells a gun, fire-works, or a jet ski to a young child, an intoxicated person, or a mental incompetent; an automobile to a person known to be an unlicensed driver or per-haps an habitual drunkard; or gasoline to a very young child or a clearly intoxicated driver, the seller may be subject to liability for negligently supplying a chattel to a person likely to use it in an unreason-ably dangerous manner.

For example, in *Moning v. Alfono*, 254 N.W.2d 759 (Mich. 1977), a retail merchant sold a slingshot to an 11-year-old boy who shot a pellet that rico-cheted off a tree into his friend's eye. In a negligent entrustment action against the retailer, wholesaler, and manufacturer of the slingshot for marketing it directly to children, the court held that a jury could find that such a sale created an unreasonable risk of harm to the injured boy.

Yet most courts have refused to apply, much less expand, the principle of *Moning*. While the basic idea of allowing a cause of action against retailers for negligent entrustment makes good sense, most courts, troubled by the implications of broadly al-lowing such claims, have held that it usually is *not* negligent simply to sell such products as bows and arrows, CO_2 cartridges, ordinary darts, lawn darts, or even slingshots to children. See *Carbone v. Alag-na*, 658 N.Y.S.2d 48 (App. Div. 1997) (slingshot). Compare *Vic Potamkin Chevrolet, Inc. v. Horne*, 505 So.2d 560 (Fla. Dist. Ct. App. 1987) (no negligent entrustment for selling car to clearly incompetent driver), aff'd, 533 So.2d 261 (Fla. 1988).

Tortious Misrepresentation and Breach of Warranty

A retail dealer is subject to liability for tortious misrepresentation, including fraud, negligence, and strict liability in tort for misrepresentation.

Retailers, of course, are as liable as manufacturers or any other "seller" for breach of warranty under Article 2 of the UCC. Consequently, retailers are subject to liability for breach of express warranty, the implied warranty of merchantability, and the implied warranty of fitness for particular purpose—subject to the normal limitations based on disclaimers, privity, notice, and limitations on remedies, all as addressed in chapter 4.

A retail seller is subject to liability for breaching its own express warranties, but it often is said that a retailer bears no responsibility for the failure of a *manufacturer's* express warranties. Yet, under UCC § 2–314(2)(f), a seller is subject to liability for breach of the implied warranty of merchantability for selling a mislabeled product if representations on its container or label prove false. And a retailer is liable for breach of a manufacturer's express warranties that it "adopts" if it affirmatively asserts that it stands behind them.

Strict Liability in Tort

The most significant retailer issue in modern products liability litigation is whether retailers are subject to strict liability in tort for the sale of defective products. In *Vandermark v. Ford Motor Co.*, 391 P.2d 168 (Cal. 1964) (Traynor, J.), the court ruled that the retail dealer of a new car was strictly liable in tort for injuries to the plaintiff when the brakes on his car failed and he crashed into a pole. As "an integral part of the overall producing and marketing enterprise," and as sometimes the only member of that enterprise available to injured consumers, retailers properly should "bear the cost of injuries resulting from defective products." Because retailers can pressure manufacturers to make safer products, they are well positioned to improve product safety, and "they can adjust the costs of such protection between them in the course of their continuing business relationship." Id. at 171–72.

Vandermark's application of the doctrine of strict products liability in tort to retailers was validated in comment *f* to § 402A, which provides that retailers are covered by the strict liability doctrine. Since that time, with little dissent, courts have widely applied the strict tort doctrine to retailers and other non-manufacturing distributors of defective products.

Yet legislative reformers have questioned the fairness of holding retailers strictly liable for design and other defects over which they have no control, such as the uncrashworthy design of an automobile sold by a retail dealer. This has led to the enactment of statutes in many states that shield retail dealers and other non-manufacturing distributors from some or all forms of strict products liability. A number of statutes generally follow the *Model Uniform Product Liability Act* in relieving non-manufacturing sellers of strict products liability (except for their breach of an express warranty), *unless* the *manufacturer* (1) is not subject to the jurisdiction of the court, or (2) is, or is likely to become, insolvent.

Wholesalers and Other Distributors

The principles examined above, applicable to retail dealers generally, apply to wholesalers and other non-manufacturing distributors as well.

§ 15.3   RAW MATERIAL AND COMPONENT PART SUPPLIERS

Suppliers of raw materials and component parts stand at the top of the chain of distribution. Like retailers, these suppliers generally have little control over the safety of the final product into which their component products are incorporated because the design and assembly of the finished product is usually in the exclusive hands of the manufacturer-assembler. For example, a car manufacturer—which obtains sheet metal, plastic, screws, glass, carpeting, tires, batteries, and radios from many suppliers—makes most decisions bearing on the safety of the finished car.

The liability issue in these cases usually rests on whether the dangerously defective condition resides in the component *itself*, in which case the component supplier generally *is* liable for resulting harm, or whether the defect arises from the *manner* in which the final product's manufacturer-assembler *integrates* the component into the product, in which case the component supplier usually is *not* responsible for resulting harm. See *White v. ABCO Eng'g Corp.*, 221 F.3d 293 (2d Cir. 2000) (N.J. law) (question turns on whether component part itself was defective).

Thus, if a tire manufacturer supplies a defective tire to the assembler of a vehicle, and the defect in the tire causes the vehicle to crash, then the tire manufacturer (as well as the manufacturer-assembler of the entire vehicle) is properly liable for the harmful consequences of the crash. Yet, courts widely agree that suppliers of nondefective components have no duty to police the manner in which their components are integrated into finished products and so are *not* liable for dangers that manufacturer-assemblers introduce into finished products containing the components—not liable, that is, unless the component supplier substantially participates in the design of the finished product. See *Springmeyer v. Ford Motor Co.*, 71 Cal.Rptr.2d 190 (Ct. App. 1998) (supplier of defective fan blade used on Ford truck engines liable for resulting injuries because it helped Ford design and test blade).

The *Products Liability Restatement* § 5 agrees, providing that component part suppliers are subject to liability only if (1) the component itself is defective, or (2) the supplier "substantially participates" in a dangerously defective integration of the component into the design of the finished product.

§ 15.4 PARENT AND APPARENT MANUFACTURERS; FRANCHISERS

Parent corporations and trademark owners reap the commercial benefits of products designed, manufactured, and/or marketed substantially or wholly by their subsidiaries or trademark licensees. The latter, as product manufacturers themselves, are of course subject to the normal rules of products liability law. But sometimes subsidiaries are thinly capitalized, and trademark licensees and franchisees typically are small enterprises in comparison to their licensors or franchisers. This section briefly examines the liability of a parent corporation, trademark owner, or franchiser that profits from a related company's manufacture and sale of a defective product.

Parent Corporations—Alter Ego Liability

Fundamental principles of corporate law ordinarily shield *shareholders* from the debts and other liabilities of the corporation. Thus, when a parent corporation owns most or all of the stock of a financially unstable subsidiary corporation, the separate identities of the two corporations normally precludes a subsidiary's creditors—including products liability claimants—from recovering against the parent corporation.

Yet a parent's "corporate veil" may be "pierced" in certain limited situations, making the parent responsible for harm caused by the defective products of its manufacturing subsidiary. The principal derivative basis for responsibility of this type is "alter ego" liability, based on the idea that a parent may so dominate its subsidiary that they are essentially a single economic entity. "[W]hen a corporation is so controlled as to be the alter ego or mere instrumentality of its stockholder, the corporate form may be disregarded in the interests of justice." *In re Silicone Gel Breast Implants Prods. Liab. Litig.*, 887 F.Supp. 1447, 1452 (N.D. Ala. 1995). See also *Fletcher v. Atex, Inc.*, 68 F.3d 1451 (2d Cir. 1995) (Del. law) (alter ego liability requires proof that (1) parent and subsidiary acted as single economic entity, *and* (2) some injustice, unfairness, or improper conduct by defendant); *McConkey v. McGhan Med. Corp.*, 144 F.Supp.2d 958 (E.D. Tenn. 2000) (listing 11 factors pertinent to whether companies acted as single economic entity); *Simeone v. Bombardier–Rotax GmbH*, 360 F.Supp.2d 665 (E.D. Pa. 2005) (listing 10 "interrelationship" factors).

Apparent Manufacturers

The "apparent manufacturer" theory imposes the liability of a manufacturer on a seller who holds itself out to the public as the product's manufacturer, by label or advertising, in order to induce consumers to buy the product. *Restatement (Second) of Torts* § 400 provides:

> One who puts out as his own product a chattel manufactured by another is subject to the same liability as though he were its manufacturer.

This doctrine would apply, for example, to the sale by Sears of a power drill manufactured by Black and Decker, but sold by Sears under its "Kenmore" brand name. If a user were injured by a defect in the drill, he or she could hold Sears liable as if it were Black and Decker. So, if Black and Decker were subject to either negligence or strict liability, Sears, derivatively, would be liable as well. See *Hebel v. Sherman Equip.*, 442 N.E.2d 199 (Ill. 1982).

When this doctrine was first set forth in § 400 of the *Restatement of Torts* in 1934, it expressed a bold new way to hold retail sellers strictly liable in tort for production errors made by manufacturers. Yet, with the adoption of strict liability theories applicable to retailers, § 400 and the apparent manufacturer doctrine have become quaintly obsolete. While acknowledging that the rule has "little practical significance," the *Third Restatement* in § 14 nevertheless readopts this harmless but now essentially hollow doctrine.

Trademark Licensors; Franchisers

Cases involving trademarks and franchises are a species of apparent manufacturer cases in which a trademark or trade name leads consumers to believe that the trademark owner or franchiser is responsible for the quality of the product. Owners of trademarks and trade names license their marks and names to induce consumers to buy or use a product based on the reputation for product quality of the holder of the mark or name. If a person is injured by a product manufactured by one company, but bearing the name or logo of another, the question that arises is whether the trademark owner or franchiser should be allowed to commercially exploit its reputation without a corresponding responsibility to be accountable for defects in products sold under its name or mark.

The rule is clear: if the licensor exercised *substantial control* over product safety, it is subject to liability for injuries caused by a defect in the product distributed by a licensee. See *Bridgestone/Firestone N. Am. Tire v. A.P.S. Rent–A–Car & Leasing*, 88 P.3d 572 (Ariz. Ct. App. 2004); *Miller v. McDonald's Corp.*, 945 P.2d 1107 (Or. Ct. App. 1997) (franchiser could be liable under right-to-control test for injury from heart-shaped sapphire stone found in Big Mac).

The reverse, of course, is also true: a trademark owner or franchise licensor is *not* liable if it does *not* substantially control a product's safety. While some courts disagree, a trade name franchiser or trademark licensor is *not* responsible for a product defect merely because the product carries the defendant's name or logo; liability does not attach, in other words, from simply selling a name or mark to a licensee who places it on an unsafe product. See

Harrison v. B.F. Goodrich Co., 881 So.2d 288 (Miss. Ct. App. 2004).

§ 15.5   SUCCESSOR CORPORATIONS

When a manufacturer goes out of business and formally dissolves, its shareholders generally are immune from responsibility for the firm's liabilities, and there usually is no remaining entity to be responsible for injuries caused by defective products the corporation may have made and sold. Yet, sometimes a part or all of a dissolving company (the "predecessor") is sold to another enterprise (the "successor") that puts some portions of the predecessor's productive assets—its equipment, capital, labor force, marketing apparatus, and goodwill—to some continued use. Indeed, sometimes the successor uses the predecessor's productive assets to continue making and selling the same products to the same customers.

General Rule of Non-liability with Specific Exceptions

Under general corporate law principles, when one company merely acquires the assets of another, the successor entity is generally *not* responsible for the predecessor's debts and other liabilities, including products liability claims and judgments from defective products made and sold by the predecessor before the transfer. Yet, courts have recognized that a successor fairly *should* be responsible for the liabilities of a predecessor in certain situations, *if*:

the successor *consents* to undertake the predecessor's liabilities; the successor and predecessor are essentially *the same entity*; or a transfer is *fraudulently designed* to avoid liability. Thus, where one company sells its assets to another, the purchaser classically is *not* liable for the seller's products liability obligations *unless*:

(1) The purchaser expressly or impliedly *assumes such liability*;

(2) The transaction amounts to a *consolidation or merger* of the two companies;

(3) The purchaser is a *mere continuation* of the seller; or

(4) The transaction is a *fraudulent scheme* to avoid such liability.

Restatement (3d) Torts: Products Liability § 12 adopts the traditional rule of non-liability with these standard four exceptions.

New Exceptions—Continuity of Enterprise; Product Line

A number of courts have applied one or both of two new exceptions to the general rule of non-liability in order to broaden opportunities for redress for persons injured by defective products manufactured by defunct corporations that morph into successor enterprises:

(5) The "continuity of enterprise" exception, see *Turner v. Bituminous Casualty Co.*, 244 N.W.2d 873 (Mich. 1976); and

(6) The "product line" exception, see *Ray v. Alad Corp.*, 560 P.2d 3 (Cal. 1977).

Conventional wisdom, supported by the *Products Liability Restatement*, holds that the traditional four exceptions are deeply entrenched in American products liability jurisprudence and that the two upstarts ("continuity of enterprise" and "product line") were but temporary aberrations in what is otherwise an unwavering set of exceptions to the general non-liability rule for successor corporations. It appears quite true that most courts passing on the issue have rejected one or both of the two new liability-expanding approaches and adhered to the traditional four exceptions. Yet recent years have witnessed a creeping expansion in the exceptions which now can boast a quite significant following, and it is difficult to predict how courts will view the new exceptions in the future.

Successor Corporation's Duty to Warn

The issue just examined concerns the *derivative* responsibility of a successor firm for defects in goods produced by a predecessor whose assets it purchases thereafter. A different issue is whether a successor corporation, when it discovers that a predecessor's products are dangerously defective, has an *independent duty to warn* the predecessor's consumers of the danger. Some courts hold that the successor has this obligation:

> [B]y virtue of succeeding to the predecessor's interests, the successor is often in a good position

to learn of problems arising from use of the predecessor's product and to prevent harm to persons or property. When the relationship between the successor and pre-transfer purchasers of the predecessor's products gives rise to actual or potential economic benefit to the successor, it is both fair and efficient to require the successor to act reasonably to prevent such harm.

Rest. (3d) § 13 cmt. *a* (successor has independent duty of reasonable care to warn if there is a reasonable way to do so).

§ 15.6 EMPLOYERS AS MANUFACTURERS

In the early 1900s, state legislatures replaced workers' common-law claims against employers for workplace injuries with *workers' compensation statutes* that ensured speedy and no-fault compensation from employers for such accidents. The legislative trade-offs for providing workers with these benefits were (1) to restrict the amounts of compensation paid, and (2) to abolish common-law claims against employers for workplace accidents. Thus, a central feature of all workers' compensation statutes is that the benefits legislatively prescribed are the worker's "exclusive remedy" against the employer for injuries on the job.

Dual Capacity Doctrine

Industrial employers may design and manufacture products for their own use, sometimes specialty tools solely for use in their own business. Yet, some manufacturers make products not only for their own use but also for sale to the general public: a press manufacturer may use the presses on its own assembly line to make parts for presses sold to others, and a tire manufacturer may equip the trucks it uses around its factories with tires from its normal production inventory. Because such an enterprise in a real sense wears two hats, it may be said to act in a "dual capacity"—both as a manufacturer *and* employer.

Normally, if an employee is injured on the job by an unguarded punch press or a defective tire blowout, the employee may recover both workers' compensation benefits from the employer and damages in a products liability action from the manufacturer. But what if the product manufacturer is also the employee's employer? May the injured employee maintain an ordinary products liability action against the company in its capacity as manufacturer? Or is the employee limited to workers' compensation benefits as his or her "exclusive remedy" for such injuries?

The *dual capacity doctrine*, which allowed tort claims against an employer, had an intriguing yet short and narrow life in products liability law. In *Mercer v. Uniroyal, Inc.*, 361 N.E.2d 492, 496 (Ohio Ct. App. 1976), an appellate court first applied the dual capacity doctrine to a products liability case. While driving a company truck equipped with Uniroyal tires, a Uniroyal employee was injured when a tire blew out. Relying on cases from other contexts, and reasoning that "[i]t was only a matter of circumstance that the tire on the truck in which the plaintiff was riding was a Uniroyal tire rather than a Sears, Goodyear or Goodrich," the court allowed the Uniroyal employee to maintain a products liability action against his employer. Twelve days later, a California court similarly extended the dual capacity doctrine to the products liability context. See *Douglas v. E. & J. Gallo Winery*, 137 Cal.Rptr. 797, 801 (Ct. App. 1977) ("when an employer engages in the dual capacity of manufacturer of a product for sale to the public, the employer assumes all of the duties and liabilities of such manufacturer").

Yet other states uniformly rejected the dual capacity doctrine in products liability litigation. Even in California and Ohio, which spawned the doctrine in this context, it quickly ran out of steam. In 1982, the year after the California Supreme Court had approved the doctrine in *Bell v. Industrial Vangas, Inc.*, 637 P.2d 266 (Cal. 1981), that state's legislature effectively abolished it. And the Ohio Supreme Court restricted the doctrine substantially in the following year. Thus, the doctrine "flourished in only two states, Ohio and California, and even there for only a few years, from 1977 to 1983." 6 *Larson's Workers' Compensation Law* § 113.01[4]. Courts in recent cases continue to reject the rule, and it seems safe to proclaim that the dual capacity doctrine essentially is dead.

Intentional Employer Misconduct

One possible escape from the exclusive remedy rule, applicable to a very narrow class of cases in which an employee is injured by a dangerously defective product supplied by his or her employer, is to prove that the employer *intended* to harm the employee. If an employer intentionally harms a worker, the worker in most states may maintain a tort action against the employer. See *Laidlow v. Hariton Mach. Co.*, 790 A.2d 884 (N.J. 2002) (exception might apply if plaintiff could prove employer desired or knew with substantial certainty that tying up safety guard would injure employee); *Beauchamp v. Dow Chem. Co.*, 398 N.W.2d 882 (Mich. 1986) (research scientist could maintain claims for intentional misrepresentation, fraudulent concealment, assault, and intentional infliction of emotional distress against his employer chemical company for injuries from his on-the-job exposure to Agent Orange).

Yet, fearful that a flexible intentional harm exception might cause a precipitous erosion of the exclusive remedy principle, most courts interpret this exception very narrowly as allowing common-law claims only if a plaintiff can prove that the employer truly intended to harm the employee, at least in the sense of knowing to a substantial certainty that the employee would be injured.

§ 15.7 MISCELLANEOUS MARKETING PARTICIPANTS

This chapter so far has examined the major types of non-manufacturing suppliers who often play an important role in a product's chain of distribution. Other types of marketing participants sometimes contribute in a secondary way to the sale and distribution of products.

Product Certifiers and Endorsers

Some enterprises, notably Underwriters Laboratories, stimulate demand for particular products by certifying or endorsing the safety or general quality of products that pass their inspection process. Such tools or other products (such as stepladders) may then be marketed with a "UL" seal of approval. Though Underwriters Laboratories is nominally a nonprofit testing organization, financial support for this large enterprise comes from manufacturers whose product marketing is materially enhanced by a UL certification. Because endorsements by Underwriters Laboratories and other certifiers of product quality may figure materially in a consumer's purchasing decisions, and because such certifications sometimes may mislead consumers as to a particular product's safety, courts from time to time have addressed the nature and scope of a product certifier's responsibility for injuries from products it has endorsed.

The most prominent products liability case concerning a product endorser's liability is *Hanberry v. Hearst Corp.*, 81 Cal.Rptr. 519 (Ct. App. 1969), briefly mentioned in the discussion of negligent misrepresentation. The plaintiff purchased a pair of shoes that were defective in manufacture and design, in that they had a low co-efficient of friction on vinyl surfaces, making them slippery and unsafe, which caused the plaintiff to slip, fall, and injure herself on her kitchen floor. The shoes had been advertised in the defendant's magazine, Good Housekeeping, as meeting the "Good Housekeeping's Consumers' Guaranty Seal" that the magazine claimed was its "Consumers' Guaranty." The magazine further represented that "[w]e satisfy ourselves that products advertised in Good Housekeeping are good ones and that the advertising claims made for them in our magazine are truthful."

The plaintiff sued the publisher, Hearst, for negligent misrepresentation, breach of warranty, and strict liability in tort. She alleged that she bought the shoes on the strength of the advertisement in the magazine; that the Good Housekeeping seal was affixed to the shoes and the box in which they came; that Hearst either failed to test, investigate, or even examine the type of shoes she bought or, that if it did, it did so negligently; and that "Hearst's issuance of its seal and certification as to the shoes was not warranted by the information it possessed." The trial court dismissed the plaintiff's complaint on demurrer. Id. at 521.

On appeal, the *Hanberry* court allowed the negligent misrepresentation claim but denied the claims for breach of warranty and strict liability in tort.

On the negligent misrepresentation claim, the court observed that the Good Housekeeping seal enhances the value of its advertisements "because its seal and certification tend to induce and encourage consumers to purchase products advertised in the magazine and which bear that seal and certification." Id. at 522. Because the very purpose of the seal and certification was to suggest that the defendant had taken reasonable steps to ensure itself of the product's quality, the plaintiff had properly alleged a negligent misrepresentation claim.

But the claims for breach of warranty and strict liability in tort were inappropriate, in the court's view, because the seal implied merely that the defendant had approved the general type of product (presumably its design and possibly its warnings and instructions), not the particular pair of shoes purchased by the plaintiff. If the plaintiff's shoes had a manufacturing defect, the defendant's endorsement could not fairly be interpreted to cover such a defect.

Although the cases are sparse, other courts agree that certifiers and endorsers are subject to liability for negligent misrepresentation, but that such defendants ordinarily are not subject to liability for breach of warranty or strict liability in tort because certifiers do not "sell" products nor control product safety.

Trade Associations

Manufacturers and retailers often form industry-wide trade associations to perform a variety of functions, from serving merely as an information clearinghouse to performing a wide-ranging assortment of services, such as conducting and sponsoring product testing, research studies, workshops, and technical symposia; developing and recommending design specifications, construction techniques, and packaging and handling procedures; promoting plant safety; collecting, analyzing, and furnishing various safety and other information; and lobbying governmental entities for beneficial legislation. Trade associations are sometimes defendants in products liability litigation.

Because trade associations do not make or sell products, they are not subject to strict liability in tort or for breach of warranty for defective products sold by members of such associations. Whether trade associations owe a duty of care to customers of their members, subjecting them to claims of negligence for harm to such third parties, is a more difficult question. All courts agree that a trade association that neither designs, tests, conducts safety research on, sets standards for, manufactures, nor sells its members' products does not owe an affirmative duty of care to protect the customers of its member companies from defects in the products that the companies make and sell.

However, if a trade association promulgates standards affecting safety for its members to use, some courts have found a duty of care to ultimate customers. See *Jappell v. American Ass'n of Blood Banks*, 162 F.Supp.2d 476 (E.D. Va. 2001); *Meneely v. S.R. Smith, Inc.*, 5 P.3d 49 (Wash. Ct. App. 2000); *King v. National Spa & Pool Inst., Inc.*, 570 So.2d 612 (Ala. 1990). Yet most courts, reluctant to force such useful organizations to don the burdensome mantle of rule-making organizations, have refused to find a duty even when a trade association plays some role in the development and promulgation of safety standards. See *Tuttle v. Lorillard Tobacco Co.*, 377 F.3d 917 (D. Minn. 2003) (no duty absent proof that Smokeless Tobacco Council manufactured, sold, or designed cigarettes, or set standards).

Sometimes plaintiffs claim that trade associations are basically a front for civil conspiracies to obstruct legislation and litigation and, more generally, to frustrate the principles of products liability and safety. Though the litigation against the tobacco industry may plausibly support this type of charge, most courts reject such claims in most contexts on both substantive and First Amendment grounds. See § 11.3, above.

Other Marketing Participants

Many cases involving miscellaneous defendants address the issue of whether the particular type of defendant is subject to strict products liability in tort or liability for breach of warranty. Because most secondary participants in product marketing do not design, manufacture, market, or sell products to consumers, they generally are *not* subject to strict products liability, either in tort or warranty. Such defendants ordinarily neither "sell" nor "otherwise distribute" such products, as variously required for UCC Article 2 warranties, *Restatement (Second) of Torts* § 402A, and *Restatement (Third) of Torts: Products Liability* §§ 1 and 20.

Strict products liability normally applies only to commercial sellers, and even then only to their regular, rather than occasional, products sales. Section 402A does not apply to *isolated noncommercial sales*, such as an individual's one-time sale of a used car, nor does it apply to "sales of the stock of merchants out of the usual course of business, such as execution sales, bankruptcy sales, bulk sales, and the like." Cmt. *f.* Nor do such secondary defendants ordinarily qualify as "merchant" sellers for purposes of the implied warranty of merchantability.

Strict liability in tort does not apply to *nonprofit standards-setting organizations* that merely establish safety standards for products but which neither manufacture nor sell such products. Such entities may be subject to liability in negligence, however, under *Restatement (Second) of Torts* § 324A. See *Wissel v. Ohio High Sch. Athletic Ass'n*, 605 N.E.2d 458 (Ohio Ct. App. 1992).

Auctioneers are not strictly liable in tort for products that they auction. See *New Tex. Auto Auction Servs., L.P. v. Hernandez*, 249 S.W.3d 400 (Tex. 2008). But they may be subject to liability for fraudulent misrepresentation or for breach of implied warranty of merchantability if they regularly auction merchandise of a particular type and hold themselves out as being experts in the field, particularly if they fail to reveal the identity of their principal.

The liability of *sales representatives*, *agents*, and *brokers*, is less clear, although normally they are not subject to strict products liability.

CHAPTER 16

SPECIAL TYPES OF
TRANSACTIONS AND
PRODUCTS

Table of Sections

§ 16.1   Special Types of Transactions and Products—
          Generally.
§ 16.2   Lease, Bailment, and License Transactions.
§ 16.3   Service Transactions.
§ 16.4   Repaired, Rebuilt, and Reconditioned Products.
§ 16.5   Used Products.
§ 16.6   Electricity.
§ 16.7   Real Estate.
§ 16.8   Publications.
§ 16.9   Blood.
§ 16.10 Miscellaneous Transactions and Products.

---

§ 16.1 SPECIAL TYPES OF
TRANSACTIONS AND PRODUCTS—
GENERALLY

Some products liability litigation involves transactions other than the typical *sale* of a *new chattel*, the paradigm around which most products liability law is centered. The principal issue examined here is whether the usual principles of products liability

457

law, particularly the doctrine of strict liability, should be extended from the new chattel sale situation to contexts where other policies and principles may predominate. In some of these situations, the differing objectives and doctrinal borders of products liability, premises liability, professional malpractice, public health, free speech, and other areas of the law are brought into sharp relief. For a more thorough examination of special types of transactions and products, see Owen, Products Liability Law ch. 16 (2d ed. 2008).

§ 16.2 LEASE, BAILMENT, AND LICENSE TRANSACTIONS

Leases

Consumers and businesses to a large extent are shifting away from purchasing many types of products, notably automobiles, and are acquiring them instead by means of short-term and long-term leases. In general, products liability principles that govern a supplier's *sale* of a product also apply to product *leases*. But some jurisdictions have not yet completed breaking down the barriers between the law governing product sales and leases.

Theory of Liability

Negligence. Ordinary negligence principles govern the liability of lessors of defective products that injure lessees and other people. Lessors must exercise reasonable care to inspect their products for defects, remove those discovered, and warn lessees of hidden hazards. See Rest. (2d) § 408.

Warranty—Article 2. By its terms, "Article 2—Sales" of the UCC applies only to true *sales* transactions, which suggests that it was not intended to apply to lease transactions in which the lessor retains title to the goods. See *Leake v. Meredith*, 267 S.E.2d 93 (Va. 1980) (no implied warranties in lease of aluminum extension ladder that collapsed). However, by one means or another, most courts have extended Article 2 warranties to lease transactions. See *Baker v. City of Seattle*, 484 P.2d 405 (Wash. 1971) (warranty principles applied to golf cart that overturned due to defective brakes).

Warranty—Article 2A. In 1987, a new "Article 2A—Leases" was promulgated and promptly enacted into law in a number of jurisdictions. Amended in 1990, almost all states enacted this article, which closely mimics Article 2 and explicitly applies to personal property "lease" transactions. In 2002–2003, Article 2A was revised again, though the states so far have largely ignored these more recent revisions.

Strict Liability in Tort. *Cintrone v. Hertz Truck Leasing & Rental Serv.*, 212 A.2d 769 (N.J. 1965) (Frances, J.), involved a claim against a rental company for injuries to a passenger in a rental truck when the brakes failed. The court ruled that commercial lessors should be subject to strict liability in tort just like sellers of new products, because:

● Rental vehicles are subjected to harder use than new vehicles offered for sale;

- Commercial lessors have more opportunity to inspect vehicles for defects than consumers who necessarily rely on lessors to discover and correct defects prior to leasing vehicles to the public;

- Lessors impliedly represent that their vehicles are fit for use and will remain so during the rental period; and,

- The law should place maximum incentives on lessors of cars and trucks to minimize dangers to persons on the highways.

Modern courts widely agree, holding commercial lessors of new and like-new products subject to strict liability in tort to the same extent as manufacturers and other sellers, an approach certified by § 20(b) of the *Products Liability Restatement*. See *Sappington v. Skyjack, Inc.*, 512 F.3d 440 (8th Cir. 2008) (Mo. law) (scissors lift); *Ruzzo v. LaRose Enters.*, 748 A.2d 261 (R.I. 2000); *Samuel Friedland Family Ents. v. Amoroso*, 630 So.2d 1067 (Fla. 1994) (rental sailboat at hotel).

Financial Lease Transactions

In a financial lease transaction, a financial institution takes title to a chattel and leases it to the user as an alternative to loaning funds and taking a security interest in the chattel. While financial lessors technically do "lease" chattels, their role is to provide financial services to their "lessees," not to ensure the safety of the products. Thus, except in unusual cases where a financial lessor actively participates in marketing a product, financial lessors (who have little control over product safety) are not liable for injuries caused by defects in products they finance. See *Massey v. Cassens & Sons, Inc.*, 2007 WL 2710490 (S.D. Ill. 2007).

Bailments and License Transactions

In General

Traditionally, product leases were regarded as "bailments for hire." In modern practice, lease transactions often are set forth in formalized contracts, whereas product bailment and license transactions (which frequently overlap) normally are much more casual—such as a hotel providing chairs in its rented rooms; a Laundromat providing washers and dryers; a bowling alley providing balls and shoes; a skating center renting roller skates; a restaurant providing wine glasses and other eating implements; and an amusement park providing go-carts, Ferris wheels, and other rides.

In many ways resembling short-term *leases*, bailment and license transactions have some distinguishing characteristics:

- They generally are less formal than true chattel lease transactions;
- The user often does not pay a specific fee for the product's use; and
- The product's use is often restricted to the supplier's premises.

Products liability law involving bailments and licenses, including how these transactions may differ, is in somewhat of a muddle. Such transactions involve the temporary transfer of a product's possession from the owner to a user, so that there never is any "sale." Yet, some courts have applied strict liability in tort to such transactions, particularly if the transfer is characterized as a "bailment." See *Golt v. Sports Complex, Inc.*, 644 A.2d 989 (Del. Super. Ct. 1994) (uncrashworthy go-cart at sports complex: bailment); *Garcia v. Halsett*, 82 Cal.Rptr. 420 (Ct. App. 1970) (boy's arm injured while removing clothes from washing machine that failed to stop when door was opened: license). *But see Greenwood v. Busch Entm't Corp.*, 101 F.Supp.2d 292 (E.D. Pa. 2000) (by providing plaintiff license to use its water slides, defendant provided service, not product). Compare *Reeder v. Bally's Total Fitness Corp.*, 963 F.Supp. 530 (E.D. Va. 1997) (no warranties, even under UCC Article 2A, on health club's stomach curl machine; patrons are merely business invitees on club's premises, not bailees or lessees of machines).

Demonstrators, Loaners, and Giveaways

If a seller provides a user with a demonstrator, a loaner, or even a product giveaway as part of its marketing scheme, then the product has entered the stream of commerce, and the supplier is subject to strict liability in tort. See *Beattie v. Beattie*, 786 A.2d 549 (Del. Super. Ct. 2001) (dealership strictly liable for defective "demonstrator vehicle" furnished to customer for test drive); *Johnson v. Stanley–Bostitch, Inc.*, 2000 WL 709480 (E.D. Pa. 2000) (pneumatic nail gun loaner provided by manufac-

turer as business incentive to customers who purchased large quantities of nails and fasteners).

Tie-In Products

When a licensor (or bailor) provides a product as
a service to its customers without charging a separate fee for the use of the product, whether strict
liability in tort should apply is difficult to determine. If the use of the licensed (or bailed) product is
necessary or "integral" to the sale of some *other*
product—such as a defective wine glass provided by
a restaurant, or a defective propane gas container
provided by a gas supplier—then courts generally
have considered the provision of the *tie-in* product
subject to strict liability in tort. Yet, when a product
seller allows its customers to use an ancillary product without charge and merely as a *convenience*—
such as a hotel bed or shower mat, a grocery cart,
or a bowling ball—most courts have reasoned that
strict liability in tort does not apply because the
product has not entered into the chain of distribution, especially if the product must remain on the
defendant's premises.

Statutory Reform

Products liability reform statutes often address
lease, bailment, and license transactions directly or
indirectly. A popular type of reform statute exempts
non-manufacturing product suppliers from strict liability if the manufacturer is solvent and subject to
the jurisdiction of the court.

§ 16.3 SERVICE TRANSACTIONS

The modern world increasingly requires specialists to help select, adapt, and install the products that consumers need and want. Architects, engineers, and building contractors create structures to house people and business firms; doctors and other health professionals select drugs, use hypodermic needles, and implant medical devices and prostheses; and plumbers and electricians select and install home heaters. When such specialists make mistakes, or when they use or install defective products, negligence law (including professional malpractice) establishes their basic responsibilities for resulting harm. The special question addressed here is whether and when service providers may also be subject to strict products liability.

As a starting point, it is axiomatic that strict products liability principles *do* apply to the commercial distribution of new chattels. At the other end of the spectrum, strict liability doctrine does *not* apply to the provision of pure services. In between, of course, lie a large number of sales-service hybrid transactions; in between resides the devil.

In deciding whether strict liability should apply to mixed sales-service transactions, courts search for the "essence" of a transaction to ascertain whether the sale or service aspect *predominates*. If a transaction principally involves a product sale, then strict liability principles are appropriate; if service aspects predominate, then negligence alone applies. Though courts occasionally heap explicit policy analyses on top of these doctrinal principles, the weight of most decisions rests on the principles themselves. See *In re Dow Corning Corp.*, 220 F. App'x 457, 459 (9th Cir. 2007) (Cal. law) (California courts look to the " '*essence*' of the transaction"); *Brandt v. Boston Scientific Corp.*, 792 N.E.2d 296 (Ill. 2003) (where hospital surgically implanted in plaintiff pubovaginal sling, thrust of transaction was provision of service, not sale of good).

Professional Services

Courts broadly refuse to apply strict liability rules to doctors, dentists, hospitals, and other health care providers, or to architects, engineers, and other design professionals, for damages from providing professional services. See *G.J. Palmer v. Espey Huston & Assocs.*, 84 S.W.3d 345 (Tex. App. 2002) (engineering firms that designed artificial harbor not liable for strict products liability or breach of implied warranty); *Milford v. Commercial Carriers, Inc.*, 210 F.Supp.2d 987 (N.D. Ill. 2002) (designer of auto trailer, who had no role in manufacture, not subject to strict products liability); *Bruzga v. PMR Architects, P.C.*, 693 A.2d 401 (N.H. 1997) (architects who designed facility not strictly liable for suicide in psychiatric cell because they provided a professional service, not a product).

City of Mounds View v. Walijarvi, 263 N.W.2d 420 (Minn. 1978), a claim for defects in a building designed by the defendant architects and engineers, explained that all professionals—architects, doctors, engineers, and lawyers—are immune from strict liability because they deal in "inexact sciences" involving "random factors which are incapable of precise measurement" and which require the exercise of skilled judgment by the professional. Id. at 424. The indeterminate nature of professional decisions precludes consistently perfect results: "doctors cannot promise that every operation will be successful; a lawyer can never be certain that a contract he drafts is without latent ambiguity; and an architect cannot be certain that a structural design will interact with natural forces as anticipated." Id. Clients are protected against simple, routine errors by negligence law, and modern products liability law cannot be borrowed because the contexts are so different. Unlike mass producers of defective products, architects usually work one-on-one with their clients and build a single "product," so they do not have a manufacturer's opportunity to test prototypes to discover latent defects. Thus, negligence malpractice actions are sufficient protection against architectural errors, and there is no room for implied warranty or strict liability guaranteeing clients good results.

Patients in a number of cases have tried to hold doctors and hospitals strictly liable for "selling" defective medical products for which the patients must pay, either directly or indirectly. Almost all the decisions have rejected such claims (in both tort and warranty) against health care providers for providing defective pharmaceutical drugs, pacemakers, silicone breast implants, jaw implants, joint prostheses, and other products surgically implanted, prescribed, used, or provided by such professionals. Courts reason that strict products liability is inappropriate because the defendants are predominantly providing medical services, not selling products, and because they are themselves merely product *users*, not suppliers. See *Conway v. A.I. DuPont Hosp. for Children*, 2007 WL 560502 (E.D. Pa. 2007) (surgically implanted heart stent); *Condos v. Musculoskeletal Transplant Found.*, 208 F.Supp.2d 1226 (D. Utah 2002) (bone tissue); *In re Breast Implant Prod. Liab. Litig.*, 503 S.E.2d 445 (S.C. 1998) (Toal, J.).

Non-Professionals—Product Installers

Like professionals, non-professionals who provide hazardous products together with their services are also subject to the normal rules of negligence. Cases involving product installations against plumbers, electricians, and contractors mirror the service and sales-service hybrid cases discussed above. Thus, most courts search for the *essence* or *predominant purpose* of the transaction to determine whether it was more in the nature of a service transaction, involving at most an incidental sale of a defective product, or primarily a sales transaction in which the installer was in the chain of product distribution.

If a plumbing contractor sells and installs for a homeowner a new hot water heater that explodes because of a manufacturing defect, the homeowner may seek recovery from the plumber for "selling" a defective product. Especially if the plumber separated the heater price from the plumbing services in billing for the project, the transaction to a large extent will have involved the commercial supply of a defective product, and the plumber will have played a significant role in the chain of distribution. In such a case, the plumber was the necessary final link in the chain of distribution to the ultimate consumer. Just as a tire dealer that sells and installs a defective tire is subject to the strict liability of a retailer, so too is a plumber, electrician, contractor, or other tradesperson who sells a defective product that it installs. See *ACandS, Inc. v. Abate*, 710 A.2d 944 (Md. Ct. Spec. App. 1998) (supplier-applier of asbestos fireproofing spray). *But cf. Hinojasa v. Automatic Elevator Co.*, 416 N.E.2d 45 (Ill. App. Ct. 1980) (strict liability does not extend to installer who did not also sell defective elevator).

Other Services

In other contexts, courts have refused to extend strict products liability law to a large miscellany of service providers who in some respect provide "products" to their patrons—health clubs, for providing defective exercise equipment; amusement ride operators, for providing defective rides; ski facilities, for providing defective ski lifts; travel agents, for providing defective trips fraught with unexpected dangers; and baseball stadiums, for providing defective protection from foul balls. Such providers are liable, of course, for their negligence. But, because they are not commercial suppliers of products in the chain of distribution, they appropriately are immune from strict products liability.

Statutory Reform

The scope of many products liability statutes is limited to product "sellers," a category from which pure service transactions, together with some sales-service hybrid transactions, generally are excluded. Some statutes more specifically exclude claims arising out of transactions that predominantly involve product services.

§ 16.4   REPAIRED, REBUILT, AND RECONDITIONED PRODUCTS

Because those who *repair* products do not "sell" them, they are subject to liability for negligence but not for breach of sales warranties nor for strict liability in tort. See Rest. (2d) § 404.

To increase their useful lives, products may be "refurbished," "reconditioned," "rebuilt," or "remanufactured." These descriptions are terms of art that carry special meaning: each level implies greater work by the renovator which generates a heightened expectation of reliability and safety by purchasers of such goods. The type and extent of product improvement thus moves along a sliding scale, from a basic clean-up and minor fix-up, at the "refurbishing" end, to a major remake, often accompanied by a product sale and warranty, at the "remanufacturing" end.

So, simple refurbishing generally gives rise to negligence liability alone, and strict products liability generally does not apply to products furnished with only such basic upgrades. See *Whitaker v. T.J. Snow Co.*, 953 F.Supp. 1034 (N.D. Ind. 1997). When restorers sell rebuilt and remanufactured products to compete with new products; buyers fairly expect them to have nearly the reliability and overall quality of new goods; and rebuilders and remanufacturers have the opportunity and duty to rebuild or remanufacture their products to demanding standards, subjecting them to whatever testing and quality control is reasonably called for in the circumstances. Buyers of rebuilt and remanufactured products thus are entitled to the same legal protection from harm from manufacturing defects as buyers of new products. See *Stillie v. AM Int'l, Inc.*, 850 F.Supp. 960 (D. Kan. 1994).

Between simple refurbishing and complete remanufacturing lie a broad range of product upgrade services, called reconditioning, overhauling, or something else. Because of the wide scope of possible services, including a lesser or greater repair or replacement of worn parts, the cases are very fact-specific. In such cases, most courts use some rough form of the essence-of-the-transaction or predominant-factor test examined above for sales-service hybrid transactions. Thus, if a particular renovation called for mostly skill and effort inputs from the renovator, so that it is predominantly a service transaction, then it should be treated as a service transaction for which negligence, not strict products liability, will apply. See *Levine v. Sears Roebuck & Co.*, 200 F.Supp.2d 180 (E.D.N.Y. 2002) (repair of dishwasher door). If, on the other hand, a renovator substantially transforms a product from a used one into basically a new one—as by rewiring, replacing or reconfiguring many important parts, and otherwise reconstructing important aspects of the product—then this rebuilding or remanufacturing usually should subject the supplier to strict products liability for manufacturing defects. See *Bell v. Precision Airmotive Corp.*, 42 P.3d 1071 (Alaska 2002) (engine overhaul).

Most of the cases involve manufacturing defects, and the waters muddy considerably when design and warning defects are involved. Not distinguishing between different types of defects, *Products Liability Restatement* § 8 in no uncertain terms provides that remanufactured products are subject to the normal rules of products liability applicable to sellers of new products. And statutes in at least four states include "remanufacturer" or "rebuilder" in the definition of "manufacturer," subjecting such parties to the principal provisions of such statutes.

§ 16.5 USED PRODUCTS

Sellers of used products are liable for negligence. In appropriate cases, Article 2 warranties may also accompany used product sales. See *Gaston v. Bobby Johnson Equip. Co.*, 771 So.2d 848, 852 (La. Ct. App. 2000) (though implied warranty of quality "does not apply as extensively as with new products, it requires that even used equipment operate reasonably well for a reasonable period of time"); UCC § 2–314 cmt. 3 (sales contracts for used goods include such obligations as are "appropriate to such goods").

On the applicability of strict liability in tort, the decisions are sharply split. Following *Peterson v. Lou Bachrodt Chevrolet Co.*, 329 N.E.2d 785 (Ill. 1975) (used car), most courts refuse to apply the doctrine to such sales. See *Tillman v. Vance Equip. Co.*, 596 P.2d 1299 (Or. 1979); *Kotz v. Hawaii Elec. Light Co.*, 83 P.3d 743 (Haw. 2004). At least a couple reform statutes (Idaho, Wash.) explicitly exclude used products from coverage. However, a fairly large minority of courts, following *Turner v. International Harvester Co.*, 336 A.2d 62 (N.J. Super. 1975), hold that strict liability in tort *does* apply to used product sales. See *Jordan v. Sunnyslope Appliance Propane & Plumbing Supplies Co.*, 660 P.2d 1236 (Ariz. Ct. App. 1983); *Frey v. Harley Davidson Motor Co.*, 743 A.2d 1 (Pa. Super. Ct. 1999) (new-used dealer who cut jumper wire subject to strict liability in tort).

Products Liability Restatement § 8 provides that sellers of defective used goods are liable generally for negligence; for manufacturing defects and product malfunctions when a seller's marketing causes buyers to expect the safety of a new product; for any type of defect in a remanufactured product; and for noncompliance with applicable safety statutes and regulations.

§ 16.6 ELECTRICITY

Invisible and elusive, electricity is hard to comprehend. Its mysterious character puts in question of whether electricity should be considered a "product" at all, subject to the principles of products liability law. Yet, a majority of courts hold that electricity is a product that may subject its suppliers, electrical utility companies, to strict liability in tort for selling it in a defective condition. See *Hanus v. Texas Utils. Co.*, 71 S.W.3d 874 (Tex. App. 2002); *Bryant v. Tri–County Elec. Membership Corp.*, 844 F.Supp. 347 (W.D. Ky. 1994). These courts reason that once electricity passes through a customer's meter, it is a product sold into the stream of commerce and so is subject to strict liability. Such cases typically involve power surges, causing personal injury or property damage from the excessive flow of electricity into a building.

Yet, a quite substantial minority of courts refuse to apply strict liability to electrical injuries, reasoning that the provision of electricity is a *service* rather than the sale of a product, whether the harm is caused before or after the current passes through a consumer's meter. See *Universal Underwriters Ins. Group v. Public Serv. Elec. & Gas Co.*, 103 F.Supp.2d 744 (D.N.J. 2000); *Wyrulec Co. v. Schutt*, 866 P.2d 756 (Wyo. 1993).

When a plaintiff is electrocuted by hitting a high-voltage transmission line with some tall object—the boom of a crane, mast of a boat, or a ladder—courts widely agree that negligence alone is the proper basis of liability. Strict products liability does not apply because electricity in high-voltage transmission lines is still under the ownership and control of the supplier and is not yet a "product" in the "stream of commerce," nor is it "sold" until it passes through a customer's meter. See *Martinez v. Duke Energy Corp.*, 130 F. App'x 629 (4th Cir. 2005) (S.C. law); *Smith v. Florida Power & Light Co.*, 857 So.2d 224 (Fla. Dist. Ct. App. 2003).

§ 16.7   REAL ESTATE

Products liability law conventionally is defined as the liability of suppliers for harm from defects in their *chattels*. Chattels, of course, are *personal* property as distinguished from *real* property. Thus real estate, including any fixtures attached to it, would not appear to be a proper subject of "products" liability law. Probably most courts thus refuse to apply strict products liability in tort to claims involving defects in land, houses, and other structures attached to the land. See *Martens v. MCL Constr. Corp.*, 807 N.E.2d 480 (Ill. App. Ct. 2004) (strict liability in tort does not apply to buildings and indivisible components thereof such as bricks, beams, and railings).

Similarly, because UCC Article 2 applies only to "goods," it does not apply to real estate transactions. Also, a number of products liability reform statutes (Ga., Ind., N.J., Wash.) provide that real estate is not a covered "product," and statutes in other states (Ark., Tenn.) use other means to exclude real estate and fixtures from coverage.

Yet a few states have applied products liability principles to certain real property transactions. In the landmark case of *Schipper v. Levitt & Sons, Inc.*, 207 A.2d 314 (N.J. 1965), an infant was severely scalded by excessively hot water from a faucet in the bathroom sink because the developer had failed to install an inexpensive mixing valve to reduce the temperature of water drawn from the boiler. The court held the developer strictly liable for the injuries, reasoning that mass-builders can better bear the risk of construction defects than consumers, that "there are no meaningful distinctions between Levitt's mass production and sale of homes and the mass production and sale of automobiles, and that pertinent overriding policy considerations are the same."

Following *Schipper*, a handful of courts applied strict liability in tort to builder-vendors of residential homes. See *Bednarski v. Hideout Homes & Realty, Inc.*, 711 F.Supp. 823 (M.D. Pa. 1989) (plaintiff's son killed and home destroyed in fire originating in electrical outlet). And several courts applied this doctrine to manufacturers of prefab homes and structures. See *Bastian v. Wausau Homes, Inc.*, 620 F.Supp. 947 (N.D. Ill. 1985) (defective baseboard heater); *Kaneko v. Hilo Coast Processing*, 654 P.2d

343 (Haw. 1982) (temporary weld in prefab building failed, and iron worker injured in collapse).

Many courts apply strict products liability to defective products incorporated as *fixtures* in homes or other structures, such as a heating and air conditioning system, a hot water heater, windows, roof-covering system, and driveway paint. Some courts make a simple "product" *vs.* "real estate" division, while others use policy analysis to decide whether the goals of strict products liability are served by extending strict liability to a particular situation. See *Nichols v. Agway, Inc.*, 720 N.Y.S.2d 691 (App. Div. 2001) (water heater); *Menendez v. Paddock Pool Constr. Co.*, 836 P.2d 968 (Ariz. Ct. App. 1991) (strict liability policies did not apply to custom swimming pool installer).

§ 16.8   PUBLICATIONS

A number of products liability claims have been brought against publishers for injuries attributable to information or thoughts communicated in books, magazine articles, films, records, computer games, websites, and aeronautical charts. Except for cases involving defective navigational charts and publications providing contract killer information, these actions have been barred.

Books, Magazines, and Print Media

Almost uniformly, courts refuse to apply products liability principles, particularly a rule of strict liability, to the publication of dangerously false information. Decisions typically conclude that the message, as distinct from the packaging of the message, is not a "product" within the meaning of *Restatement (Second) of Torts* § 402A. Courts thus have rejected strict liability claims against publishers of a liquid diet book, for the death of a woman from complications associated with the diet; a medical textbook, for injuries to a nursing student from following a constipation remedy described in the textbook; a travel guide, for injuries to a swimmer injured in hazardous beach conditions not mentioned in the guide; a metal-smithing book, for injuries from the explosion of a caustic substance mixed according to the book's instructions; and other publications for harmful results spurred by the written word. See *Way v. Boy Scouts of Am.*, 856 S.W.2d 230 (Tex. App. 1993) (content of *Boys' Life* magazine, and advertising supplement for shooting sports, not "products"); *Winter v. G.P. Putnam's Sons*, 938 F.2d 1033 (9th Cir. 1991) (Cal. law) (mushroom encyclopedia: content of book not "product"); *Walters v. Seventeen Magazine*, 241 Cal.Rptr. 101 (Ct. App. 1987) (publishers not liable for plaintiff's toxic shock syndrome caused by Playtex tampons advertised in magazine).

The one situation where courts have allowed tort claims against such publishers is for the promotion of contract killing. Several courts have allowed such claims against *Soldier of Fortune Magazine* for publishing advertisements of contract killers, see *Braun v. Soldier of Fortune Magazine, Inc.*, 968 F.2d 1110

(11th Cir. 1992) (Ga. law), and one court allowed a tort law aiding-and-abetting claim against the publisher of a "how-to" book for contract killers that included precise instructions, meticulously followed by a hit man, detailing gruesome techniques for such projects. See *Rice v. Paladin Enters.*, 128 F.3d 233 (4th Cir. 1997) (Md. law) (after suit allowed, settled for millions of dollars).

Navigational Charts

Courts have also allowed claims against a publisher of aeronautical charts containing false information that causes a pilot to crash. See *Fluor Corp. v. Jeppesen & Co.*, 216 Cal.Rptr. 68 (Ct. App. 1985) (jet pilot crashed into mountain not depicted on approach chart, though lower mountain was). Noting the total reliance pilots necessarily place on the accuracy of navigational charts, courts have distinguished them from other types of publications because the very purpose of such charts is to portray precise *physical* phenomena rather than ideas. Such cases may fit more comfortably in the law of misrepresentation and express warranty, but there seems little practical harm in allowing these meritorious claims under the conventional product defect umbrella.

Games, Music, Video Games, and Websites

No decision allows a products liability claim against a distributor of a game, recording, movie, video game, or Internet website. In an action against the publisher and manufacturer of the game "Dungeons and Dragons" for the suicide death of a player, the court upheld the defendants' First Amendment defense and further ruled that the defendant-publishers had no duty to warn mentally fragile persons of the possibly dangerous consequences of playing the game. See *Watters v. TSR, Inc.*, 904 F.2d 378 (6th Cir. 1990) (Ky. law) ("the doctrine of strict liability has never been extended to words or pictures [and] other courts have looked in vain for decisions so expanding the scope of the strict liability doctrine"); *Davidson v. Time Warner, Inc.*, 1997 WL 405907 (S.D. Tex. 1997) (no case law supported products liability claim against rap artist for murder of police officer suggested in recording; such a claim would raise constitutional problems).

Courts have rejected a number of claims against manufacturers of video games and other visual entertainment products, often concluding that products liability principles do not apply to them because they are not "products," and mentioning First Amendment concerns. See *James v. Meow Media, Inc.*, 300 F.3d 683 (6th Cir. 2002) (violent movie, video games, and obscene Internet websites that allegedly caused Kentucky high school shootings); *Sanders v. Acclaim Entm't, Inc.*, 188 F.Supp.2d 1264 (D. Colo. 2002) (violent movie and video games that allegedly caused high school shootings in Columbine, Colorado); Rest. (3d) § 19(a) (a "product is tangible personal property").

§ 16.9   BLOOD

No "product" could be further from a typical, commercially manufactured chattel than human blood. In *Cunningham v. MacNeal Memorial Hosp.*, 266 N.E.2d 897 (Ill. 1970), the court held a hospital that supplied hepatitis-infected (hence "defective") blood strictly liable in tort despite the defendant's inability to detect or prevent the virus. *Cunningham* was widely criticized for discouraging the collection and sale of blood, undermining the market in this uniquely valuable commodity so necessary to public health. Not only did other courts refuse to apply strict liability in tort or warranty to the sale of defective blood, but the Illinois legislature promptly overruled *Cunningham* by statute. And other state legislatures, if they had not already done so, passed similar laws restricting the responsibility of blood suppliers to negligence.

Today, every state exempts blood suppliers from strict liability, in warranty or tort, for supplying infected blood. Almost all states accomplish this exemption from strict products liability through "blood shield statutes" which prohibit strict liability actions by providing that the supply of blood is a service (rather than a sale) or by more directly stating that the supply of blood products does not give rise to liability unless the supplier was at fault. See *Scher v. Bayer Corp.*, 258 F.Supp.2d 190 (E.D.N.Y. 2003) (strict liability in tort and warranty claims dismissed against commercial supplier of allegedly defective blood derivative product, Hyp–

Rho(D), used to prevent hemolytic disease in new-born children of Rh–Negative mothers and Rh–Positive fathers; case allowed to proceed on negligence claims).

Modern litigation has mostly involved AIDS transmitted by transfused blood and blood products. The blood shield statutes preclude strict liability in tort and warranty claims in such cases. See *Christiana v. Southern Baptist Hosp.*, 867 So.2d 809 (La. App. 2004) (blood shield law in effect at time of transfusion protected hospital that supplied blood from patient's strict liability claim). Accordingly, these cases normally are based on negligence; but, because of the difficulties of proving negligence, such claims generally fail. See *Johnson v. American Nat'l Red Cross*, 578 S.E.2d 106 (Ga. 2003) (negligence claims against blood bank for HIV and fear of HIV failed).

§ 16.10 MISCELLANEOUS TRANSACTIONS AND PRODUCTS

Casual Sales

It is fundamental that claims for breach of the implied warranty of merchantability and strict liability in tort apply only to harm from products that have been *commercially* distributed. *Restatement (Second) of Torts* § 402A(1)(a) applies only if "the seller is engaged in the business of selling such a product," and the *Products Liability Restatement*, which applies only to commercial transactions in the normal course of business, explicitly excludes "casual sales." See Rest. (3d) § 1 cmt. *c*. Courts refuse to apply strict products liability to occasional commercial sales, and there is even less reason to apply this doctrine to a private party who, on one occasion, sells his or her neighbor a pound of sugar or a car. See Rest. (2d) § 402A cmt. *f*.

Animals

The cases are split on whether strict liability in tort applies to animals. Most courts hold that "living things do not constitute 'products' within the scope of the strict tort liability doctrine which requires that a product's nature be fixed when it leaves the manufacturer's or seller's control." *Kaplan v. C Lazy U Ranch*, 615 F.Supp. 234 (D. Colo. 1985) (horse is not a "product"). Thus, courts have been particularly reluctant to hold defendants subject to liability for the natural proclivities in animals, such as the tendency of a "fractious" horse to expand its lungs while being saddled, or a dog to bite. See *Blaha v. Stuard*, 640 N.W.2d 85, 89 (S.D. 2002) (yellow Lab; "living creatures have no fixed nature and cannot be products as a matter of law"); *Whitmer v. Schneble*, 331 N.E.2d 115 (Ill. App. Ct. 1975) (after giving birth, Doberman bit child).

But negligence remains a viable claim against the seller of a fractious horse, and most courts have allowed recovery on some basis for the sale of animals—such as a duckling, puppy, parakeet, or skunk—infected with diseases transmitted to the owner, sometimes on the theory that the animal is a defective product and sometimes on simple negligence principles such as the failure to warn. The *Products Liability Restatement* states that "when a living animal is sold commercially in a diseased condition and causes harm to other property or to persons, the animal constitutes a product for purposes of this Restatement." § 19 cmt. *b*.

Toxic Contaminants

Toxins that escape from products into the environment can seriously harm people and property. As noted in connection with the destruction and disposal of products at the end of their useful lives, a complex set of federal and state laws and regulations, including products liability law, govern liability for harm resulting when such toxins are released. One such toxin is the chemical methyl tertiary butyl ether (MTBE), added to gasoline during the refining process, that may leak from service station storage tanks and contaminate ground water. Whether the doctrine of strict liability in tort should apply to a water company's damage claim against the gasoline refiner in such a situation involves a host issues, including whether strict liability applies only to ultimate users and consumers, whether such a plaintiff should be allowed recovery as a bystander, and whether relief is limited to persons injured after retail sale or an equivalent transaction. Reasoning that manufacturers are subject to strict liability once they place a defective product in the stream of commerce, and that storage in possibly faulty containers is a foreseeable use of gasoline once it is placed on the market, a California court ruled that policy reasons support holding a refiner strictly liable for failing to warn of the foreseeable risk of noxious harm to the water supply if a gas station's storage tanks allow the contaminant to leak into the ground. See *Nelson v. Superior Ct.*, 50 Cal. Rptr.3d 684 (Ct. App. 2006).

CHAPTER 17

AUTOMOTIVE LITIGATION

Table of Sections

§ 17.1   Automotive Litigation—Generally.
§ 17.2   Defects That Cause Accidents.
§ 17.3   Crashworthiness.
§ 17.4   Indivisible Harm and Damages Apportionment.
§ 17.5   Plaintiff Fault.

———

§ 17.1   AUTOMOTIVE LITIGATION— GENERALLY

Many products liability cases involve claims against manufacturers of cars, sport utility vehicles, vans, trucks, motorcycles, and other motor vehicles alleging that defective conditions in such products caused injuries to the plaintiffs. The usual victims in such accidents are the drivers and passengers in the allegedly defective vehicles, but sometimes an accident vehicle injures someone in another vehicle or a pedestrian. Automotive products liability cases may be divided into two major categories: (1) accidents caused by automotive defects, and (2) aggravated injuries caused by a vehicle's failure to be sufficiently "crashworthy" to protect its occupants in an accident.

In many respects, automotive products liability cases are no different from any other type of products liability case. But certain issues that may affect the outcome of automotive products liability litigation—crashworthiness, apportionment of damages, and the role of plaintiff fault—involve special considerations. This chapter explores the most important, recurring, special issues in automotive products liability law. For a more thorough examination of automotive litigation, see Owen, Products Liability Law ch. 17 (2d ed. 2008).

§ 17.2   DEFECTS THAT CAUSE ACCIDENTS

Many automotive products liability cases involve accidents that allegedly result from some defect in the vehicle. Most of the cases considered in this section involve claims of defects in one of a vehicle's essential control mechanisms or components, such as its steering, brakes, accelerator, transmission, engine, suspension system, and wheels or tires.

Manufacturing Defect Claims

When the sudden malfunction of a new vehicle leads to a crash, as in both *MacPherson v. Buick Motor Co.*, 111 N.E. 1050 (N.Y. 1916) (defective wooden wheel), and *Henningsen v. Bloomfield Motors, Inc.*, 161 A.2d 69 (N.J. 1960) (defective steering), the cause of the accident typically is some type of manufacturing defect. If the vehicle is badly damaged, it may be difficult (if not impossible) to discover precisely what went wrong. In such cases, a plaintiff may turn to *res ipsa* or the malfunction doctrine, previously discussed. Yet accident reconstructionists (though they may disagree) usually can ascertain the precise defect that caused a crash. See *Castaldi v. Land Rover N. Am., Inc.*, 2007 WL 4165283 (E.D.N.Y. 2007) (misaligned brake light switch deactivated brake shift interlock, causing rapid acceleration); *Cooper Tire & Rubber Co. v. Tuckier*, 826 So.2d 679 (Miss. 2002) (tire); *Smith v. Ford Motor Co.*, 215 F.3d 713 (7th Cir. 2000) (Ind. law) (steering).

Design Defect Claims

Design defects (often with piggy-backed warning defects) are the other principal cause of automotive accidents claims in products liability litigation. Since design defects infect the entire product line, threatening the safety of thousands of persons, some design defects have become quite notorious. Control problems in the Corvair, publicized by Ralph Nader in the 1960s in *Unsafe at Any Speed*, is one example. Accelerator sticking problems in certain Audis led to claims in the 1970s, as did the rollover tendencies of certain Jeeps in the 1970s and 1980s; the Suzuki Samurai, Ford Bronco II, and other SUVs in the 1980s and 1990s; and the Ford Explorer in the late 1990s and early 2000s. This kind of rollover litigation resulted from the relatively high center of gravity in many SUVs, combined with their narrow track width and sometimes light weight, which made some models quite unstable and apt to roll over in sharp steering maneuvers at highway speeds. See *Jonas v. Isuzu Motors Ltd.*, 210 F.Supp.2d 1373 (M.D. Ga. 2002) (1993 Isuzu Rodeo rolled over). For other types of design defects, see *Estate of Edward W. Knoster v. Ford Motor Co.*, 200 F. App'x 106 (3d Cir. 2006) (N.J. law) (sudden acceleration); *Bourgeois v. Garrard Chevrolet, Inc.*, 811 So.2d 962 (La. Ct. App. 2002) (brakes); *Jarvis v. Ford Motor Co.*, 283 F.3d 33 (2d Cir. 2002) (N.Y. law) (cruise control); *General Motors Corp. v. Sanchez*, 997 S.W.2d 584 (Tex. 1999) (transmission).

§ 17.3 CRASHWORTHINESS

An issue that cuts across nearly every automotive accident, regardless of its cause, is the extent to which the design of the vehicle protected the safety or aggravated the injuries of the occupants during a vehicular accident. This is the issue of automotive "crashworthiness," one of the most important aspects of design defectiveness in modern American products liability law.

Crashworthiness in General

Congress aptly defines automotive "crashworthiness" as "the protection a passenger motor vehicle gives its passengers against personal injury or death from a motor vehicle accident." 49 U.S.C. § 32301(1). A vehicle's capacity to offer such protection is a function of its ability to withstand and absorb the physical stresses of a collision combined with its ability to prevent additional ("enhanced" or "aggravated") injuries occupants may sustain in a "second collision" with the vehicle's interior. Thus, a vehicle's crashworthiness depends on whether:

- Its structure can absorb the forces of a crash without collapsing into the passenger compartment against the occupants;

- Its dashboard and head restraints are appropriately padded, rather than being made of solid steel;

- The glass in its windows crumbles harmlessly, rather than fracturing into lethal slivers;

- The steering wheel telescopes to absorb the force of a collision with the driver's chest, rather than remaining rigid as a wall;

- The edges and ends of knobs, levers, and other protrusions are rounded and covered by protective material, rather than being left as sharp and pointed steel;

- The fuel tank is located in a safe position and securely protected against the varying insults it may encounter in different types of collisions;

- The doors and windows have sufficient latches to hold them closed in accident situations, to keep the occupants contained, rather than popping open and allowing the occupants to be flung outside;

- The airbags protect the occupants from injury, rather than activating spontaneously or with explosive force; and

- The safety belts, harnesses, and head rests effectively restrain and protect the occupants rather than serving as instruments of death.

The Crashworthiness Duty

Whether manufacturers have a duty to design crashworthy vehicles was a major issue of products liability law in the late 1960s and early 1970s. The controversy originated in *Evans v. General Motors Corp.*, 359 F.2d 822, 824 (7th Cir. 1966) (Ind. law), which held that "[a] manufacturer is not under a duty to make his automobile accident-proof or fool-proof." Reasoning that the "intended purpose" of automobiles does not include their participation in collisions, a split panel of the 7th Circuit Court of Appeals ruled that GM did not have a duty to equip its cars with side frames to protect the occupants from foreseeable collisions.

After critical reviews of *Evans* in the law journals, the 8th Circuit joined issue in *Larsen v. General Motors Corp.*, 391 F.2d 495 (8th Cir. 1968) (Mich. law), which rejected GM's "intended use" argument. Citing data on the high rate of serious injuries and deaths from automotive accidents (52,500 deaths and 1.9 million disabling injuries in 1966), including the fact that many or most cars eventually are involved in at least one accident causing injury or death, the *Larsen* court concluded that car manufacturers have a duty of due care, as an extension of their general duty to make their products reasonably safe for normal use, which includes reasonable safety for the crash environment. Today, the crashworthiness doctrine is the law in every American jurisdiction.

How Crashworthy?

Establishing that manufacturers have a *duty* to design their cars to be crashworthy does not resolve the far more complex matter of deciding the *limits* of that design obligation. Manufacturers are not expected to make their vehicles crash-proof and able to protect occupants in accidents of every type, such as when a small car crashes head-on into an 18–wheeler truck at highway speeds. Even *Larsen* recognized that "manufacturers are not insurers," that "all risks cannot be eliminated nor can a crash-proof vehicle be designed," and that the crashworthiness duty extends only to eliminating *unreasonable* risks and requires only "*reasonable* steps in design . . . to minimize the injury-producing effect of impacts."

All courts now agree that a manufacturer's obligation to produce a "crashworthy" vehicle is bounded by a reasonable balance of the costs and benefits of reducing various risks of injury. In short, "crashworthy" means reasonable—not perfect—automotive crash safety. See *Carillo v. Ford Motor Co.*, 759 N.E.2d 99 (Ill. App. Ct. 2001) (seat design); *Nissan Motor Co. v. Nave*, 740 A.2d 102 (Md. Ct. Spec. App. 1999) (design of steering column); *Soule v. General Motors Corp.*, 882 P.2d 298 (Cal. 1994) (design of floorboard and wheel assembly).

Because of the different ways in which accidents can occur, automotive engineers must balance a vehicle's safety in one type of crash against its safety in other types of crashes; making it safer for one type of accident may make it more *dangerous* for another type of accident. It is thus axiomatic that a design which allows or enhances one type of hazard in order to prevent another, greater hazard is not defective. This widely accepted principle of design defectiveness receives unequivocal expression in the *Products Liability Restatement*: "When evaluating the reasonableness of a design alternative, the overall safety of the product must be considered. It is not sufficient that the alternative design would have reduced or prevented the harm suffered by the plaintiff if it would also have introduced into the product other dangers of equal or greater magnitude." § 2 cmt. *f*; see also § 16 cmt. *b*.

Contexts

Courts have applied the crashworthiness doctrine in a large variety of contexts. Probably the most recurring type of case involves the *structural* integrity of a vehicle's body—the resistance of vehicles to impacts from different directions, including the ability of a vehicle's roof, lift-gate latch, or some other component to withstand the forces of a roll-over. Some crashworthiness cases involve dangerous design aspects of a vehicle's *interior*, such as the presence of sharp or hard objects inside a vehicle that can aggravate injuries to occupants in a collision. Other cases have involved claims challenging

the safety of a vehicle's *exterior* design for present-
ing untoward risks to bystanders who may encounter a sharp side vent or unyielding side-view mirror.

Some of the most notorious crashworthiness cases
have involved the ability of a vehicle's fuel system
to withstand certain types of collisions. It was the
vulnerability of the Ford Pinto's fuel system that
generated the $125 million punitive damage verdict
in *Grimshaw v. Ford Motor Co.*, 174 Cal.Rptr. 348
(Ct. App. 1981), a 1979 verdict that was eclipsed
two decades later by another California jury's levy
of a $4.8 *billion* punitive damages assessment for
locating the Chevrolet Malibu's gas tank behind the
rear axle close to the rear bumper, causing the car
(as in *Grimshaw)* to burst into flames when hit at
high speed from the rear. *Anderson v. General Motors Corp.*, 1999 WL 1466627 (Cal. Super. Ct. L.A.
Cty. 1999). Both punitive damages verdicts were
substantially reduced by the trial courts, but both
were partially allowed to stand.

Finally, safety devices such as head restraints, lap
and shoulder belts, and airbags must operate properly and should not expose occupants to an unexpected and unreasonable risk of harm. Thus, a
vehicle may be uncrashworthy if its roll bar collapses; its headrest contains a sharp metal edge that
strikes the driver's skull and kills him when the
vehicle is rear-ended; its lap or shoulder belts cause
severe abdominal injuries, paralysis, brain damage,
or death; or its airbag activates unnecessarily, fails

to deploy, deploys too late, or deploys with excessive force, injuring or killing an occupant.

§ 17.4   INDIVISIBLE HARM AND DAMAGES APPORTIONMENT

As examined in the preceding section, the crashworthiness doctrine maintains that vehicular manufacturers have a duty to afford as much protection as reasonably possible against the risks of "second collisions" between a vehicle's occupants and its interior. But liability for such additional ("enhanced" or "aggravated") injuries does not render the manufacturer responsible for other injuries that the occupant would have suffered anyway from the first collision. Thus, assuming that the first collision was caused by something other than an automotive defect, such as driver error or dangerous highway conditions, the manufacturer of an uncrashworthy vehicle is *not* responsible for the injuries caused in the *initial* accident but it *is* responsible for any *additional* injuries attributable to the uncrashworthy feature of the vehicle.

This basic apportionment principle is simple, logical, and fair: a manufacturer should pay for the damage caused by defects in its vehicles, but not for damages caused by something else. When this kind of division of injuries between the first and second collisions is feasible, it clearly must be done, and the manufacturer's responsibility will be limited to those damages resulting from the uncrashworthy aspect of the vehicle.

For example, if a truck is driven through a red light and smashes into the passenger door of a car entering the intersection, the force of the first collision may break the arm of a passenger in the car and may also cause the car to roll over, injuring the passenger's head when the roof collapses. If the door was adequately designed but the roof structure was not, the passenger may recover against the manufacturer for his head injuries caused by the uncrashworthy roof but not for his broken arm caused in the first collision when the truck struck the door. Probably all courts agree with this commonsense result, and it is embraced by *Products Liability Restatement* § 16(b).

In violent collision situations involving severe injuries, however, ascertaining which injuries were caused by the first collision and which are attributable only to the second collision is often difficult or impossible. Thus, deciding who has the *burden of proof* on damages apportionment—who has the burden to show which damages were caused by the vehicle's uncrashworthy feature—may effectively determine whether recovery is allowable in serious crashworthiness cases.

The first case expressly to address the apportionment burden-of-proof problem in crashworthiness cases was *Huddell v. Levin*, 537 F.2d 726 (3d Cir. 1976) (N.J. law), in which the plaintiff driver was killed when his Chevrolet Nova, which had run out of gas, was hit from behind at 50–60 mph by another car. The plaintiff died from brain injuries caused by the impact of his head against the head restraint. In an action against GM, the plaintiff contended that the head restraint was defective because the sharp edge of the "unyielding metal allowed for excessive concentration of forces against the rear of the skull," and that it "was designed much like an airplane wing, with the front 'ax-like' portion aimed directly at the rear of the head." The jury decided for the plaintiff, but the Third Circuit reversed, ruling that plaintiffs in crashworthiness cases must prove three things:

(1) The existence of a feasible, alternative, safer design;

(2) The injuries that would have resulted from such an alternative design; and

(3) The *extent* of the enhanced injuries caused by the *defective* design.

Because the plaintiff's expert had only testified that a properly designed head restraint would have been "survivable," and because the plaintiff offered no proof of the probable extent of injury had such a restraint been used, a majority of the court ruled that the plaintiff had failed to carry his burden of proof showing the extent to which the design defect had caused his damages.

But then the federal circuits began to split. *Fox v. Ford Motor Co.*, 575 F.2d 774 (10th Cir. 1978) (Wyo. law), and *Mitchell v. Volkswagenwerk, A.G.*, 669 F.2d 1199 (8th Cir. 1982) (Minn. law), both rejected *Huddell*, reasoning that automotive manufacturers, like other defendants, are jointly and severally liable for indivisible injuries (such as paraplegia and death) where there is no reasonable basis for determining causation between them. Thereafter, the number of jurisdictions following *Huddell*'s approach has diminished and a growing majority of courts—including an intermediate appellate court in New Jersey, the state whose law was predicted in *Huddell*—now follow the *Fox–Mitchell* approach of holding manufacturers of uncrashworthy vehicles responsible for indivisible injuries.

Thus, in most states today, a plaintiff must establish that an uncrashworthy design feature was a substantial factor in aggravating his or her injuries, after which the manufacturer is liable for all such injuries that it is unable to prove were not caused by the vehicle's uncrashworthy design. See *Boryszewski v. Burke*, 882 A.2d 410 (N.J. Super. Ct. App. Div. 2005); *Trull v. Volkswagen of Am., Inc.*, 761 A.2d 477 (N.H. 2000); Rest. (2d) § 433B(2); Rest. (3d) § 16 cmt. *d* ("The defendant, a wrongdoer who in fact has caused harm to the plaintiff, should not escape liability because the nature of the harm makes such a determination impossible.").

§ 17.5   PLAINTIFF FAULT

Manufacturers naturally seek to introduce evidence of driver fault in automotive products liability litigation—such as intoxication, speeding, erratic driving, failing to wear a seatbelt, falling asleep, overloading the vehicle, failing to keep the tires inflated or otherwise to maintain the vehicle. Such evidence may undercut the plaintiff's prima facie case on cause in fact and proximate causation, establish affirmative defenses, diminish the plaintiff's damages, or intangibly tarnish the plaintiff.

The general role of plaintiff fault in products liability litigation, including the defenses of contributory negligence, assumption of risk, product misuse, and comparative fault, was previously considered. But courts and legislatures have confronted a number of special issues involving the fault of drivers and other plaintiffs in automotive products liability cases.

Accident Causation

Evidence of a driver's misconduct is relevant in a products liability action if, but only if, it contributed in some way to cause the accident or the plaintiff's injuries. Assume, for example, that a drunken driver is injured while driving erratically and at excessive speed when one of his tires blows out. If the tire failed due to the speed and erratic driving caused by the driver's intoxication, then evidence of the plaintiff's misconduct would be relevant to causation and the standard misconduct defenses. But if the accident occurred solely because the tire failed, and the tire failed solely because it was manufactured in a defective condition, then the driver's misconduct simply has no bearing on any issue in the case. That is, evidence of a plaintiff's bad behavior usually should be excluded if it was not a cause in fact of the accident or resulting injuries.

A driver's misconduct implicates two principal causation issues—cause in fact and proximate cause. Sometimes the actual cause of an accident is hotly in dispute, with the plaintiff claiming that the accident was caused by some defect in the vehicle and the manufacturer asserting that the failed component in the vehicle was caused by the violence of the accident which itself was caused by the driver's misconduct. In *Hardy v. General Motors Corp.,* 710 N.E.2d 764 (Ohio Ct. App. 1998), the driver of a Corvette was injured when he lost control of his car and struck a tree while attempting to negotiate a curve at between 104 and 111 mph. The plaintiff's expert testified that a tie rod broke due to a fatigue fracture, causing the plaintiff to lose control; whereas the defendant's engineers testified that the tie rod broke when the vehicle hit the tree. Affirming a directed verdict for the defendant, the court ruled that the evidence clearly established that the loss of control was caused by the driver's dangerous driving, not by any defect in the car. Other courts similarly have allowed evidence of the driver's speeding and erratic driving, or recklessly jamming on the brakes in a high-speed turn, to support the defendant's theory of accident causation, but not to prove the plaintiff's contributory fault. See *Daye v. General Motors Corp.*, 720 So.2d 654, 660 (La. 1998) ("In reality, plaintiff's vigorous application of the brakes while driving through a blind curve on a substandard two-lane country road at a breakneck speed—and not his reliance on the promotional information—was the cause of the accident.'').

As for *proximate* causation, a driver's claim may be barred on grounds that his or her misconduct was the "sole proximate cause" of an accident if the misconduct was clearly the dominant cause of the injuries, trivializing any uncrashworthy aspect of the vehicle. Courts thus have allowed evidence of a driver's speeding while intoxicated, or speeding at 110–120 mph on underinflated tires. See *Mazda Motor Corp. v. Lindahl*, 706 A.2d 526 (Del. 1998) (driver killed when car failed to negotiate curve and plunged down embankment, tumbling end over end through air, and striking ground several times before it came to rest; claim for defective design of seats denied).

Crashworthiness Cases

A difficult issue that has sharply split the courts is whether a driver's fault in causing an accident may be considered, as a matter of proximate cause or comparative fault, in apportioning damages for enhanced injuries in *crashworthiness* cases. A closely divided decision, *Reed v. Chrysler Corp.*, 494 N.W.2d 224 (Iowa 1992), illustrates the issues. An intoxicated plaintiff injured his arm in the rollover of a Jeep CJ–7 which he claimed was uncrashworthy because its top was made of brittle fiberglass rather than steel like similar vehicles. Ruling that the intoxication evidence should have been excluded, a five judge majority reasoned that a driver's misconduct in causing an accident is "beside the point" because the purpose of the crashworthiness duty is to reduce injuries in "accidents precipitated for myriad reasons." The four judges in dissent thought the majority missed the point: because a claimant's fault in causing an accident also causes any aggravated injuries, usual comparative fault rules also apply to such enhanced injury claims.

This issue is a close and difficult one, as illustrated not only by the sharp division of the court in *Reed*, but by the nearly equal division of the decisions which continue to go both ways. The commentators are also hopelessly divided, some viewing driver fault as irrelevant to claims for enhanced injuries, others viewing such conduct as no different in this context than any other. The *Third Restatement* addresses this issue ambiguously, and neither logic nor doctrine provides a clear resolution. The debate, in other words, is inconclusive.

Failure to Use Seatbelts and Other Safety Devices

One of the easiest and most effective ways to increase one's life expectancy, and to improve the general level of automotive safety, is to buckle up one's seatbelt. Put another way, occupants of automotive vehicles who fail to use their seatbelts significantly increase their risk of being seriously injured or killed in accident situations. For these reasons, state legislatures began requiring manufacturers to install seatbelts in automobiles in the early 1960s. Today, all states except New Hampshire (state's motto: "Live Free or Die") have mandatory seatbelt *use* statutes applicable to adults, and the national seatbelt usage rate is about 80%.

Seatbelt Defense at Common Law

Defendants in ordinary car accident litigation have long sought to introduce evidence that the plaintiff failed to use an available seatbelt to try to establish that the plaintiff, rather than the defendant, is responsible for those injuries which a seatbelt would have prevented. During the 1960s and 1970s, most courts were hostile to the "seatbelt defense" for a variety of reasons. During the 1980s and 1990s, however, spurred by the spread of comparative fault and mandatory seatbelt legislation around the nation, a number of courts adopted some form of seatbelt defense. Today, much of the litigation on seatbelt nonuse has shifted to questions of statutory interpretation, and so the applicable statutes must be examined.

Seatbelt Use Statutes

How seatbelt use or nonuse may affect a civil case depends on the state's particular statute. Most statutes *bar* evidence of *nonuse*, but they vary considerably in their specifics and may:

- Prohibit the use of seatbelt nonuse evidence in civil litigation to reduce ("mitigate") a plaintiff's damages;
- Permit such evidence to reduce a plaintiff's damages;
- Permit such reductions, but with a cap; or
- Leave the matter to the courts.

Because of their many differences, it is not too helpful to generalize on whether or how such statutes may be specifically applicable to automotive products liability litigation.

One recurring seatbelt issue is whether states that prohibit evidence of seatbelt *nonuse* also bar a manufacturer from introducing evidence of seatbelt *availability*, as in a rollover case, to prove the *crashworthiness* (i.e., nondefectiveness) of the vehicle. Plaintiffs argue that this type of evidence improperly *suggests* nonuse, as when the jury knows that the plaintiff was thrown from the vehicle, such that seatbelt "availability" evidence is really just an end-run around the prohibition against nonuse evidence. Manufacturers respond that they should be permitted to defend the safety of their products viewed as a whole, and it is difficult to deny that safety belts are a central component of the overall "safety package" provided by a vehicle's design engineers. See *Daly v. General Motors Corp.*, 575 P.2d 1162, 1175 (Cal. 1978) (defendant not limited to narrow rebuttal of plaintiff's design defect theory (because driver's outside door button protruded, door would pop open if handle bumped object), and jury could consider availability of seatbelts and other safety features in deciding whether vehicle was crashworthy as a whole; "a product's components are not developed in isolation, but as part of an integrated and interrelated whole").

Other Safety Devices

While the discussion to this point has concerned an occupant's failure to wear a seatbelt, a person's failure to use *other* kinds of safety devices may raise similar issues in products liability litigation. Thus, a parent's failure to buckle a child into a child-restraint seat logically may bar or reduce the *parent*'s claim for medical expenses and other derivative damages from the child's injury to the same extent as if the parent had failed to use his or her own seatbelt. The *child*'s claim for injuries should not, of course, be barred by the parent's failure to perform his or her parental duties. Yet, apportionment principles may require that the trier of fact be permitted to apportion some responsibility to the parent in such a case.

Motorcycle helmets are another safety device mandated in many but not all jurisdictions, and the failure of a motorcycle rider to wear a helmet logically raises issues similar to those applicable to seatbelt nonuse.

CHAPTER 18

PUNITIVE DAMAGES

Table of Sections

§ 18.1 Punitive Damages—Generally.
§ 18.2 Functions of Punitive Damages.
§ 18.3 Forms of Manufacturer Misconduct.
§ 18.4 Basis of Liability.
§ 18.5 Problems and Recurring Criticisms.
§ 18.6 Judicial and Legislative Reform.
§ 18.7 Constitutional Limitations.

§ 18.1 PUNITIVE DAMAGES— GENERALLY

"Punitive" or "exemplary" damages are money damages awarded to a plaintiff in a private civil action, in addition to and apart from compensatory damages, assessed against a defendant guilty of flagrant misconduct. A jury (or judge, in the absence of a jury) may, in its discretion, render such an award in cases in which the defendant is found to have injured the plaintiff maliciously, intentionally, or with a "conscious," "reckless," "willful," "wanton," or "oppressive" disregard of the plaintiff's rights. The purposes of such damages are usually said to be (1) to punish a defendant for

505

outrageous conduct, and (2) to deter the defendant and others from similarly misbehaving in the future. Sometimes, though infrequently, punitive damages are assessed against manufacturers of defective products.

Manufacturers have a powerful hold on product safety. Normally, manufacturers exercise this power responsibly to prevent defective products from reaching or remaining on the market. Occasionally, however, manufacturers abuse their control over product safety and market defective products in flagrant disregard of public safety. One manufacturer of color televisions, for example, included in each set a high voltage transformer it learned was causing frequent fires and refused to spend the $1 per unit it knew would eliminate the hazard. See *Gillham v. Admiral Corp.*, 523 F.2d 102 (6th Cir. 1975) (Ohio law). In another case, a major drug company submitted fabricated test data to the FDA to obtain approval of a new drug. Approval was granted, and hundreds of persons developed cataracts as a result. See *Toole v. Richardson–Merrell, Inc.*, 60 Cal.Rptr. 398 (Ct. App. 1967).

The liability rules of products liability law address the question of when a manufacturer or other supplier should bear responsibility for actual damages suffered by the victim of a product accident. Modern products liability law is based at least nominally on no-fault principles, and the normal liability rules do not address problems at the other end of the culpability scale when harm results from a manufacturer's sale of a defective product in conscious or reckless disregard of consumer safety. Nor has the criminal law filled this void. Punitive damages help to expose this form of gross misconduct, to punish manufacturers guilty of such flagrant misbehavior, and to deter all manufacturers from acting with similar disregard for public safety.

No aspect of modern products liability law provokes as much controversy as large awards of punitive damages. The most notorious verdict of this type in recent years was the $2.7 million in punitive damages awarded to an 81-year-old woman severely scalded when she spilled a cup of McDonald's hot coffee in her lap. See *Liebeck v. McDonald's Rests.*, 1995 WL 360309 (D.N.M. 1994). The claim was based on McDonald's failure to warn customers that it served its coffee exceedingly hot, 180–190°, far hotter than coffee sold by most of its competitors despite its receipt of more than 700 complaints of burns, sometimes in the third degree. While upholding the jury's finding that punitive damages were warranted on these facts, the trial court remitted the award to $480,000, three times the compensatory award.

Punitive damages have been awarded for the sale of a wide range of other dangerous products—an IUD especially prone to cause septic abortions and even death; a tire knowingly made from bad stock rubber that could cause the tread to separate; an automatic nail gun that activated too easily; a disposable butane cigarette lighter that children frequently used to start fires; an unstable 3–wheel all-terrain vehicle that too easily tipped over; an overly-absorbent tampon that caused toxic shock syndrome; a helicopter prone to engine failure; a multi-piece truck tire rim that could easily be misassembled and explosively fly apart; cotton flannelette fabric for a child's nightgown not treated with flame retardant chemicals; a football helmet that failed to protect a high school football player against brain damage; and a number of cases in which pharmaceutical manufacturers marketed dangerous drugs or medical devices without warning about their hazards and sometimes with outright fraudulent representations to the medical profession, the public, and the FDA. Such decisions represent only a sampling of the several hundred cases in which juries have awarded punitive damages in products liability litigation.

Not only are punitive damages awarded in a wide variety of situations, but sometimes the awards are very large, occasionally amounting to tens or even hundreds of millions (and, in a couple of cases, *billions*) of dollars. While the number of large punitive damage verdicts in products liability cases has increased in recent decades, such awards are still very uncommon, being awarded in roughly 2% of all products liability cases, and the increasing frequency of such awards may well be a thing of the past. Studies reveal that most such awards are moderate in size and usually well deserved.

Moreover, the largest punitive damages awards typically are remitted substantially or reversed by trial or appellate courts, or both, particularly now that the Supreme Court has declared that excessive punitive damages awards may violate due process. For example, in a case against the manufacturer of a helicopter that crashed due to a defect that the manufacturer knowingly concealed, the jury assessed punitive damages of $175 million, which the trial court remitted to $87.5 million, and which the appellate court remitted further to $26.5 million. See *Barnett v. La Societe Anonyme Turbomeca France*, 963 S.W.2d 639 (Mo. Ct. App. 1997). Even twice reduced, however, $26.5 million remains a very large award. Thus, the threat of massive punitive damage awards truly is the "big stick" of modern products liability litigation. For a more thorough examination of punitive damages, see Owen, Products Liability Law ch. 18 (2d ed. 2008).

§ 18.2 FUNCTIONS OF PUNITIVE DAMAGES

In order to determine whether punitive damages are appropriate in particular cases, it is necessary to understand the objectives of such awards. Though courts typically refer only to "punishment" and "deterrence" as the purposes of such damages, this commonly stated duality of goals masks the nuanced variety of specific functions served by punitive damages. While the various overlapping functions may be formulated and subdivided in any number of ways, it may be helpful to identify five separate objectives: (1) retribution; (2) education;

(3) deterrence; (4) compensation; and (5) law enforcement.

Retribution

When courts refer to the "punishment" function of punitive damages, they generally mean retribution, perhaps the most fundamental basis for punishment in any form. Punitive damages have an important retributive, restitutionary role in forcing flagrant offenders to repay their "debts" to, and restore the equality of, victims and society.

The retributive needs of victims and society may be substantial when manufacturers sell defective products in flagrant disregard of serious risks of injuries to consumers. Awards of punitive damages in such cases help assuage a victim's feelings of helplessness and frustration over the apparent futility of holding an anonymous corporation accountable for its serious, damaging misdeeds. Further, punishing manufacturers guilty of intentional or reckless breaches of their safety obligations should tend to diminish whatever unfair competitive advantages such companies otherwise might obtain.

Education

Punitive damages serve to educate individual offenders and society by sensationalizing the consequences of serious misbehavior in a manner that informs and reminds defendants and society at large that a particular right–duty legal value not only exists, but that it is given staunch protection by the law.

Due to the elusive nature of product "defectiveness" in design and warning cases, manufacturers in pursuit of profits are naturally tempted to press ever closer toward (and sometimes over) the amorphous line that separates lawful from unlawful conduct. Yet, manufacturers should not be permitted blithely to close their eyes to the consequences of safety decisions they know may unreasonably endanger many persons. Accordingly, occasional judicial declarations that certain types of product safety decisions are not only improper but intolerable provide useful information; the publicity afforded large assessments of punitive damages announces that the push for profit must always leave fair room for safety.

Deterrence

Many courts and commentators believe that the predominant purpose of punishment in general, and punitive damages in particular, is deterrence—the prevention of similar misconduct in the future. The two-part deterrence message punitive damage awards provide manufacturers is that the law: (1) will not tolerate the acquisition of illicit profits from exploiting the vagueness and resulting under-enforcement of the liability rules; and (2) will force an enterprise that has marketed a product in flagrant disregard of consumer safety to disgorge all ill-gotten gains, and possibly much more. In a nutshell, punitive damages put all manufacturers on notice that the price of getting caught, discounted by the risk thereof, may well exceed the value of the booty.

Compensation

Although it frequently is asserted that punitive damages are not designed to compensate the plaintiff, such damages do indeed serve a variety of important compensatory roles. Such awards serve to reimburse a plaintiff for losses not ordinarily recoverable as compensatory damages—actual losses the plaintiff is unable to prove or for which the rules of damages do not provide relief including, most importantly, attorneys' fees and other costs of bringing suit. In addition, such awards serve the restitutionary purpose that underlies the retributive function, as seen above, and their provision of "extra" money is what fuels the private prosecutor engine of the law-enforcement function discussed below.

Law Enforcement

Punitive damages are frequently criticized for providing "windfalls" to plaintiffs in addition to compensating them for losses they actually sustained. In a sense this characterization is accurate, but in another sense it is not. The windfall characterization ignores the crucial restitutionary and compensatory effects of such awards, discussed above, and it overlooks the important fact that the very purpose of prospective windfalls is to help motivate reluctant victims (and their lawyers) to press their claims and so enforce the rules of law. That is, punitive damage awards serve as a kind of bounty, inducing injured victims to serve as "private attorneys general," increasing the number of wrongdoers who are pursued, civilly prosecuted, and eventually "brought to justice."

If public confidence in the legal system is to be maintained, flagrant breaches of the rules of behavior need to be punished and deterred. As discussed in connection with deterrence, punitive damages are a powerful instrument in enforcing compliance with the basic safety principles of products liability law. Together, law enforcement and the other punitive damages functions combine to present a compelling case for allowing such awards in situations where the profit motive has blinded a manufacturer to its product safety obligations.

§ 18.3 FORMS OF MANUFACTURER MISCONDUCT

Manufacturers have committed various forms of misconduct in making and selling products that juries and courts have found flagrantly improper and, hence, deserving of punitive damages. The cases reveal six categories of manufacturer misbehavior that recur with some frequency: (1) fraud; (2) knowingly violating safety standards; (3) failing to conduct adequate tests to uncover dangerous defects; (4) failing to design away known dangers; (5) failing to warn of known dangers; and (6) failing to issue post-sale warnings. Most cases in which punitive damages are assessed involve some combination of these different forms of misbehavior.

Fraud

Many punitive damages assessments in products liability cases involve fraudulent misrepresentations by manufacturers. In *Axen v. American Home Prods. Corp.*, 974 P.2d 224 (Or. Ct. App. 1999), a pharmaceutical company sold a drug called Cordarone that was beneficial for heart conditions but which permanently injured some people's eyes. The company had known of this serious side-effect for years and, despite repeated letters from the FDA threatening criminal prosecution unless it stopped understating the hazard as involving merely a possible eye nerve inflammation, the company continued to market and sell the drug as so misrepresented. The plaintiff took the drug for three months and went blind. Concluding that the jury could find that the defendant "deliberately placed misleading information on its packaging in order to preserve sales," the court upheld a punitive damages verdict of $20 million.

Knowingly Violating Safety Standards

Evidence that a manufacturer knew its product violated a formal safety standard, yet marketed it anyway to cut costs, is proof that the manufacturer acted with conscious disregard of the possibility that the product might be dangerously defective.

Rosendin v. Avco Lycoming, Civ. No. 202,715 (Cal. Super. Ct. Santa Clara Cty. 1972) arose out of the crash of an executive jet when its engine failed. The manufacturer of the engine overhauled and resold it twice after its initial sale, both times "zero timing" it and giving the new owners a new warranty and certificate stating that it complied with "all [FAA] regulations concerning zero timing engines." Strict federal regulations governed the tolerances of parts in zero-timed engines represented to be "rebuilt," and the defendant's service manager conceded that at least one resale violated FAA regulations because the company had equipped its engines with secondhand parts that met only the lower tolerances the FAA permitted for "overhauled" engines rather than the safer tolerances required for genuinely "rebuilt" zero-timed engines. Evidence also revealed that the defendant had ignored the regulations because it considered them too stringent and too expensive. On this evidence of the defendant's knowing breach of a governmental regulatory safety standard, together with its effort to mislead consumers, the jury awarded $10.5 million punitive damages to the sole survivor.

Failing to Conduct Adequate Tests to Uncover Dangerous Defects

A manufacturer's research, testing, and quality control procedures may be so inadequate as to manifest a flagrant indifference to the possibility that the product might expose consumers to unreasonable risks of harm. In *Deemer v. A.H. Robins Co.*, Case No. C-26420 (Kan. Dist. Ct. Sedgwick Cty. 1975), the jury awarded compensatory and punitive damages to a woman injured when the defendant's Dalkon Shield IUD had to be surgically removed after perforating her uterine wall. Among other things, the complaint alleged inadequate testing. Testimony before a congressional committee investigating the cause of the many injuries and deaths from this product revealed that A.H. Robins had marketed the Dalkon Shield after clinically testing the product for a "pathetic" average insertion time of only 5.5 months. Considering the delicacy and importance of the human organ into which the device was to be inserted for extended periods, and the risks involved if the device proved dangerously defective, proof that pre-marketing clinical testing had been seriously inadequate suggested the manufacturer's flagrant disregard of consumer safety. See also *Sufix, U.S.A., Inc. v. Cook*, 128 S.W.3d 838 (Ky. Ct. App. 2004) ($3 million punitive damages award upheld for grossly deficient testing of defective weed trimmer).

Failing to Design Away Known Dangers

A number of punitive damages assessments have been based largely upon a manufacturer's failure to adopt a simple design solution to a substantial safety problem plainly demanded by the simplicity and economy of the easy "fix." Thus, a manufacturer of silicone gel breast implants that knows they are prone to leak and break may be subject to punitive damages if it refuses to "dip" the envelope more than once to reduce the risk of rupture, retaining the "single dip method" of production because it is "easier" and "cheaper." *Hopkins v. Dow Corning Corp.*, 33 F.3d 1116 (9th Cir. 1994) (Cal.

law) (affirming $6.5 million punitive award). And punitive damages may be assessed if a radial saw manufacturer knows that a lower blade guard is necessary to prevent amputations yet refuses to follow the rest of the industry in installing the guard as standard equipment rather than selling it merely as an optional accessory, "because of the nominal additional cost." *Sears, Roebuck and Co. v. Kunze*, 996 S.W.2d 416 (Tex. App. 1999) (affirming $2 million punitive award to plaintiff who lost four fingers while using defendant's power radial saw).

Failing to Warn of Known Dangers

If a manufacturer withholds information about a serious product hazard in order to protect the marketing of its products, a punitive damages assessment appropriately punishes the defendant and makes clear that such behavior will not be tolerated by society nor profitable for the manufacturer. A large proportion of punitive damages verdicts awarded in products liability cases have been based at least in part on the manufacturer's failure to warn consumers of a serious product hazard of which it was aware, including:

- A heart medication manufacturer's decision not to warn that its product might cause vision loss, for fear of losing profits;

- A silicone breast implant manufacturer's failure to warn of the suspected defectiveness of its implants and the adverse results of its laboratory tests;

- A chemical preservative manufacturer's warning merely of irritation, burns, and allergic reaction, and its failure to warn that inhalation could be deadly, after discovering nine other incidents of death or injury; and

- Asbestos product manufacturers' failure to warn of the extreme hazards of inhaling asbestos dust for years after they learned of the often fatal risk.

Failing to Issue Post–Sale Warnings

Punitive damages awards are sometimes based on a manufacturer's failure to issue post-sale warnings of product hazards. If a manufacturer knows that its products are failing and producing severe injuries, or failing in a way likely to do so, its refusal to act promptly to adopt reasonable remedial measures suggests that it has little concern for consumer safety. See *Lovick v. Wil–Rich*, 588 N.W.2d 688 (Iowa 1999) (punitive damages warranted in action against manufacturer of cultivator, where manufacturer failed to institute post-sale warning campaign, despite its knowledge of numerous similar accidents involving its cultivators).

§ 18.4 BASIS OF LIABILITY

Punitive damages are awarded to remedy a conscious, reckless, or willful and wanton violation of a person's rights. Accordingly, punitive damages are not recoverable on their own, but rest instead upon the flagrant violation of some underlying substantive right and duty. There is, in other words, no independent cause of action for punitive damages; such damages must piggy-back instead upon one of the traditional products liability claims for compensatory damages. Thus, a plaintiff's entitlement to compensatory damages is widely held to be a prerequisite to recovery on a punitive damages claim. See *Watson v. Ford Motor Co.*, 2007 WL 4216975 (Ohio Ct. App. 2007).

Warranty

A long-established rule prohibits the award of punitive damages in *contract* actions. Since warranty actions today sound principally in contract rather than in tort, punitive damages are unavailable for breach of warranty. See *Robinson Helicopter Co. v. Dana Corp.*, 129 Cal.Rptr.2d 682, 701 (Ct. App. 2003) ("This rule is based in part upon the important policy concern of providing predictability in commercial transactions and respecting the freedom of contract by restricting a contracting party to its contractual remedies for breach."), rev'd on other grounds, 102 P.3d 268 (Cal. 2004); UCC § 1–106(1) ("penal damages" not available for breach of warranty).

Strict Liability in Tort

Early in the development of products liability law, a number of commentators argued, and a very few courts held, that punitive damages claims are inconsistent with claims for strict products liability in tort. The argument put forth, still sometimes made today, is that a punitive damages claim based on allegations of aggravated fault is conceptually incompatible with a strict products liability action where the manufacturer's care, or absence thereof, is irrelevant to liability for compensatory damages.

While the incompatibility argument contains some superficial appeal, it rests on the false premise that punitive damages claims must be established by facts identical to those supporting the underlying claim for compensatory damages. Only one punitive damages state (S.C.) still bars such damages in strict products liability in tort, based on a narrow interpretation of that state's products liability statute. Thus, punitive damages are recoverable today, in the great majority of jurisdictions, in products liability actions brought in strict liability in tort.

Basis of Punitive Damages Claim

Most products liability decisions addressing punitive damages have applied traditional common-law and statutory standards that generally provide for punitive damages liability, such as "willful and wanton"; "malice, oppression, or gross negligence"; or "ill will, . . . actual malice, or . . . under circumstances amounting to fraud or oppression." Courts sometimes define the proscribed misbehavior as conduct that is in "conscious," or "reckless," or "flagrant" disregard of consumer safety or of a product's defectiveness.

§ 18.5   PROBLEMS AND RECURRING CRITICISMS

Punitive damages are subject to a number of criticisms:

- That they confuse tort and criminal law; that manufacturers and innocent shareholders are unfairly subjected to vicarious liability for them;

- That insurance against them destroys their punitive effect; that their liability standards are hopelessly vague; and

- That the standards for assessing their amounts are unfair.

Some merit lies in each of these criticisms which are elsewhere examined extensively. See Owen, Products Liability Law § 18.5 (2d ed. 2008). These problems have led to a number of important reforms by courts and legislatures, outlined in the remaining sections.

§ 18.6   JUDICIAL AND LEGISLATIVE REFORM

The various problems with punitive damages, including those just mentioned, suggest a rather compelling need for reform. A number of such "reforms" have been afoot, all supposed to improve the logic and fairness of punitive damages law.

Refining the Standards of Liability and Measurement

A basic reform some courts and legislatures have adopted is to narrow and refine the formal standards for both punitive damages *liability* and the *amount* of such awards. Definitions of the proscribed misconduct and standards of measurement for such awards are improved by tying them explicitly to the goals of punitive damages applicable in the products liability context.

Prima Facie Case Showings

Statutes in several states (Cal., Fla., Minn.) require a plaintiff to make a prima facie showing of the defendant's liability for punitive damages before punitive damages may be pleaded, discovery of wealth may proceed, evidence of wealth may be admitted, a provisional cap on the amount of a punitive damages award may be removed, or the amount of punitive damages may be argued to the jury.

Close Judicial Scrutiny

In recent decades, trial courts in products liability cases frequently have ruled for manufacturers on punitive damages claims on motions for summary judgment, directed verdict, and judgment notwithstanding the verdict. Appellate courts, too, particularly since the Supreme Court began applying due process constraints on punitive damages in the 1990s, have increasingly subjected such awards to

close scrutiny, reversing them when unwarranted
on the record.

Standard of Proof

Because punitive damages judgments are extraordinary and harsh, most states in recent years, by legislation or common law, have raised the standard of proof from "preponderance of the evidence," the ordinary standard for civil litigation, to a "clear and convincing" standard of proof. This is an important reform that reflects the intermediate position of punitive damages, a "quasi-criminal" remedy, between the civil and criminal law.

Compliance with Government Standards

Some states (Ariz., N.J., Or., Utah) have statutes providing a defense to punitive damages for pharmaceutical manufacturers whose drugs comply with applicable FDA regulations. At least one state more broadly exempts manufacturers and sellers of any type of product from liability for punitive damages if they comply with federal statutes and administrative regulations. See N.D. Cent. Code § 32–03.2–11(6). Other states (Colo., Kan., Tenn., Utah) provide a regulatory compliance shield for manufacturers of all products with respect to liability for compensatory damages, raising a rebuttable presumption of nondefectiveness or non-negligence.

Remittitur

Another common mechanism of judicial control, which courts have exercised from the very inception of punitive damages in products liability litigation, is the remittitur of excessive awards—by granting a defendant's request for a new trial (or reversing and remanding for a new trial, in the case of an appellate court) unless the plaintiff accepts a reduction in the punitive damages award to some specified amount. See *Buell–Wilson v. Ford Motor Co.*, 73 Cal.Rptr.3d 277 (Ct. App. 2008) (issuing remittitur conditioning affirmance of punitive damages judgment of $75 million on plaintiffs' acceptance of reduction to $55 million, after trial court had remitted jury award of $246 million punitive damages to $75 million); *Bocci v. Key Pharms., Inc.*, 76 P.3d 669 (Or. Ct. App. 2003) (denying defendant's motion for new trial conditioned on plaintiff's accepting remittitur of $57 million punitive damages verdict to $3.5 million).

Multipliers and Other Caps

In an effort to bridle jury discretion to prevent run-away punitive damages awards, some states have adopted various arbitrary measurement approaches that reduce or remove discretion from the trier of fact. The most common is to *cap* punitive damages at some *multiple* of the compensatory award—at one (Colo.), two (Conn., N.D., Okla.), three (Fla., Nev.), four, or five (N.J.) times compensatory damages. Some jurisdictions use other measures to cap punitive awards, such as absolute dollar amounts (Va.: $350,000; Kan.: $5 million), the defendant's gross income (Kan.), a percentage of the defendant's net worth (Miss.), or the amount (or some multiple thereof) by which the defendant profited from the misconduct (Okla., Kan.). Most statutes combine two or more limitations, as by limiting such damages to the *greater* of some dollar amount, such as $250,000, *or* some multiple of (such as 3 times) the compensatory award. Compare *Exxon Shipping Co. v. Baker*, 128 S.Ct. 2605 (2008) (adopting a punitive damages limit of one times compensatory damages for maritime cases).

Single Award

A recurring problem with punitive damages awards in products liability litigation is that a defendant may be subject to repetitive awards for a single design or warning defect. Accordingly, a small number of states (e.g., Ga., Fla., Ohio) have enacted "one-bite" reform legislation that limits punitive damages to one punishment for a single act or course of conduct.

Splitting Awards with State

Some states, to capture the supposed "windfall" portion of punitive damages awards from plaintiffs and in recognition of the public policy purposes of punitive damages, provide that some portion of such assessments go to the state. The statutes, variously called "split-recovery" or "state-extraction" statutes, have varied in the amount of the award that goes to the state: 35% (Fla.); 50% (Alaska, Kan., Mo., Utah); 60% (Or.); 75% (Ga., Iowa); and a percentage within the court's discretion (Ill.). The statutes vary on whether particular state agencies are designated as the recipients of such recoveries or whether the state's share simply goes into its general treasury.

A split-recovery statute was successfully attacked on state constitutional grounds in one state (Colo.), but courts in a number of other states (Fla., Ga., Iowa, Mo.) have upheld such statutes against various state and federal constitutional attacks. Because the *state* shares in the punitive damages award under this type of statute, a very large award may violate the Excessive Fines Clause of the 8th Amendment, an issue left open by the Supreme Court. See *Browning–Ferris Indus. v. Kelco Disposal, Inc.*, 492 U.S. 257 (1989).

Bifurcation

Some courts and legislatures require or permit, upon the defendant's (or any party's) motion, that the punitive damages issue be bifurcated at trial, so that the jury's decision on liability and compensatory damages will not be contaminated by the plaintiff's evidence and argument on the defendant's wealth and other punitive damages matters. Some jurisdictions bifurcate all punitive damage issues from the basic liability and compensatory damages issues; others segregate only the determination of the *amount* of punitive damages, leaving the issue of liability therefor to be decided in the preliminary proceeding along with liability for (and the amount of) compensatory damages. Fed. R. Civ. P. 42(b) accommodates bifurcation of punitive damages by permitting federal courts to order separate trials of claims and issues for convenience, expedition, economy, or to avoid prejudice.

Judicial Determination of Amount

At least three states (Conn., Kan., Ohio) have statutes allowing juries to determine a defendant's *liability* for punitive damages, but transferring to the court responsibility for determining their *amount*. This shift of responsibility is designed to prevent the perceived risk of biased juries rendering run-away punitive damage awards. Challenges to these statutes for violating the state constitutional right to jury trial met with mixed results: the Ohio Supreme Court struck down its statute, while the Kansas Supreme Court upheld its statute, reasoning that punitive damages were merely a discretionary remedy of the common law not subject to the right to jury trial.

Written Explanations

Punitive damages problems may be minimized if courts are required to provide explicit justifications—in the record or by opinion—for allowing, upsetting, or remitting such assessments. A number of jurisdictions now require courts (trial courts in some states, appellate courts in others) to explain punitive damages rulings. The importance of this reform should not be underestimated, and it would seem to be a necessary fairness bedrock for the administration of punitive damages law.

§ 18.7 CONSTITUTIONAL LIMITATIONS

Courts and commentators long have questioned the fairness of assessing civil penalties for conduct described so vaguely as "malicious," "reckless," or "willful and wanton," with no real ceiling on the size of the assessments, and without the procedural safeguards used in criminal cases to assure the propriety of punishment. Beginning in the 1990s, to address concerns over the increase in multi-million dollar awards of punitive damages and the widespread perception that such damages are too often assessed arbitrarily and unfairly, the United States Supreme Court constitutionalized the law of punitive damages. In a series of decisions, the Court in some detail has examined the fairness of procedures for assessing punitive damages and determining their amounts.

Haslip

In *Pacific Mutual Life Insurance Co. v. Haslip*, 499 U.S. 1 (1991), the Court held that the 14th Amendment's Due Process Clause requires that punitive damage assessments be supported by proper procedures. Juries must base such awards on the purposes (usually punishment and deterrence) of such awards; trial courts must assure that juries fulfill their obligations; and appellate courts must closely monitor the lower courts to ensure that punitive damages are "reasonable in their amount and rational in light of their purpose to punish [and] deter" so that such awards "are not grossly out of proportion to the severity of the offense" and to the compensatory damages. Id. at 22. *Haslip* thus established a *procedural* due process structure for punitive damages determinations.

BMW v. Gore

In *BMW of North America, Inc. v. Gore*, 517 U.S. 559 (1996), the Court began its *substantive* due process inquiry into standards for determining whether large punitive damage awards are constitutionally *excessive*. An Alabama dentist recovered $4,000 in compensatory damages against BMW for selling him a car as "new" without disclosing that it had been repaired and partially repainted after being damaged in transit by acid rain. Following the suggestion of plaintiff's counsel, the jury calculated punitive damages by multiplying the compensatory damages by 1000, the approximate number of cars BMW had refinished and sold as new across America, for a total punitive award of $4 million. The Alabama Supreme Court, concluding that the jury may have improperly based its award on the defendant's conduct outside the state, reduced the punitive damages award to a "constitutionally reasonable" amount of $2 million.

Reversing, a 5–justice majority of the United States Supreme Court agreed with the Alabama high court that a jury could not properly impose *extraterritorial* punishment on the defendant, based in part on conduct in states where the conduct was legal, which would violate principles of state sovereignty and comity. When Alabama's state interests

alone were considered, the *Gore* majority viewed the
$2 million penalty as grossly excessive and, hence,
violative of due process.

Actors must be provided with fair *notice*, the
Court reasoned, not only of the type of conduct that
is punishable but also the *severity* of the possible
penalty. For this purpose, *Gore* identified three
"guideposts" of adequate notice to help discern
whether a particular punitive award is "grossly
excessive" and, hence, violative of due process:

(1) **Reprehensibility.** The degree of *reprehensibility* of the defendant's conduct, the most important guidepost;

(2) **Ratio.** The reasonableness of the relationship
(the *"ratio"*) of the punitive award to the compensatory award; and

(3) **Other Penalties.** A comparison of the punitive award with *other penalties*, civil and criminal,
authorized in such cases.

Although the Court reiterated that it was "not
prepared to draw a bright line marking the limits of
a constitutionally acceptable punitive damages
award," it concluded that the $2 million punitive
damages award was out of all proportion to the
goals of punitive damages under each of the three
indicia.

Cooper Industries

*Cooper Industries, Inc. v. Leatherman Tool
Group, Inc.*, 532 U.S. 424 (2001), an unfair trade

practices case, changed the standard of federal appellate review of the constitutionality of punitive damages awards from abuse of discretion to *de novo* review.

State Farm

The Court's next treatment of the constitutional aspects of punitive damages law was *State Farm Mutual Automobile Insurance Co. v. Campbell*, 538 U.S. 408 (2003), an insurance bad-faith failure-to-settle case. On evidence of the company's widespread practices of preying on the vulnerabilities of its own insureds, the jury returned verdicts of $2.6 million in compensatory damages and $145 million in punitive damages, which the trial judge remitted, respectively, to $1 million and $25 million. Reinstating the full $145 million punitive damages verdict, the Utah Supreme Court concluded that it was warranted under the three *Gore* measurement guideposts because the defendant's nation-wide scheme to cheat its policyholders was reprehensible, coupled with the company's "massive wealth" and the improbability of its being caught and punished due to the clandestine nature of its activities.

State Farm appealed to the Supreme Court, arguing that the $145 million punitive damages assessment was excessive and violated due process because the Utah courts had improperly considered conduct outside the state and had otherwise violated the due process principles set forth in *Gore*. Agreeing, the Supreme Court reversed and remanded, stating that the case was "neither close nor difficult" under *Gore's* guideposts for avoiding constitutionally excessive punitive damages awards.

Reprehensibility

The *State Farm* court acknowledged the impropriety of the defendant's scheme but explained that due process precluded courts from basing punitive awards on misconduct, especially conduct outside the state, unrelated to the plaintiff's harm. Noting that a much lower award would have adequately protected Utah's interest in punishing and deterring State Farm's relevant misconduct that occurred in Utah, the Court observed that the case was improperly "used as a platform to expose, and punish, the perceived deficiencies of State Farm's operations throughout the country." Unfortunately, the majority ignored considerable reprehensibility evidence of State Farm's serious misconduct, detailed in Justice Ginsburg's dissent, relevant to the company's abusive practices in this case.

Ratio

As for the second guidepost, the ratio between punitive and compensatory damages, the Court "decline[d] again to impose a bright-line ratio which a punitive damages award cannot exceed." While signaling that "few awards exceeding a single-digit ratio ... will satisfy due process," the Court observed that due process may permit greater ratios in certain circumstances—for particularly egregious misconduct resulting in small economic damages, where the injury is hard to detect, or where the misconduct causes physical injuries. In all cases, however, "courts must ensure that the measure of punishment is both reasonable and proportionate to the amount of harm to the plaintiff and to the general damages recovered." Because State Farm eventually paid the plaintiffs' excess liability, their losses were mostly emotional, leading the Court to determine that the generous $1 million compensatory damages award contained a substantial punitive component such that a large punitive award would be constitutionally inappropriate. (On remand, the Utah Supreme Court reduced the punitive damages award to slightly more than $9 million, a ratio of about 9 to 1. See *Campbell v. State Farm Mut. Auto. Ins. Co.*, 98 P.3d 409 (Utah 2004). The U.S. Supreme Court denied State Farm's subsequent petition for *certiorari*.

Comparison to Other Penalties

Finally, the Court explained that the very large punitive damages award was unjustified by *Gore*'s third guidepost which compares the punitive award to other civil and criminal penalties that may also apply to the defendant's misconduct which, in Utah, was a mere $10,000 fine for fraud.

For these reasons, the Court concluded that the $145 million punitive damages assessment was "neither reasonable nor proportionate to the wrong committed, and it was an irrational and arbitrary deprivation of the property of the defendant." Id. at 429.

Philip Morris USA v. Williams

Williams I. After *State Farm,* the Supreme Court vacated and remanded a number of products liability cases for reconsideration. One such case was *Williams v. Philip Morris Inc.*, 48 P.3d 824 (Or. Ct. App. 2002), a case against a cigarette manufacturer brought by the widow of a man who died of cancer from smoking the defendant's cigarettes. In addition to $800,000 in compensatory damages, the jury awarded the plaintiff $79.5 million in punitive damages, which the trial court remitted to $32 million. The Oregon Court of Appeals reinstated the jury's full $79.5 million punitive award, but, in an order without opinion, *Philip Morris USA Inc. v. Williams* (*"Williams I"*), 540 U.S. 801 (2003), the Supreme Court vacated and remanded for reconsideration in light of its decision in *State Farm*.

Williams II. On remand from *Williams I*, after reconsidering its prior opinion, the Oregon Court of Appeals again reinstated the full $79.5 million punitive damages award, reasoning that the defendant's reprehensibility justified a punitive damages award well in excess of a single-digit ratio and met the *Gore–State Farm* due process guidelines. See *Williams v. Philip Morris Inc.*, 92 P.3d 126 (Or. Ct. App. 2004). The Oregon Supreme Court affirmed, concluding that due process warranted the jury's very large assessment against Philip Morris for its "extreme and outrageous" conduct. *Williams v. Philip Morris Inc.*, 127 P.3d 1165 (Or. 2006).

In *Philip Morris USA v. Williams* (*"Williams II"*), 127 S.Ct 1057 (2007), the United States Supreme Court vacated and remanded, side-stepping the excessiveness issue by ruling that the Oregon trial court should have instructed that, in considering the reprehensibility of the defendant's conduct, the jury could consider the defendant's conduct on other Oregonians, but that the jury could not punish the defendant "directly" for harming such "nonparty victims." To do the latter, reasoned the Court, would contravene due process by magnifying the risks of arbitrariness, uncertainty, and lack of notice that surround awards of punitive damages. In dissent, Justice Stevens, remarked, "This nuance eludes me."

Williams III. On remand, the Oregon Supreme Court again reaffirmed its prior decision upholding the trial court's award of $79.5 million punitive damages, this time on an independent state ground that the defendant's requested instruction on due process at trial had misstated other aspects of Oregon law. *Williams v. Philip Morris Inc.*, 176 P.3d 1255 (Or. 2008). In this manner, the Oregon court avoided the due process question raised by the United States Supreme Court in its opinion.

The defendant again petitioned for *certiorari*, which the Court granted, *Philip Morris USA Inc. v. Williams*, 128 S.Ct. 2904 (2008), to consider the question of whether a state court may interpose a "state-law procedual bar that is neither firmly established nor regularly followed" after the Court "has adjudicated the merits of a party's federal claim and remanded the case to state court with instructions to 'apply' the correct constitutional standard." *Philip Morris USA v. Williams*, Appellate Petition for a Writ of Certiorari, 2008 WL 795148 (U.S. 2008). A decision in *Philip Morris USA Inc. v. Williams* ("*Williams III*") is expected in the 2008–2009 term.

Constitutional Doctrine in the Products Liability Context

One must question how meaningfully the due process excessiveness principles of *Gore* and its progeny may be applied to products liability cases involving personal injury or death. In *Gore*, the Supreme Court noted that the reprehensibility of misconduct is affected by certain "aggravating factors," including whether the conduct threatened merely economic interests or health and safety; whether the defendant acted with "trickery and deceit"—with "deliberate false statements, acts of affirmative misconduct, or concealment of evidence of improper motive"; and whether the defendant engaged in repetitive misconduct, whether it was a "repeat offender."

Products liability cases in which punitive damages are levied almost always involve a significant threat to human safety; trickery and concealment frequently pervade these cases; and many involve a manufacturer who continues to market its product, while continuing to tout its safety, despite increasing proof that it is dangerously defective. The fact that each of *Gore*'s aggravating factors commonly exists in products liability cases involving large punitive damages awards—cases in which multi-million dollar punitive damages awards are assessed against multi-billion dollar, multi-national manufacturers of defective products—frustrates the usefulness of these guideposts in this context. Stated otherwise, *Gore*'s excessiveness guideposts provide manufacturers and the courts with little useful guidance as to how due process may limit punitive damage awards in products liability cases.

Gore's most helpful lesson is its central theme, underscored by the Court's shift to a standard of *de novo* review in *Cooper Industries*, that reviewing courts must closely examine the culpability and other punitive damages evidence in relation to the principles and goals of punitive damages law—particularly if the size of a particular award raises "a suspicious judicial eyebrow," which may indeed be all that due process truly should require. One should not minimize the importance of this due process requirement—commenced in *Haslip* and continued in *Gore, Cooper Industries*, and *State Farm*—that courts must scrutinize the evidence closely to assure that the procedures by which punitive damages are assessed are fair to the defendant.

From *Haslip* to *Gore, State Farm*, and *Williams*, the Supreme Court has continued to emphasize the due process problems in punitive damage awards many times the size of compensatory awards. Lower courts seem to be getting the message, evidenced by their lowering high-multiple punitive awards, in an attempt to comport with due process ratio principles, to much lower "reasonable" multiples of compensatory damages. This development reflects the fact that courts and lawyers are now focusing closely on the various constitutional dimensions of punitive damages, from the fairness of the procedures by which such assessments are made and reviewed, pursuant to *Haslip* and *Williams*, to the various standards for testing their excessiveness developed in and applied by *Gore* and *State Farm*.

*

INDEX

AFFIRMATIVE DEFENSES
Generally, 383–386
Airbags, federal preemption, 425–426
Airplanes, federal repose statute for small airplanes, 430
Assumption of risk. User misconduct defenses, below
Cigarettes, federal preemption, 424–427
Comparative fault. User misconduct defenses, below
Contributory negligence. User misconduct defenses, below
Express warranty, user misconduct defenses to warranty claims, 409–410
Federal preemption, 422–428
General Aviation Revitalization Act of 1994 (GARA), federal repose statute for small airplanes, 430
Limitations. Statutes of limitations, below
Misrepresentation claims, defenses to. User misconduct defenses, below
Misuse. User misconduct defenses, below
Special defenses
Generally, 415
Contract specifications defense, 417–418
Federal preemption, above
Government contractor defense, 418–419
Government standards defense, 419–421
Preemption. Federal preemption, above
Statutes of limitations, below
Statutes of repose, below
Statutory and regulatory compliance, 419–421

AFFIRMATIVE DEFENSES—Cont'd
Special defenses—Cont'd
Statutes of limitations, 428–430
Statutes of repose
    Generally, 429–430
    General Aviation Revitalization Act of 1994 (GARA), federal
        repose statute for small airplanes, 430
    Statutes of limitations distinguished, 429
    Time-certain statutes, 430
User misconduct defenses
    Generally, 383–386
    Assumption of risk, 396–402
        Strict liability claims, 400–401
    Comparative fault, 389–396
        Strict liability claims, 394–395
        Types, pure and modified, 392–393
        Warranty claims, 412
    Contributory negligence, 386–389
    Express warranty, defenses to warranty claims, 409–412
    Misrepresentation claims, defenses to, 412–414
    Misuse, 402–409
        Burden of proof, 405
        Comparative fault, 409
        Failure to follow warnings, 408
        Foreseeability limitation, 406–408
        Misrepresentation claims, defenses to, 414
        Theory of liability, 404–405
        Warranty claims, defenses to, 410–411
    Reform legislation, 385–386
    Strict liability in tort
        Assumption of risk, 400–401
        Comparative fault, 394–395
        Warranty claims, defenses to, 409–412
Warranty
    Statutes of limitations, 429
    User misconduct defenses, above

ALCOHOLIC BEVERAGES
Defectiveness, inherent product hazards, 307–308

ALLERGIC PERSONS
Warning defects, 280–281

ALTERNATIVE DESIGNS
Design Defects, this index

ALTERNATIVE LIABILITY
Multiple defendants. Causation, this index

APPORTIONMENT OF DAMAGES
Damages, this index

ASBESTOS
Causation, 345
Duty to warn, 263–264
Punitive damages, 518
Statutes of repose, 429–430
Unknowable dangers, duty to warn of unknowable risks, 315–325

ASSUMPTION OF RISK
Affirmative Defenses, this index

AUTOMOBILES AND AUTOMOTIVE LITIGATION
Motor Vehicles, this index

BAILMENTS
Special Transactions and Products, this index

BLOOD
Special Transactions and Products, this index

BOOKS
Special Transactions and Products, this index

CASUAL SALES
Special Transactions and Products, this index

CAUSATION
Generally, 337–338, 361–363
Cause in fact
Generally, 337–338
Defendant identification, tests and proof of causation, 338–340
Heeding presumption, warning cases, 359–360
Multiple defendants
Generally, 346–356
Alternative liability, 352–353
Civil conspiracy, 355–356
Collective liability theories, 348–356
Concert of action, 354–355
Concurrent causation, 346–348
Enterprise liability, 353–354
Market share liability, 349–352

CAUSATION—Cont'd
Cause in fact—Cont'd
    Tests, 338–346
        "But-for" test, 340–341
        Defendant identification, 338–340
        "Substantial factor" test, 341–342
        Toxic substance litigation, 343–346
    Warning cases, special causation issues
        Generally, 356–360
        Heeding presumption, 359–360
  Foreseeability and other tests. Proximate causation, below
Intervening and superseding causes. Proximate causation, below
Multiple defendants. Cause in fact, above
Proximate causation
    Generally, 361–363
  Conventional foreseeability categories, 369
  Foreseeability and other tests, 363–369
  Intervening and superseding causes
    Generally, 370–374
    Comparative fault, superseding causes and, 382
    Misconduct, intentional and criminal, 376–381
    Reform legislation, 376
    Substantial change, 376
    Third parties, types of, 374–375
  Misconduct, intentional and criminal. Intervening and
    superseding causes, above
    Superseding causes. Intervening and superseding causes,
      above
    Tests. Foreseeability and other tests, above
  Third parties. Intervening and superseding causes, above
Restatement (Third) of Torts: Products Liability. Defectiveness,
  this index
Superseding causes. Proximate causation, above
Warning cases, special causation issues. Cause in fact, above

CAUSE IN FACT
Causation, this index

CAVEAT EMPTOR
Generally, 6–8, 93–94

CIGARETTES
    Generally, 307–309
Federal preemption, 424–427

CIVIL CONSPIRACY
Multiple defendants. Causation, this index

COLLECTIVE LIABILITY
Multiple defendants. Causation, this index

COMPARATIVE FAULT
Affirmative Defenses, this index

COMPONENT PARTS
Raw materials and component parts. Special Transactions and
    Products, this index

CONCERT OF ACTION
Multiple defendants. Causation, this index

CONCURRENT CAUSATION
Multiple defendants. Causation, this index

CONSTITUTIONAL LAW
Punitive damages, constitutional limitations, 528–537
Statutes of repose, constitutionality, 430

CONSUMER EXPECTATIONS
Strict Liability in Tort, this index

CONSUMER EXPECTATIONS TEST
Food and drink, manufacturing defects, 217–220

CONTRIBUTORY NEGLIGENCE
Affirmative Defenses, this index

CRASHWORTHINESS
Motor Vehicles, this index

DAMAGES
    Generally, 40–41
Apportionment of damages
    Motor vehicles, 494–497
    Restatement (Third) of Torts: Products Liability, 204
Punitive Damages, this index

DEFECTIVENESS
    Generally, 173–174
Design Defects, this index
Deterioration, 329–330
Disposal and salvage, 330–332
Expert testimony, proof of defect, 180–191
Inherent product hazards, 305–309

DEFECTIVENESS—Cont'd
Limitations on defectiveness
　　Generally, 298–299
Manufacturing Defects, this index
Motor Vehicles, this index
Obvious dangers, 299–305
Post-sale duties, 332–335
Prenatal harm, 327–329
Product category liability. Inherent product hazards, above
Proof of defect
　　Government standards, 192–193
　　Industry standards—custom, 192–193
　　Recurring issues, 192–198
　　Remedial measures. Subsequent remedial measures, below
　　Repairs, repair doctrine. Subsequent remedial measures,
　　　　below
　　Safety standards, 192–193
　　Similar accidents, 193–194
　　Subsequent remedial measures, 194–195
Restatement (Third) of Torts: Products Liability, 199–200
Retrofit, post-sale duty to retrofit or recall, 334–335
Salvage, disposal and, 330–332
State of the art, 309–327
Tests
　　Design defects. Theories and Tests of Liability, this index
　　Manufacturing defects. Theories and Tests of Liability, this
　　　　index
　　Strict liability in tort. Liability Tests, this index
　　Warning defects. Theories and Tests of Liability, this index
Warnings
　　Post-sale duty to warn, 333–334
　　Warning Defects, this index

DEFENDANTS
Apparent manufacturers, 440–441
Employers as manufacturers, 446–449
Multiple defendants. Causation, this index
Parent corporations, alter ego liability, 439–440
Product certifiers and endorsers, 450–452
Raw materials and component parts suppliers. Suppliers, raw
　　materials and component parts, below
Retailers and other non-manufacturing sellers, 432–437
Successor corporations, 443–446
Suppliers, raw materials and component parts, 437–439
Trade associations, 452–454
Trademark licensors and franchisers, 441–443

DEFENSES
Affirmative Defenses, this index

DESIGN DEFECTS
Generally, 221–224
Alternative design, proof of reasonable alternative design, 233–239
Combining consumer expectations and risk-utility, 239–246
Complex designs, 243–246
Two liability prongs, *Barker*, 241–243
Constructive knowledge, Wade–Keeton test, 246–248
Consumer expectations test, 224–227
Cost-benefit analysis, fundamentals, 228–231
Definition. Restatement (Third) of Torts: Products Liability, below
Drugs, 255–260
Hand formula, risk-utility test, 228–231
Motor vehicles, design defect claims, 487–488
Optional safety devices, 251–254
Restatement (Third) of Torts: Products Liability, 200, 248–251, 257–260
Risk-utility test, 228–233
Theories and tests of liability, 224
Wade factors, burdens, benefits and utility, 231–233
Wade–Keeton Test, 246–248
Warning defects, relationship between duty to warn and duty of safe design, 265

DETERIORATION
Defectiveness, this index

DETERRENCE
Strict Liability in Tort, this index

DISCLAIMERS
Restatement (Third) of Torts: Products Liability, contractual disclaimers, 205
Warranty, this index

DISPOSAL AND SALVAGE
Defectiveness, this index

DRUGS
Design defects, prescription drugs, 255–260

DRUGS—Cont'd
Inherent product hazards, 305–309
Restatement (Third) of Torts: Products Liability, defective drugs,
        201–202
Warning defects, prescription drugs, 285–297

EARLY LAW
    Generally, 5–6
Early American law, 7–11
Early English law, 6–7

ELECTRICITY
Special Transactions and Products, this index

EMPLOYERS
Defendants. Employers as Manufacturers, this index

ENTERPRISE LIABILITY
Multiple defendants. Causation, this index

EXPERT TESTIMONY
Defectiveness, this index

EXPRESS WARRANTIES
Warranty, this index

FEDERAL PREEMPTION
Affirmative Defenses, this index

FITNESS FOR PARTICULAR PURPOSE
Warranty, this index

FOOD AND DRINK
Manufacturing Defects, this index

FOREIGN LAW
Generally, 42–43

FRAUD
Tortious Misrepresentation, this index

GENERAL AVIATION REVITALIZATION ACT OF 1994 (GARA)
Federal repose statute for small airplanes, 430

HAND FORMULA
Design defects, 228–231
Negligence, 51–53
Strict liability in tort, risk-utility test, 157–159

HEEDING PRESUMPTION
Warning cases, cause in fact, 359–360

HORSES
Generally, 482

IMPLIED WARRANTY OF FITNESS FOR PARTICULAR PURPOSE
Warranty, this index

IMPLIED WARRANTY OF MERCHANTABILITY
Warranty, this index

INCONSISTENT JURY VERDICTS
Strict liability in tort, 167–172

INHERENT PRODUCT HAZARDS
Defectiveness, this index

INTERVENING AND SUPERSEDING CAUSES
Causation, this index

INTOXICATION
Motor vehicles, intoxication and plaintiff's fault, 497–500

INTRODUCTION TO PRODUCTS LIABILITY LAW
Generally, 1–5

LEASES
Special Transactions and Products, this index

LICENSE TRANSACTIONS
Special Transactions and Products, this index

LIMITATIONS
Affirmative Defenses, this index

MALFUNCTION DOCTRINE
Manufacturing Defects, this index

MANUFACTURING DEFECTS
  Generally, 206–209
Definition. Restatement (Third) of Torts: Products Liability, below
Departure from design specifications, 211–212
Food and drink, 217–220
Malfunction doctrine, 212–217
Restatement (Third) of Torts: Products Liability, 200, 212
Theories and tests of liability, 209–211

MARKET SHARE LIABILITY
Multiple defendants. Causation, this index

MERCHANTABILITY
Warranty, this index

MISCONDUCT
Proximate causation, intentional and criminal misconduct as intervening and superseding causes, 376–381
Punitive Damages, this index
User misconduct. Affirmative Defenses, this index

MISREPRESENTATION
Affirmative Defenses, this index
Tortious Misrepresentation, this index

MISUSE
Affirmative Defenses, this index

MOTOR VEHICLES
Generally, 485–486
Apportionment of damages, 494–497
Crashworthiness, 488–494
Defectiveness, defects that cause accidents, 486–488
Design defect claims, 487–488
Federal preemption, 425–426
Indivisible harm, 494–497
Manufacturing defect claims, 486–487
Plaintiff fault
Generally, 497–504
Causation, accident, 498–500
Crashworthiness cases, 500–501
Intoxication, 498–500
Safety devices, failure to use seatbelts and other safety devices, 501–504

NEGLIGENCE
Generally, 45–48
Breach, 48
Cost-benefit analysis, determining due care, 50–53
Design, due care in, 54–56
Due care. Standard of care, below
Duty, 46–48
Expert in the field, manufacturers held to standard of, 49
Foreseeability, responsibility limited by reasonable foreseeability, 49–50
Hand formula, 51–53

NEGLIGENCE—Cont'd
Industry standards. Proof of negligence, below
Instructions, due care in marketing, 56
Manufacture, due care in, 53–54
Misrepresentation, negligent. Tortious Misrepresentation, this
     index
Proof of negligence
     Generally, 56–68
   Custom, industry standards as, 56–58
   Industry standards, 56–58
   Res ipsa loquitur, 64–68
   Statute, violation of 58–64
Res ipsa loquitur. Proof of negligence, above
Resurgence of negligence, 69–71
Standard of care, 48–56
Statute, violation of. Proof of negligence, above
Strict liability vs. negligence. Strict Liability in Tort, this index
Warnings, due care in marketing, 56

NEGLIGENCE PER SE
Proof of negligence, generally, 58–64

NEGLIGENT MISREPRESENTATION
Tortious Misrepresentation, this index

NOTICE
Warranty, notice of breach. Warranty, this index

OBVIOUS DANGERS
Defectiveness, this index

PARENT CORPORATIONS
Alter ego liability, 439–440

POST-SALE DUTIES
Defectiveness, this index

PREEMPTION
Affirmative defenses. Federal Preemption, this index

PRENATAL HARM
Defectiveness, this index

PRESCRIPTION DRUGS
Drugs, this index

PRINT MEDIA
Books, magazines, and print media. Special Transactions and
    Products, this index

PRIVITY OF CONTRACT
Early law, 7–11
Warranty, this index

PRODUCT CERTIFIERS AND ENDORSERS
Defendants, this index

PROOF OF DEFECT
Defectiveness, this index

PROXIMATE CAUSATION
Causation, this index

PUBLICATIONS
Special Transactions and Products, this index

PUNITIVE DAMAGES
    Generally, 505–509
Amount of punitive damage awards. Problems and recurring
    criticisms, below
Basis of liability, 518–520
Constitutional limitations, 528–537
Controversy, 507–509
Functions, 509–513
    Compensation, 512
    Deterrence, 511
    Education, 510–511
    Law enforcement, 512–513
    Retribution, 510
Misconduct, forms of manufacturer misconduct
        Generally, 513–518
    Design out, failure to design out known dangers, 516–517
    Failure to warn, 517–518
    Fraud, 514
    Post-sale failure to warn, 518
    Safety standards, knowingly violating, 514–515
    Testing, failure to test to uncover dangerous defects, 515–516
Problems and recurring criticisms, 521
Reform, judicial and legislative, 521–527

RAW MATERIALS
Special Transactions and Products, this index

REAL ESTATE
Special Transactions and Products, this index

REFORM LEGISLATION
User misconduct defenses. Affirmative Defenses, this index
Intervening and superseding causes. Causation, this index
Negligence, resurgence in reform statutes, 71
Punitive Damages, this index
Warranty, this index

REPAIRED, REFURBISHED, RECONDITIONED, REBUILT, AND REMANUFACTURED PRODUCTS
Special Transactions and Products, this index

REPOSE
Affirmative Defenses, this index

RES IPSA LOQUITUR
Negligence, this index

RESTATEMENT (SECOND) OF TORTS § 402A
Strict Liability in Tort, this index

RESTATEMENT (THIRD) OF TORTS: PRODUCTS LIABILITY
Generally, 198–205
Defectiveness, this index
Strict Liability in Tort, this index

RETAILERS AND OTHER NON–MANUFACTURING SELLERS
Defendants, this index

RISK-UTILITY TEST
Strict Liability in Tort, this index

SERVICE TRANSACTIONS
Special Transactions and Products, this index

SPECIAL TRANSACTIONS AND PRODUCTS
Animals, 482–483
Bailments, 461–463
Blood, 480–481
Books, magazines, and print media, 476–478
Casual sales, 481–482
Electricity, 473–474
Games, music, video games, and web sites, 478–479
Installers, product, 467–468
Landlords, 474–476
Leases, 458–463

SPECIAL TRANSACTIONS AND PRODUCTS—Cont'd
License transactions, 461–462
Navigational charts, 478
Professional services, 465–467
Publications, 476–479
Raw material and component part suppliers, 437–439
Real estate, 474–476
Refurbished, reconditioned, rebuilt, and remanufactured
     products, 469–471
Repaired products, 469–471
Service transactions, 464–469
Toxic contaminants, 483–484
Used products, 471–473

STATE OF THE ART
Defectiveness, this index

STATUTES OF LIMITATIONS
Affirmative Defenses, this index

STATUTES OF REPOSE
Affirmative Defenses, this index

STRICT LIABILITY IN TORT
    Generally, 126–127
Abnormally dangerous products, strict products liability vs. strict
    liability for abnormally dangerous products, 164–165
Affirmative Defenses, this index
Alternative tests, 160–164
Comparison with other liability theories, 164–172
Consumer expectations test, 150–155
Defect-specific tests, 162–164
Deterrence and risk-spreading, 146–148
Hand formula, 157–159
History, 127–134
Inconsistent jury verdicts, 167–172
Judicial efficiency, 145
Negligence, strict liability vs. negligence
      Generally, 165–167
    Juries, strategy, and inconsistent verdicts, 167–172
    Resurgence of, 69–71
Policies and rationales, 143–148
Restatement (Second) of Torts § 402A, 134–143
Restatement (Third) of Torts: Products Liability, 200
Risk-utility test, 155–159
Tests, liability tests

STRICT LIABILITY IN TORT—Cont'd
Tests—Cont'd
>Generally, 149–150
Consumer expectations test, above
Hand formula, above
Risk-utility test, above
Tortious Misrepresentation, this index
Verbal standards test, 160
Wade–Keeton test, 246–248
Warranty, strict liability vs. warranty, 169–172

SUCCESSOR CORPORATIONS
Defendants, this index

SUPERSEDING CAUSES
Causation, this index

THEORIES OF RECOVERY
Misrepresentation. Tortious Misrepresentation, this index
Negligence, this index
Strict Liability in Tort, this index
Warranty, this index

TORTIOUS MISREPRESENTATION
>Generally, 72–74
Fraud, 74–80
Negligent misrepresentation, 81–83
Strict liability, 83–85

TOXIC SUBSTANCE LITIGATION
Cause in fact, proving, 343–346

TRADE ASSOCIATIONS
Defendants, this index

TRADEMARK-HOLDERS AND FRANCHISERS
Defendants, this index

USED PRODUCTS
>Generally, 471–473
Restatement (Third) of Torts: Products Liability, 202

USER MISCONDUCT DEFENSES
Affirmative Defenses, this index

WARNING DEFECTS
>Generally, 261–265
Adequacy of warnings, 268–277

WARNING DEFECTS—Cont'd
Adequacy of warnings—Cont'd
Content, substantive, 270–271
Foreign language, 272–273
Form, procedural, 271–272
Nonverbal, 274–275
Overpromotion, 275
Warnings pollution, 276–277
Definition. Restatement (Third) of Torts: Products Liability, below
Persons to be warned, 277–281
Allergic persons, 280–281
Bystanders, 279–280
Prescription drugs and medical devices, 285–297
Restatement (Third) of Torts: Products Liability, 200
Sophisticated users and bulk suppliers
Generally, 281–285
Bulk suppliers, 283–284
Restatements, 284–285
Sophisticated users, 282–283
Theories and tests of liability, 265–268

WARNINGS
Causation, this index
Defectiveness, this index
Warning Defects, this index

WARRANTY
Generally, 86–88
Affirmative Defenses, this index
Anti-disclaimer legislation. Reform legislation, below
Disclaimers
Generally, 106–117
Express warranties, 108–109
Implied warranties, 109–117
Safe-harbor, 111–114
Unconscionability, 115–117
Express warranties
Generally, 88–89
Breach, 89–90
Fact *vs.* opinion, "puffs," 90–92
Reliance, basis of the bargain, 92–93
Fitness for particular purpose. Implied warranty of fitness for particular purpose, below
Implied warranty of fitness for particular purpose
Generally, 96–99

WARRANTY—Cont'd
Implied warranty of fitness for particular purpose—Cont'd
    Buyer's reliance, 99
    Fitness for particular purpose, 96–98
    Seller's knowledge, 98–99
Implied warranty of merchantability
      Generally, 93–96
    Ordinary purpose, 94–96
Limitations of remedy
      Generally, 117–121
    Failure of essential purpose, 119–120
    Repair or replacement, 119
    Unconscionability, personal injury, 120–121
Magnuson–Moss Federal Warranty Act, 123–125
Merchantability. Implied warranty of merchantability, above
Notice of breach, 105–106
Personal injury damages exclusions, unconscionability of
    limitations. Limitations of remedy, above
Privity of contract. Third-party beneficiaries and privity of
    contract, below
Reform legislation
    Magnuson–Moss Federal Warranty Act, above
    Personal injuries to consumers, disclaiming responsibility for,
      121–122
    State anti-disclaimer statutes, 122–123
Strict liability vs. warranty. Strict Liability in Tort, this index
Third-party beneficiaries and privity of contract
      Generally, 100–105
    Employees, 104–105
    Horizontal privity, 102–105

WORMS
Generally, 217

†